AN INTRODUCTION TO AGRICULTURAL ECONOMICS

AN INTRODUCTION TO AGRICULTURAL ECONOMICS

S.A.R. BILGRAMI
Department of Economics,
Jamia Millia Islamia,
New Delhi.

Himalaya Publishing House
ISO 9001:2015 CERTIFIED

First Edition : 1996
Second Revised &
Millennium Edition : 2000
Reprint : 2006, 2010, 2011, 2013
2015, 2017, 2018, 2023
Reprint : 2026

Published by : Mrs. Meena Pandey
for **HIMALAYA PUBLISHING HOUSE PVT. LTD.,**
Vishal Industrial Estate, 1st Floor, Office No. 63/64,
Bhandup Village Road,Subhash Nagar (Opp. CEAT Tyres),
Nahur (W), Mumbai - 400 078. **Phone:** 022-35131464/65/66/67
E-mail: himpub@bharatmail.co.in; **Website:** www.himpub.com

Branch Offices :

New Delhi : "Pooja Apartments", 4-B, Murari Lal Street, Ansari Road,
Darya Ganj, New Delhi - 110 002.
Phone: 011-23270392, 23278631; Fax: 011-23256286

Nagpur : Kundanlal Chandak Industrial Estate, Ghat Road,
Nagpur - 440 018. Phone: 0712-2721215, 2721216

Bengaluru : Plot No. 91-33, 2nd Main Road, Seshadripuram, Behind
Nataraja Theatre, Bengaluru - 560 020.
Phone: 080-41138821; Mobile: 09379847017, 09379847005

Hyderabad : No. 3-4-184, Lingampally, Besides Raghavendra Swamy
Matham, Kachiguda, Hyderabad - 500 027.
Phone: 040-27560041, 27550139

Chennai : No. 34/44, Motilal Street, T. Nagar, Chennai - 600 017.
Mobile: 09380460419

Pune : "Laksha" Apartment, First Floor, No. 527, Mehunpura,
Shaniwarpeth (Near Prabhat Theatre), Pune - 411 030.
Phone: 020-24496323, 24496333; Mobile: 09370579333

Cuttack : Plot No 5F-755/4, Sector-9, CDA Market Nagar,
Cuttack - 753 014, Odisha. Mobile: 09338746007

Kolkata : 3, S.M. Bose Road, Near Gate No. 5, Agarpara Railway Station,
North 24 Parganas, West Bengal - 700109.
Mobile: 9674536325

Printed at : Infinity Imaging System, New Delhi. On behalf of HPH.

PREFACE

This book is intended primarily for students of agricultural economics. It provides an elementary statement of some of the analytical tools used in agricultural economics. Main objectives is to provide a theoretical foundation for use in analysis of agricultural economic problems. We believe that students can obtain greater benefits from studies in agriculture and economic development, agriculture production economics, agriculture distribution economics and some important issues related to agriculture in developing economies. The book has been so designed as to serve the requirement of students both at the undergraduate and post-graduate levels, as also the teachers, researchers and agronomist alike. Pure theoretical and analytical treatment of the book provide an exhaustive discussion on principles of agricultural economics.

The book is broadly divided into four sections. The introductory part deals with the definition, nature, scope and peculiar characteristics of agricultural economics. The role and contribution of agriculture in economic development of a nation with special reference to developing economies have also been discussed in the concluding part of this section.

Part second is concerned primarily with problems involved in production decisions. Here emphasis is placed upon the principles of production economics. Attempt is made to provide an elaborate analysis of the theory of agricultural production and profit maximisation, ample of illustrated tables and diagrams are also provided.

Section three is concerned with the forces affecting the demand for farm products. Here emphasis is placed upon the principles of consumer behaviour. The effect of changes in income and price upon consumption are discussed. The characteristics of demand for farm products and the importance of foreign trade are also discussed. Changes in economic conditions and its impacts on farmers over-time are also included in this section. Changes in the supply of agricultural commodities are discussed from the stand-point of technological change in agricultural production. Changes in demand are analysed from the stand-point of changes in numbers and composition of population and from the growth and distribution of incomes among economic sector.

The fourth and the last section deals with some important problems and issues in relation to agriculture in developing countries. These are : land reforms, green-revolution, farm-size and productivity, marketable and marketed surplus, surplus-labour, agricultural planning strategy, agricultural taxation and mechanisation.

In writing this book, we have heavily relied upon a large number of sources and we express our sincere thanks to their authors and publishers. We are indebted to our colleagues and students for numerous suggestions for improving the content of this book. Thanks are also due to a number of libraries including Zakir Hussain Library, Jamia Millia Islamia, Ratan Tata Library, Delhi School of Economics, Library of Institute of Economic Growth and Library of Planning Commission (Yojana Bhawan). In the end we express our sincere thanks to Mrs. Farida Naz who typed the script, and M/s Himalaya Publishing House for publishing this book.

JAMIA MILLIA ISLAMIA **S.A.R. BILGRAMI**
JAMIA NAGAR,
NEW DELHI.

CONTENTS

PART I

PART II

PART III

PART IV

PART - I

Introduction

(i) ECONOMICS AND AGRICULTURAL ECONOMICS

(ii) DEFINITION, NATURE AND SCOPE OF AGRICULTURAL ECONOMICS

(iii) PECULIARITIES OF AGRICULTURE

(iv) PLACE OF AGRICULTURE IN DEVELOPMENT ECONOMICS: A HISTORICAL PERSPECTIVE

(v) AGRICULTURAL DEVELOPMENT MODELS: A BRIEF NOTE

(vi) AGRICULTURE AND ECONOMIC DEVELOPMENT

(vii) CONCLUDING REMARKS

INTRODUCTION

Agricultural economics as a separate branch of economics is a recent addition to economic literature. Various books on agriculture had been written in the past and many problems of farm economics had been given considerable attention, but well thought out effort on agricultural economics as a separate discipline started only in the beginning of 20th century. It was only after the depression of 1890's which seriously affected farm activities that organised farm groups and developed interest in farm management problems. This new field of agricultural interest was later known as agricultural economics. The emergence of industrial revolution stimulated the growth of agriculture and facilitated understanding of its importance. This stimulation and understanding of the growth of agriculture gradually resulted in the evolution of agricultural economics as a separate discipline. The importance of this discipline has recently grown so much that we have now separate agricultural universities, centres and colleges and agricultural economics is treated as an inseparable part of the academic programmes.

We know that the producers, processors and consumers of farm products face constantly changing economic conditions. In this book our focus is on the agricultural aspects of economics to know, how changes in economic conditions affect producers, processors, and consumers of agricultural products. To understand these agricultural aspects in details, we must therefore, first understand the working of the whole economic system.

Economics and Agricultural Economics

The science of economics deals with the problem of choice between alternatives. The problem of choice arises because resources are scarce before ever-growing desires. Economic problem arises when the question is raised: how the scarce resources should be allocated to get maximum satisfaction? Every economic system concentrates on this question.

There are five basic functions which any economic system perform if the economy is to grow and develop. One is to determine what goods and service are to be produced. In the production of goods and services, producers assume that their products will be consumed. This means that some method must be established so that consumers may convey their preferences to producers concerning the kind and the quality of goods they like to consume and which the producers would like to produce. That is, some criteria must be introduced for transmitting the desire of consumers to producers.

To conform the wishes of consumers an organisation is needed in relation to produce goods and services. Organisation is needed because resources are limited and it is necessary to have some method of dividing available scarce resources among producing units in such a manner that could permit these units to produce those goods and services which are in great demand. This means that by transferring resources from one use to another, more goods and services could be produced for reaching at higher and higher level of satisfaction. This is the second important economic function of a system.

A third important function which an economic system must perform is to distribute the product. Owners employ their resources in the production of commodities for the market or sell their resources to others engaged in production. The price system directs resources to those uses where the returns are greatest. Returns from the sale of the product are distributed among resource owners through prices established for resource services. These payments are given special names in economics. Payments for labour services are called "Wages". Payments for the use of land are called "Rent". Payments for the use of capital are called "Interest". And payments for management are called "Profit". If the productive potential of an economy is to be explored, these rewards to the owners of resources must be high enough so that they could get better incentive.

If an economy is growing, it has to maintain or increase its production over-time for the maintenance and expansion in plant and equipment. This is the fourth important function of an economic system. New and additional goods and services cannot be produced unless the economic system is organised in a manner which permits the production of these goods and services. This means that some incentives for research, innovation and invention are needed if new and improved goods and services are to be made available for consumption.

At any point of time, the amount of commodities and services is fixed. Obviously, consumption cannot exceed the stock of commodities available. The economic system must be so organised that consumption at any point in time should be restricted to the stock of goods and services available. This is the fifth function of an economic system and is essentially a rationing function. Here consumption is adjusted according to the available stock of goods and services.

Among all the five functions discussed above, the first four may be viewed as an expression of preferences of the consumers and an adjustment of production to fulfil the desires of consumers. The last fifth function takes the stock of goods and services as given and adjust the amount of consumption accordingly. All these functions are the essential elements for a smooth functioning of an economy.

These functions of an economic system must be perform by any economic system irrespective of its political organisation. In a capitalist system the owners of resources, i.e., land, labour, capital and enterprise are free to enter into the production or sell their services to others. In such free enterprise exchange economy owners of the resources are paid for the use of their services/resources and have the freedom to spend the money to buy goods and services offered for sale. In a centrally controlled economy all resources are owned by the state and the decisions of production and distribution are taken by the central authority.

To sum up, economics may be defined as the science of analysing the use of limited and scarce resources to achieve desired ends. It is a social-science which studies "human behaviour as a relationship between ends and scarce means which have alternative uses". As such economics decides alternative ways of using scarce resources to satisfy human needs for which there are varying degrees of preferences. The questions: What tc produce? How to produce? For whom to produce? are centred around this basic theme of economics.

DEFINITION, NATURE AND SCOPE OF AGRICULTURAL ECONOMICS

Agricultural Economics: Agriculture is one sector of the total economy. Agricultural economics is an applied field of economics which analysis the principles of choice applied to the use of scarce resources such as land, labour, capital and management in the farming and allied agricultural activities. It decides what should be produced, which crops should be raised to maximise profit and what should be the price of the product. As a social science, agricultural economics is concerned with the allocation of scarce resources among the uses associated with producing, processing and consuming the farm products. The problem of allocating scarce means for diversified uses is more crucial in agriculture than any other sector because the land which is the basis of all agricultural pursuit is highly limited. Hence, the theoretical frame of agricultural economics should be such which could provide plausible methods and procedures of using such precious and limited resource for the maximum satisfaction of society. Agricultural economics is, therefore, both theoretical and applied in its character. It is theoretical because it deals with the development of principles of resource economics, production economics and distribution economics.

It is an applied science as well as it deals with the application of these principles in diversified production, consumption and distribution activities related to agriculture.

Nature and Scope: The scope of agricultural economics is very wide. A number of forces are actively involved in agricultural activities whether it is production, processing, marketing or consumption. Some of them are physical and are taken care by soil-scientists, geologists, soil-chemists and physicians. Some other forces are biological which are studied by animal and plant physiologists, geneticists, entomologists, pathologists and bacteriologists. Agriculture is also governed by some economic and sociological forces. Agriculture is a vocation as well as a way of life. This unique characteristic refers a relationship between economics and sociology. And it is with this relationship that agricultural economists deal. There are some relationships which are of purely economic nature. Input-output relationship, cost and revenue relationship, production decisions, price-decisions, maximisation of output/profit or least-cost combination of inputs, income-distribution and trade are some aspects where economists pay attention. Demographic structure, working conditions, customs, traditions and rituals of rural population and their impact on the thinking of rural masses and on their way of living are some sociological aspects where sociologist show their keen interest.

Thus, the scope of agricultural economics, as Tailor pointed out, "deals with the principles which underline the farmer's problem of what to produce and how to produce it, what to sell and how to sell it in order to secure the largest net profit for himself consistent with the best interest of society as a whole. More specifically, it treats of the selection of land, labour and equipment of a farm, the choice of crops to be grown, the selection of livestock, enterprises to be carried on, and the whole question of the proportions in which all these agencies should be combined. These questions are treated primarily from the point of view of costs and price."[1] Although Tailor deals with the subject in broader prospective, yet the whole treatment rests only on the problem of production. And as such an impression emerges that agricultural economics has nothing to do with the problem of consumption and distribution of farm products. But this is not true. Consumption, processing and distribution economics is as important for farm people as it is for them to understand the economics of their farm production. They are, therefore, part of the economics of agriculture.[2]

The scope of agricultural economics, is, thus, not confined to only production economics. It is equally related with the problem of distribution and consumption. It includes the questions: what to distribute;

among whom to distribute and on what basis to distribute; what to consume and how much to consume. Agricultural economics also includes the participation and functioning of Government in agriculture. "To neglect the public management, public aid, and public regulation", as Black reveals, "as arts of the agricultural economics would be almost like leaving mechanics out of the agricultural economics would be almost like leaving mechanics out of a course of physics".[3] Of course, the role of the Government cannot be neglected as in the process of production, distribution and consumption and overall upliftment of the rural masses. It provides infrastructure, technical know-how, aid and assistance on one hand and regulates input and output prices in the interest of both the consumer and the producers on the other. Thus, Government participation is a relevant part of the study of agricultural economics and as such it should also be included in the scope of agricultural economics.

To be specific the scope of agricultural economics include the production, distribution, consumption and Government activities in relation to agriculture and farm enterprises. The main problem is of choosing the most profitable activity. The task of agricultural economist is to point out what is best to do in the economic interest of rural community under the given conditions. The scope is very vast which include every phase of national activities that affect farmers in their efforts to make a happy and prosper living.[4]

Agriculture economics is both a social-science as well as a natural science. As a social-science we study farmers' activities, decisions and functioning which are greatly influenced by society. The society, in turn, is also affected by the farmer's decisions. Since farmers' decisions are to some extent affected by his own psychology, social institutions and other religious taboos, their activities cannot be measured in such a precise manner as are possible in a laboratory experiments. In this respect, agricultural economics is subject to all such influences which exist within the domain of social-sciences.

As a natural science agricultural economics deals with a thorough examination and evaluation of scientific innovations in relation to agricultural activities. Since agricultural economics is an applied science, the practical wisdom of an agricultural economist seems to be more useful than the volume of his theoretical knowledge. The nature of agricultural economics is unique as all the practical aspects of agriculture are controlled and governed by nature. In no other economic phenomenon as in agriculture is the nature so strongly, directly and closely involved. The problem of maximisation of output is therefore more complex in agriculture in comparison to other sectors.

Obviously the solution is too more uncertain. Varying agro-climatic conditions, soil-fertility lead to inter-regional and intra-regional heterogeneity in the production conditions. This creates the problem of differential achievements under varied geo-economic conditions. The problem of agricultural production is, therefore, complex and multi-dimensional.

Seasonality is another unique factor that distinguishes agricultural production activities from other non-agricultural production activities. Naturally, market fluctuations are more sharp and frequent in agriculture sector in comparison to non-agricultural sectors. The nature of agricultural activities is such that it involve the whole family in pursuit of livelihood, it becomes a way of life, a culture, besides, of course, a means of livelihood. The very word "agriculture" reflects that it is more a culture, a way of living rather than a profession and a business enterprise.

SOME PECULIARITIES OF AGRICULTURE

Agricultural economics does not present a different set of economic principles and methodology relevant to only agriculture. The general framework of economic theory is applicable just as much to agriculture as it is applicable to any other sector such as industry. The analysis of demand and supply, equilibrium, cost and revenue, markets, maximisation of profit etc. is as valid in agriculture as in industry. When all the general principles of economics are applicable to agriculture the basic question arises: What is the need of studying agricultural economics separately?

True, goals of production and the need for management decisions in relation to the allocation of inputs are strikingly similar between agricultural and industrial production. However, there are substantial differences in the natural conditions under which production is carried on in the agricultural and industrial sector. And this necessitated a separate study of agricultural economics. Agriculture possesses some unique and peculiar characteristics which in turn makes the agricultural economics as a separate branch of study.

(i) Agriculture is a unique industry in the sense that it is only agriculture where a mode of life, a culture, and profession, a business all are combined together. This combination no longer exist in industry or in any other sector. Agricultural activities are such that involve the whole family for the pursuit of livelihood. And as such it is more a way of life than merely an industry or business enterprise. It is on this ground that agriculture is more influenced by sociological, political and sentimental elements.

(ii) Agriculture is known as basic industry. Basic in the sense that it provides food for all without which nobody can live. Basic in the sense also that industrial growth depends on it as it provides major raw material for their growth and expansion. No other sector takes such strategic responsibilities of growth and development. Agriculture is also unique in the sense that it produces net surplus production over cost. However it is also true that its production activities are makred with uncertainties, limitations and immobilities. Agriculture, being a biological activity is always subject to the vagaries of nature. Here man's association with nature is more close, intimate and many sided. Weather, climate, rainfall, temperature, moisture, chemical properties of soil, latitude, altitude all serve a limiting factors is man efforts to develop agriculture according to his own plan. Man has hardly control over them. Here nature decides the level of output. When production is not controllable serious maladjustments are likely to occur because at times more production is needed, agriculture fails to produce it. Hence, the whole economy suffers with shortages and high-prices. When prices are high and farmers wish to produce more he is not capable of producing more. And at other time, more products are produced than are required, making the whole production activity unprofitable. This trend refers towards the immobility of agriculture.

(iii) Agriculture is immobile in the sense that it cannot adjust their output and organisation in accordance with the market fluctuation immediately, while the other sectors such as industry can do it easily. Expansion and contraction in their case is more a function of time and technique. But in agriculture the adaptability of any such change is slow and therefore, it is immobile and inflexible. A farmer neither can take immediate advantage of technological changes nor can be benefitted from the changes in taste fashion and mode of life. Besides, factor limitation like area of land also places svere limitation on the efforts of man to expand his activities. But no manufacturing unit suffers from such limitation.

(iv) Due to these limitations and immobilities, the Law of Diminishing Returns is more pronounced in agriculture than in any other industry. Other industries which are more flexible gains remunerative returns on fresh application of capital and they yield increasing returns.

(v) Production in agriculture is also highly immobile. Other industries can adjust their production at a short notice in response to the changing pattern of market demand. But this is not possible in agriculture. Here production has its own fixed time and farmer has to wait for it whatever may be the demand position of these products. The economic life of a plant may be 10 years, 20 years, 30 years or even more. Once planted, the planter is in no position to alter the course of production. Hence, according to the changes in prices, cost and demand, a producer is unable to adjust his output, the area of crop or the level of output. In industries, such adjustments are easy and possible. The cost structure may be changed, production level can be adjusted through contraction and expansion and even the output can safely be preserved to take the advantages of market conditions. In agriculture many products are perishable and can't be stored for a longer period. Hence, agriculture faces greater price and demand risks in view of its inability to make quick adjustment in supplies according to change in demand.

(vi) Agricultural production activity is seasonal. Output comes out only at a specific period and, therefore, turnover is slow. Production in industries are not seasonal. Their production is a continuous flow which may be raised or slowed down according to the changes in demand. On demand side, most of the agricultural products like cereals, pulses show an inelastic demand. The demand for some processed commodities like sugar, butter, and some other commodities like fish, meat, eggs, fruits are comparatively elastic. But the demand for such commodities specially in developing countries is urban-biased. The transportation, storage, distribution and marketing etc. of such commodities create another set of problems in relation to maintain a proper supplies according to the changing pattern of demand.

(vii) Many agricultural commodities are joint products like wheat, milk, mutton, wool etc. because they are the part of the same plant or the same animal. The costs attributable to the various products cannot be separated as they often can be produced in industry even when several products are produced in the same plant. Hence, in agriculture it is rarely justifiable to consider the supply of any product in isolation.

(viii) Agriculture also require far larger proportion of land in relation to its employment of other factors than does industry. Moreover, it is also scattered over a large area with uneconomical and small-size units. This raises organisational problems which are absent in industry. Hence, the benefits of large-scale organisation better known as economies of scale and the division of labour are not possible in agriculture, specially in the agricultural sector of developing countries.

(ix) Agricultural activities are so complex, varied and diversified that no other activities such as industrial, commercial, trade or business can hardly compete it. It includes not only arable crops but also livestock, plantation, pastures, horticulture, fisheries, forestry, animal-husbandry, poultry, dairy, sheep-farming and cattle-rearing. All have some outstanding features of their own. All have their own culture and contribution to the economy.

(x) Farming has been the oldest and the chief occupation of mankind the world over. Other occupations evolved in the process of civilization. Even to-day more than half the world's labour force is directly engaged in agricultural occupation. Thus on occupational side, agriculture is the biggest industry of the world.

PLACE OF AGRICULTURE IN DEVELOPMENT ECONOMICS: A HISTORICAL PERSPECTIVE*

Economists have traditionally analysed agricultural development in terms of its relationship to the growth of the overall economy. Early theoretical literature on the place of agriculture in development economics can be traced to as far back as the eighteenth century in the writings of the physiocrats. They viewed agriculture as the engine of economic growth, and that agriculture is the only activity capable of generating a surplus large enough to stimulate growth in other sectors of the economy. According to them only agriculture turned out a "net

* This part draws heavily on Eicher C.K. & Staatz J.M. Edited work: Agricultural Development In The Third World, The Johns Hopkins University Press, London, 1984, Part 1 (Agricultural Development Ideas In Historical Prespective) and Part III models of Agricultural development by Ruttan V.W. and Introduced Innovation Model of Agricultural Development by Ruttan V.W. and Havamiy) pp 3-71

product" over and above its cost of production and it is only in agriculture that nature labours along with man and by her bounty yields not only what the agricultural labourer or the farmer consumes, but also a surplus which nourishes the other classes of society. Hence, agriculture plays the most strategic role in economic development. Manufacture and commerce were regarded as "sterile" class as they enhanced the value of raw material only enough to pay for the labour and capital used in the process of production.

Importance of agriculture in economic development was also recognised by the classical economists such as Adam Smith, Ricardo and Malthus. Adam Smith's basic economic growth model refers only to the agricultural sector.[5] Food, according to him is the conditional factor in the growth of the economy and hence technical improvement in agriculture is the pivotal point for sparking of development in other sectors of the economy. Ricardo considers agriculture as the most important sector of the economy. The difficulty of providing food for an expanding population serves as the focal point for the entire analysis of both, Ricardo and Malthus. But classical economists believed that diminishing marginal returns to agricultural land would eventually lead to over-all economic stagnation or the "steady-state". Thus, the law of diminishing returns from land dominates the economic scene and governs the fortunes of all classes. Shortage of land, according to Ricardo, would set a limit upon the expansion of agriculture and, hence, upon the whole economy.

Although the problem of economic growth and development has been the subject of serious discussion among the economist since the beginning of mercantilism, development economics as a separate branch of economics has come into existence only since 1950. The history of economic development ideas can roughly and broadly be divided into the two phases:

(i) An era of economic growth and modernisation when the subject of economic development is treated as growth in average per capita output. This growth trend has been found during 1950's and 1960's; and (ii) The era of growth with equity start around 1970. This is growth with social-justice phase where the economist are concerned with broader objectives such as equitable distribution of income and wealth, elimination of unemployment, poverty and hunger and host of other subject. Agriculture's role in economic development has been profoundly changed during these two phases.

AGRICULTURE IN DEVELOPMENT ECONOMICS: 1950-69

Most of the Western economists of 1950's did not pay much attention towards agriculture, they did not view agriculture as an important contributor to economic growth. I.M.D. Little, for instance, comments in his survey of development economics: "It is fairly obvious from the reading their work that the leading development economists of the 1950's knew little about tropical agriculture or rural life". They viewed traditional agriculture as a passive sector that would decline in importance as industrial growth absorbed an increasing share of production and employment.

Economic development was considered as the process of structural transformation of the economy where agriculture's relative share of the national product and of the labour force both declines. Economic development was presumed as a process that facilitates transformation, specially of labour, from traditional agriculture to industry which is considered the engine of growth. Agriculture was treated merely a "black-box from which people, and food to feed them, and perhaps capital could be released".

Ideas on development economics were deeply and strongly influenced by W. Arthur Lewis's article: "Economic Development with unlimited Supplies of Labour" appeared in 1954. He presented a two sector model of expansion of an economy – a modern capitalist exchange sector and a non-capitalist sector dominated by subsistence farming. A fundamental relationship between the two sectors is that when capitalist sector expands, it draws labour from the subsistence sector. The subsistence agricultural sector is described as the "self-employment sector" which did not hire labour or use reproducible capital. This model explains and analyse how the transfer of labour from subsistence agriculture sector, where the marginal productivity of labour is considered to be zero, to the capitalist sector facilitates capitalist expansion through reinvestment of profits. The labour supply facing the capitalist sector has been considered "unlimited". It is unlimited in the sense that when capitalist sector offers additional employment opportunities at the existing wage rate, the numbers willing to work at this wage rate will be greater than the demand. That is the supply curve of labour is infinitely elastic at the ruling wage.

In tracing out the process of economic expansion, Lewis emphasises the reinvestment process of the capitalist system. As the capitalist sector expands labour is withdrawn from capitalist sector into wage employment, the surplus of the capitalist then becomes even larger. There is still more reinvestment of profits and the process continues on, progressively absorbing the surplus labour from the subsistence sector. This process of capital formation comes to an end when capital accumulation catches up with population, so that there is no longer surplus labour in the subsistence sector left to be absorbed in the industrial sector. Beyond this point real wages no longer remain constant, instead, rise as capital formation occurs. In other words, expansion in the capitalist sector continued until earning in the two sectors were equated. At this point of equilibrium it will now be in the interest of the producers in the subsistence sector to compete for labour since the marginal product of labour will no longer be below the institutional wage. When this point is reached, the agricultural sector is said to have been commercialised and a dual sector model is no longer relevant. The growth proceeds in one-sector. Lewis model has been later on extended by Ranis. fei (1961, 1963 and 1964) and Jorgenson (1961).

The relative neglect of agriculture was reinforced by two other developments. Paul Prebisch and Hans Singer independently formulated the thesis that there is a secular tendency for the terms of trade to run against countries that export primary products and import manufacturing goods. This led them to conclude that the scope for development through agriculture and other primary exports was limited and hence the tendency to down-play agriculture's potential role in development was reinforced.

The publication of Albert Hirschman's book: "The Strategy of Economic Development" in 1958 also affected development economist view of agriculture. In this book he introduced the concept of linkages as a tool of investigating how investment in one type of economic activity induced subsequent investment in other income-generating activities. He explained the linkage effect as "the investment-generating forces that are set in motion, through input-output relation, when productive facilities that supply inputs to that (productive) line or utilise its output, are inadequate or non-existent. Backward linkages lead to new investment in input-supplying facilities and forward linkages to investment in out-put using facilities". He asserted that "agriculture certainly stands convicted on the count of its lack of direct stimulus to the setting up new activities through linkage effect the superiority of manufacturing in this respect is crushing". He, therefore, argued that investment in industry would generally lead to more rapid and more broad based economic growth than in agriculture.

The views expressed by the development economists in early 1950's clearly indicates that their main attention was to focus on the contribution of agriculture to over-all economic growth instead on analysing the process of agriculture growth per se. They stressed on inter-sectoral resource transfers, particularly of labour, from traditional agricultural sector to the modern industrial sector. In this respect, they viewed agricultural sector as a passive sector that declines its importance as industrial growth absorbs an increasing share of production and employment.

In the early 1960, Johnston, Mellor and several other agricultural economist stressed the fundamental role that agriculture potentially could play in economic development and the importance of understanding the process of agricultural growth per se if that potential was to be exploited. Johnston and Mellor drew insight from Lewis model and stressed the importance of agriculture as a motive force in economic growth. They pointed out five important contributions to the structural transformation of third world economies. Agriculture provides labour, capital, foreign exchange and food to a growing industrial sector and also provides a market for industrial goods produced within the economy. Johnston and Mellor's article and W.H. Nicholl's article: "The Place of Agriculture In Economic Development" (1964) were instrumental in encouraging economists to view agriculture as a potential positive force in economic development and helped to stimulate debate on the interdependence of agricultural and industrial growth. This in turn developed growing interest in the empirical measurement of inter-sectoral resource transfers during the course of development.[6] Numerous attempts were also made to develop specifications of the agricultural sector in economic growth models and to model developed carefully the dynamics of growth within the agricultural sector. A brief survey of these models is given in the next part of this chapter.[7]

The Growth-With-Equity Era Since 1970

Around 1970 development economics began to give greater attention to employment and the distribution of real income. The focus shifted from per capita output growth to more equitable distribution of income, expansion of employment and eradication of poverty. The main reason was a growing awareness among development economist that even in countries where rapid economic growth had not contributed to social turmoil, the benefits or economic growth often were not trickling down to the poor and the income gap between rich and poor was widening. Even where the incomes of the poor were rising, they were rising so slowly that the poor would not be able to afford decent living for at least another generation.

This awareness led them to realize that merely increasing per capita income is not enough to solve the problems of poverty and malnutrition. Economist, political leaders and the leaders of the major donor agencies argued that greater explicit attention is needed towards employment, income distribution and basic needs such as nutrition, health and housing. This orientation of development economics in the early 1970 implied a much greater role for agriculture in development programmes.

Majority of the population of the Third World Countries is poor and live in rural areas. Food prices, in such countries, are the major determinant of the real income of both the rural and the urban poor. Since the productivity of agriculture in the Third World is low, the income level is also very low and this is a major cause of poverty. Moreover, because urban industry provided few jobs for the rapid growing labour force, planners concentrated on ways to create productive employment in rural areas. These findings tend to realise that agriculture has to play more important role in development programme. And merely two-sector models of 1950's and 1960's are not enough to understand its contribution. Policy-makers needed a more detailed understanding of rural economies. Consequently the late 1960's and early 1970, there has been a rapid expansion of micro-level research on agricultural production, marketing, farmer decisions, rural factor, markets and rural non-farm employment.[8]

Hayami and Ruttan's induced innovation model of agricultural development was a major contribution of 1970's.[9] They argued that there are multiple technological paths to agricultural development. Each path indicates different mix of factors of production and changes in relative factor prices can guide to choose the most efficient path. This implies that countries with different factors endowment would have different efficient growth paths and the import of technology in full-scale from industrialised countries to these developing countries would lead to highly inefficient pattern of growth.

1970 also witnessed empirical researches on interdependence between agricultural and non-agricultural growth. In this respect Mellor, Johnston and Kilby's work is noteworthy. Mellor argued that employment-oriented strategies of development inherent in the new high-yielding grain varieties is possible. His analysis is based upon empirical evidence from India. Mellor emphasized that the new varieties could also raise the incomes of foodgrain producers and in turn could generate increased effective demand for a wide variety of labour-intensive products. The potential growth in employment is laying outside the foodgrain sector, producing labour-intensive goods such as dairy product, fruit and other consumer product and agricultural inputs. This expanded employment is made possible by the simultaneous increase in effective demand for these products and the increased supply of expensive wage goods in the form of foodgrains.

Johnston and Kilby focussed their attention on the factors affecting the rate of labour transfer between sectors and the level and composition of inter-sectoral commodity flows. They argued that the size distributionof farms is critical determinant of the demand for industrial products in a developing economy. To them broad-based agricultural growth is more effective than estate production in stimulating the demand for industrial products and speeding structural transformation of the economy. Their analysis supported the view that concentrating agricultural development efforts on the mass of small farmers in developing countries, rather than promoting a bimodal structure of small and large farms, would lead to faster growth rates of both aggregate economicoutput and employment.

A large number of studies during 1970's have been done on evaluatingthe performance of labour markets in low-income countries. Thesestudies found that at peak periods of the agricultural cycle there is little unemployment in rural areas, while at other periods, there are labour surpluses. The studies also revealed that earlier researches frequently had overestimated the size of these surpluses because they failed to take account of the time devoted to rural non-farm enterprises.

Rural to urban migration has also been an important area of study during 1960's and 1970's. The rate of rural-to-urban migration in most developing countries far outstripped the rate of growth of urban employment. This is the main reason of urban unemployment. Hence the policy makers shifted their attention from trying to transfer surplus labour from agriculture to industry to reducing excessive expansion of urbanization. In this area Todaro's study (1969) is significant. He proposed a model which was later on extended by Harvis and Todaro in 1970. In this model they argued that a migrant's decision to migrate is motivated primarily by the difference between his/her expected urban income and the prevailing rural wage. The model explains that attempts to reduce urban unemployment by creating more urban jobs actually results more urban unemployment. And this is because the potential migrants believe that their chances of getting an urban job have increased. Hence, urban employment programmes induced greater rural-to-urban migration. Haris and Todaro, therefore, argued that urban unemployment could best be addressed by reducing the incentives to migrate to cities. For example, this could be done by raising rural income via a broad range of agricultural and rural developmentprogrammes.

Rapid urbanisation and income growth put increasing pressure on markets for agricultural products, particularly food, during 1960's and 1970's. In response, researches and economists undertook a number of studies to evaluate the performance of agricultural product markets and suggested improvements. These studies analysed how insufficient infrastructure and lack of reliable public information system often reduced market efficiency and lowered farmer's incentives to specialise for market production. Studies criticises state monopolies in the domestic food trade and suggests that the state should provide public goods — better information system, standardised weights and measures etc. – to facilitate private trading, price stabilisation and regulation of international trade.[10]

One more area of interest during the late 1960's and the 1970's has been the farmer's decisions whether or not to adopt new crop varieties and farming practices. This research stressed the need to understand how Government policies could simultaneously affect both the production and the consumption decisions of small farmers. These studies, for example, showed that marketed surplus of a crop might, in some circumstances, actually declined as the crop price was increased, because the price increase would raise farm family income, some of which would be spent on the goods whose price had risen.

1970's also witnessed concentrated efforts towards Integrated Rural Development Programme (IRDP) in almost all developing economies. IRDP attempts to combine in one project elements to increase agricultural production and improve health, education, sanitation and a variety of other social services. Like Community Development Programme (CDP) of 1950's, IRDP of 1970's expanded social services much faster than they expanded the economic base to support them. Moreover, the inability of IRDP projects to increase agricultural production rapidly often suffered by the lack of appropriate technical support. By 1980, many supporting agencies like World Bank and the U.S. Agency for International Development (USAID) had retreated from IRDP or had redesigned these projects to give greater emphasis to agricultural production.[11] This led to conclude that the rise and decline of IRDP (1973-80) was in some way very similar to the fate of CDP in the 1950-57.[12]

Another important area of research, a part of IRDP, has been the basic needs approaches for rural development. This approach was popularised by the ILO and by the World Bank economists. The basic needs approach holds that development projects should give priority to increasing the welfare of the poor through improving their nutrition level, education, housing and health, rather than merely focusing on increasing aggregate growth rates. Although investment in health, education, nutrition and housing can contribute to the welfare of the poor and to the rate of growth, the experience with this approach suggests that low-income countries also need an appropriate economic base to finance these investment. By the early 1980 many economist once again giving greater emphasis to economic growth and to different types of development activities such as investment in irrigation and health. This shift of emphasis does not mean a rejection of the growth-with-equity philosophy of 1970. Instead, it reflects an increasing recognition of the impossibility of achieving a decent living for the rapid growing populations simply by redistributing existing resources. This led World Bank to shift to a more growth-oriented strategy in the early 1980's and the basic needs approach faded into the background.[13]

The broad-based researches done on agricultural growth and rural development during 1970 and early 1980 actually analyses agricultural and rural development issues in broader macro-economic framework. They also encourage to move towards more interdisciplinary approaches to solve the problems. The micro-level researches on different aspect of agricultural and rural development during 1970's contributed to an accumulation of knowledge about the behaviour of farmers, constrain on the expansion of farm and non-farm production, income and employment, the linkages between agricultural researches and extension institutions and the complexity of the agricultural development process. During 1970's and 1980's, it has been realised that agriculture is not a passive sector. It is a major contributor to economic growth and stability.

A Brief Note on Agricultural Development Models

Before 19th century the increase in food production was mainly the function of the area under cultivation. The increase in food production was obtained by bringing new land into cultivation. By the end of this century the increase in food production had become the function of higher yields from increased output per hectare. This transition from a resource-based to a science-based system of agriculture has been occurred within a single century. In a few countries this transition began in the 19th century. In most of the present developed countries it did not start until the first half of this century. In most of the developing countries it started only since mid century. The technology associated with this transition, particularly the new seed – fertilizer technology, has been referred to as the "green-revolution" in the developing world.

The literature on agricultural development can be classified into following six models: (1) the frontier, (2) the conservation, (3) the urban-

* This part draws heavily on: Ruttan W.V., "Models of Agricultural Development". In Agricultural Development in the Third World (Edi) op. cit Chapter 2 pp 38-45.

industrial impact, (4) the diffusion, (5) the high-pay off input and (6) the induced innovation. A brief statement of each model is as under:

Frontier **Model:** From the beginning of the civilization expansion of the area cultivated or grazed has represented the dominant source of increase in agricultural production. In the earlier phase of the history, the discovery of new continents such as North and South America and Australia became increasingly important source of food and agricultural raw materials for the development of the metropolitan countries of Western Europe. Later on intensification of land use in villages, establishment of new villages agricultural colonization and opening of forest or jungle land to cultivation in Europe, Asia and Africa continued the process of increasing agricultural production by the expansion of area cultivated.

In favourable soil conditions such as in the great river basins and plains, new villages gradually intensified their system of cultivation. In the favourable soil conditions such as in hilly and upland regions new areas were opened up to shifting cultivation or nomadic grazing.

the

The limits of frontier model were quickly realised under the condition of rapid population growth. Crop yields were low in terms of output per unit of seed rather than per unit of crop area. Output per hectare and per man-hour tended to decline. Up to 1960, there were few areas of the world where this model could present an efficient source of growth. 1960's saw "closing of the frontier" in most areas of Southern Asia.

Conservation Model: The conservation model of agricultural development evolved series of advances in crop and livestock husbandry. The application of law of diminishing returns to labour and capital was introduced. The model also emphasized the evolution of a sequence of increasingly complex land and labour intensive cropping systems, the production and use of organic manures, and labour-intensive capital formation in form of drainage, irrigation and other physical facilities to more effectively utilize land and water resources. The inputs used in this conservation system of farming – land improvement, agricultural labour force, physical capital, animal power and plant nutrients – were all largely produced or supplied by the agricultural sector itself.

This model has capable in many parts of the world of sustaining rates of growth in agricultural production in the range of 1.0% per year over relatively long period of time. And it was the only approach to intensification of agricultural production available to the most of world's farmers. The model remains an important source of productivity growth in most poor countries and an inspiration to agrarian fundamentalists and the organic farming movement in developing countries.

Urban-Industrial Impact Model: Initially the model was developed in Germany by J.H. Von Thuman. He explained geographic variations in the intensity of farming system and the productivity of labour in an industrializing society. Later on, the model was extended to explain the more effective performance of the input and products markets linking the agricultural and non-agricultural sectorsin regions characterised by urban-industrial development than in regions where the urban economy had not made a transition to the industrial stage.

The rationale of the model was develop in terms of more effective input and product markets in areas of rapid urban-industrial development. It is said that industrial development stimulated agricultural development by expanding demand for agricultural products, supplying industrial inputs needed to improve agricultural productivity and drawing away surplus labour from agriculture. The empirical tests of the urban-industrial impact model have repeatedly confirmed that a strong-non-farm market is an essential pre-requisite for improving labour productivity and the incomes of the rural population. This model appears to be more relevant for rapidly growing less developed countries.

Diffusion Model: The spreading out of agricultural products and animals from the new-world to the old – rubber, maize, potatoes and cassava – and from the old world to the new – wheat, sugar, and domestic animals was an important by-product of trade during fifteenth to the nineteenth century. The diffusion approach is based upon the empirical observation of substantial differences in land and labour productivity among farmers and regions. In this view, agricultural development is considered to be based upon effective dissemination of technical knowledge and upon narrowing of the productivity differences among farmers and among regions.

The diffusion model provided the basis of the research and extension effort in farm management and production economics. It also helped in providing the intellectual foundation of the research of agricultural economics and rural sociology as a separate subdisciplines linking the agriculture and the social sciences. During 1960, the limitation of diffusion model as a basis for the design of agricultural development policies became apparent as technical assistance and rural development programmes based on this model failed to generate either rapid modernisation of traditional agricultural communities or rapid

High-Pay Off Input Model: The inadequacy, limitation and failure of aforesaid models led to a new perspective in 1960 and that was transforming a traditional agricultural sector into a productive source of economic growth through investment on making modern and high-pay off inputs available to farmers in poor countries. This view was developed by T.W. Schultz in his book; Transforming Traditional Agriculture. He insisted that farmers in traditional societies remained poor because there were only limited technical and economic opportunities available to them. The new, high-pay off inputs provide them: (1) new technical knowledge; (2) new technical inputs and (3) technique of using new inputs effectively.

This model has been accepted with great enthusiasm. New high-productivity grain varieties has been successfully developed in Mexico and new High-Yielding rice varieties has been developed in the philippines. These varieties were highly responsive to industrial inputs such as fertilizer and other chemicals and to more effective soil and water management. The high returns associated with these new varieties and the associated technical inputs and managements practices have led to rapid diffusion of the new varieties among farmers in a number of countries in Asia, Africa and Latin-America. India is one of such countries where H-Y-V programmes has been successfully adopted.

Induced Innovation Model: The high-pay off model also showed various limitations and was incomplete on various counts. It was incomplete in the sense that it failed to incorporate fully the mechanism where resources are allocated among education, research and other public and private sector economic activities. It failed to explain how economic conditions induce the development and adoption of an efficient set of technologies for a particular society. Not it attempted to explain the process by which input and product-price relationships induce investment in research in a direction consistent with a nation's particular resource endowments.

These limitations led Yujiro Hayami and V.W. Ruttan to develop a model of agricultural development in which technical change is treated as endogenous rather than an exogenous factor to the development process.[14]

The productivity levels of the farmers in most advanced countries are high which reflects the level of technical progress achieved by these countries. These levels are not available in most low-productivity countries. They can be made available by investing on agricultural research needed to develop technologies appropriate to the countries natural and institutional environment and by investing on physical and institutional infrastructure needed to realise the new production potential opened up by technological advances.

It has been historically proved that technology has been developed to facilitate the substitution of relatively abundant (hence cheap) factors for relatively scarce (hence expensive) factors of production. The constrains imposed on agricultural development by an inelastic supply of land have been removed by the development of High-yielding crop varieties designed to facilitate the substitution of fertiliser for land. Similarly, the constraints imposed by an inelastic supply of labour in most advanced countries have been removed by technical advances leading to the substitution of animal and mechanical power for manpower.

Developing countries which are incapable of evolving technical and institutional innovations in agriculture suffers two major constraints on its development of productive agriculture. One is that they are unable to take advantage of advances in biological and chemical technologies suited to labour-intensive agricultural systems. And second is that their size of farming is small and hence the imported technology will not work productively. The imported technology will be useful only under conditions of large-scale agricultural organisation.

During the last two decades number of developing countries have begun to establish to institutional capacity to generate technical changes based upon national and regional resource endowments. A new system of international crop and animal research institutes has also emerged which became both important source of new knowledge and technology and increasingly effective communication links among the developing national research systems.

The lag in shifting from a natural-resource-based to science-based system of agriculture continues to be a source of national differences in land and labour productivity. Lags in the development and application of knowledge is also an important source of differences in regional productivity within the countries. In countries like India differential rates of technical change have been an important source of the widening disparities in the rate of growth of total agricultural output, in land and labour productivity and in incomes and wage rates among regions. Hence, productivity differences in agriculture are increasingly a function of investments in science and industrial capacity and in the education of rural people sector than of natural resource endowments.

The effects of education on productivity are particularly important during periods in which a nation's agricultural research system begins to introduce new technology. In a condition of static technology, the gains from education to be realised are few in rural areas. Rural people who lived for generations with the same resources and with the same technology have learned from long experience what their efforts can get out of the resources available to them. The skill which the children acquire from their parents are worthwhile. Formal schooling has little economic value in agricultural production.

This situation changes as soon as the new technical opportunities are available. Technical changes need the acquisition of new husbandry skill; acquisition from non-traditional sources of additional resources such as new-chemicals, new-equipment new-seed and new-skills in dealing with both natural resources and input and product market institution linking agriculture with the non-agricultural sector. The process by which new knowledge can alter the rate and direction of technical change in agriculture are, however, substantially greater than the knowledge of the processes by which resources are brought to bear on the process of institutional innovation and transfer. Yet, the need for viable institutions to support more rapid agricultural growth and rural development is more compelling to-day than a decade ago.

AGRICULTURE AND ECONOMIC DEVELOPMENT

A close contact between agriculture and economic development has been discussed in the previous two parts – "Place of Agriculture In Development Economics: A Historical Perspective" and "A Brief Note on Models of Agricultural Development". While the first part deals with the gradual changing attitude of the economists in viewing the role of agriculture in economic development, the second part explains, in brief, the stages of the penetration of agriculture in the development process in various farms of models.

The importance of agriculture in the economic development of any country, developed or developing, is born out of the fact that it is the oldest and the most basic of all human professions and is the primary sector of the economy which not only provides the basic ingredients necessary for the existence of mankind but also provides the basic raw materials for the development of important and essential industries which when transformed into finished products serve as basic necessities and comforts of human race. In a preponderantly agrarian economy like India, agriculture plays a most strategic role in maintaining the high rate of economic growth. Basically, agricultural production must be increased to keep pace with population growth. When economy moves towards industrialisation, the urbanisation also expands quickly. This may then be expected to bring with it rising per capita demand for food, based on the increasingly high per capita incomes.

In addition to supplying food, agriculture also provides many raw materials to our most important industries. The fate of our textiles, silk, wool, leather, sugar, tobacco, edible oil, food processing, brew and many more crucially affected by the supply of raw materials produced in agricultural sector. Hence, the pace of advance in a wide range of consumer goods manufactures is eventually be affected by the pace of agricultural development.

Moreover, agriculture also generates exports surpluses in order to earn foreign exchanges. These foreign exchange are used to finance the import of capital goods and certain kinds of industrial raw materials.

However, agriculture is not only a supplier of goods for domestic and export needs but is also a supplier of production factors such as labour and capital. A rapidly growing industrial sector necessarily require some labour force which the rural sector provides abundantly. Moreover, in one form or other, agriculture is called upon to save and hence it finances a significant part of the investment for an expanding industrial, transport and other sectors.

In brief the crucial significance of the agricultural sector in the economic development is that it constitutes an important source of supply of goods, manpower, capital and saving as well as of earning foreign exchange.

These contributions can be summed-up under four broad headings:

(i) Agriculture production contribution,

(ii) Agriculture market contribution,

(iii) Agriculture factor contribution, and

(iv) Agriculture foreign exchange contribution.

Production Contribution: The growth of product within the agricultural sector itself is the first and the basic contribution to economic development. An increase in the net output of agriculture represents a rise in the product of the country since the latter is the sum of the increase in the net products of several sectors. Hence, agriculture product not only keeps a growing population alive but also keeps alive the other sectors and so the nation as a whole. This is quite obvious that if agricultural output — food and raw material — does not keep pace with the rate of population and industrial growth, the nutritional level of the growing population and the expansion of the most of consumer-goods industries both will adversely be effected. The nutritional level either will be lowered or will be maintained by increasing food imports. Similarly, the expansion of the consumer-goods industries will also be possible on importing strategic raw materials. Spending meager foreign exchange reserves on food and raw material would mean hampering the imports of most important capital goods and technology which is crucial but in short supply in the initial stages of economic development. Poor agricultural performance in terms of output, thus, declines the macro-dimensions of growth rate.

The slow growth of agricultural output, amidst high rate of population growth and industrialisation process, generates inflationary pressures. Aggregate demand for farm output increases on two fronts. It increases because of population growth and because of rising of per capita income. Since all developing countries show relatively high income elasticity of demand for food, most part of the increased income has been spent on food and other essential consumption goods. On the basis of the growth of population, income and income elasticity for the increase in the demand for food can be measured as[16]

$$Gr = Pr + (YED)Yr$$

Where Gr = the rate of growth of food demand.

Pr = the rate of growth of population

Yr = the rate of growth of per capita income

YED = Income elasticity of demand for food

If suppose "Pr" is 2.5 per cent, "Yr" 3.5 per cent and "YED" is .5, then "Gr" will be 4.25 per cent. If YED is higher than .5, say .9, then Gr will be 5.6 per cent. Thus, to keep pace with the growing demand for food, agriculture production must increase by 4.25 per cent or 5.6 per cent respectively. According to NSS, YED IN INDIA is 0.8 Keeping this income elasticity and possibilities of increase in population and per capita consumer expenditure in view, Planning Commission has estimated that demand for agricultural commodities is likely to increase at the rate of 4.7 per cent per annum. Accordingly, the nation can remain self-reliant in agriculture only if agricultural output rises at least at the rate of 5 per cent per annum. If domestic food production is not growing by these rates and imports are also limited by foreign exchange constraints, both the absolute and relative price of food will tend to rise. Such inflationary pressure is more burdensome to those poor nations who spend more than 50 per cent of the income on food. This leads to the conclusion that increasing food and raw material output is crucial to achieve a sustained multi-dimensional rate of growth.

Simon Kuznets[17] examines the product contribution of agriculture in terms of its share to the growth of total net or gross product and to the growth of product per capita. Algebraic notation of it is given as under:

Pa = output of agricultural sector (Sector A)

Pb = output of all other sector (Non Agricultural Sector B)

P = Total output Pa + Pb

Δp = Increment in total output

ra = Rate of growth of Pa

rb = Rate of growth of Pb, so that

$p_a 1 = p_a o\,(1 + ra)$, the subscripts are referring to time

$p_b 1 = P_b o\,(8 + rb)$

Then $\Delta p = P_{ara} + P_{brb}$

The equation for the share of agricultural output in the growth of total output is therefore:

$$r = \frac{Pa\ ra}{\Delta\ p} = \frac{1}{1 + \left(\frac{Pb}{Pa} \times \frac{rb}{ra}\right)}$$

Kuznets pointed out that the product contribution to the economic growth of a country will be higher, if: (1) the share of agriculture in country's labour force is larger and (2) the ratio of product per worker in agriculture in relation to non-agricultural sector is also higher. When economic growth moves towards industrialisation the share of agriculture in the labour force decreases and hence there will be a continuous decrease in the proportional contribution of agriculture to economic growth.

Several important conclusions in regard to the contribution of agriculture to net-outpuut have been drawn by Kuznets **Firstly,** "so long as the rate of growth of the non-agricultural sector is higher than that of agriculture, all other conditions being equal, the proportional contribution of agriculture to the growth of total product will decline".[18] Indian economy proves it well. A study indicated: "A point to be noted from the point of view of structural changes is that contribution of agriculture to the growth is still very large, in spite of its low growth related to other sectors. Out of over 5 per cent of total growth during the eighties, 1 per cent point has come from agriculture, a little over 0.9 percentage point has come from registered manufacturing and 0.44 percentage point share come from unregistered manufacturing. Thus, the manufacturing, registered and unregistered together, share for the first time during the eighties, increased their contribution to growth to 1.36 percentage points which is more than the contribution of agriculture".[19] Since the contribution of non-agricultural sector to total growth is higher than the agricultural sector, the share of agriculture to Gross

Domestic Product (GDP) at 1980-81 prices also shows a declining trend. The share of agriculture to GDP during 1950-51 to 1952-53 was 55.13 per cent. During 1960-61 to 1962-63 it was 49.18 per cent, 1970-71-1972-73 42.94 per cent and during 1980-81-82-83, it was only 37.37 per cent.[20]

Secondly, ... "if the rate of growth of the non-agricultural sector is increasingly higher than that of agriculture, the decline in the share of agriculture in the growth of total product would be even greater.[21] The percentage rate of growth of manufacturing in India, registered and unregistered together, has been 12.49 per cent during 1950-51 – 60-61, 9.18 percentage during 1960-61 – 1970-71, 9.26 per cent during 1970-71 – 1980-81 and 14.53 per cent during 1980-81 to 1988-89. As against it the share of agriculture in the growth of GDP has been 1.55 per cent, .99 per cent, .77 per cent and 1.00 per cent during the same decades. The overall declining trend is higher in case of agriculture as against the increasing percentage contribution of manufacturing sector.

Thirdly, "if we assume that the rate of growth of country-side product is constant over-time...and if...the rate of growth of the non-agricultural sector is higher than the rate of growth of agriculture, then either "rb" or "ra" or both, must decline over-time".[23]

Let us now turn from product contribution of agriculture to the growth of country-wide product per worker. This is more useful sectoral analysis. The increment in a country's aggregate product per worker is the sum of: (a) the increment in product per worker in agricultural sector; (b) the increment in product per worker in the non-agricultural sector; and (c) the change in the share of the non-agricultural sector in the labour force which usually shows a rise during the period. According to Kuznets the level and movements of the proportional contribution of agriculture to additions to country-wide product per work may be of three types. **Firstly,** "this proportional contribution will be larger, the larger the terminal share of agriculture in the country's labour force, and the higher the ratio of product per worker in agriculture to that in non-agricultural sector. And if we permit the rate of growth product per worker in the "A and non-A" sectors to differ, the proportional contribution of the agricultural sector will be larger, the higher the ratio of the rate of growth of product per work in the A-sector to that in the non-A sector".

Secondly, "Insofar as in the course of economic growth the share of agriculture in the labour force declines, there will be a continuous decline in the proportional contribution of agriculture to the growth in the country-wide product per worker"...and

Thirdly, "if we assume that the country-wide product per worker grows at a constant percentage rate, the continuous shift of the labour force from the agricultural sector with its lower product per worker to the non-agricultural sector with its high product per worker must be accompanied by a decline in the rate of growth of product in the agricultural sector, or in the non-agricultural sector, or in both".[24]

These statements and conclusions can be examined on the basis of long-term records on product, labour and product per work in agricultural and non-agricultural sectors. The statistical analysis in most of the developing countries reveals that as such the economics obtain a high rate of economic growth along with structural shift, the proportional contribution of agriculture declines rapidly. Studies based on NSS and CSO data seem to be quite relevant in relation to the conclusion drawn by Kuznets.[25]

Increase in agricultural production is a virtual precondition of sectoral diversification and hence of development itself. A growing surplus of agricultural output is required to: (1) increase supplies of food and raw material at non-inflationary prices; (2) widen the domestic market for industrial goods through increased purchasing power within the rural sector; (3) facilitates inter-sectoral transfers of labour and capital for industrial development; and (4) increase foreign exchange earnings through increasing agricultural exports.

Agriculture's Market Contribution

A sector makes a contribution to an economy when it provides opportunities to other sectors to emerge and grow. These opportunities may be provided through the medium of trade where a part of its product, either in domestic or foreign markets, is offered in exchange for goods produced by the other sectors at home or abroad. This may be called market contribution.

The market contribution of agricultural sector as Kuznets explains, can be made by: (1) "Purchasing some production items from other sectors at home and abroad; (2) selling some of its product, not only to pay for the purchases under (i) but also to purchase consumer goods from other sectors or from abroad, or to dispose of the product in any way ofher than consumption within the sector".[26] Hence, the sectoral terms of trade explains the market contribution of a sector with the other sector.

In the early stages of the economic growth, this market contribution of agriculture to economic growth is found larger as it account for a greater share of the net output of the economy. Hence, the magnitude of the trade with other sectors will also be larger and will have greater bearing on the economic base of the country. But as the process of growth proceeds and the economy moves towards industrialisation, the share of agriculture declines in both product and labour force and as a result the proportionate market contribution of agriculture began to decline. Thus, agricultural market contribution will be high in the early stage of growth and gradually declines as growth proceeds.

In the process of economic development agriculture provides a market for the product of non-agricultural sectors. Rapid industrialisation itself depends on how rapidly agricultural income is rising and, in turn, is rapidly increasing the demand for industrial goods. In the early stages of economic growth, rising incomes in the agricultural sector can expand the market not only for the light consumer goods such as radios, bicycles, kitchen wares, readymade garments, electric-appliances and construction materials, but for the agricultural inputs as well such as tractors, pumping sets, electric motors and other machines, fertilisers, seeds and pesticides. The need to purchase these new goods from other sectors would mean an increasing marketisation of the production process within the agricultural sector. It provides the level of purchases of the agricultural sector from the other sectors.

Agriculture not only expands the market for industrial consumption goods and various modern agricultural inputs, but has been the main supplier of labour, raw material and savings to non-agricultural sector. Various consumer goods industries such as textile, silk, wool, tea, coffee, rubber, tobacco, sugar, edible oil, food processing industry, paper, paints depends upon the crucial raw material supplied by the agricultural sector. Agriculture also provides cheap labour to various non-agricultural sector such as industries, transport and construction.

In this trading process, other economic activities such as research, construction and transport also expand equally. As the markets expands, transport construction market-research and many other activities receive the full benefits of trading process. Thus, agricultural sectors sell its product, labour and capital to other sectors and in turn, purchase some goods and services from them. This trading process expands the market for both and develops transport, research, construction and various marketing and trading institution.

On international market side, agriculture's contribution is also of strategic importance. Each country has some products in which she has a comparative advantage. This is mainly because of the bounty of nature. In agriculture natural endowment has greatest weight and as such in the initial stages of growth, it remain a major source of export and played a strategic role in expanding international markets and enhancing the export reserves.

Agriculture Factor Contribution

Factor contribution of agriculture to economic growth occurs when some resources are transferred from agriculture to non-agricultural sectors of the economy.

(a) Capital Contribution

The factors which are usually transferred from agriculture to non-agricultural sectors are capital and labour. In case of capital, two different types of transfers occur. These may be compulsory or forced or may be voluntary. Sources of capital for economic development are conveniently divided into three categories – foreign-aid, foreign commercial investment and domestic savings. Studies prove that the burden of domestic saving is likely to fall heavily on the agricultural sector. "The greater the extend to which a low-income country chooses not to receive or cannot receive foreign aid and foreign commercial investment the greater the extent to which it must draw upon its own resources, chiefly from the dominant agricultural sector".[27]

The contribution of the agricultural sector to capital formation may be marshaled in four ways. Firstly, it may be extracted by the Government through the medium of taxes such as land tax and agricultural income-tax. Secondly, agricultural production may be increased sufficiently to bring about a relative decline in agricultural prices and hence favour increased profits in the non-farm sector which, in turn, bring about favourable effects on savings and investment in that sector. Thirdly, agriculture may form capital directly within its own sector and minimise its own demands for capital from other sectors. And fourthly, agriculture may invest directly in other sectors – perhaps after its own development has increased demand for products from other sectors.[28]

Among four categories while the first one is the compulsory or forced extraction of capital resources from agriculture, the latter one are voluntary. Japan and the former USSR present the classic example of forced extraction of capital resources from agriculture. In an economy where agricultural sector is poverty stricken and income disparities are large, landless labourers and small land holders are in abundance, forced and compulsory methods of extracting capital may not be called appropriate. In such countries, substantial aggregate capacity for capital contribution lies with only few rich farmers whose percentage is very small. Forced method can only be justified only to that small segment of the rural community. Voluntary categories obviously, go in favour of the majority of the poor peasantry class.

Utilisation of rural savings for the capital formation of other sector is an other important part of capital transfer from rural to non-rural sector. If we have a data on saving and capital formation in agriculture and non-agricultural sectors, there is no problem in measuring the extent to which saving originating in agricultural sector contribute the financing of capital formation in other sectors of the economy. But such data is very scanty in most of the developing countries and we can only speculate the magnitudes of such contribution. We know that in the initial stage of economic growth the share of agriculture in total GDP is large. And the per capita income is distinctly lower than in the non-agricultural sector. Hence, the share of domestic saving originated in agricultural sector will be a function of: (I) "the share of agriculture in total income, (II) the lower level of real income in agriculture in comparison to other sectors, and (III) the relative propensity to save of the rural population and of the other sectors in the economy". If we assume that the share of agricultural sector in total national income is 60 per cent, its share in labour force is 75 per cent and savings is 5 per cent of its income which is only half of the income of non-agricultural sector, the total domestic saving would then amount to 7 per cent of national income of which 4 per cent would be originated in the non-agricultural sector and 3 per cent in the agricultural sector.[29]

The flow of savings out of the agricultural sector for the capital formation of the other sectors depends largely upon the relative needs of these sector for capital. These needs are reflected in differential rates of return. The incremental capital output ratio (ICOR) might suggest how much capital is needed to secure additional output. The available data reveals that in all developed countries the ICOR for the agricultural sector is not too different from the national ratio. If we assume this situation to be valid for the early stages of economic growth, the allocation of savings would largely depend upon the relative rates of growth of the agriculture and non-agricultural sector.[30]

Thus, to know whether or not there will be a flow of savings from the agricultural sector to finance capital formation in the non-agricultural sector, the comparison of two fractions are essential: (i) "the ratio of additions to product of the agricultural sector to additions to the total product of the economy; and (ii) the ratio of savings originating in agriculture to all savings originating in the economy". If we assume that the rate of net saving is 7 per cent, the rate of growth of net product is 3 per cent per annum, the ICOR is 2.3 to 1, and the rate of growth of non-agricultural sector is four times that of the product of the agricultural sector, the required capital formation in the agricultural sector will be only 27 per cent of the total capital formation needed; whereas savings originated in agricultural sector are 43 per cent of the total savings. On this basis a flow of savings originating in the agricultural sector into the capital formation in the non-agricultural sector would be somewhat less than a quarter of the non-agricultural sector.[31]

This is purely an illustrative example where the variable used in the discussion require an empirical test. The rate of growth of non-A-sector may be more than four times that of sector-A. And the ICOR for sector-A may also be distinctly lower than the ICOR of non-A sector. There are some cases where in some periods agricultural output may increased significantly with little or no capital investment. In all such cases, the flow of savings from agriculture to finance capital formation elsewhere would be relatively larger than what is illustrated in the example.[32]

In India when we look at the growth rate and saving together, we find that growth rate had a tendency to decline a little over the three decades (1950-73) and then jump to higher levels in eighties, while the savings were also rising except the decade eighties.[33] During 1950-51 to 1989-90 the ICOR trend in India has been fluctuating. It was lowest (2.9) during 1950-51 to 1955-56, but increased to 3.40 during 1956-57 – 1960-61 and 5.43 during 1961-62 – 1965-66. During 1966-67 – 1970-71, there was a little decline. It was 3.43 during this period. But again in the two subsequent periods 1971-72 to 1975-76 and 1976-77 – 1980-81. ICOR has been constantly rising. It was 5.80 and 6.70 respectively. The period starting from 1981-82 shows a sudden decline. It was 4.14 during 1981-82 to 1985-86 and slightly above 4, that is 4.04, during 1985-86-1990-91. Thus the decade of eighties shows significantly higher growth rate with significantly lower ICOR.[34]

The development of infrastructure and capabilities over the earlier three decades certainly has been used to advantage in the decade of eighties. Still there is vast scope of utilisation of resources already created particularly in the areas of fertilisers, irrigation, power, credit and transport. If concerted effort is made to improve the utilisation of existing capabilities, ICOR will decline in India and the cost of production will also come down.[34(a)] If this trend continued in future decades, the flow of savings from agriculture to finance capital formation elsewhere would also be larger.

Labour Contribution: Migration of labour force from agriculture to non-agricultural sector is another important contribution made by agriculture to the economic growth of a country. Two important aspects have to be discussed. First, the magnitude of the migration and second, the factors involved in such migration.

The feasibility of accelerating development through the transfer of labour from agriculture to industry is subject to the following conditions: (I) The size of surplus reservoir of agricultural labour force; (II) The quality of rural migrants as potential industrial worker; and (III) the supplies and prices of non-labour inputs and other components of the demand for industrial labour.[35]

In many LDCs the rate of migration to cities and towns is higher than the growth of urban and industrial employment. Several development models are based on the mobilisation of surplus agricultural labour force for productive employment outside the agriculture. This "surplus" is supposed to take the form of "disguised unemployment".[36]

A brief survey of some of the important models is as under:

Lewis Model: Lewis has made the following important assumptions to develop his model:

(i) The economy is divided into two sectors. One is backward, predominantly rural sector – subsistence sector. And the other is well-developed capitalist sector.

(ii) The developed capitalist sector utilises capital stock which is reproducible, and capitalist receive payments for such utilisation. On the other hand, the backward agricultural sector utilises non-reproducible capital – for example land.

(iii) The labour supply in the backward agricultural sector is infinite. Labourers, particularly unskilled are available in abundance. This is very crucial assumption of the Lewis model. It implies that the real wage in the subsistence agricultural sector is constant and the marginal productivity of labour is approximately equal to zero. It means that if some workers are removed from crops producing activities total output will remain the same.

(iv) Production technologies differ and as such per capita output is higher in the capitalist sector and low in the backward agriculturist sector.

(v) The economy has very little capital with unlimited supply of unskilled labour. In this situation, it is difficult to promote economic growth as the skill constraint could be very severe. Such constraint, however, can be removed by education and training, that is, by investment on human capital. With little capital, economic growth can take place through transfer of "surplus" labour from agriculture to industry. It is argued that a rise in the demand for labour in the industrial sector does not rise wages because the supply of labour is infinitely elastic with respect to wages.[37]

The transfer of 'surplus' from subsistence agricultural sector to developed capitalist sector should be beneficial to both. After the transfer, the backward agricultural class experiences an improved land: Labour ratio; and the modern capitalist class (industrial sector) obtains labourers which it requires to increase output. The wage in the capitalist sector is determined by what labour earns in the subsistence sector. Capitalist wage is generally higher than the subsistence earnings in order to compensate labour for the cost of transferring and to induce labour to leave the traditional life of the subsistence sector.[38]

The amount of labour that can be transferred will depend upon the amount of capital stock available and the numbers of labour. The rate of transfer will depend upon the rate of growth of profit (or surplus) within the capitalist sector. Lewis argues that profits or surplus generated in the industrial sector are usually invested by the capitalist. This may not be always true. He does recognise the possibility of some "leakages" from the profits, but these "leakages" are supposed to be very small. He emphasises that the key to the process of economic expansion is the use of the capitalist surplus. Following diagram shows the operation of the Lewis model.[39]

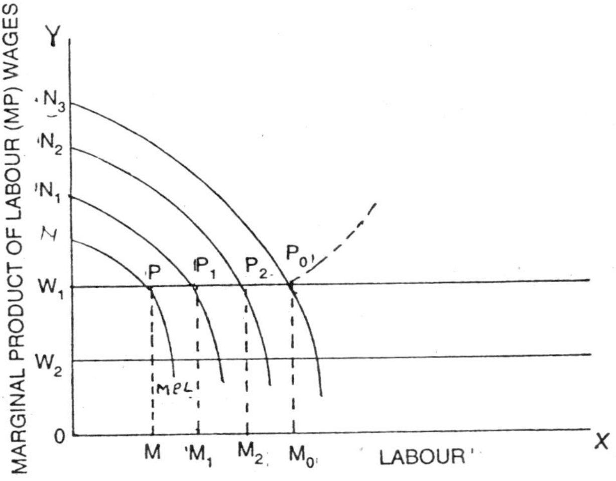

Fig. 1. Marginal Product of Labour (MP) / Wages

In this diagram the horizontal axis measures the amount of industrial labour and the vertical axis measures the marginal productivity and wages. The MP curve measures the marginal productivity of labour. The fixed subsistence wage is shown by OW_S. The industrial wage is equal to OW_1 where $OW_1 > OW_S$. The industrial sector employed labour up to the point where wages are equal to MP_L. Hence P is the initial point of equilibrium and OM amount of labour is employed. The size of profit or surplus within the advanced industrial sector is given by the difference between ONPM and OW_1PM. That is W_1NP. This is total wage bill. Hence, profit is equal to W_1NP.

We assume that capitalists will reinvest all their profits. Then marginal productivity curve will shift to M_1 P_1. Employment will now go up to OM_1 and the size of profits will rise to W_1 N_1 P_1. The real wage will remain fixed at OW_1.

The process will continue to operate until all the surplus agricultural labour is absorbed into the industrial sector. The point of exhaustion of surplus labour is Po with employment OMo. After that point the level of wages will start to rise indicating in the diagram by the dashed line. This implies that after Po, the supply of labour from agriculture to industrial sector will be less than perfectly elastic and it is competing with the industrial sector for more labour. This phase, according to Lewis, is commercialisation of agriculture. Such commercialisation will take place because: (i) of the rise of profits in the capitalist sector, and (ii) the rise of the level of real wages.

Although Lewis model has been considered as one of the pioneering efforts in the development of dual economy, various criticisms are levelled against it.[40]

Firstly, the process of exhaustion of surplus labour may come to an abrupt end because of relative change in the distribution of factor shares. For example, the level of real wages, instead of remaining constant, may rise before commercialisation point (Po) because: (i) of the operation of minimum wages laws; (ii) Government intervention; (iii) trade union activities and (iv) a rise in productivity. Moreover, surplus labour may also be found in the industrial towns and cities. It may not be confined to agricultural subsistence sector. This urban surplus labour has to be absorbed within the industrial sector and this may adversely effect the process of labour transfer from agriculture to industry. But in Lewis model, the labour transfer is not between rural and urban sector, instead, between backward and advanced sector. And the backward sector is not confined to agriculture only but also includes unorganised urban activities.

Secondly, the assumption that the marginal productivity of labour is always near or equal to zero in subsistence sector is also not true. Various empirical studies tend to suggest that the $MP_L > O$.[41] If this is true, then there will be a positive opportunity costs due to transfer of labour from agriculture to industry since such transfer will reduce the level of agricultural output. However, some empirical studies have suggested that a fall in labour supply has led to a fall in agricultural output. Such studies confirms the Lewis-type-hypothesis of a surplus agricultural labour.[42]

Thirdly, many have raised the question of study of Schultz because: (i) the study is not comprehensive enough; (ii) MP_L could be positive in some forms and negative in other; (iii) MP_L could be positive and negative in different seasons of agricultural crop production; (iv) random elements (weather) could probably account for such a fall in output when labour has been displaced.[43]

Fourthly, this is also observed that Lewis-model operates in a specific way which allows employment to grow with reinvestment of surplus or profit. But suppose capitalist, instead of adopting labour-intensive technique, adopts capital-intensive technique of production. In under-developed countries landlords may try to introduce technical progress by mechanisation of agriculture – tracterisation. An increase in capital intensity in under-developed agriculture will rise marginal productivity (MP) per capita and this will shift the MP curve. But this shift may fail to raise the level of employment.[44]

In view of these criticism others have tried to modify or extend the basis of Lewis-model in different ways. Some major contributions come from Fei and Ranis and Jorgenson.

Ranis And Fei Model: The basic aim of RF-model is to demonstrate that by transferring "surplus" labour from agriculture to industrial sector, an economy can be fully commercialised and developed. In Lewis-model, much attention is not paid to the role of agriculture in promoting industrial and economic growth. Actually, the model ignores agricultural sector altogether and consider it as simply a reservoir of labour. RF-model places greater emphasis on the desirability of increasing productivity in the agricultural sector and in its commercialisation. They develop the thesis that agricultural sector not only supplies manpower for industrial development, but a substantial proportion of saving as well for the development process.

RF-model assumes a Lewis-type economy which is characterised by the presence of surplus labour. The level of wages in agricultural sector is assumed to be fixed. The supply curve of labour in the industrial sector is infinitely elastic since the opportunity costs of displacing labour is zero or very small.

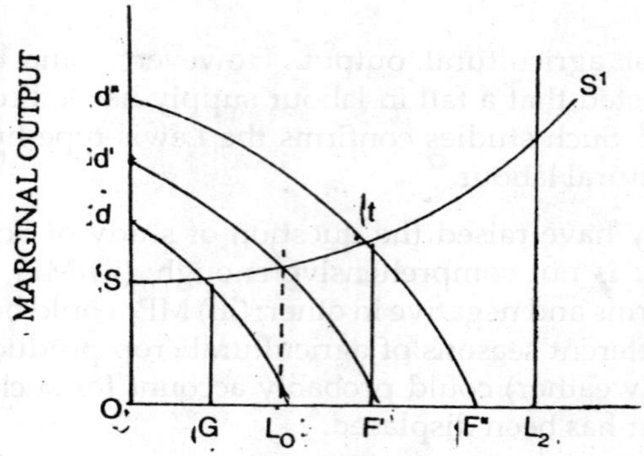

Fig. A

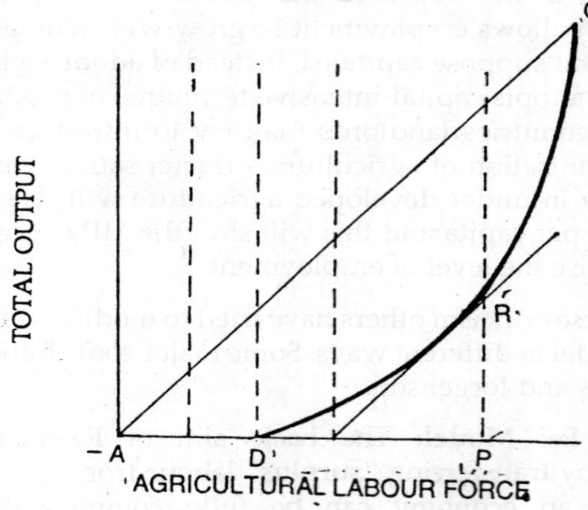

Fig. B

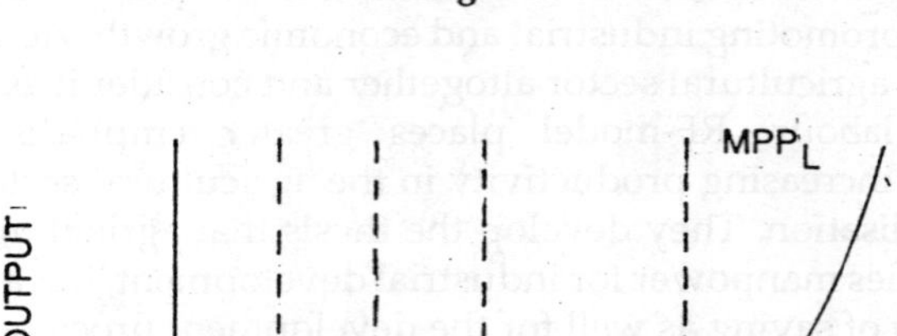

Fig. 2 C

With these assumption the RF-model of economic development consists of three stages of economic growth. In the first stage, it is assumed that the labour supply is infinitely elastic and hence the supply of labour is invariant with respect to changes in the level of wages. Surplus labour with zero or near zero marginal productivity is transferred from agricultural to the industrial sector. Diagram on next page shows that the elasticity of labour supply is infinity, and real wages and marginal product, measured in the vertical axis, remain fixed at a constant institutional wage (CIW). The marginal productivity of labour (MP) is shown by the slope of the production function in figure 'B'. The slope of production function between A and D is flat. This implies that MP is equal to zero. Figure 'C' in the diagram also depict zero marginal product between O and C. In this figure the constant institutional wage is given by OW whereas the average product is given by WVQ. Growth takes place through reinvestment of profit by the capitalist. The d's in figure 'A' refers this reinvestment of profit. And the transfer of surplus labour is depicted by OC = AD. This transfer is completed when the surplus labour is exhausted and MP begins to rise. Up to this stage, there is little difference in the operation of the RF and the LeFig. Cel.[45]

DP in the figure 'B' and CH in figure C shows the completion of this process. This is the second stage of economic development. But wages remain higher than both average product (AP) and marginal product (MP). Since MP in agriculture is positive, the opportunity cost of labour transfer from agriculture to industry would also be positive.

And this is so because of foregone output in agriculture. Hence beyond the point 't' in figure 'A' the supply curve of labour ceases to be completely elastic as it begins to rise.[46]

The economy is fully commercialised at the point E in figure 'C' where MP = CIW. In figure 'B' the corresponding point is indicated by the tangent to the production function at the point 'R'. Hence sections CH in figure 'C' and DP in figure 'B' mark the completion of the second stage of economic development. As long as the supply exceeds OL_2 (in Fig. A) it is in the interest of labourers to leave since such a departure will imply a fall in crop yield by an amount less than the level of wages. But below OL_2 it is in the interest of landlord to keep the labourer on his farm. In this sense in RF-model, the points E, R and L_2 signify points of commercialisation.[47]

So long as the number of labour taken off the land does not exceed OL_0, (Fig. A) total wages fall in proportion to the labour transfer. However total output does not fall as the MPL is zero. This is indicated by the flat section of the production function, in figure 'B'. The surplus is

WL which is proportional to the size of labour force in urban area. If we assume along with RF that landlord will sell all the surplus in the market, then the per capita food for the industrial worker remains the same at W, which is the agricultural subsistence wage. This means that each agricultural worker goes to industry with the same amount of food for his consumption as before.

As the supply of labour in industry is greater than OL_0 a further transfer of labour from agriculture to industry will result in a fall of agricultural output. Hence, beyond this point, "surplus" for every industrial worker will began to decrease. This will result in a rise in the relative price for food and this is why the supply curve of labour in the industrial sector will begin to rise. Thus, Lewis-type model is valid only up to L_0, after that such model no longer functions for the industrial sector since 'unlimited' labour supply at zero opportunity cost ceases to be available. At point L_2 both sectors have commercialised as the value of MP_1 in both sectors have been equalised and wages too, in both the sectors, will be equal to the MP_1.[48]

In the industrial sector a positive surplus or profit will permit capital formation and raise the MPC. This will shift the demand curve for labour to the right. Technical progress in industry will expedite the whole process. As wages in the industrial sector begin to rise in the industrial sector beyond the point L_0, investment and the rate of economic growth will tend to fall. Even if landlords will use substantial proportion of their profit, from the sale of agricultural goods to the urban sector, for investment in industries, it may not be adequate to take the economy to the point like L_2, that is, the point of full commercialisation.

At this stage innovation and technical progress is essential to introduce in agriculture, because such progress will shift the production function in agriculture upwards. The fall in agricultural surplus will thus be offset by the generation of more output and price of agricultural good will remain unchanged. However, landlords will be induced to introduce innovation in agriculture if the price of agricultural goods is allowed to rise initially. Subsidisation of input costs by the Government may also provide further incentives to landlords to introduce technical progress. But in underdeveloped countries the portrait of such dynamic landlords is difficult to envisage.[49]

In RF-model the speed with which surplus labour can be transferred from agriculture to the industrial sector depends upon: (i) the rate of population growth; (ii) the nature of technical progress in agriculture; and (iii) the growth of industrial capital stock which is determined by the rate of growth of profit in the industrial sector and the growth of surplus generated within the agricultural sector. In contrast to the LeFig. Cel Ranis - Fei argue that a balanced growth of both the industrial and the agricultural sector is necessary to avoid stagnation of the rate of economic growth. On policy ground, the growth of agriculture is as important as of industry and the rate at which labour is transferred from the agricultural sector to the industrial sector must be high than the overall rate of growth of population.[50]

Various comments have been made on assumption and operation of RF-model. Some important points are as under. Firstly, like Lewis R.F. also assume that marginal productivity in agriculture is zero in the initial phase of economic development. This assumption is questioned in view of empirical evidence obtained by Mehra, 1966, Desai & Mazumdar, 1970 and Sen 1975. Secondly, the role of money and prices has been neglected. But we know that the credit policies play an important role in easing bottlenecks on the growth of agriculture and industry. Thirdly, RF have not made any distinction between wage-based labour and family-based labour. Fourthly, they do not attempt to discuss the nature and causes of stagnation that characterise the economics of LDCs. A clear understanding of backwardness would have been very useful for policy formulation. Fifthly, RF-model assume a closed economy which denies the possibility of importing food and raw material. Sixthly, RF did not analyse the role of capital in agricultural production. This is an omission. Many who believe in a significant role of capital will find difficult to over-look. In fact, some even may argue that the slow growth rate of industries can be explained by slow growth rate in agricultural productivity in LDCs. Under such circumstances, it is very important to raise agricultural productivity and surplus in the first place. As Jorgenson points out for the expansion of the industrial sector in developing countries it is essential not only to generate an agricultural surplus but also to maintain it through technical progress. And seventhly, RF-model completely neglected the role of the service sector in the absorption of surplus labour. In many LDCs the service sector has played an important role in providing employment.[51]

Jorgenson Model: In contrast to Lewis and RF-model, Jorgenson assumes that 'surplus' labour may exist in LDCs but in the sense of zero MPL in agriculture. The framework of analysis is dualistic which consists of an industrial and agricultural sector. Total output in agricultural sector is a function of land and labour and is subject to an operation of law of diminishing return. Jorsgenson assumes that "transfer of labour from agriculture will result in a decline in agriculture production" and then create "a problem of feeding the increasing urban population. As a result the transformation may be delayed not only by a shortage of capital for non-form jobs, but also by a shortage of food to support the non-form work force". Hence, it has been suggested that "the process of capital formation cannot proceed without technological change in the agricultural sector to increase productivity of the labour force remaining in agriculture so that it may feed itself and the new recruits to the urban labour force". Various empirical evidences (Schultz 1964, Kao, Anschel, and Eicher 1966 and Mellor 1963) supports Jorgenson's basic assumption.[52]

In many LDCs since the output elasticity with respect to changes in labour is relatively stationary, the productivity of labour will remain constant. Hence, it is important either to accelerate the rate of technical progress or to reduce the rate of growth of population. Measures can be taken to take care of both problems at the same time to make significant impact on poverty and development. When the rate of change in output due to technical progress is higher than the rate of growth of labour, a positive growth of agricultural output per worker will be assured. But when both rates are equal the economy will stagnant at a low level equilibrium trap.[53]

A number of criticism have been levelled at the Jorgenson model. The model appears to be inadequate as it emphasis "a situation in which the entire agricultural population is living at a minimum subsistence level. If this is so, the only output that can be withdrawn from agriculture is that resulting from the increased production or that which is consumed by workers to be withdrawn from agriculture". But the empirical evidence shows that "much of the rural population in low-income countries enjoys incomes well above the minimum requirements for subsistence. Thus, in theory, the agricultural sector may be taxed for support of growing urban population even if agricultural production declines with the agricultural labour force"[54]. Further, this model like RF-model, overlooked the important role that service class plays in promoting sectoral as well as overall growth of both agriculture and industry. Without proper facilities of credit, transport, marketing, education, health, communication, growth rates in both sectors could be significantly reduced.[56]

CONCLUDING REMARKS

All the three models discussed above emphasis the need to examine the role of both the agricultural and industrial sector to promote economic growth. In these models basic emphasis is that rising population, increased urbanisation and rising per capita income will put pressure on agriculturer's capacity to produce. If there is no agricultural surplus, continuation of economic development will cause an increase in the prices of agricultural commodities in companion to non-agricultural commodities and as such the terms of trade will change in favour of agriculture. Technological change, innovation, mechanisation help to improve agricultural productivity.

Unfortunately some economists have neglected the vital role that a developed agriculture can play in the promotion of economic growth. Lewis has not paid much attention to the mechanism of development within the agrarian sector. He consider it as merely a reservoir of labour. In other two models – RF and Jorgenson – the structural interdependence of the agricultural and non-agricultural sectors is being highlighted. But some of assumptions have not been sustained in practice. Actually, Lewis and RF-models have not emphasised the crucial role of population growth. In Jorgenson model population is given its due weightage.

Some important conclusions may be drawn as under: (i) Expansion of non-agricultural sector is reliant on domestic agriculture, not only for a sustained increase in the supply of food, but also for raw materials used in manufacturing products. Kuznets terms it "production contribution". (ii) Because of the strong agrarian and rural bias of the economy during the early stages of economic growth, the agricultural population inevitably forms a substantial proportion of the home market for the product of the domestic industry, including the market for producer goods as well as consumer goods. Kuznets termed it "market contribution". (iii) Because relative importance of agriculture in the economy declines with economic growth and development, agriculture is seen as a principal source of capital for investment elsewhere in the economy. The development process, thus, evolves the transfer of surplus capital from agriculture to the non-agricultural sector. Similarly, development also entails the transfer of surplus labour from agriculture to non-agricultural occupation. Kuznets call these "agriculture's factor contribution". (iv) Agriculture is also capable of contributing beneficially to the balance of overseas payments either by augmenting the country's export earnings or by expanding the production of import substitute. This is "foreign exchange contribution" of agriculture.[56]

Thus, according to Kuznets, "if agriculture itself grows, it makes a product contribution; if it trades with others, it renders a market contribution; if it transfer resources to other sectors, these resources being productive factors, it makes a factor contribution".[57]

REFERENCES

1. Taylor H.C., *Outlines of Agricultural Economics*, Macmillan.
2. Black J.D., *Introduction to Economics for Agriculture*, Macmillan 1953 p. 14.
3. *Ibid.,.*
4. Forster G.W and Leoger M.C, *Element of Agricultural Economics*, Prentice Hall, 1951 p. 24.
5. Hicks J., *Capital and Growth* 1965 Chapter IV.
6. See Millor J.W., *"Agricultural Development and Inter-sectoral Transfer of Resources"*. In *"Agricultural Development in the Third World"* (Edi) Eicher C.K. and Staatz J.M. *Op. Cit.* Chapter-9 p.p. 136-44.
7. See for detailed Study: Johnston B.F., *"Agriculture and Structural Transformation in Developing Countries: A Survey of Research"*, *Journal of Economic Literature* 1970; Reynolds L.G., *"Agriculture in Development Theory (Edi 1975)*. New Haven Yale University Press.
8. See Stevens R.D., *"Tradition and Dynamics in Small-Farm Agriculture"* (Edi), Iowa State University Press 1977.
9. Ruttan V.M. and Hyayami Y., *"Induced Innovation Model of Agricultural Development"* In Eicher C.K. and Staatz J.M., *Agricultural Development in the Third World*, (Edi) *Op. Cit* Chapter 4. pp. 59-73.
10. For detailed study see: Uma Lele: *"Considerations Related to Optimum Pricing and Marketing Strategies in Rural Development. In Decision-Making and Agriculture*, (Edi) by T. Dams and K. Hunt, 1977, Lincoln: University of Nebraska Press; Uma Lele and Candler W., *Food Security in Developing Countries: National Issues. In Agricultural Development in the Third World*, (Edi) Eicher C.K. and Staatz J.M. *Op. Cit* (Chapter 14) pp. 207-219.
11. For detailed study see: Ruttan V.W, *"Integrated Rural Development: A Skeptical Perspective"*, ***International Development Review*** 1975; Johnston B.F. and Clark W.C, *Redesigning Rural Development: A Strategic Perspective*. John Hopkins University Press, 1975.
12. See – Holdcroft L.E, *The Rise and Fall of Community Development* 1950-65: *A Critical Assessment. In Agricultural Development in the Third World* (Edi) *Op. Cit* (Chapter 3) pp. 45-58.
13. See: Streeten P, *"Development Ideas in Historical Perspective. Economic Growth and Resources Vol. V*, edited by Irma Adelman, 56-67, St. Martin's Press, N. York, 1979.
14. For detailed study See: V.W. Ruttan and Hyayami 4, *"Induced Innovation Model of Agricultural Development"*, *In Agricultural Development in the Third World"* (Edi) *Op. Cit* (Chapter 4) pp. 59-73.
15. S. Kuznets, *"Economic Growth and the Contribution of Agriculture"*, ***International Journal of Agrarian Affairs***, Vol 3, 1961; See also: *"Economic Growth and the Contribution of Agriculture. Note on Measurements"*, In Eicher E. and Witt L., (Edi) *"Agriculture in Economic Development"*, Vora & Co, Bombay, 1964 pp. 102-19; Ghatak. S. and Ingersent K, *"Agriculture and Economic Development"*, Select Book Service Syndicate, N. Delhi 1964, Chapter 3 pp. 26-69.

16. Mellor J.W., *The Economics of Agricultural Development*, Cornell University Press, New York 1966 Chapter 3 and 4.
17. Kuznets S., *"Economic Growth and the Contribution of Agriculture, Notes on Measurements"*. In Eicher C. and Lawrence W. (Edi) *Op. Cit.*.
18. *Ibid.,*.
19. Hashim S.R, *"Forty Years of Indian Economy: Structure and Dimensions of Growth.* ***The Indian Economic Journal*** *Vol 38 No. 3* January – March 1991 pp. 5-6.
20. *Ibid.*, p.11. (Table 4)
21. Kuznets S., *Op. Cit.*
22. Hashim S.R., *Op. Cit.* pp. 12-13 (Table 5,6)
23. Kuznets S. *Op. Cit.*
24. Kuznets S. *Ibid., Op. Cit.* p.108.
25. For Example See Das Gupta A.K., *"Agriculture and Economic Development in India"*. Associate Publishing House New Delhi 1973 (Chapter I, III, IV, V and VI).
26. Kuznets S, *Op. Cit.* pp. 109-110.
27. Mellor J.W. *"The Economics of Agricultural Development"*, *Op. Cit.* p 84.
28. *Ibid.,*.
29. Kuznets S., *Economic Growth and the Contribution of Agricultural*: Notes on Measurement *Op. Cit.* pp. 115-16.
30. *Ibid.,*. p. 116.
31. *Ibid.,*. pp. 116-17.
32. *Ibid.,*. p. 117.
33. Hashim S.R., *Forty Years of Indian Economy: "Structure and Dimension of Growth"*, *Op. Cit.* p. 3.
34. *Ibid.*
34. (a) *Ibid.,*. pp. 3-4.
35. Ghatak S. and Ingersent K., *"Agriculture and Economic Development"*, *Op. Cit.* p.50.
36. *Ibid.*, pp. 51-52. See for detailed Study: *"Nurkse R, Problems of Capital Formation in Under-developed Countries"*, Oxford 1953; Lewis W.A, *"Economic Development With Unlimited Supplies of Labour"*, Manchester School Economics & Social Studies, 1954; Ranis, G and Fei, J.C.H., *"A Theory of Economic Development"*, ***American Economic Review***, 1961 (reprinted in Eicher & Witt, 1964 *Op. Cit.*); Ranis, G and Fei, J.C.H., *Development of the Labour Surplus Economy*, Theory & Policy. Economic Growth Centre, Yale University, 1967; Jorgenson D.W., *"The Development of A Dual Economy"*, ***Economic Journal***, June, 1971, *Kao Charles H.G., Kurt R., Anschel and Eicher C.K., "Disguised unemployment in Agriculture; A Survey"*. In Eicher C.K. and Witt L. (Edi) *Agriculture in Economic Development" 1964*; Todaro M.P., *"A Model of Labour Migration and Un-*

employment in Less Developed Countries", **American Economic Review** 1969 Schultz T.W., *Transforming Traditional Agriculture*, Yale University Press. New Haven 1964.

37. Ghatak S and Ingersent K., *"Agriculture and Economic Development"*, *Op. Cit.* pp. 98-99.
38. *Ibid.*, p. 99.
39. *Ibid.*, pp. 99-100
40. *Ibid.*, pp. 101-105.
41. Mehra S., *"Surplus Labour in Indian Agriculture"* In Parmit Chaudhuri (Edi) *Reading in Indian Agricultural Development*, George Allen & Unwin London 1966; Desai, M. and Mazumdar, D, *"A Test of Hypothesis of Disguised Unemployment"*, **Economics**, 1970; Sen A.K., *Employment, Technology, Development*, Oxford 1975.
42. Schultz T.W. *Transforming Traditional Agriculture*, Yale University Press, New Haven 1964.
43. Ghatak S and Ingersent K., *Agriculture and Economic Development. Op. Cit.* p.101 see also reference No. 41.
44. *Ibid.*, p. 103.
45. *Ibid.*, p. 105.
46. *Ibid.*, p. 106.
47. *Ibid.*,
48. *Op. Cit* pp. 106-8.
49. *Ibid* p. 108.
50. *Ibid.*, pp. 108-109 pp. 108-109.
51. *Ibid.*, pp. 109-112; For the criticism of RF-model see also: Oshima H.T, *"The Ranis-Fei Model of Economic Development: Comment"*, ***American Economic Review** Vol 53*, June 1953. Reprinted in Eicher C and Witt L, (Eds) *Op. Cit.*
52. Mellor J.W, *"Towards a Theory of Agricultural Development"*, In South-Worth H.M. and Johnston B.F, (Edi) *Agricultural Development and Economic Growth*, Cornell University press (London) 197; pp. 25-27; Ghatak S and Ingersent K, *Op. Cit.* pp. 111-113; Kao C.H.C. Anschel K.R. and Eicher C.K, *Disguised unemployment in Agriculture: A Survey. Op. Cit*; Schultz T.W, *Transforming Traditional Agriculture. Op. Cit.*
53. Ghatak S and Ingersent K. *Op. Cit* p.113.
54. Mellor J.W. *"Towards a Theory of Agricultural Development" Op. Cit* p. 26.
55. Ghatak S. and Ingersent K. *Op. Cit.* p. 114.
56. *Ibid.*, pp. 26-27.
57. Kuznets S, *Economic Growth and the Contribution of Agriculture: Notes on Measurement. Op. Cit.* p. 114

PART - II

PRODUCTION ECONOMICS

(i) PRODUCTION ECONOMICS. A CONVENTIONAL APPROACH

(ii) ISOQUANT-ISOCOST PRODUCTION FUNCTION: A NON-CONVENTIONAL APPROACH

(iii) MULTIPLE OUT-PUT WITH ONE INPUT ANALYSIS

(iv) COST, REVENUE AND PROFIT MAXIMISATION

(v) RISK AND UNCERTAINTY IN FARMING

(vi) COB-DOUGLAS PRODUCTION FUNCTION: A CRITICAL EVALUATION

1

PRODUCTION ECONOMICS

Production Function: (Conventional Approach)

In economics production function generally refers to a "process whereby some goods and services called inputs are transformed into other types of goods and services called outputs". Production function is, therefore, a process of conversion of certain inputs into a consumable outputs. From technical point of view it refers to a quantitative relationship between input and output. It describes the way in which the quantity of particular product depends upon the quantities of particular inputs used. For example, a farmer may produce 100 quintals of rice if he use 8 kg. of seed on one acre of land. If he use 10 kg. of seed on the same plot of land, the yield might be increased, say 118 kg. The input and output relationship indicate how the production of rice vary as the seed input is changed. This indicates that production function "provides information concerning the quantity of output that might be expected when particular inputs are combined in specific manner".[1] The chemical, physical, and biological properties of inputs determine the kind and amount of outputs which will be received from particular combinations of inputs.

There are many possible combinations of inputs. Obviously, all production functions are not known. It is the job of research and experimentation to discover the production functions which are physically, chemically and biologically possible. Once production has been discovered, it provides useful information for making decisions. An important point to note is that producers do not control the production functions. They can only choose between alternative functions. Economic considerations arise from the fact that a choice between alternative production functions must be made. If a producer is interested in maximizing net revenue from the given resources, he will wish to employ some production function in preference to other.

One of the simplest production decisions is to know the effects of varying the quantity of one input on the amount of product or output produced. If Y_1 stands for the product and X_1 for the input, the production function $Y_1 = f(X_1)$ tells decision makers that amount of Y_1 depends upon, or is a function of, the amount of X_1 used in producing Y_1. This expression $Y_1 = f(X_1)$, however, does not explain the amount by which Y_1 changes as X_1 changes. Hence, information must be available concerning not only kind but also the quantities of inputs used to produce particular quantities of products. Since production is not the function of one input, but of various inputs, say, land, capital, labour, seed, fertilizers, machinery etc., the production function, in real sense, can be expressed as:

$$Y_1 = f(X_1, X_2, X_3, X_4, X_5, ..., X_n).$$

Here producer needs to know the quantitative relation between inputs and outputs. If a farmer knows that in producing corn nitrogen fertilizer is essential, then he must also know the amount of nitrogen to apply in the production of corn. This information that corn is produced by the combination of land, labour, fertilizer, capital, seed, organisation, water etc. is incomplete and unfruitful unless the farmer knew something about the manner in which these inputs must be combined in order to produce corn.

That is, he must know how and when the land should be prepared, fertilizer and water should apply, seed should sow. Hence, "the kind and amount of product which a farmer produces depend upon the kind and quantities of inputs used in production and the way in which they are combined".[2]

When a farmer is confronted with the question how much nitrogen (fertilizer) is to be used in corn production he may consider the other inputs as given and constant in specified kinds and quantities. Then the production function can be expressed as:

$$Y_1 = f(X_1, X_2, X_3, X_4 ....X_n).$$

That is the amount of Y_1 output, say corn, depends upon or is a function of X_1 (nitrogen), while the amount of all other inputs X_2, X_3, X_4....X_n as land, labour, irrigation, seed etc are considered as given and constant

Now, the manner in which the amount of Y_1 varies as the amount of X_1 varies depends upon the amount of X_1 used. There are three types of relationship between Y_1 and X_1. One possibility is that there is a constant relationship between the application of X_1 and the amount of Y_1 produced. This is a linear relationship which can be expressed as:

$$Y_1 = a + bx_1.$$

For example if farmer expects 1 quintal of wheat for each 2 kg of fertilizer applied, this can be expressed as $Y_1 = a + 0.5\ X_1$ where "a" is the intercept which indicates production of wheat without fertilizer applied and 0.5 indicates that Y_1 increases by 0.5 for every increase of 1 kg. fertilizer. Suppose that "a" equal to 30 quintal that is, the farmer expects 30 quintal of wheat without the application of fertilizer. The production function would then be $Y_1 = 30 + 0.5\ X_1$ and the relationship between Y_1 and X_1 would be as explained in the following diagram.

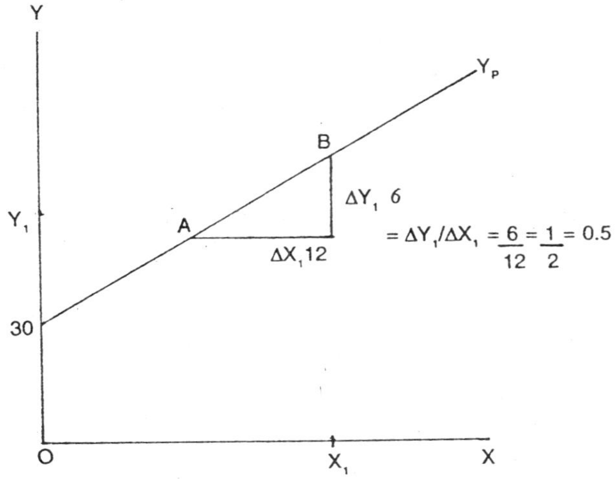

Fig. 1

We see that the production function is a straight line which shows that it has the same slope throughout its entire range. The slope of a line is defined as the vertical distance divided by the horizontal distance or Y divided by X. In our diagram, going from the point 'A' to 'B' the change in Y_1, that is ΔY_1, is 6 and the change in X_1, that is ΔX_1, is 12. Thus, the slope of the line – production function – between A and B is $\Delta Y_1/\Delta X_1$ or 6/12 or 1/2 or 0.5. Since the production function is a straight line, the slope 1/2 or 0.5 is found at any point on the curve. The amount of product increases by the same amount for each additional unit of input. It is, therefore, said that there are constant returns from the input being varied in the production of particular commodity. Once the manner in which the output varies in relation to the quantity of input has been determined, this relationship can be expressed in tabulation form. The following table shows constant relationship between X_1 and Y_1.

X_1	Y_1	Slope of the line $\Delta Y_1/\Delta X_1$
0 kg	30 Quintals	0
25 "	42.5 "	12.5/25 1/2 or 0.5
50 "	55.0 "	12.5/25 1/2 or 0.5
75 "	67.5 "	12.5/25 1/2 or 0.5
100 "	80.0 "	12.5/25 1/2 or 0.5
125 "	92.5 "	12.5/25 1/2 or 0.5
150 "	105.0 "	12.5/25 1/2 or 0.5

This can also be expressed as:

$$\Delta Y_1/\Delta X_1 = \Delta Y_2/\Delta X_2 = \Delta Y_3/\Delta X_1 .... = \Delta Y_n/\Delta X_1$$

This kind of relationship is seldom found in agriculture when only one factor is varied with respect to all other factors.

Another type of relationship which we observe is when each successive input of the variable resource adds more to the total product than the previous input. Where this is true, we say that there are increasing returns from the input. This case is illustrated in the following hypothetical table and the diagram.Here as inputs are added, ΔY_1

X_1	ΔX_1	Y_1	ΔY_1	$\Delta Y_1/\Delta X_1$		
5	—	10	—	—		
15	5	22	12	12/5	or	2.5/1
20	5	48	26	26/5	or	5.2/1
25	5	75	27	27/5	or	5.5/1
30	5	110	35	35/5	or	7.0/1
35	5	150	40	40/5	or	8.0/1
40	5	200	50	50/5	or	10.0/1

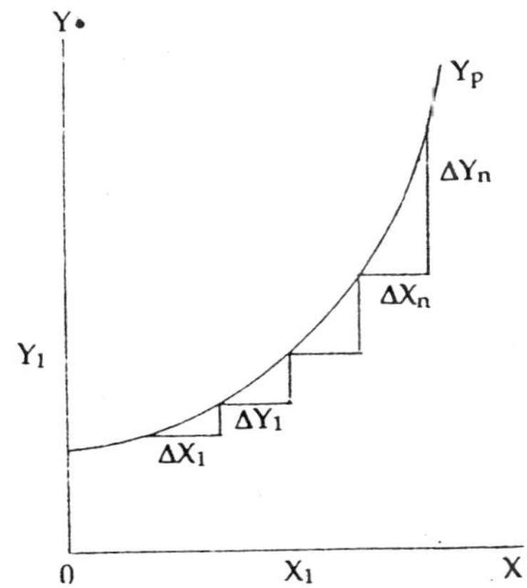

Fig. 2

increases for any given ΔX_1. The production function curve Y_p is convex to the X-axis and its slope becomes steeper as inputs are added. The triangles illustrate increasing returns; while return from first units of input is 2.5, the return from second unit is 5.2, and similarly the return from last unit of input is 10. Each additional unit of input adds more to output than the previous unit. This relationship can be expressed as:

$$\Delta Y_1/\Delta X_1 < \Delta Y_2/\Delta X_2 < \Delta Y_3/\Delta X_3 .... < \Delta Y_n/\Delta X_n$$

Since $\Delta X_1 = \Delta X_2 = \Delta X_3 ..... = \Delta X_n$, the ratio of $\Delta Y/\Delta X$

will go on increasing as more and more units of input are added. Increasing returns take place because in the beginning the quantity of fixed factor is abundant in relation to the quantity of the variable factor and as a result when more and more units of variable factor are added to the fixed factor, it is used more intensively and effectively. In other words, in the initial stages the productivity of factor is not fully explored and as a result it gives more production as more units are added. Centuries ago Adam Smith had also pointed out division of labour as the main cause of increasing returns. So the high degree of specialisation is also an important reason of higher productivity and more production.

A third type of relationship which we observe in production function is one where each additional unit of input results in a smaller increase in product than the preceding units. This can be illustrated in the following hypothetical table and a graph.

X_1	ΔX_1	Y_1	ΔY_1	$\Delta Y_1/\Delta X_1$
5	—	10	—	—
10	5	18	8	8/5 = 1.6/1
15	5	25	7	7/5 = 1.4/1
20	5	31	6	6/5 = 1.2/1
25	5	35	4	4/1 = .8/1
30	5	38	3	3/5 = .6/1
35	5	40	2	2/5 = .4/1
40	5	41	1	1/5 = .2/1

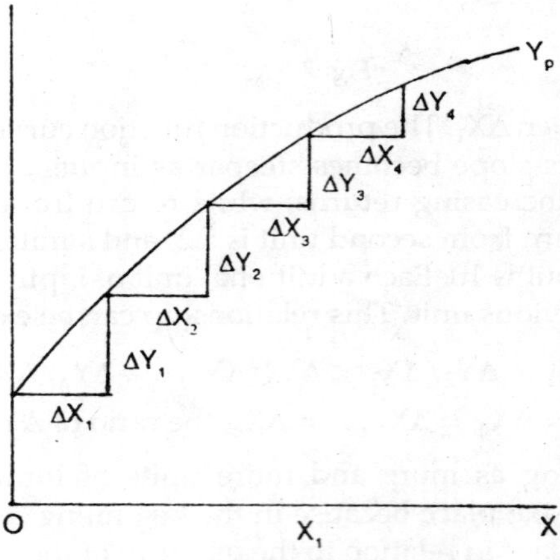

Fig. 3.

Table presents a case of diminishing returns. If the first input adds 1.6 units of output the last unit. adds only .2. In the whole series every additional unit adds less than the preceding unit. The slope of production curve Y_p becomes smaller as more inputs are added or in other words:

$$\Delta Y_1/\Delta X_1 > \Delta Y_2/\Delta X_2 > \Delta Y_3/\Delta X_3 .... > \Delta Y_n/\Delta X_n$$

Since $X_1 = X_2 = X_3 .... = X_n$, the ratio of $\Delta Y/\Delta X$ goes on decreasing as more units of X are applied.

This law is applicable in all practical situation of agricultural production. As doses of variable factors are increased we will soon reach a stage where returns are maximum. But beyond this point, further increase of the dose of variable factor will yield diminishing returns because the fixed factor such as land then becomes inadequate in relation to the quantity of the variable factor such as labour. It means, after the point of inflection, contribution to production made by the variable factor becomes less and less because additional unit of variable actor has to work with less and less fixed factor. The phenomenon of diminishing returns is, thus, closely related to indivisibility of fixed factors. Indivisibility refers that equipment is available only in minimum sizes or in definite ranges of size.

Since the law of diminishing returns refers to situations in which the proportions of the inputs are varied, it is also called the law of variable proportions. The law of variable proportions is a technological law which describes a physical relationship between inputs and outputs. Therefore, we cannot determined the quantity of particular variable inputs which could yield the greatest net revenue from a production of a commodity. For this price information is essential along with the knowledge of the physical relationship. This price information along with the physical relationship will help us to determined the level of output that will yield maximum net revenue. This problem has been explained and analysed in the next chapter.

Total, Average and Marginal Product

By summing the quantity of output produced by different quantities of one variable input, we can get a total production. From this total output two more products can be estimated. One is the average and the other is the marginal product. The average product (AP) is defined as the ratio of the total product (TP) to the quantity of input used in producing that amount of product. This can be expressed as:

$$AP = Y_1/X_1$$

If 10 points of input produce 40 units of output, the AP will be 40/10 or 4.

The marginal product (MP) is defined as the addition to product resulting from the addition of one unit of the input. This can be expressed as: $MP = \Delta Y_1/\Delta X_1$

Thus MP for a unit of input is the change in product divided by the change in input. In other words, it is the rate of change in total product as the quantity of input increases. Mathematically, MP is the first derivative of the total product. It may be calculated by constructing a tangent to a total product curve and determining the slope of the tangent at the point in question. The hypothetical schedule of TP, AP and MP and their related curves have been explained as under:

$$MP = \Delta Y_1/\Delta X_1.$$

Input X_1	*Total Product* *TP*	*Average Product* *AP* (Y_1/X_1)	*Marginal Product* *MP* $(\Delta Y_1/\Delta X_1)$
0	0	—	—
1	10	10	10
2	28	14	18
3	42	14	14
4	52	13	10
5	60	12	8
6	66	11	6
7	70	10	4
8	72	9	2
9	72	8	0
10	70	7	–2

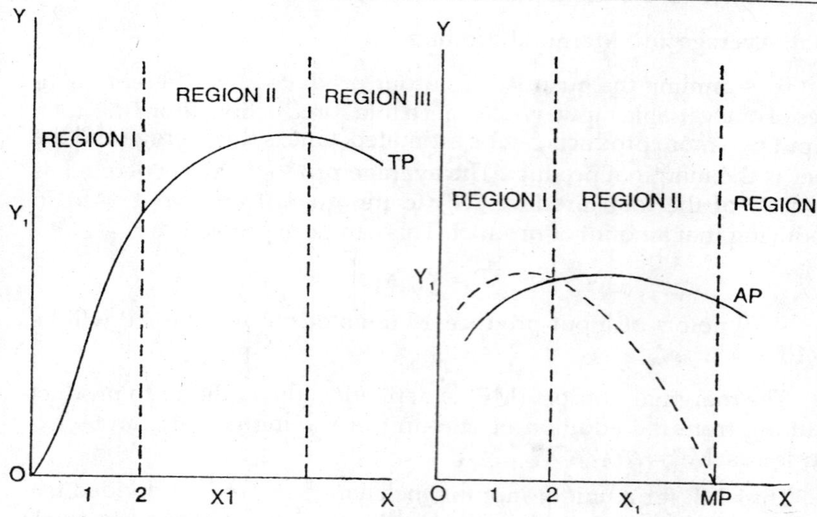

Fig. 4

Since both the average and the marginal products are derived from the total product, both are also related to the shape of the total product curve. Thus, when the TP is increasing at an increasing rate, the MP is also increasing and when TP is increasing but at a decreasing rate, the MP is decreasing. The derivation of AP and MP curves from the TP are given as under:

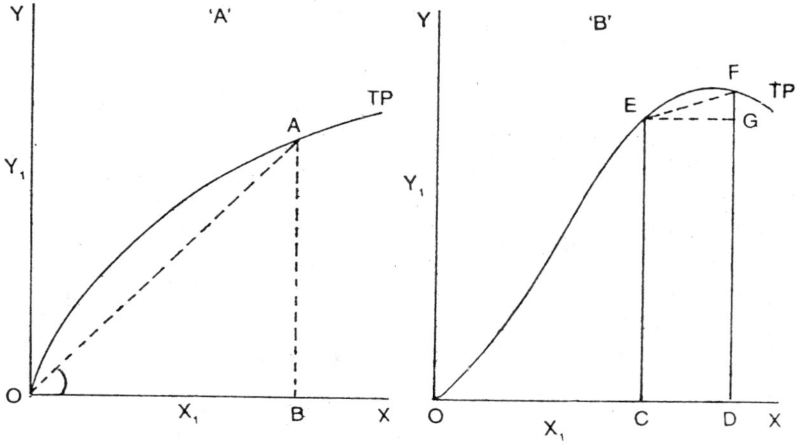

Fig. 5

In figure A OB is the input level and the corresponding level of output is AB. At this level APP is measured by the ratio Y_1/X_1 or AB/OB. We know AB/OB is also the tangent of the angle A OB which is derived by drawing a line from the origin O through point A on the production function. Therefore, APP = tan A OB. Point E in figure 'B' is the point where tan A OB is maximum. MP is measured in figure B. The distance CD represents one unit of input. Therefore, FG distance can be measured as MP. Here MP = FG/EG = tan F E G which indicates the slope between the points E and F. A combined figure of TP, AP, and MP and their relationship has been given as under:

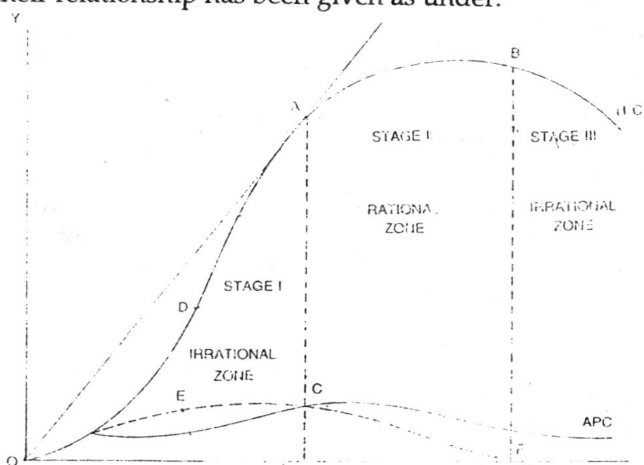

Fig. 6

Diagram shows that so long as TPP rises at an increasing rate, MPP is also rising and production curve is concave upwards. Beyond point D TPC is rising, but at a diminishing rate. Corresponding to TPC, MPC starts declining. Beyond point E on MPC curve, this declining trend can be visualised. TPC is highest at point B and at that point MPC falls to zero (point F). Beyond this point if variable inputs are further added, TPC will fall absolutely and MPC becomes negative. MPC starts declining beyond point D and it intersect APC at point C which is the point of maximum value of AP. This intersection refers the equality of MP and AP at maximum AP. The relationship between AP and MP thus, can be analysed on three propositions:

(i) In the beginning total product rises at an increasing rate, average and marginal products also increase but MP rises at a faster rate than AP. Here production curve is concave upwards.

(ii) When AP reached at maximum and is constant MP = AP.

(iii) Beyond this maximum point AP starts falling, but MP falls more than AP.

These relations can be expressed as:

when AP is rising MP > AP

when AP is maximum and constant MP = AP

when AP is falling MP < AP.

Rational and Irrational Zone of Production Function

The input-output relations discussed above can be divided into three regions in such a manner that we can isolate the portion in which production is most profitable. Stage 1 is characterised by an increasing output per unit of input. When the supply of variable factor is increased in the initial stages, we get increasing returns because fixed factors are made to work to their full capacity. Economists attributed increasing returns to the economies of scale and specialisation. In this stage the average product is increasing. Hence, the marginal product must be greater than the average product. To maximise his profit, a farmer can continue to increase variable factor as long as the average productivity is increasing. In this way, he may go at least to the point of highest average product in the application of inputs.

In stage III the product curve is declining since the marginal product or the amount of product added by additional units of input is negative, we can say that it is not profitable to operate with a combination of resources existing in this region. Here a farmer is incurring greater cost, as he is utilising more of the variable inputs but receiving less output.

A farmer whose rational aim is to maximise profit would find two of the above stages, Ist and IIIrd as irrational. In stage I farmer cannot stop production because in doing so he will suffer a loss. A farmer can increase his profit by switching over to stage II in which the total product is still rising. Thus, for profit maximising, production in stage I is irrational. Similarly stage IIIrd is also irrational, because here a farmer is incurring greater cost but receiving less returns. And this is so because the total output is declining.

We may conclude, that for profit maximisation stage II is the only stage where maximum level of resource use occurs. Regardless of factor cost and product price, the chosen level of input application should be somewhere in the range between maximum APP and zero MPP and this range falls in stage II[3]. In this region, the total output is increasing; the marginal product is decreasing and is positive, and is less than the average product; and the average product is decreasing. The small farmers who has limited funds may operate in a range of increasing returns to capital and they are not irrational producers. They can maintain production in stage I since they do not have enough resources to extend production into stage II.

Best Level of Resource Use: Our analysis of three stages shows that production will pay the farmers to produce somewhere within stage II. But the question is where? or what is the most economical level of input application? Hence, in order to determine at what level in stage II a producer should operate to maximise net revenue, he must have information regarding the price of the product and the price of the input.

Once a physical production has been derived, the amount of revenue from a particular production process can be determined by multiplying the quantity of product produced by the price of the product. And in this way, the production function has been converted into a revenue function. For example, if PY_1 is the price of a product, the total revenue (TR) received from particular level can be derived. Similarly, by multiplying the marginal product by the price of the product, we can determine th amount by which the total revenue changes as inputs are added. I. is known as value of the marginal product (VMP). In the same manner, by multiplying the average product by the price of the product, the value of the average product (VAP) can be determined for particular levels of input. Thus VAP is the value of the product per unit of input at any particular level of input.

If a farmer knows the price of the input (cost) and the value of the marginal product (VMP) he can determine the most profitable level of input. If a farmer buy inputs at a given price (Px_1) he will continue to add additional units of the inputs until the value of the marginal product is just equal to the price of the input. Here it is assumed that the cost of applying the input is included in the price of input and that the price of the input does not change as additional units are applied. At this point, the additional cost of an input is equal to an additional revenue which the input yields. Beyond this level, if more inputs are added, the added costs will be greater than the added return. On the other hand, if fewer units of inputs are used, the value of the marginal product of the input will be greater than the price of the input. This situation refers that the return which the producer gets from the additional unit of input is greater than the cost. These situations have been expressed in the following diagram.

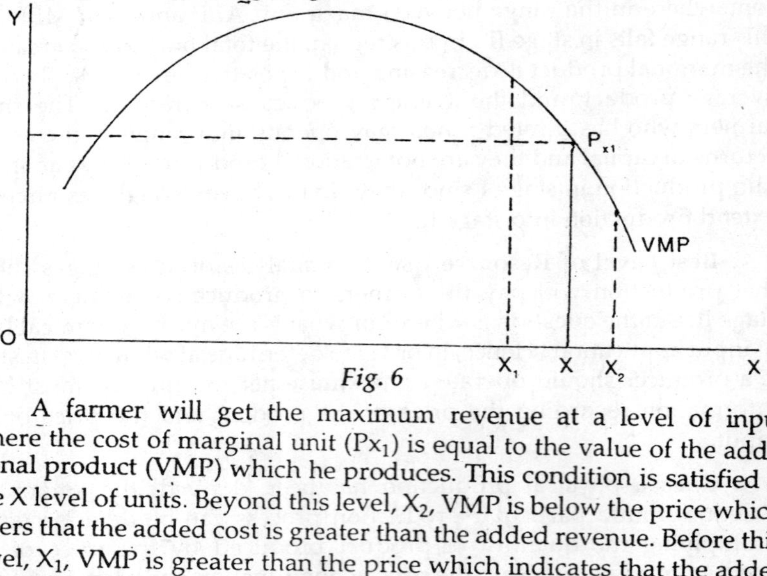

Fig. 6

A farmer will get the maximum revenue at a level of input where the cost of marginal unit (Px_1) is equal to the value of the additional product (VMP) which he produces. This condition is satisfied at the X level of units. Beyond this level, X_2, VMP is below the price which refers that the added cost is greater than the added revenue. Before this level, X_1, VMP is greater than the price which indicates that the added value of marginal product is higher than the added cost and as such the farmer can increase the level of inputs upto X.

We see from the above analysis that the basic condition for maximisation of net revenue is that where the price of the marginal product is equal to the price of the input. This can be expressed as:

$$P_{Y1} (\Delta Y_1/\Delta X_1) = P_{X1}$$

This refers that the added return from the last unit should equal to the cost of adding that unit. We can also express the same condition as:

$$Py_1 \; \Delta \, Y_1 = Px_1 \, \Delta \, x_1,$$

Where $Py_1\ \Delta Y_1$ is the added revenue and $Px_1\ \Delta X_1$ is the added cost. Another way of expressing the condition of maximising revenue is that the ratio of the price of the input to the price of the product shall be equal to the marginal product of the input. And this can be written as:

$$P_{X1}/P_{Y1} = \Delta_{Y1}/\Delta_{X1}.$$

All these three conditions of maximising revenue are related with the application of a single variable X_1 to Y_1 while the level of other inputs are considered unchanged. There are three major factors that affect the most profitable level of an input. These are: (i) price of the output (P_{Y1}), (ii) price of the input (P_{X1}) and (iii) physical production relationship as it affects the marginal product (Δ_{Y1}/Δ_{X1}). Input and output prices change frequently. Since the most profitable level of an input to use in the production of a commodity depends upon the price of that commodity as well as the price of input, changes in prices of either of these affect the most profitable level of input used.[4]

To what extent, changes in prices affect the most profitable level of input? It depends upon the form of production function. If the production function is linear, the MP is constant and AP = MP. Under such condition, if VMP > P_{X1}, it pays to add the input in an infinite amount. On the other hand, if P_{X1} > VMP, it does not pay to use any of the input. The P_{X1} may also be equal to VMP. In this case, the producer is neither in loss nor in gains by varying the amount of input used.[5]

Under conditions of diminishing returns, MP decreases as inputs are added. Therefore, the amount that pays a producer to change an input in response to price changes depends upon the manner the marginal product varies. If Px_1 increases the value of the ratio Px_1/Py_1 is also increased. The MP is now less than the ratio of the price of the product to the new price of the input. In order to make MP again in ratio of the price of the input to the price of the product, the producer must alter the MP, Px_1 or Py_1. A single producer cannot change Px_1 or Py_1. Therefore, if he wants to make $P_{X1}/P_{Y1} = \Delta Y_1/\Delta X_1$ he must increase $\Delta Y_1/\Delta X_1$. In order to increase MP in a region of diminishing returns, it is necessary to decrease the quantity of the input used. Hence if PX_1 increases relative to PY_1 the amount of input which it pays to use and, consequently, the amount of 'Y_1' which it pays to produce decrease.[6]

On the other hand, a decrease in Px_1 decreases the ratio Px_1/Py_1 and MP becomes greater than the ratio of the price of the input to the price of the product. In this case, in the region of decreasing marginal returns, it pays to add additional units of the inputs and, consequently, to increase production of Y_1. The effects of a change in the price of a commodity are comparable to those of a change in the price of an input.

If there is an increase in Py_1, the ratio Px_1/Py_1 decreases. If the MP of X_1 is to be brought into equality with the new price-ratio, a decrease in Py_1 results in an increase in the ratio Px_1/Py_1 and it is profitable to reduce the amount of X_1.[7]

Input Demand Curve: If information regarding prices and production function is given, a producer can determine how much of an input pays him to use. We know, from the above analysis, that the amount of input which it pays to use changes as the price of input changes, even though the price of the product remain constant. In the process of determining the most profitable unit of input for different input prices, a demand schedule for inputs is derived. "This demand schedule shows the maximum quantities of an input which it will pay to purchase at alternative prices of the input". The intersection of the price line and VMP curve determines the most profitable level of input. Thus, VMP curve is, in itself the demand curve for an input in the production of one commodity.[8]

Elasticity of Production

The elasticity of production "Ep" refers to the percentage increase in output as compared to the percentage increase in input and can be computed as:

$$Ep = \frac{\Delta Y/Y}{\Delta X/X} \text{ or } \left(\frac{\Delta Y}{Y}\right) \bullet \left(\frac{\Delta X}{\Delta X}\right) \text{ or } \left(\frac{X}{Y}\right) \bullet \left(\frac{\Delta Y}{\Delta X}\right)$$

Following table provides an analysis of production elasticity.

X_1 *units*	Y_1 *units*	*Ep*
0	0	—
1	100	—
2	160	0.60
3	230	0.70
4	270	0.40
5	285	0.15
6	295	0.10
7	305	0.10
8	308	0.03
9	312	0.04
10		

It is evident from the above table that as the input X_1 increases from 1 to 2,Y_1 increases from 100 to 160. It means that against 100 per cent increase in input, the output has increased only 60 per cent. Therefore,

Ep = 60/100 = 0.6. Similarly, between second and third unit of output, the Ep is calculated to 0.7. In case of Ep following points are important:

(1) A production function with an elasticity 1.0 throughout indicate constant returns to scale. It refers that 1 per cent increase in input is always accompanied by a 1 per cent increase in output.

(2) When the elasticity is 1.0 MP and AP are equal.

(3) A production function for which the elasticity is less than 1.0 throughout refers diminishing returns.

(4) The elasticity is more than 1.0 upto the maximum average product and less than 1.0 between the maximum average and maximum total product..

(5) It becomes less than Zero when the total product declines.[9]

Effects of Changes in Technology

To know the effect of changes in technology on the most profitable level of production, we should observe the manner in which the change in technology brings change in the shape of the total production curve. If the change in technology increases the marginal product, it is profitable to expand the quantity of input used. There is a possibility that a technological change may increase the total product for some levels of input but will not increase MP at these levels. If this is the case, the value of the MP will remain the same for both the methods of production, and the level of input at which the value of the MP = Px_1 is unchanged. Here, it is profitable to expand production of the commodity, but it is not profitable to expand of input used.

REFERENCES

1. Bishop C.E. and Toussaint W.D., *Introduction To Agricultural Economic Analysis*, John Willey & Sons - N. York 1958 pp. 29-30.
2. *Ibid.*, p. 31.
3. Robertson C.A., *An Introduction to Agricultural Economic And Farm Management*, Tata McGraw Hill, Bombay, 1971, p. 11.)
4. *Ibid.*
5. Bishop C.E., Toussaint W.D., *Introduction To Agricultural Economic Analysis, op cit.* p. 46-48.
6. *Ibid.* p. 48.
7. *Ibid.* p. 48.
8. *Ibid.* p. 51.
9. Heady O.E., *Economics of Agricultural Production and Resource Use*, Prentice Hall New Delhi, 1964, p. 50.

2

ISOQUANT-ISOCOST PRODUCTION FUNCTION: A NON-CONVENTIONAL APPROACH

In the introductory part — Chapter-1 the production function has been discussed at traditional lines. In this chapter, an attempt has been made to analyse it with the help of isoquant-isocost approach.

As we have discussed in the previous chapter that agriculture production process needs different types of inputs. These inputs may further be classified into different varieties, types and sizes. For examples, fertilizers may be of different varieties, seeds may be of different types, and machines may be of different sizes. A farmer must choose the particular combination of inputs which would be most profitable to use. That is, he has to make a choice among alternative combinations. He will certainly prefer a combination that maximises his returns. He may choose the amount of hay and grain to be used in feeding dairy animals or the amount of fertilizers to be used in growing wheat. He has to decide whether to use machines on farm or use manpower or animal power. A choice can also take place between hired and family labour. Thus, the problem of best combination of inputs certainly arises and this problem is not only concerned within similar factors (family and hired labour) but even within dissimilar factors (labour and machine, hay and fertilizers) as well.

We start with a situation of two variable inputs. It can be expressed as: $Y_1 = f(X_1, X_2/X_3, X_4 ... X_n)$. That is, production depends upon the amount of X_1 and X_2 used while the other inputs are held constant at particular level. The problem is to determine the amount of X_1 and X_2 to use in the production of Y_1.

Iso-Product or Isoquant Curve

In the production process the same level of out-put can be obtained by various combinations of X_1 and X_2 inputs. When this is possible, the producer may be able to reduce the cost of producing a particular level of output by changing the combination of inputs used. The curve which provides equal amount of product with various combinations of X_1 and X_2 is known as Iso-product or Isoquant or equal-product contour. This will be useful, as we shall see below, in choosing the combination of input which will yield a level of output at a minimum cost. A hypothetical table given below explains this situation.

X1 units		*X2 units*	*Y1 output*
1	+	20	100 quintal
2	+	16	100 quintal
3	+	12	100 quintal
4	+	9	100 quintal
5	+	7	100 quintal
6	+	6	100 quintal

A farmer can produce 100 units of Y_1, say 100 quintals of wheat, by applying any one of the combination of inputs X_1 and X_2. If this schedule is plotted, we get a curve which is known as iso-quant or iso-product curve. This is also known as product indifference curve.

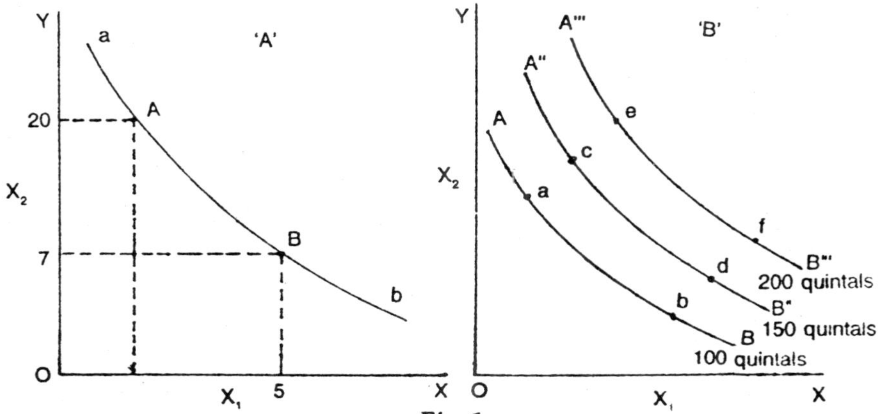

Fig. 1

In diagram "A" a b is the iso-cost curve which shows all possible alternative combinations which can produce 100 units of Y1. Point 'A' on this curve shows that 1 unit of X_1 and 20 units of X_2 can produce 100 quintal of Y_1. The same level of output can be obtained by applying 5 units of X_1 and 7 units of X_2 at point 'B'. The producer has no difference in choosing either of the combinations as both provides the same level of output. Diagram "B" shows various iso-product curves showing different levels of output. Curve A B shows iso-product level of 100 quantals, curve A" B" shows iso-product level of 150 quintals, and curve A''' B''' shows iso-product level of 200 quintals.

The substitutability of two inputs determines the shape of iso-quant. In case the two inputs are perfect substitutes, the shape of the isoquant would be a straight line. Perfect substitutability is difficult to find in agriculture. A tractor and a man (driver) may be an example of this situation. An addition of a tractor will require an additional driver. But, this is not always true. A farmer may have two tractors of different sizes and may have capabilities to perform different tasks. In this situation perfect substitutability between machines and labour does not occur.

Two inputs may be a good substitute or they may be a poor-substitute. If they are good substitutes the isoquant would be slightly curved and convex to the origin and if they are poor-substitutes, the curve will have a steep curvature. Two inputs may also be used in a fixed proportion. This situation refers that they are absolutely non-substitutable and isoquant is of right angle. All these shapes of isoquant are explained in the following diagram:

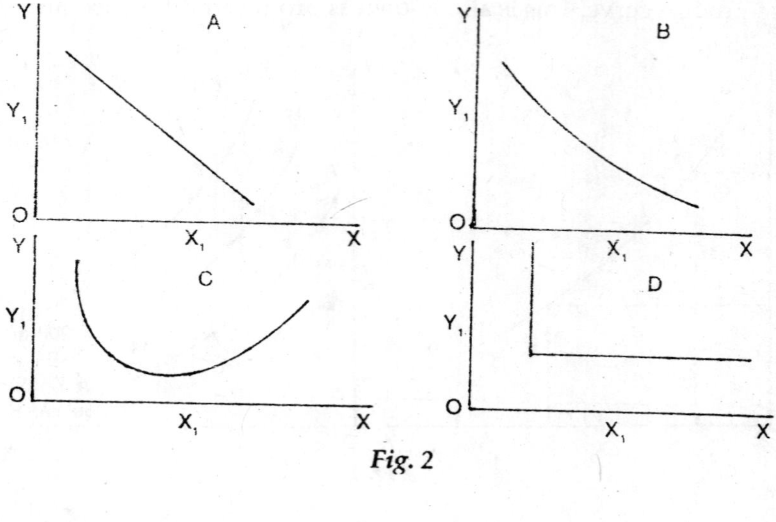

Fig. 2

There are thus three broad categories of input combinations:

(1) Inputs which combine in fixed proportions; (2) Inputs which may be substituted in a constant ratio; and (3) Inputs for which the rate of substitution varies according to the combination of the input used.

Inputs in Fixed Proportion

Some products can be produced only if inputs are mixed in a fixed proportion at all level of output. Inputs which combine in such a way presents no economic problem insofar as choosing the optimum proportion of inputs is concerned. Water is an example where, at every level, hydrogen and oxygen is mixed in a fixed proportion. The contour lines are simply points which farther out from the origin representing higher level of output. It has been explained in the following diagram.

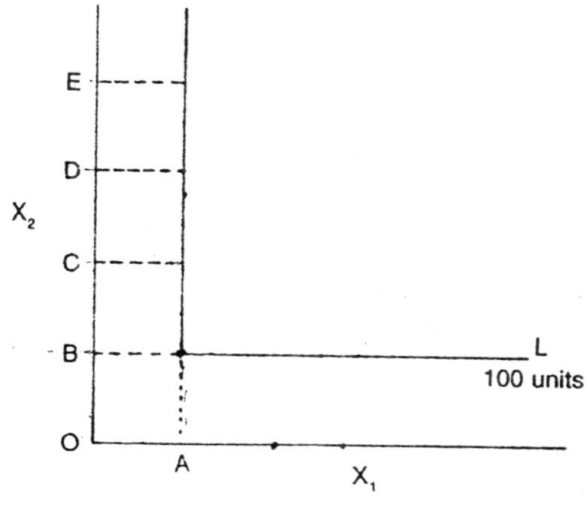

Fig. 3

Here 100 units of output requires an input OB of X_2 and OA of X_1. If input of X_2 is increased to OC or OD or OE while X_1 is held constant at OB the output remains stable at 100. Hence both X_1 and X_2 inputs are limitational factors because output is limited by the input of either.

Inputs with Constant Rate of Substitution

In the process of production two inputs may substitute at a constant rate. It refers that the rate at which two inputs can be exchanged in the production of a particular level of output is constant regardless of the level of output or of the proportion in which the factors are combined.

This rate of substitution indicates the amount by which X_2 is exchanged to offset a change in the amount of X_1 in order to maintain same production level. When production level is held constant, the constant factor substitution rate refers that one unit increase in X_1 results in one unit decrease in X_2. It is commonly known as Marginal Rate of Substitution (MRS) between inputs and is denoted by $\Delta X_1/\Delta X_2$ which is the slope of the product contour at any point. Family labour and hired labour, two different brands of seed or fertilizer which are basically identical, two brands of the same machines etc. are some important examples where the rate of substitution is found constant. When inputs can be exchanged at a constant rate, only one should be used. It depends upon the relative prices and the rate at which the inputs can be exchanged. The following hypothetical table and diagram explain the constant rate of substitution between X_1 and X_2.

MRS Table

	X_1	X_2	ΔX_1	ΔX_2	$\Delta X_2/\Delta X_1$		*(MRS)*
1	0	45	-	-	5/10	=	0.5
2	10	40	10	5	5/10	=	0.5
3	20	35	10	5	5/10	=	0.5
4	30	30	10	5	5/10	=	0.5
5	40	25	10	5	5/10	=	0.5
6	50	20	10	5	5/10	=	0.5
7	60	15	10	5	5/10	=	0.5
8	70	10	10	5	5/10	=	0.5
9	80	5	10	5	5/10	=	0.5
10	90	0	10	5	5/10	=	0.5

In this table the substitution ratio is constant throughout the range. This has been expressed in the following diagram.

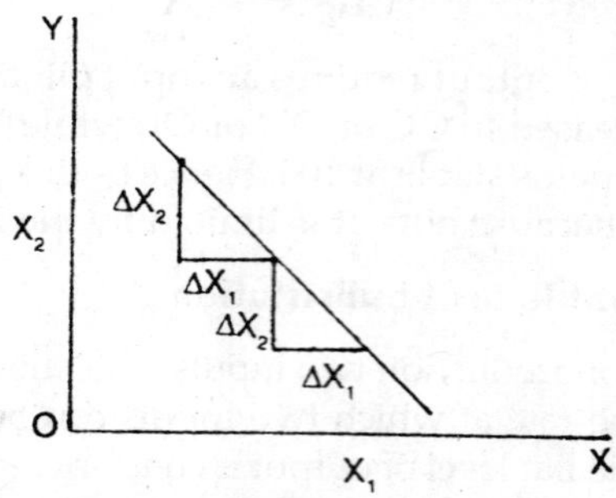

Fig. 4

Inputs with Varying Rate of Substitution: In most cases, factors substitute for each other at diminishing rates because they are incomplete substitutes for each other. The amount of X_1 required to offset the loss of one unit of X_2 while maintaining production constant increases as the amount of X_1 used increases. That is $\Delta X_2 / \Delta X_1 > \Delta X_2' / \Delta X'_1$ The slope of the iso-product curve becomes less steeper as more X_1 is used in relation to X_2. Agriculture presents many examples. Hay and grain substitute in this manner in the production of milk. A buffalo fed entirely on hay would produce the same quantity of milk with a small addition of grain and a relatively large decrease in hay. Here as more and more grain is added, the additional grain replaces less and less hay. This has been explained in the following diagram.

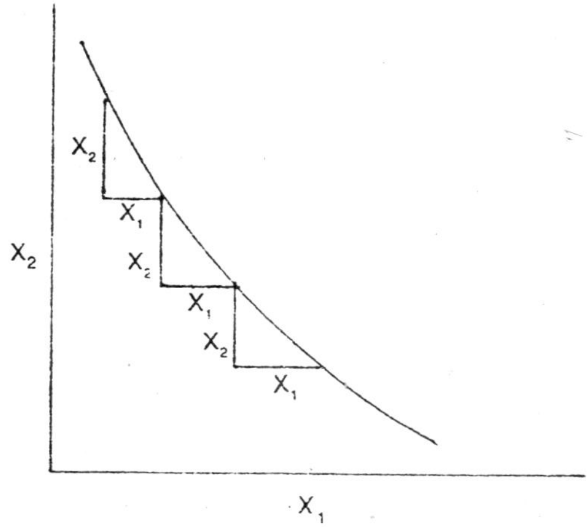

Fig. 5

Optimum Factor Combination or Least-Cost Combination of Inputs

The marginal rate of substitution (MRS) as discussed above is a physical phenomenon. It explains how much of one input can be removed with the output remaining at the same level if one unit of the other input is added. Since the concept is physical, it cannot explain the combination of input which will minimize cost in the production of a given quantity of output.

Hence to know the variable inputs that could give a certain amount of product at a minimum cost, a farmer must know the rates at which the inputs can be exchanged in the market in addition to the rate at which they can be exchanged in production. In other words, in order to achieve this least-cost combination of inputs, the farmer must know the prices of these inputs. The prices of inputs are represented by the iso-cost lines. This line shows the quantity of either input and combination of both inputs which can be purchased for a given cost. When prices of inputs which farmers buy do not change as the quantity purchased increases, the rate of substitution of two inputs in the market is the ratio of the prices of the two inputs. If the price of wheat is Rs. 6 per k.g and of rice Rs. 3 per kg. the rate of substitution of wheat for rice is 2 to 1. Thus PX_1/PX_2 is the rate of substitution in the market. It is this ratio, compared with the physical substitution ratio $\Delta X_2/\Delta X_1$ which tells the farmers how to choose his optimum input combination.

The combination of inputs which yields a quantity of output at least cost is, therefore, that combination where physical rate of substitution is equal to the price ratio of the inputs. In other words: $\Delta X_2/\Delta X_1 = PX_1/Px_2$. This statement which gives least-cost combination of inputs can also be expressed as: $PX2\ \Delta\ X2 = PX1\ \Delta\ X_1$. That is the cost of adding X_2 is equal to the reduction in cost from using less of X1. If $pX_2\ \Delta\ x_2 > Px_1 > x_1$, adding x_1 and decreasing x_2 will decrease cost. If $Px_2\ \Delta X2 < Px1\ \Delta\ x1$ adding x2 and decreasing X_1 will decrease cost in producing given quantity of output. Unless $\Delta\ X_2/\Delta\ X_1 = PX_1\ /(Px_2)$ it is possible either to increase output with the same cost or to decrease the cost of obtaining the same level of output.[1] The following hypothetical table will help to understand the least-cost combination of inputs.

Combination of Least-Cost Combination of Two Inputs to Obtain Equal Product

Y_1 = Rs. 10							Y_1 = Rs. 20
X_1	X_2	$\Delta X_2/\Delta X_1$	*Cost (Rs.)*	X_1	X_2	$\Delta X_2/\Delta X_1$	*Cost (Rs.)*
0	80		800	0	120		1200
6	56	24/6 = 4	680	10	80	40/10 = 4	1000
12	38	18/6 = 3	620	20	50	30/10 = 3	900
18	24	14/6 = 2.3	600	30	30	20/10 = 2	900
24	12	12/6 = 2.0	600	40	14	16/10 = 1.6	940
30	4	8/6 = 1.3	640	50	6	8/10 = 0.8	1060
36	0	4/6 = 0.7	660	60	0	6/10 = 0.6	1200

Px_1 = Rs. 20 – Px_2 = 10

In the above table, two different combinations of inputs produce either 10 or 20 units of output at least-cost. If we go from the combination of 20 X_1 and 50 X_2 to 30 X_1 and 30 X_2 in the production of 20 units of output, the MRS or $\Delta X_2/\Delta X_1$ is 2. It refers that in this range 2 units of X_2 can be replaced by one unit of X_1 without changing the level of output. But the cost of X_1 is twice as much as X_2. Since X_1 costs twice as much as X_2 for each unit, and 2 units of X_2 will replace one unit of X1, the cost of either input combination must be the same when we move to another input combination.

A revenue earned by a producer and the cost accrued are associated with each least-cost input combination. A producer wishes to know the level of output where TR-TC is greatest. In the table the least-cost combinations for either 10 or 20 units of product are given. For the production of 10 and 20 units, the cost is Rs. 600/-and Rs. 900/-. Suppose the product price is Rs. 80/-, the revenue from the production of ten and twenty units are Rs. 800/- and Rs. 1,600/- respectively. In this way the net revenue (TR-TC) for producing ten and twenty units is Rs. 200/- and Rs. 700/- respectively. A producer is receiving more revenue in producing twenty units than ten units. Hence, to choose the amount of product which would yield the greatest net revenue, a producer would proceed in the same manner to compare the net revenue for other level of output each produced with minimum cost. The graphic explanation of minimum-cost combination is given as under:

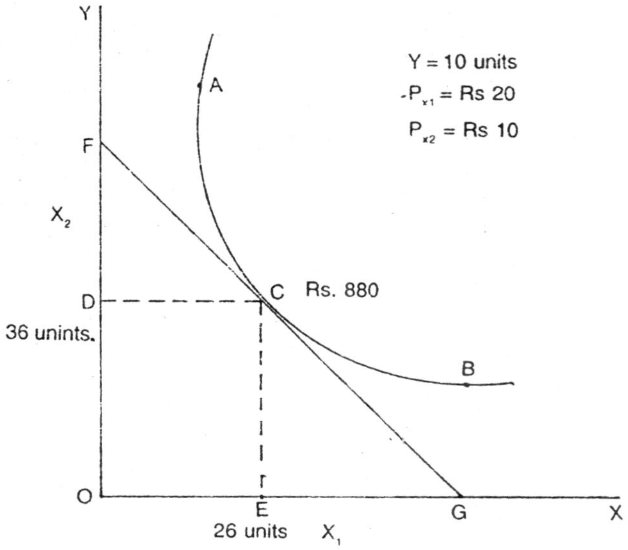

Fig. 6

The least-cost combination picture with two variable inputs has been presented in this diagram. This diagram depicts both the iso-cost and iso-product curves. The line FG is the iso-cost curve, the slope of which indicates the price of X_1 in terms of X_2 and all points on the line presents the same total cost. The highest total output that can be produced from an outlay represented by the iso-cost line FG is determined by the point of tangency C between FG and iso-product curve. Suppose it is 10 units. Thus, the lowest total cost at which 10 units can be produced is by using OE units of X_1 and OD units of X_2.

Thus to achieve the aim of locating the least-cost combination of two inputs, a farmer must go to a point of tangency between iso-cost and iso-quant, because it is the point where iso-cost comes into contact with highest isoquant, (maximum output with minimum cost); and an isoquant comes in contact with the lowest iso-cost curve (given output at the minimum cost) we know where iso-cost and isoquant will meet together, the slope of both the curves will be equal, or in other words at point C the slope of the product contour $\Delta X_2 / \Delta X_1$ is equal to the slope of the iso-cost curve PX_1 / Px_2. Ten units of product cannot be produced at less cost because no combination of X_1 and X_2 below Rs. 880 iso-cost curve will produce 10 units of product. Two other points A and B can also produce 10 units, but at higher cost.

More Than Two Inputs: One Output with Multiple Input Analysis:

In the long-run all inputs may be variable. When more than two inputs are considered, the least-cost analysis will become more complex. However, the condition for the least-cost combination of three or more inputs can be explained in mathematical forms.

It has been explained earlier that the optimum combination of inputs X_1 and X_2 where $PX_1\ \Delta X_1 = PX_2\ \Delta X_2$. It is also true that $PX_1\ \Delta X_1 = PX_3\ \Delta X_3$ for the least-combination of inputs X_1 and X_3. It shows that for any number of variable inputs, the optimum condition is attained where $PX_1\ \Delta X_1 = PX_2\ \Delta X_2 = PX_3\ \Delta X_3 ..... = Px_n\ \Delta\ x_n$. It refers that "inputs are combined in such proportions that the reduction in costs from reducing the amount of one input is equal to the cost of adding another input in sufficient amount to maintained output".[2]

This condition for least-cost combination can also be analysed on the basis of maximizing net revenue. The condition for maximizing net revenue with one variable input is that VMP = PX_1 or $Py_1\ (\Delta y_1 / \Delta X_1 = Px_1$. Similarly $Py_1\ (\Delta Y_1 / \Delta X_2) = Px_2$ is the optimum condition of using X_2. From these two equations it can be seen that:

$$[PY_1\ (\Delta Y_1 / \Delta X_1)] / PX_1 = 1$$
$$[PY_1\ (\Delta Y_1 / \Delta X_2)] / Px_2 = 1$$

Since both equations are equal to 1 they are also equal to each other and this can be expressed As: $[Py_1\ (\Delta Y_1/\Delta X_1)]/\ PX_1 = [PY_1\ (\Delta Y_1/\Delta X_2)]/\ PX_2$. Here, both X_1 and X_2 are used to produce Y_1. Dividing both side of PY_1 and extending to 'n' variable we get: $(\Delta Y_1/\Delta X_1)/PX_1=(\Delta Y_1/\Delta X_2)/\ PX_2=(\Delta Y_1/\Delta X_3)/Px_3 ....=(\Delta Y_1/\Delta X_n)/PX_n$.

Here $X_1, X_2, X_3 .....\ X_n$ variables are used in production of Y_1. This equation explains that a product is produced at least-cost when the marginal products of the inputs are proportional to the price of the inputs. If all inputs have the same price, but some inputs are more productive than the other, a producer will, obviously, purchase the more productive inputs. The additional purchase of such high productive inputs and their use will decrease their marginal product until the ratios of the marginal product to inputs prices are the same for all inputs. Thus, equality of the ratios of the marginal products of the variable inputs to their prices is a basic condition for minimum cost of producing a particular quantity of product using "n" variable inputs.[3]

Most Profitable Level of Output: The minimizing of cost for producing a particular level of output does not necessarily mean that the level of output is also most profitable. To determine the most profitable level of output, the producer compares cost and revenues for various level of output, all of which are produced at least-cost combination of inputs. A condition for profit maximization is that $MC = PY_1$. We know that $MC = PX_1\ /\ (\Delta Y_1\ /\ \Delta X_1)$; therefore $(\Delta Y_1/\ \Delta X_1)\ /\ PY_1$ must be the same as $1/MC$. Hence, a farmer would expand his output until

$$= \frac{\Delta Y_1/\Delta X_1}{PX_1} = \frac{\Delta Y_1/\Delta X_2}{PX_2} = \frac{\Delta Y_1/\Delta X_3}{PX_3}$$

$$= \frac{\Delta Y_n/\Delta X_n}{PX_n} = \frac{1}{MC} = \frac{1}{PY_1}$$

FOOTNOTES & REFERENCES

1. Bishop C.E, Toussaint W.D. *Introduction to Agricultural Economic Analysis, op. cit. p.* 96.
2. Bishop C.E:, Toussaint W.D. *Introduction To Agricultural Economic Analysis, op. cit.* p. 99.
3. *Ibid., pp.* 99-100.
4. *Ibid.,* p. 100.

3

MULTIPLE OUT-PUT WITH ONE INPUT ANALYSIS

In the previous two chapters we have discussed the problem of choice in the form of one input for one output, two inputs for one output and multiple inputs for one output. Here we are going to alter the situation. Now we are going to discuss the problem of choice in the form of multiple output with one input and multiple output with multiple inputs.

If the stock of input is known and given, a producer has to decide which crop he should produce from the given stock of resources. Taking into account the condition of soil, weather and the amount of available resources, a list of all possible productions can be raised. A farmer can produce a large number of possible crops. But the question is: which combination of crops he is going to choose? A rational producer is that whose aim is to maximise profit. He is required to derive the optimum economic combination of products.

Production Possibilities: One simple production possibility is that a producer may produce Y_1 and Y_2 using the same input X_1. Here the amount of X_1 that can be used to produce Y_1 depends upon the amount of X_1 that goes to produce Y_2. It means the amount of Y_1 depends on the amount of Y_2 or we can say $Y_1 = f(Y_2)$. The relationship between any two product can be expressed graphically by considering the amount of inputs used as constant. By assuming the amount of inputs constant, we can show what happens to the quantity of each product as inputs are transferred from Y_1 to Y_2 or vice-versa. We can explain the effect of producing more of Y_1 on the production of Y_2 by a production possibilities or an iso-resource relationship. It shows the maximum amount of one output say, Y_1 which can be produced for particular level of another product, say, Y_2 from given quantity of inputs. A hypothetical production function for two product Y_1 and Y_2 using the same input can explain the production possibilities.

Input X_1	*Production of* Y_1	*Production of* Y_2
0	0	0
10	14	22
20	26	40
30	36	56
40	44	70
50	50	82
60	54	92

This table shows two separate production functions using the same X_1. Effect of using X_1 to produce either Y_1 or Y_2 is different . The input X_1 can be used to produce either Y_1 or Y_2 or a combination of them. If 60 units of X_1 are available to produce Y_1 or Y_2 or combination of both, we can produce them in such a manner that a maximum of one is obtained for any level of the other. This has been explained in the following table.

Production Possibilities for 60 Units of X_1

X_1 used in Production		*Output*		*MRS* ($\Delta Y_2/\Delta Y_1$)
Y_1	Y_2	Y_1	Y_2	
0	60	0	92	——
10	50	14	82	10/14 or 0.7
20	40	26	70	12/12 or 1.0
30	30	36	56	14/10 or 1.4
40	20	44	40	16/8 or 2.0
50	10	50	22	18/6 or 3.0
60	0	54	0	22/4 or 5.5

If 60 units of X_1 is available for the production of Y_1 and Y_2, a producer can determine various combinations of two products as have been shown in the table, in such a manner that a maximum of one is obtained for any level of the other. If producer uses all 60 units in the production of Y_2 he obtains 92 units of Y_2 and does not get any unit of Y_1. He shifts 10 units of X_1 to the production of Y_1 and receives 14 units of Y1 production. But in doing so he receives 82 instead of 92 units of Y_2. He produces 82 units of Y_2 by 50 units of X_1. In like manner, he can produce various other combinations.

The way in which two products are substituted for each other is important from economic point of view. The rate of substitution shows how much one product can be reduced in order to produce one additional unit of the other product.

Product-Product-Relationship:

Farm products may have different product relationship with each other. These may be classified as: Joint-product, complementary, supplementary and competitive product.

A: Joint Products: This class of products refers that if a given quantity of one is produced, the amount of the other is fixed by nature. It includes such combination as milk and butter, lamb and wool, cotton and cotton seed, wheat and straw. All agricultural products are mostly joint product. The combinations of Y_1 and Y_2, therefore, are simple points as shown in the following figure. The points a, b, c, d, e, represents possible combination of Y_1 and Y_2 at five different levels of resources.

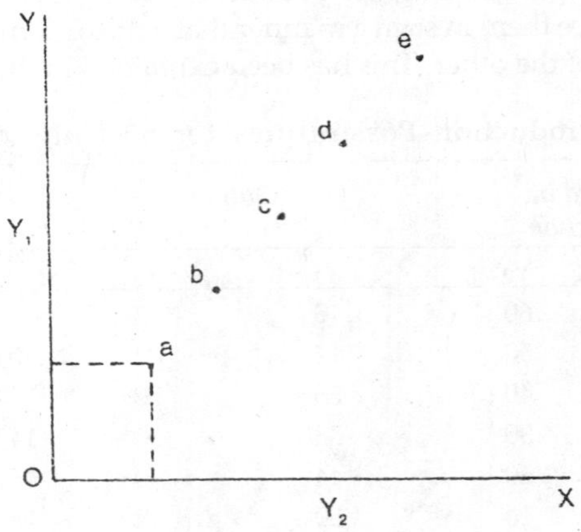

Fig. 1

For a short period analysis, two products are treated as one and, therefore, no economic decision is made with respect to product combination. In the long-run, however, adjustment can be made in the combination, say wool and mutton, by selecting alternative breeds of sheep, if the price of one product is higher than the other. Once this adjustment is made, the proportions of the two products are again fixed.

B: Competitive Products: If the resources are limited all crops and livestocks become competitive at some point. With two competitive products, the use of given resources to produce more of one necessitates a reduction in the amount of other product. When two products are competitive, they may substitute either at a constant rate or at increasing rate. This is true only in the short-period and under constant rate of substitution. Two varieties of the same grain fall under this category. Here MRS in production of two varieties is constant regardless of crop-land area engaged in one variety or the other. This has been explained in the following diagram.

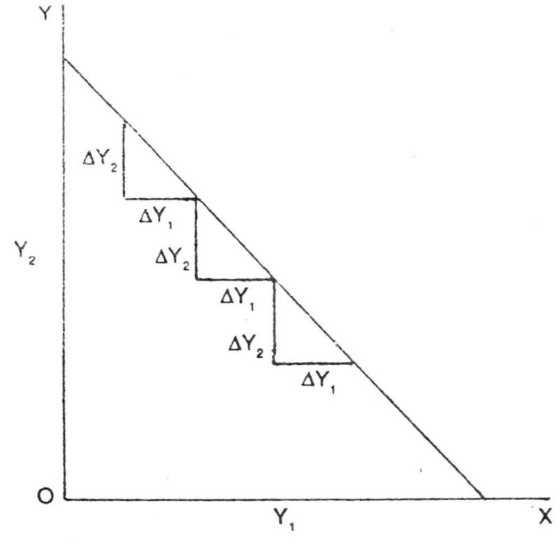

Fig. 2 Competitive-Products Substituting at Constant Rate

If two products are produced with the same resources and they are substituted at constant rate, only one of the products should be produced to obtain maximum net revenue. For example if one variety of wheat yields 100 quintal on a particular soil and another 90 quintal, the first one will be preferred as long as production costs and price per quintal are equal for both varieties.

However, over a longer period of time, this constant MRS between products may not be continued. The effect of one crop on another in rotation changes MRS. Where for obtaining an additional unit of a product, a decreasing quantity of the other product is needed, only one product is preferred. A combination of two such product will never yield maximum net revenue. The reason is that every successive increase of the one unit requires less and less unit of the other. This has been explained in the following diagram.

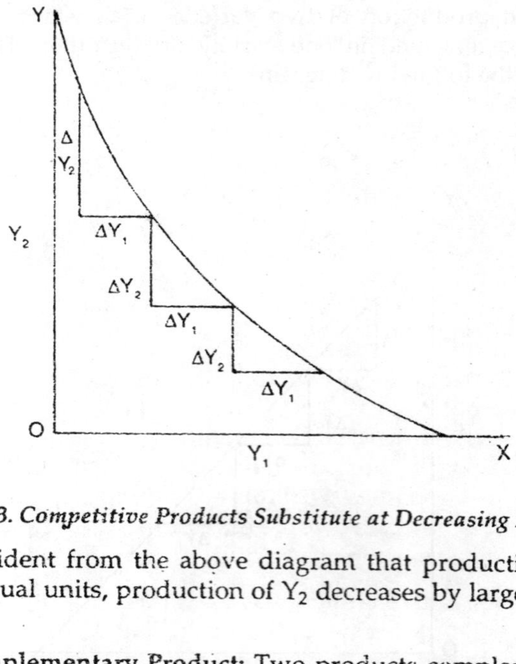

Fig. 3. Competitive Products Substitute at Decreasing Rate

It is evident from the above diagram that production of Y_1 increases in equal units, production of Y_2 decreases by larger and larger amounts.

C: Complementary Product: Two products complement to each other when an increase in one, results in an increase in the other, maintaining the resources at the same level.[1] Forage and grain or hay crops which adds nitrogen and other organic matter to the soil and thus increases per acre grain yields come under this category. Within certain limits, both grain and forage crops can be increased together as we shift land and labour from grain to hay. This complementary relationship has been expressed in the following diagram:

The range of complementarily is from A to B. In this range, the production of Y_1 and Y_2 both may be increased simultaneously. The MRS between the two product is, therefore, positive. But this complementary relationship will not be continued over all possible combination of two product. This relation ends at point B. This complementary relation gives way to competition. After some time, a transfer of resources from Y_2 to Y_1 or Y_1 to Y_2 must cause a reduction of either Y_1 or Y_2. For example, if we extend forage for enough in rotation, grain production must decline. Thus, beyond OC any further increase in production of Y_1 must decrease the production of Y_2. How much beyond OC a producer will go in producing Y1 is determined by relative prices of Y_1 and Y_2.

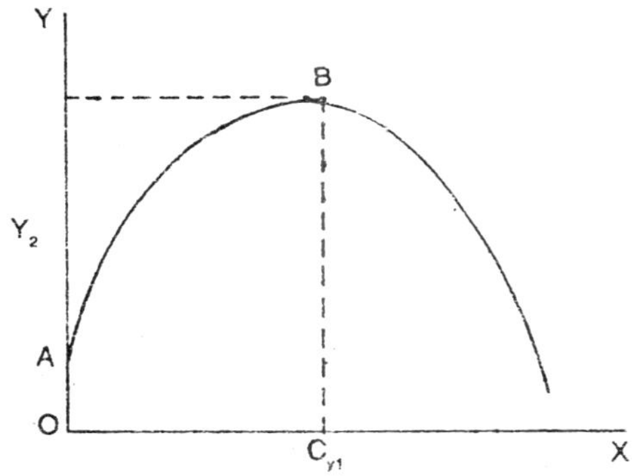

Fig. 4. Range of Complementarity

D: Supplementary Product: This relationship between the two products exists when, with constant resources, output of one can be increased without gain or the loss in the other product. This is the borderline case between competitive and complementary goods. Poultry farms, dairy enterprises, labour and machine are some examples of supplementary product. see Fig. 5. S

Two products are supplementary in two places. Production Y_1 can be increased without reducing Y_2 in the range AB. From D to C production Y_2 can be increased without affecting Y_1. Range BC is competitive within which a rational producer will operate.

All the four relationship discussed above can be expressed in a summary form:

MRS	Relationship
$\Delta Y_1 / \Delta Y_2$ or $\Delta Y_2 / \Delta Y_1 <$ Zero	Competitive
$\Delta Y_1 / \Delta Y_2$ or $\Delta Y_2 / \Delta Y_1 =$ Zero	Supplementary
$\Delta Y / \Delta Y_2$ or $\Delta Y_2 / \Delta Y_1 >$ Zero	Complementary

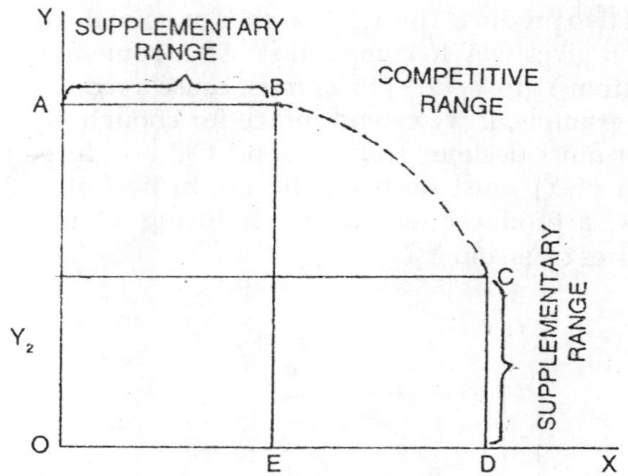

Fig. 5

Optimum Combination of Two Products: A rational producer, as we have already explained, operates in the range where products are competitive. Before deciding the profit maximising product combination he takes into account the total revenue based on the prices of two products. If prices of Y_1 and Y_2 are Py_1 and Py_2, the total revenue of the two products will be

$$TR = Y_1 . P_{y1} + Y_2 . P_{y2}$$

TR can be depicted by a straight line which is also known as iso-revenue or price line and is defined as the locus of product combinations that will earn the same revenue. The slope of the line is given by Py_1/Py_2.

The problem before farmers is to choose the most profitable resource allocation when two or more products are to be produced. The simple method is to calculate total net revenue which the producer can obtain from different combinations and choose the one which brings him the highest returns. Following table demonstrates the solution of maximising net revenue.

It is evident from the above table that the combination of 15 units of Y_1 and 44 units of Y_2 yields the maximum revenue Rs. 560. It refers that the maximum net revenue obtainable with a given amount of inputs is where MRS between two products is equal to the price ratio or $\Delta Y_2/\Delta Y1 = Py1/Py_2$. As inputs are transferred from Y_2 to Y_1, $\Delta PY_1 \Delta Y_1 > Py_2 \Delta Y_2$, more inputs should be added to produce Y_1 and hence less Y_2 should be produced. If, on the other hand, $PY_1 \Delta Y_1 < PY_2 \Delta Y_2$ adding inputs to Y_2 will be profitable.

Determination of Most Profitable Combination of output (with 60 units of X_1 used)

Output Y_1	*Output Y_2*	ΔY_1	ΔY_2	*$PY_1.Y_1$ (Rs. 8 per Kg)*	*$PY_2.Y_2$ (Rs. 10 per Kg)*	*Total Revenue*
0	50	–	–	–	500	500
5	48	5	– 2	40	480	520
10	47	5	– 1	80	470	550
15	44	5	– 3	120	440	560
20	38	5	– 7	160	380	540
25	26	5	–12	200	260	460
30	8	5	–18	240	80	320
35	0	5	– 8	280	0	280

The maximum return combination from production of two commodities can be shown with the help of production possibility curve and iso-revenue line.

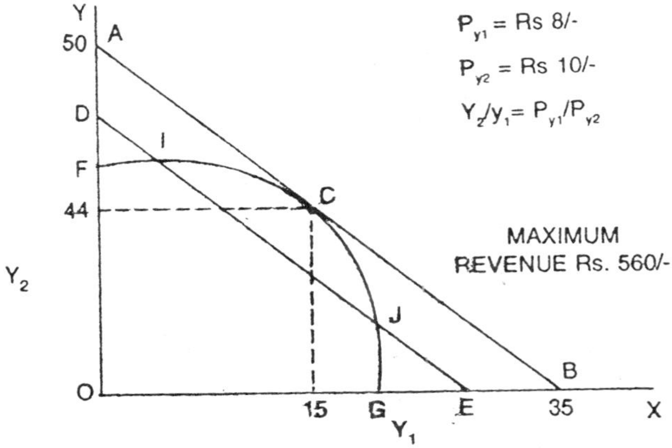

Fig. 6 Maximum Revenue Rs. 560/-

The maximum total revenue obtainable is found where iso-revenue line A B is tangent to the production possibility curve F G. They are tangent at point C which shows the combination of 15 units of Y_1 and 47 units of Y_2. This combination yields maximum revenue of Rs. 560. At point C, the slope of production possibility curve is equal to the price ratio i.e., $\Delta Y_2/\Delta Y_1 = PY_1/PY_2$. All other combinations such as point I and J mean that the loss in revenue from the reduction in production of one product exceeds the gain in revenue from increasing the production of the other product.

Optimum Combination of Many Products: As resources at the disposal of farmer increases he may wish to expand his output.

The pattern of expansion can be explained by the expansion path shown below:

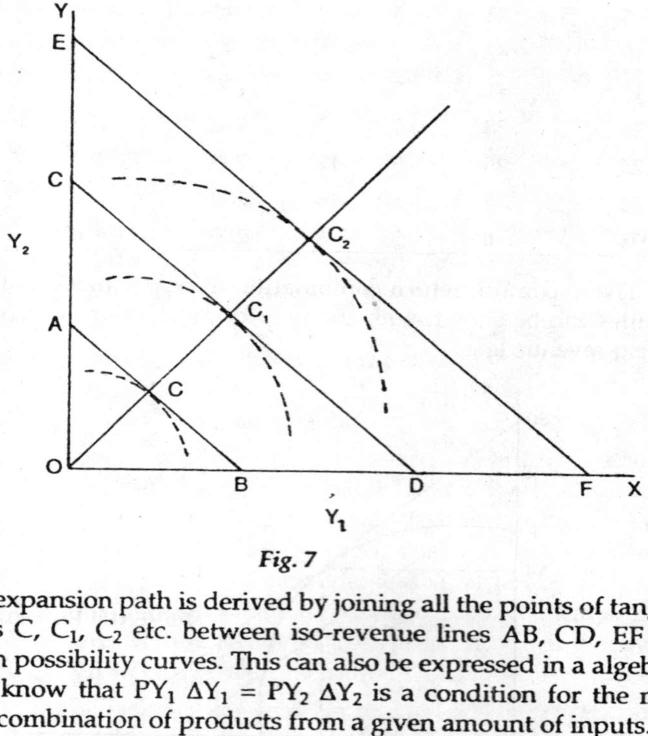

Fig. 7

This expansion path is derived by joining all the points of tangency such as C, C_1, C_2 etc. between iso-revenue lines AB, CD, EF and production possibility curves. This can also be expressed in a algebraic form. We know that $PY_1\ \Delta Y_1 = PY_2\ \Delta Y_2$ is a condition for the most profitable combination of products from a given amount of inputs. We have also explained that optimum combination of product is achieved where the value of the marginal product of a unit of X_1 in the production of Y_1 is equal to the price of X_1, that is PX_1, $(\Delta Y_1/\Delta X_1) = PX_1$. It is also true that $PX_2\ (\Delta Y_2/\Delta X_1) = PX_1$ is the most profitable condition of using X_1 in producing Y_2. Thus, the value of the marginal product (VMP) of X_1 in producing both Y_1 and Y_2 is equal to PX_1. And this is the condition of maximising net revenue. In other words $PY_1\ (\Delta Y_1/\Delta X_1) = PY_2\ (\Delta Y_2/\Delta X_1)$. Many inputs are used in the production of more than two products. Then we obtain the most profitable combination of products when:

$$PY_1\ (\Delta Y_1/\Delta X_1) = PY_2\ (\Delta Y_2/\Delta X_1) = Py_3(PY_3/\Delta X_1) = \ldots\ldots = PY_n\ (\Delta Y_n/\Delta X_1)$$

That is the value of the last unit of any one resource engaged in producing any product must be equal for all product.[2] Suppose labour can be transferred from one use to another where the return is greater, revenue would be increased in this process of transferring labour. This transfer would be continued until the return of the last unit of labour is equal in both uses. This is the only condition of maximising net revenue. It refers that, with a resource limitation, the input price which is relevant is not always the market price but is the opportunity return of using the resource elsewhere. In any event, maximum net revenue is possible when VMP of an input is equal in all uses. Both concepts are identical when we consider the price of the input to be the opportunity return.[3]

Specialization and Diversification: After explaining the maximisation condition, we are now discussed why some farmers or some areas specialise in producing one product and some farmers or some areas diversify their products. Forms of product combination, complementary, supplementary and competitive etc. provide the answer. Diversification of products exists where complementarity or supplementarity is found among the products. Where the products are competitive and substitute at a constant rate, production is less diversified. If products are competitive and have a constant MRS, specialisation is the general rule.[4]

In plain regions grain crop is competitive and can be substituted at a constant rate. Thus, wheat which yields highest returns per acre, tends to be the major and sometime the only crop grown. However, there is supplementarity between wheat and other grains is some areas became seeding and harvesting dates are not the same. To take the advantage of the situation grains other than wheat are grown in many parts of the plains. Risk element is another consideration which diversifies the crop. Diversification is considered a means, for reducing risk. Since farming is highly competitive business, it is difficult to keep all farmers up-to-date on new development in numerous farming activities.

As a result, many farmers realise that they can do a better job of keeping themselves up-to-date by concentrating on one or two main production activities. Farmers who specialise in the production of one commodity can also take advantage of any economies of size which exists in producing that particular commodity. New machines and equipment reduce the average costs at increased level of output. Those who are producing single commodity or in other words are specialised in a single commodity, often greatly reduces the average cost of producing that commodity. If the same farmer produces two commodities, the average cost of production for each commodity may increase than for either commodity if it is produced alone and on large scale. Thus, increasing capital investment and economies of scale in production creates incentives for specialisation in agricultural production.[4]

REFERENCES

1. Heady E. O. *op. cit.* p. 211.
2. Bishop C.E., Toussaint W.D., *Introduction To Agricultural Economic Analysis. op. cit.* p. 123.
3. *Ibid.*, pp. 124-25.
4. *Ibid.*, p. 125.

4

COST, REVENUE AND PROFIT MAXIMISATION

A rational farmer who aims at profit maximisation view production decisions from the costs angle. He is interested in cutting costs as a means of increasing profits. In this chapter we are going to analyse the cost side, the revenue side and the profit maximisation side of the production activities.

Cost Analysis: When we speak of costs of producing a commodity we frequently refer to the expenses incurred in producing that commodity in a particular time period. Without referring the amount and the time any reference to cost is, thus, meaningless. Further, cost of production often becomes a policy issue when producers complain that the prices they receive for their products do not cover the cost of production. It means cost of production and the prices of commodities both are closely related.

The expenses or cost-outlays for productive services are directly related to the laws of production. That is the cost structure is determined by the nature of production function as well by the level of prices and the nature of the market for productive services. Moreover, in economics the concept of cost is more broader than the layman's concept of cost which is more close to mere accountancy.In accountancy the concept of cost is related with paid-out costs such as wages, bills to purchase seed, fertilisers, pesticides and machines etc. An economist, besides all such paid out cost, is also concerned with the imputed costs. These are the costs which refers to farmers own labour, feed for livestock etc. are not covered by any monetary transaction and yet do represent a use of real resources which, if not used in one type of production, might have been used to produce something else.[1] This is the opportunity return or the opportunity cost. The opportunity return for family labour is the return which the family could get for its labour in other employment.

The term cost is used in many ways. A terminological clarity is essential to distinguish various concepts of cost so that one should know when to use which.

Real and Money Costs: Alfred Marshall defined the real cost in a philosophical way. He says: "the exertions of all the different kinds of labour that are directly or indirectly involved in making it together with the abstenences or rather the waiting required for saving the capital used in making it". The concept of real cost is, no doubt, real as it refers the efforts and sacrifices undergone by producer in producing certain commodities but the main problem with this concept is that efforts and sacrifices are subjective phenomenon and hence cannot be measured accurately. Modern economists seldom employs this term; instead they accept cost in money terms. Money cost of a product means the aggregate money expenditure incurred on various items during the process of production and sale.

Social or Opportunity Costs and Private Costs

In recent times social or opportunity costs has become more popular. If one commodity X has been produced with the given amount of resources, the social cost or opportunity cost of X commodity will be the commodity Y which has been sacrificed. If a farmer produces paddy instead of maize, the social cost of raising paddy will be the amount of maize sacrificed in the process.

Private costs of production, on the other hand, include the explicit as well as implicit costs. Explicit costs are the actual money expenses incurred directly in raising a farm commodity and implicit costs are the money value of those inputs which are supplied by the farmers themselves. It includes the money value of their labour, managerial services, interest on their invested capital and rent on their own lands.

Fixed and Variable Costs: In production we are generally concerned with a planning period which is divided into short-run and long-run periods. There are number of ways in which production can be varied depending upon the length of period under consideration. A short-run period refer a period which is long enough to permit desired changes in output without altering the size of the plant. The long-run period is that period which is sufficiently long for output to be altered by varying either the size of the plant or by making a more intensive or a less intensive utilization of the existing plant.[2]

In line with these two lengths of period, there are two major costs, known as fixed and variable costs. Costs which incurred even if there is no output are known as fixed cost. These are the costs which do not changes with changes in output and hence have no bearing on the decisions of increasing or decreasing the production. In short-run some costs are fixed such as land, taxes, insurance, machinery, tube well maintenance etc. and some may vary. But in the long-run, however, all costs become variable, because more opportunities are available to arrange all the factors of production, including plants and machinery. Thus, fixed costs will be at maximum when the output is zero and their incidence will go on decreasing as output is extended beyond the zero level.[3]

Variable cost incurred when production is carried on. Thus, these costs are the costs of adding the variable inputs. The amount of these costs depends upon the kinds and quantities of input used. In short these are the "farming expenses" during the production process. These costs include payments such as wages to hired labour, price of seed, fertilisers, fuel, power, pesticides, and transport etc. Since variable costs change with the level of output, total variable cost increases with the level of farm output. Variable costs, therefore, play an important role in maximising net revenue. If the farmers are to carry on the production the variable cost must be less than the selling price.

Fixed costs plus variable costs make the total cost. Total costs are necessary in estimating net revenue since net revenue is equal to total revenue minus total costs. If total revenue is less than the total costs, producer will not stay in production. A hypothetical cost is given on table 1.

Table 1
Hypothetical Cost Table Showing Relationship Among Various Cost Concepts (in Rupees)

OUTPUT Y_1	FIXED cost (Rs.)	VARIABLE cost ($P_{X1} X_1$)	TOTAL cost (FC + VC)	AVERAGE VC (VC/Y_1)	AVERAGE FC (FC/Y_1)	AVERAGE TC (TC/Y_1)	CHANGE In OUTPUT (ΔY_1)	CHANGE In COST (ΔVC)	MARGINAL Cost ($\Delta VC/\Delta Y_1$)
0	40	0	40	—	—	—	—	—	—
10	40	10	50	1.0	4	5	10	10	1.0
28	40	20	60	0.71	1.43	2.14	18	10	0.56
42	40	30	70	0.71	0.95	1.67	14	10	0.71
52	40	40	80	0.77	0.77	1.54	10	10	1.00
60	40	50	90	0.83	0.67	1.50	8	10	1.25
66	40	60	100	0.91	0.61	1.52	6	10	1.67
70	40	70	110	1.0	0.57	1.57	4	10	2.50
72	40	80	120	1.11	0.57	1.67	2	10	5.00

Adopted From: Bishop C.E., Toussaint W.D. P. 74.

Total and Average Cost Analysis: Total cost of production is the sum of total variable cost (TVC) and total fixed cost (TFC). Total variable cost refers to those factors of production — labour, capital, equipments, fertilisers, seed, pesticides etc. — whose supplies vary with the change in output. These costs are also referred as "direct costs", "prime costs", and "special costs". Total fixed cost, on the other hand, represents the sum of expenditure incurred irrespective of the level of output. Table shows that whatever the level of output fixed cost remains the same.

variable costs may be converted into average variable costs (AVC) by dividing total variable costs by the number of units produced. That is:

$AVC = \frac{TVC}{Y_1}$. It refers variable cost per unit output.

Similarly total fixed cost may also be converted into average fixed cost by dividing it with the number of output produced. That is:

$$AFC = \frac{TFC}{Y_1}.$$

It is clear from the table that AVC starts falling as soon as production is extended from zero to normal capacity output. It is due to the increasing returns. But once normal capacity is achieved, it starts rising beyond that point become the law of diminishing returns began to operate. This has been shown as under:

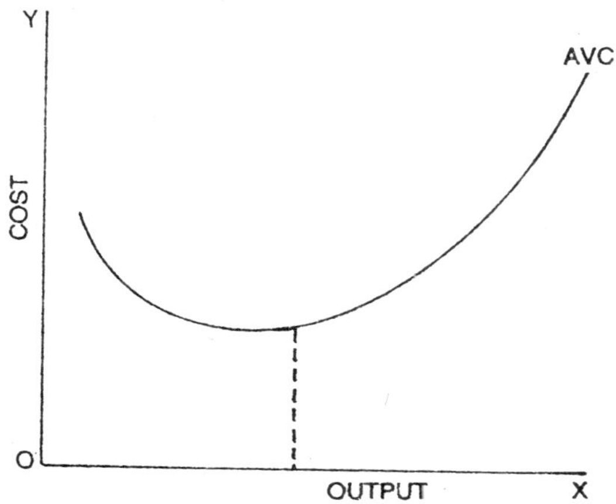

Fig. 1

Average total cost (ATC) can be calculated by dividing the total cost (TC) by the number of units produced. That is:

$$ATC = \frac{TC}{Y_1}$$

Since total cost is also the sum of AVC + AFC. that is:

$$ATC = \frac{TC}{Y_1}$$

$$TC = TVC + TFC$$

$$ATC = \frac{TVC + TFC}{Y_1}$$

$$= \frac{TVC}{Y_1} + \frac{TFC}{Y_1}$$

$$= AVC + AFC$$

Derivation of TC curve from TFC and TVC is depicted in the following figure:

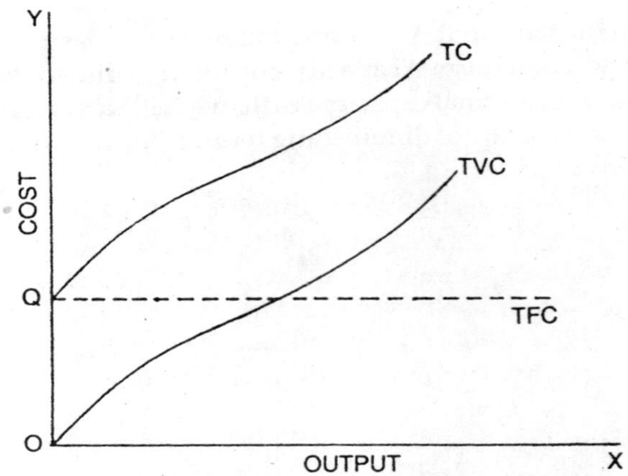

Fig. 2.

Since TFC remains unchanged whatever is the level of output TFC will be parallel to X-axis. TVC starts from the origin showing that at zero level of output, TVC will also be nil. TVC starts rising as output increases. TC starts from Q which shows that even if no output is produced a farmer will have to pay fixed cost to the extent of O Q. Average total cost (ATC) has been depicted in the following diagram.

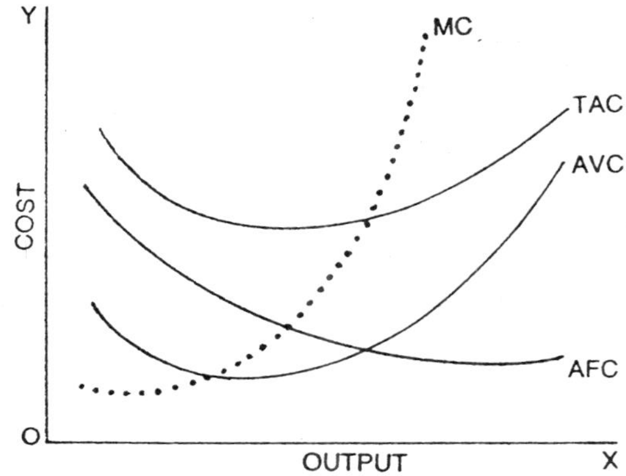

Fig. 3

As we know ATC is the sum of AVC + AFC. AFC is maximum when production is nil, but starts falling as production is increased. AVC starts falling as soon as production is extended beyond zero to normal capacity level of output and, as we have stated earlier, it is due to the increasing returns. But beyond the normal capacity, AVC will start rising because of the operation of law of diminishing returns. The vertical distance between ATC and AVC curves measures the amount of fixed cost per unit. This distance steadily diminishes as output rises which shows that fixed costs are spread over more and more units of the output.

Marginal Cost Analysis: MC shows a change in cost associated with an increase of one unit in output. That is it refers the addition to the total cost by the last unit of output. It can be expressed as:

$$MC = \frac{\Delta TC}{\Delta Y_1}$$

Since FC do not vary with output, marginal cost are always zero. It means that marginal costs are necessarily marginal variable costs and a change in fixed cost will leave marginal costs unaffected. Since marginal cost is marginal variable cost, our previous formula can be expressed as:

$$MC = \frac{\Delta VC}{\Delta Y_1}$$

Marginal cost plays an important role in deciding whether to continue production or not. A farmer will be willing to extend production so long as his revenue from the last unit produced is higher than the added cost incurred on producing that unit. Marginal cost is related to marginal product. This can be expressed in the following manner:

$$M C = \Delta \text{ Cost} / Y_1$$

$$\Delta \text{ Cost} = P X_1 \Delta X_1$$

$$\text{Therefore MC} = PX_1 (\Delta X_1/\Delta Y_1)$$

$$\text{by inverting MC} = \frac{PX_1}{\Delta Y_1 / \Delta X_1}$$

$$\Delta Y_1 \Delta X_1 = MP$$

$$\text{Therefore MC} = PX_1/MP$$

It shows an inverse relationship between MP and MC. That is when MP is at maximum MC is at a lowest point. Similarly, MC also has a definite relationship with ATC and AVC. When ATC and AVC curves will fall MC curve will be below them. And when they will rise MC is greater than both the curves. MC is equal at the low points of both the curves. MC and AFC have no relation at all. FC has no bearing on the additional cost as more output is produced.[4]

Cost Curves and Production Curves

The nature and the shape of TC curves depends upon the nature of production function, provided that the prices of inputs do not vary as the quantity of input purchased varies. In other words total cost curves is considered similar to the linear production function. How the production function and the total cost curve are related can be expressed in the following diagrams:

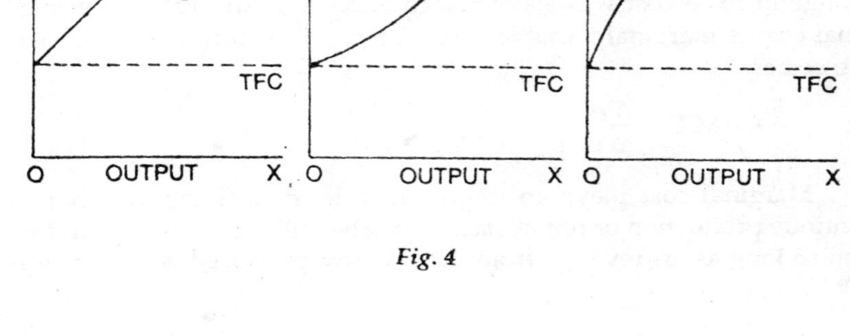

Fig. 4

In each figure the portion below the dotted line is fixed cost and the portion above the dotted line is variable cost. Figure 1 shows total cost curve for a linear production function. It shows constant marginal productivity. Figure 2 shows total cost function where the relationship is one of diminishing marginal productivity. Figure 3 illustrates the total cost function reflecting increasing returns throughout. A complete cost function which include both the increasing as well as decreasing returns is shown in the following diagram No. 4.

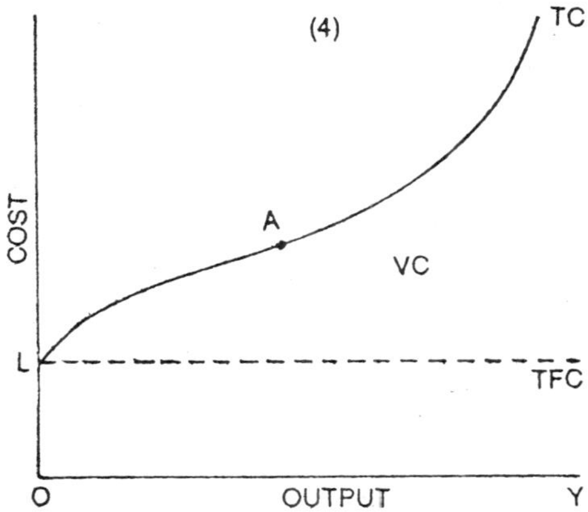

Fig. 5

Here the total cost between L A increases with a decreasing rate over the range of outputs consistent with increasing return on the production function and then from point 'A' onwards it shows an increasing rate over a range of output which indicate decreasing returns or production function. Point 'A' is the turning point, indicating the change in TC rate on the increase in production.

Revenue Function: After having some knowledge of cost concepts, now we study the concept of revenue since profit of the farmer is determined by the difference between total revenue and the total cost. If the price of a commodity does not vary along with the quantity producer sells, total revenue increases in proportion to increases in output. Hence TR schedule to output is a straight line, the slope of which is the price of the commodity.

Revenue refers the receipt obtained by the farmer from the sale of commodities at various prices. The revenue concept presents three forms namely, total revenue (TR), average revenue (AR) and marginal revenue (MR). The total amount of money that the farmer receive from the sale of products is known as total revenue or gross revenue. TR vary with the level of sales. Total revenue may be obtained by multiplying the quantity sold with the price of the commodity. Average revenue is the price per unit of a commodity and may be calculated by dividing total revenue with the number of units sold. This relationship shows that the average revenue curve is identical with the demand curve that relates price to output. Marginal revenue refers to the change in total revenue resulting from an increase in the sales of product by one unit. All forms of revenues have been expressed in the following table:

	Total Product	PY_1 = Rs. 5			PX_1 = Rs. 10	
	Y_1	TR	AR	MR	TC	Net Revenue (TR-TC)
0	0	0	—	—	0	0
1	10	50	50	50	10	50-10=40
2	28	140	70	90	20	140-20=120
3	44	220	73.3	80	30	220-30=190
4	54	270	69.3	50	40	270-40=230
5	60	300	60.0	30	50	300-50=250
6	66	330	55.3	30	60	330-60=270
7	70	350	50	20	70	350-70=280
8	72	360	45	10	80	360-80=280
9	72	360	40	0	90	360-90=270
10	70	350	35	-10	100	350-100=250

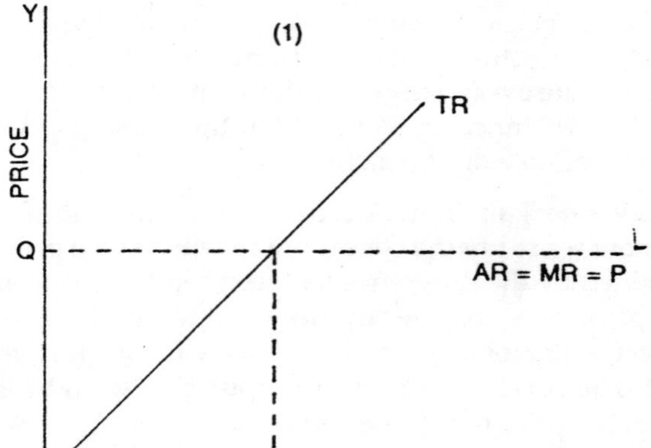

Fig.6

In a competitive condition, the amount of output sold by one producer has no bearing on market price. Agriculture is a competitive industry, and the amount sold by one farmer has no important influence on the existing market price. Since there are large number of buyers and sellers, farmers receive the same price per unit whether they sell 10 units or 100 units. In other words each unit sold adds the same amount to the total revenue or gross income. Accordingly, the TR curve for an individual farmer is linear indicating that each unit of grain sold adds the same amount to the gross revenue. [Fig. 6]

Since the total revenue curve is linear, AR and MR are identical and constant at the market price as shown by the line Q L. The price curve will also be horizontal to X-axis and MR will be equal to AR.

Profit Maximisation: A farmer who seeks to maximise net revenue will try to produce that level of output at which the difference between TR and TC is greatest. This is the level where revenue is equal to marginal cost (MR = MC). The reason is quite clear; MR and MC refers additions to TR and TC. Hence it pays the farmer to produce one unit of output as long as the marginal cost is less than the marginal revenue. In doing so, he is adding less to total costs than the total revenue. Production of one additional unit is always unprofitable if MC > MR since more is added to total cost than to the total revenue. Thus farmer should not produce if the total revenue does not equal or exceed total variable cost. And farmer will expand output when MR > MC and he keeps on expanding output until MR = MC.[5]

The above conditions can be depicted in the following two diagrams.

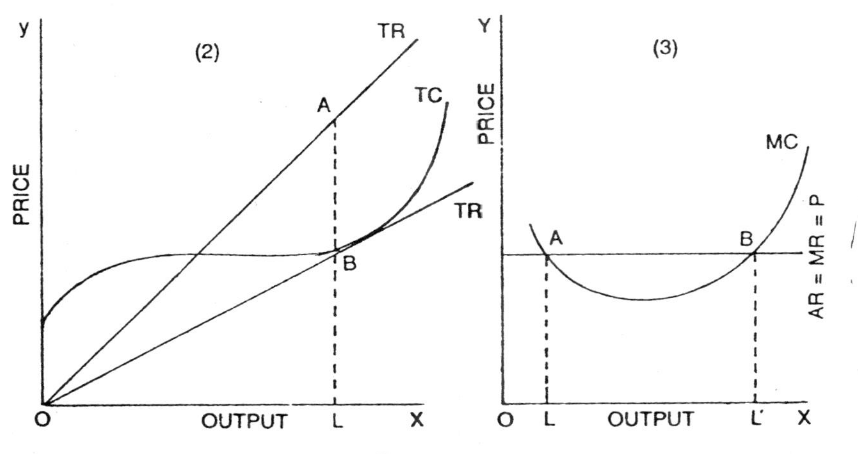

Fig.7

Figure 2 shows TR and TC curves. The slope of TR curve shows the price or AR. Two curve TR and TR′ indicate price difference. Maximisation of net revenue is possible where the difference between TR and TC is greatest. In figure difference A B between T R and T C is greatest and hence O L level of output will provide maximum net revenue. If more output is produced, the added cost will be greater than the added return. And if fewer units of output are produced, some net revenue will be forgone since additional revenue from increased output exceeds the additional cost. Thus maximum net revenue can be obtained where MR — MC is greatest.

There are three important conditions for the profit maximisation. These are:

(i) One condition for maximum net revenue is that MC must be equal to the price of the product. (MC = MR).

(ii) Second condition is that MC must be rising. If this is not true and MC is falling the produce will operate under condition of maximum loss; and

(iii) A third condition is that total revenue must be greater than total variable cost or in other words AR (price) be equal or greater than AVC.

All these three conditions have been depicted in figure No. 2. Under conditions of competition, a farmer cannot influence the market price. As such the TR is linear and both AR and MR curves are identical and constant at market price as has been explained in figure No. 1. In this figure OP level of output is that level where MC is equal to the price of the product or MR = MC.

The other two conditions have been explained in figure No. 3. In this figure OL′ is the level of output where profit is maximised. It is because as output is increased upto OL′ each additional unit produced is adding more to revenue than to the cost. If a farmer extend output beyond OL′ each successive unit of output will add more cost than revenue. Marginal cost is also equal to marginal revenue at OL′ level, but this level is not profit maximising level because if output is extended beyond OL level, MR > MC which is contrary to the condition 2. Moreover, it is also necessary that MC curve must cut the MR curve from the below. At OL level MC curve is cutting the MR curve from the above. Hence only OL′ level satisfies both the conditions.

Long-Run and Short-Run Analysis: Fixed cost which amount Rs. 40 in our example cannot be changed in the short-run. Thus in the short-run farm's production is profitable if his PY_1 > AVC. But in the long-run every cost is variable cost. The size of the operation may change. New machines and equipments can be purchased, new capital may be invested. Moreover, prices may also be changed. Thus ATC, as shown in the previous table as well as in the diagram represents only one particular size of the plant. These curves may be different for some other size of operation. For example FC curve for a 20 acre farm will be lower than for a 100 acre farm. Since AC curves show cost per unit of output, the AC curves for 20 acre will also be lower than the AC curves for 100 acre. This situation has been depicted in the following diagram.

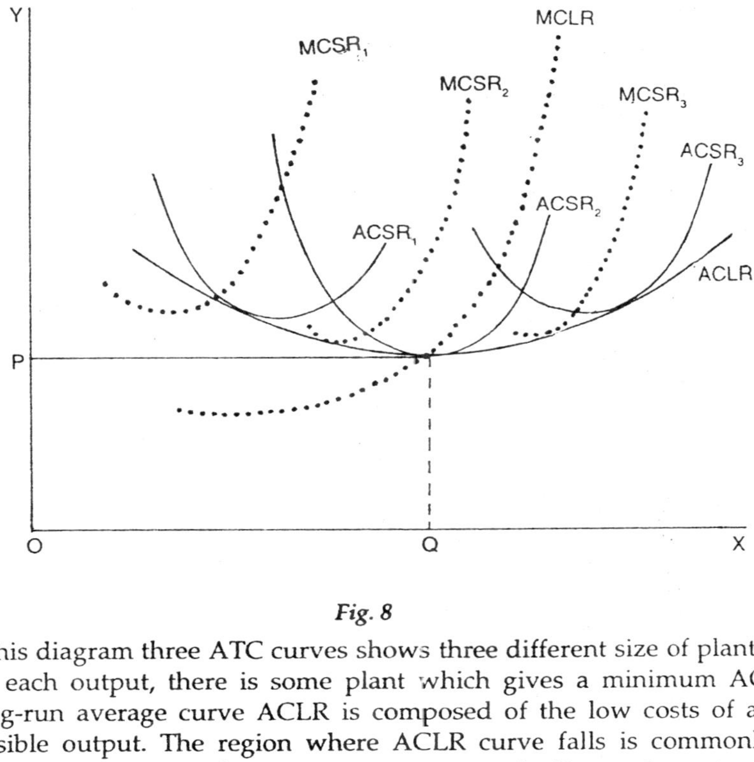

Fig. 8

In this diagram three ATC curves shows three different size of plants. For each output, there is some plant which gives a minimum AC. Long-run average curve ACLR is composed of the low costs of all possible output. The region where ACLR curve falls is commonly known as the region of increasing returns to scale. Decreasing returns to size is that portion of the long-run curve where average cost is increasing. The long-run MC curve is shown by the curve MCLR. OQ is the level of output at which MCLR = PY1. The producer can obtain OQ level of output in either plant 2 or 3. In plant 2, the average cost per unit of output is QP, but it only PN if he remain in plant 3. It shows that plant 3 is more efficient size of this level of output. So in the long-run, plant 3 is the most efficient and that is the size of plant where

$MCLR = PY_1$. In this long-run, the supply curve is flatter than the supply curve for the short period. The reason is that as the period of time increases, the number of inputs which can be varied also increases. Thus, the response of production to changes in price is greater in the long-run rather than in the short-run.

REFERENCES

1. Heady E.O., *Economics of Agricultural Production and Resource Use, op cit.* p. 316; Bishop C.E., Toussaint W.D., *Introduction To Agricultural Economic Analysis, op cit.* pp. 68-69.
2. Bishop C.E., Toussaint W.D., *op cit.* p. 70.
3. Bishop C.E., Toussaint W.D., *op cit.*, Sandhu A.N., Singh A., *op cit.*, p. 124; I.J. Singh, *Elements of Farm Management Economics*, East-West Press, 1977, p. 32.
4. Bishop C.E., Toussaint W.D. *op cit.*, pp. 75-76.
5. Lipsey R.G., *Positive Economics*, Weidenfied And Nicolson, London 1970, p. 237.

5

RISK AND UNCERTAINTY IN FARMING

In the introductory part of the production economics, we have defined production function as a process of conversion of some goods called inputs into some other goods called output. This transformation of inputs into output requires time. Time is required to collect market informations, time is also required to organise the factors of production to produce certain commodities. And time is also needed in converting inputs into output. Here the amount of time involved in production process is different for different commodities. Among different crops, time differ. Some crops require few months and some other require almost one year. Few other agricultural productions such as coconut, teak-wood trees require several years to be ready for earnings.

Hence, longer the time period of production, the more uncertain producers are of the prices which may be received for their product. It is usually experienced that there is little relation between prices at the time of production is planned and the prices at the time of sale of the product. Moreover, risks and uncertainties are permanent phenomenon in agriculture because it faces disturbances. These disturbances may be of different types. It may be due to erratic variation in monsoons. Disturbances may also occur due to damages done by insects, diseases, storms. In a similar manner, livestocks are also subject to risk and uncertainties as the output of this enterprise is mostly influenced by laws of nature which are outside the human control. Thus disturbances in agriculture are more pronounced as the laws of nature have an upper hand in this area. In the production of non-farm products, the output level is not disturbed and output can be predicted with certainty because the kinds and quantities of inputs to be used are known. In agriculture, a farmer has some idea of the range of results to be expected from combining particular quantities of inputs in the production of a commodity. That is, he has, at the most, an idea of the highest and the lowest yields.

Risk refers to probability and hence it is a probabilisitic phenomenon. Here outcomes are unknown can be predicted only in probability forms. A farmer can solve his problem of choice by applying his prior knowledge and experience or by using statistical approach to a probability situation. The application of game theory also helps in solving probability problems. Uncertainty, on the other hand, is the phenomenon where prediction cannot be made precisely. Here the probability of outcome cannot be established in an empirical or quantitative sense because of an uncertainty of a situation. At the most a range can be guess within which an uncertainty can materialise. Since probability is absent in uncertainty it is uninsurable. Thus, while "risk refers variability or outcomes which are measurable in an quantitative manner..... uncertainty refers to future events where the parameters of probability distribution cannot be determined empirically". In other words, while risk loss due to its measurability can be controlled or reduced by various methods such as insurance, careful planning etc., uncertainty loss due to its unmeasurability cannot be controlled or reduced. Imperfect knowledge about the market conditions, yield, variance, dispersion and skewness creates uncertainties.[1]

Degree of Uncertainty: The amount of risk and uncertainty which a farmer is willing to take depends upon his calculations of probabilities of an event. Farmers may have different opinions that price-wise some products evolve greater risk and uncertainty. A farmer may also faced with questions: will monsoon be favourable this year? Will sufficient labour be available on prevailing wages? Will prices rise or fall? And so an and so truth.

The magnitude of variations, say in prices or yields, is one basis of estimating the degree of risk and uncertainty. Loss may be another basis. Some farming operations may result frequent losses. They may be called as more risky or uncertain than those which shows less frequent losses. Thus, the "dispersion of expectations" is one method of uncertainty measurement. In statistical form this dispersion can be represented by the variance, standard deviation and range of expected values. If all such measures for a commodity or price is zero, the producer will be certain about his estimates of yield or price. If, on the other hand, this dispersion is greater, anticipation will be multi-valued and the degree of uncertainty will also be high.[2]

Willingness of a farmer to take risk depends upon various factors. Some farmers, by nature, are more enterprising than the others. An enterprising farmer is more dynamic, innovative and sharp and view the situation with optimism. He, therefore, undertake the job even if it involves a high risk. On the other hand, if a farmer is sluggish conservative and view a new situation with pessimism, he will not adopt the job even if there is minimum amount of risk involved in it. Thus, the spirit of enterprise is one factor which determines the willingness of farmer to take risk.

Another important factor is the amount of capital involved. Before taking risk in adopting new venture, a farmer calculate the amount of capital that he may lose in the process. If the amount of capital involved is less, a farmer may take greater risk. If the capital involved is of larger magnitude, farmer's willingness to take risk may be low.

The economic and social status of a farmer also decides the degree of risk to be taken by a farmer. A sound economic position and high social status of a farmer tempts and strengthens his capability to take risk as, by doing so, he satisfies his ego that society expects from him a direction and a leadership in new and risky enterprises. On the other hand, a farmer who is economically not sound and socially not so high, hesitate to take any risk. His attitude will always be risk averter as his economic and social compulsions bound him to do so.

Age is also an important factor in determining the degree of risk. It is generally experienced that younger farmers have more capacity to take greater risks than the older ones who are victim of conservatism, lack of drive, fundamentalism etc. The younger ones enjoy experiments with new ideas even if the risk involved is of high magnitude.

Type of Uncertainties: In agricultural production farmers face various type of uncertainties which may broadly be classified into (1) "on-farm" and (2) "off-farm" uncertainties. On-farm uncertainties are related to production, stock of resources, family labour etc. and off-farm uncertainties are those which are concerned with the market price, Government policies, technology and institutions.

Resources uncertainty are directly related with the resources that are involved in the process of production, land, labour, capital and organisation are such resources. Productivity of a piece of land is uncertain, availability of labour is also uncertain due to sickness or terms of contact, capital is uncertain due to its non-availability in time or on agreeable terms and conditions. Other resources such as seed, fertilisers, equipments may not be timely and sufficiently available.

Yield uncertainty is an important feature of agriculture production, and arises due to imperfect knowledge. Since, agricultural production is predominated by nature, seasonal fluctuations are beyond the control of man. Uncertainties in rainfall, for example, may be of different types. It may or may not come in time. It may be excessive and scanty. It may not be spread over evenly. All such uncertainties are beyond human control. Some weather changes also change sowing and harvesting operation unexpectedly. And as a result altered the expected yields.

Among the "off-farm uncertainties" input and output price uncertainty is most important as they influence the production decisions. Among input and output price uncertainty, output price uncertainty is more important than input uncertainty, because variations in input prices may be adjusted to some extent as all inputs are not purchased or used up at once. But output price uncertainty is known only with a time lag.

Price of the products fluctuate due to uncontrolled supply and inelastic demand. A time-lag between initiation and sale of agricultural product plays an important role to change the demand and supply conditions. And as a result uncertainty prevails. Crops whose gestation period is longer still creates more uncertainties. Government policies which encourages certain commodities tend farmers to make sudden changes in price and change relative profitability of various farm enterprises.

Agricultural output also faces uncertainties on account of institutional behaviour such as functioning of credit agencies, conditions of tenure, actions and out-look of various rural agencies involved in assisting farmers.

Remedial Steps: A farmer can take different steps to safeguard against risk and uncertainty. The responsiveness of a farmer towards these steps depends upon the size of farm, amount of capital employed and the family responsibilities. The pre-cautions which the producer can take to minimize the risk and uncertainty increases the cost of output, necessitates sacrifice and results less than maximum output from given resources. Risk and uncertainty also discourage long-term capital investment and hence adversely affect the efficiency.

Some important steps through which a farmer can reduce risk and uncertainty are insurance, diversification, contracts, education, maintaining flexibility and liquidity.

Crop insurance is an important means of safeguarding farmers against loss due to weather hazards, destruction from insects and diseases and ultimately against falling production and farm income. Diversification of production is another means of minimising uncertainties. This is actually another form of insurance. It refers the production of various commodities simultaneously or production or sale of commodities at different timings. By doing so, farmer actually spread over the risk of loss over various commodities and may reduce the risk of loss. In this way, it may also reduces the variability of income. Production on contact basis is also a method of reducing risk and uncertainty. Production of broilers and vegetables for canneries is an example. Many processors prefer to know in advance about how much of a commodity they will have for processing. On that basis they often contact for the production of specified amount to be purchased at a guaranteed price. In this way production on contact basis minimizes the risks and the uncertainties. Flexibility refers the convenience with which the plan of production can be changed. A flexible plan should be such that a farmer could shift the resources from one enterprise to another enterprise in order to achieve better returns if he realises that the market conditions are becoming more favourable towards one enterprise in relation to the other. Some short duration crops such as cereals, vegetables, pulses, seasonal fruits are the examples of such flexible approach. Similarly dual purpose animals such as sheep is also an example of such flexibility. If the market is unfavourable for wool, sheep can still be marketed for meat.

Liquidity also play an important role in reducing risk and uncertainties. Liquidity refers to the maintenance of balances of money or assets that can be easily and readily converted into cash money. In this way liquidity provides flexibility. Because uncertainty does exists and farmers are unable to convert readily most of their assets into cash, it is often desirable for a farmer to hold some liquid asset. Thus, insurance, diversification, education, contact, flexibility and liquidity are some important steps through which risk and uncertainty may be minimised. All such devices involved costs and hence influences farmer's income. The adoption of all, few or any of these measures depends upon farmer's estimate of the relation between the cost and the returns.

FOOTNOTES & REFERENCES

1. Heady E. O., *Economics of Agricultural Production & Resource Use. op cit.* p.p. 440-45.
2. *Ibid,* p.449.

6

COBB-DOUGLAS PRODUCTION FUNCTION: A CRITICAL EVALUATION

Cobb-Douglas production function (C-D Function) has been universally practiced. The function is based on empirical study of the American manufacturing industry conducted by Paul H. Douglas and C.W. Cobb. It is a linear homogeneous production of the first degree where two input factors labour and capital have been taken into account for the entire output of the industry. It assumes that the logarithms of the total output of the economy is a linear function of the logarithms of the labour force and the capital stock engaged in the process of production. This can be expressed as:

$$\text{Log } Y = K + p \text{ Log } L + q \text{ Log } C$$

This can also be expressed as:

$Y = AL^{p}C^{q}$ where

Y = output

L = quantity of labour employed

C = quantity of capital employed

p and q = positive constants where $p < 1$.

This is homogeneous linear production function which implies constant returns to scale. That is $p + q = 1$. In this function, the share of labour to an increase in manufacturing industry was calculated 3/4 and that of capital 1/4. Hence C-D function ($Y = a\ L^{3/4}\ C^{1/4}$) shows constant returns to scale because the total of the values of L and C, that is 3/4 + 1/4, is equal to one. In such case of homogeneous production function if all the factors of production are increased in the same proportion, output would also increased in the same proportion.

This function, in fact, is by used by Wicksell. He gave in a footnote, the function as $P = a^{\alpha} b^{\beta} c^{\gamma}$ where $\alpha + \beta + \gamma$ was equal to 1. In C-D production function $\alpha + \beta = 1$.

The C-D function, though originally applied to industry, later began to be applied to agriculture also. The earliest application of it was made by K. Kamiya of Tokyo university in 1943. In this attempt, however, one restraint imposed by the original C-D function, that is $\alpha + \beta = 1$, was relaxed and values of α and β were determined independently of each other. Since then, the C-D production function has been extensively applied in agriculture and in majority of the cases the *restraint* of $\alpha + \beta = 1$ has been given up. Further, the number of factors included in the production function is no longer confined to only labour and capital. Now, many inputs are being used as independent variables. This can be expressed as:

$$Y = a x_1^{\alpha} \times x_2^{\beta} \times x_3^{\gamma} \ldots <$$

where $\alpha + \beta + Y$ may or may not be equal to one. According to Heady this type of function is Cobb-Douglas type production function. It is not the original C-D production function which is confined to two input production function with $\alpha + \beta = 1$. This reformation actually refers to unconstrained growth base production function.

In production economics there are three broad sources of growth, namely: (i) increases in factor supplies, (ii) increasing returns, and (iii) technical progress which in the wider sense refers to anything that increases productivity. The production function most commonly fitted to aggregate data to distinguish between these three broad sources of growth has been the unconstrained form of C-D production function. This can be expressed as:

$$Yt = Tt\ Kt^{\alpha}\ Lt^{\beta} \text{ where}$$

Yt = real output at time 't',

Tt = index of technology (total productivity)

Kt = index of the capital services at constant prices,

Lt = index of the labour input

α = partial elasticity (responsiveness) of output with respect to capital, holding labour constant,

β = partial elasticity of output with respect to labour, holding capital constant.

Changes in technology have been considered as exogenous and independent of changes in factor inputs. Hence the effect of technological progress is neutral on the factor intensity of production 'Tt', 'α' and 'β' are constants and are to be estimated empirically if the function is unconstrained. Generally, 'α' and 'β' are less than unity on the assumption of diminishing marginal productivity of factors. The sum of partial elasticities of output with respect to the factors of production gives the scale of returns or the degree of homogeneity of the functions. If: (i) $\alpha + \beta = 1$, it represents constant returns, (ii) $\alpha + \beta > 1$, it represents an increasing returns, and (iii) $\alpha + \beta < 1$, it refers decreasing returns. Geometrical expression of such degree of homogeneity may be given as under:

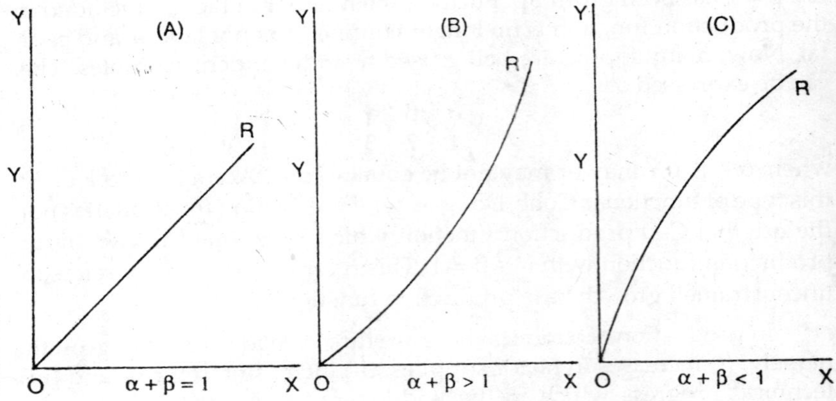

Fig. 1

Figure 'A' presents a constant returns to scale. The emerging function Y = ax1.0 is a straight line passing through the origin. Here Y is output, 'a' is the constant term, and X is the input. If the function that emerged is of the type Y = ax1.5 it will find expression of through a progressively rising curve as shown in figure 'B'. In such case marginal productivity of X input is rising. If the function happens to have a co-efficient with value less than 1, say Y = ax0.6, the function will be represented by a rising curve, progressively moving towards a maximum. This refers that the marginal productivity is constantly declining and tending towards zero. Figure 'C' presents this situation. These shapes of the production function clearly show various types of changes in the marginal productivity.

We know that the slope of a production function curve express the marginal productivity of the independent factor. In case of single input C-D production function, the marginal productivity of the independent factor is dy/dx which shows that it will remain constant, or increase or decrease, depending upon whether $\alpha = 1$, $\alpha > 1$ or $\alpha < 1$ It may be noted that the marginal products pertaining to such single variable production function of C-D type will have the same sign throughout. Either they will be positive or negative, depending upon the sign of coefficient of the variable input. Another important point to be noted is that the elasticity of production is constant over the entire input-output curve and is equal to the co-efficient of the independent variable. This can be explained as under:2

$$Ep = dy/dx \cdot \frac{x}{y}$$

for the function $Y = a\,x^{\alpha}$

$$dy/dx = \alpha\, ax^{\alpha-1}$$

$$\text{So } Ep = \alpha\, ax^{\alpha-1} \cdot x/y$$

$$= \frac{\alpha ax^{\alpha}}{Y}$$

$$\text{As } ax^{\alpha} = y$$

$$Ep = \frac{\alpha y}{Y} = \alpha$$

The introduction of one more variable in C-D function makes the diagram a bit more complicated. In case of two variables we have a production surface, instead of a production curve. The following diagram shows production surface with two variable inputs.

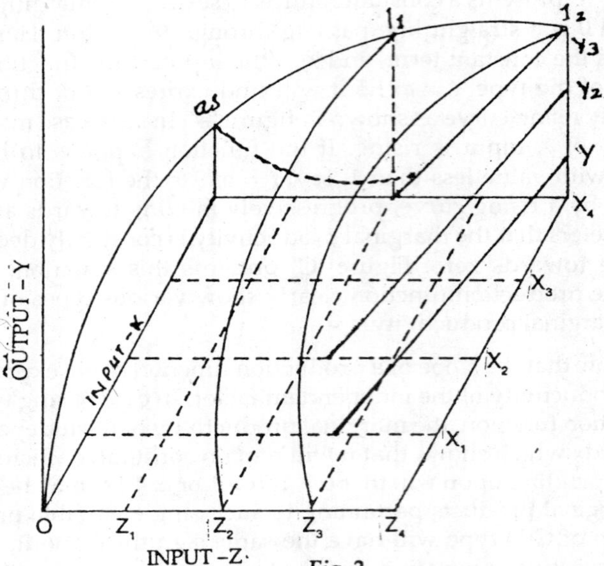

Fig. 2

In the above diagram Y is the output and Z and X are the two inputs. The diagram is of three dimensional form where quantities of inputs are measured along with horizontal axes or known as input plane and output is measured vertically or output plane. The production surface consists of a large number of production curves as shown in the diagram. For example, the curve Z2 11 indicates how the production moves when input Z is kept constant at Z_2 level and input X goes on increasing. We have different curve if we keep Z constant at different level. Similarly, we can have other curves by keeping X constant at different level and vary Z. All points on the production surface will show some combination of X and Y and we must note that if we have two variables, the number of such combination and the corresponding points on production surface will be infinite.

If this production surface represents C-D type production function then all curves for a variable factor while the other variable kept constant at some point will have the same characteristics as explained in a single variable C-D type production function. Two important and necessary characteristics are: (i) at each point on the curve, elasticity of production of the variable factor is equal to its co-efficient in the production function and (ii) marginal products of the variable in question have only plus or minus sign, regardless of the quantity of the input used or output produced. Cobb-Douglas production with three independent variables will become more complicated for purposes of diagrammatic representation.

C-D production function can also be explained with the help of isoquants. An isoquant or iso-product curve shows various combination of two inputs which produces the same quantity of a product. The C-D production function $Y = ax^{\alpha} Z^{\beta}$ shows a set of iso-quants. For a particular value of Y we, on the basis of this function, derive different combinations of X and Z. By presenting all such combinations through a curve we shall get a iso-quant. If the coefficients of X and Z that is 'α' and 'β' have positive values, the isoquants for this function will be convex to the origin throughout and at the same time asymptotic to the input Axes.

Suppose our production functions is $Y = ax^{\alpha}z^{\beta}$ where α and β both are positive. Suppose Y = Yo which shows a particular amount of output produced. Various amount of X and Z to produce Yo will be represented by an isoquant. In that case, relationship between X and Z with reference to this isoquant will be:[3]

$$X^{\alpha} = \frac{Y_0}{a\,x^{\beta}}$$

$$X = \left(\frac{Y_0}{a\,X^{\beta}}\right)^{1/\alpha} \quad \text{... (i)}$$

Now slope of this isoquant at a given point, will represent the marginal rate of substitution (MRS) of Z for X. In our case MRS of Z for X is:

$$\frac{dx}{dz} = -\frac{1}{\alpha}\left(\frac{Y_0}{a\,z^{\beta}}\right)\frac{1}{\alpha - 1} \cdot \beta \frac{Y_0}{a} \cdot \frac{1}{z^{\beta+1}}$$

$$\frac{dx}{dz} = -\frac{\beta}{\alpha}\left(\frac{Y_0}{az^{\beta}}\right)^{1/\alpha}\frac{1}{Z} \quad \text{... (ii)}$$

$$\text{Now}\left(\frac{Y_0}{az^{\beta}}\right)^{\frac{1}{\alpha}} = X \text{ proved in (i)}$$

$$\therefore \frac{dx}{dz} = -\frac{\beta}{\alpha} \cdot \frac{X}{Z} \quad \text{... (iii)}$$

The above equation of MRS for an isoquant based on C-D production function shows that as Z increases MRS will fall. And if MRS falls the isoquent will be convex to the origin. The isoquants are asymptotic to the axes of coordinates is also clear from the fact that if one variable in the above equation of the isoquant, say Z is O, value of X will be infinity and vice-versa. This means that the isoquant will meet the axis showing X at infinity which in fact refers that it is asymptotic to this axis. Similarly, isoquant on the other axis is also asymptotic.

MRS of an isoquant in case of C-D function is a linear function of the ratio in which X and Z are combined to produce the output represented by the given iso-quant. Another important feature of the isoquant of the C-D type function is that if output is increased by increasing both the inputs in equal proportions and as a result isoquant moves on a high isoquant, the MRS (dx/dz) at the point indicating the same ratio of two inputs, will remain unchanged. The diagrammatic expression of such iso-clines for C-D function will be straight lines, all passing through the origin.[4]

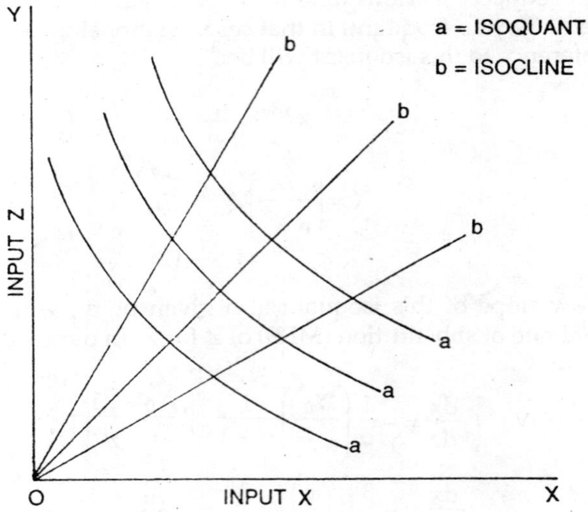

Fig. 3

Since the iso-clines are straight lines passing through the origins, these line will also coincide with scale-lines. It shows an increase in output i.e., movement to the high iso-quant when two inputs are increased in the same ratio.

Another important point needs attention. We know that for determining a point of minimum cost when a particular amount of output is to be produced, we find a point on iso-quant where its slops is the same as that of the iso-cost line. The tangency point of iso-quant and iso-cost is the minimum point of cost. If another amount of output is to be produced and is represented by a higher or lower iso-quant, the same condition has to be satisfied. In other words, the input prices remained unchanged, the optimum combinations of inputs for various levels of output will be represented by a particular iso-cline. In C-D production function, this iso-cline is straight line which implies that the ratio in which inputs are to be mixed for minimising total costs is the same for all level of output. In such production function where iso-clines are not linear or do not pass through the origin, this principle cannot be applied. So we can say that once we have been able to determine the optimum combination of inputs for producing an output according to C-D type function, the optimum combination of other levels of output are automatically determined provided prices of inputs do not change. In such case, the ratio of inputs will remain unchanged at all levels of output.

In the original C-D production function, as has been explained earlier, $\alpha + \beta$ is equal to one. This refers to constant returns to scale. Later on, this constraint was given up and we used an unconstraint production function which shows that the same of α and β could take up any value. It could be more than one or less than one. If $\alpha + \beta > 1$ it refers to an increasing returns to scale and if $\alpha + \beta < 1$ it indicate decreasing returns to scale. If we draw the iso-quant map for the C-D type production function, we can know whether the returns to scale are constant, increasing or decreasing. The iso-cline as we have seen earlier, also represents the scale line. If increase in output as shown by iso-quants is accompanied by an increase in both the input in the same proportion as that of increase in output, it will indicate the constant returns to scale. If more than proportionate increase inputs is needed for any given increase in output, it will be a case of decreasing returns to scale. If less than proportionate increase in two inputs is required, it will be case of increasing returns. In diagram, this is revealed itself by the fact that with every given increase in output, the distance between the successive iso-quants representing the given increase in output will go on increasing. And in case of increasing returns to scale, this distance will go on decreasing.[5]

C-D Function in Agriculture — A Critical Evaluation[6]

In agriculture C-D production function has been most frequently applied and has been universally practiced. The most appealing nature of this function is its linear function. Besides, it has got the additional advantage of the coefficients being the elasticities of outputs with respect to the inputs. But in the field of agriculture a serious drawback of C-D function is when one works with micro-level observations. In such case it does not allow any of its input variables to take zero value. If any of its input variables takes the zero value, output has automatically become zero. This is false assumption. Many farms uses fertilisers and irrigation water and many farms does not. If one chooses C-D production function for all such farms, he should assumed that the farms with no fertilisers and no irrigation water would have zero output. This is quite absurd logic.[7] Actually, the main reason for the extensive use of C-D production function in agriculture is its relative simplicity of estimation of parameters. But one pay a high price for this simplicity in terms of its unrealistic assumptions such as the constancy of partial and total elasticities of production and of unit elasticity of substitution between factors of production.[8] Anderson and Jodha also pointed out: "The restrictiveness enters implicitly into his test of the hypothesis of allocative efficiency so that the conditional question he is asking is effectively", "Do farmers maximize profits given that they are operating under a single C-D production function that is common to all members of the same group (i.e. common Cobb-Douglas technology)?"[9]. Thus, for using C-D technique for evaluating the allocative efficiency of the farmers two problems have to be examined: (1) Does every activity have C-D as the underlying production function? and (2) Does every member (or farmer) have the same C-D technology? Unfortunately no empirical study have touched these aspects in any detail. It is also revealed that for the C-D production function case, differences in technical efficiency cannot be separately identified from the actual profit or production functions.[10]

It is also well-known that all farms would have the same quantities of inputs and outputs if: (i) all farms have the same production function, i.e. the same technical knowledge and identical fixed factors; (ii) all farms faced the same prices in the produce and factor market; and (iii) all farms maximizes profit perfectly. But the fact is quite different. Observations reveal differences in factor intensities with varying factor productivity. It implies that (i) different farms face different factor prices; and/or, (ii) they use different technologies of production. These aspects of the problems have not been dealt with in the empirical studies and the empirical studies assumed that farmers have identical technologies and face perfectly competitive factor and product markets.[11]

Thus, the most frequently used C-D function creates serious limitations. This C-D function is being fitted to cross-section data relating to inputs and output in agriculture with not much consideration to the sampling procedure followed in collecting the data, the units in which they were measured or the aggregation that are involved in them. This exercise is being used to test hypothesises regarding such matters as returns to scale, efficiency of resource allocation etc. But this fact is being neglected that a production function fitted to cross-section data cannot be treated as an aggregate production function.[12]

Moreover, since only one combination of factor inputs can be observed at any one time, it is not possible to distinguish shifts in the function — technical progress — from moments along the function — changes in factor intensity — unless the assumption of neutral technical progress is made. This is an unrealistic assumption. Technical progress may not be neutral and therefore the effect of technical progress and changing factor intensity confused, biasing the results of the contribution of factor inputs and technical progress to growth.[13] Apart from all these weaknesses and drawbacks C-D production function has been extensively used in agriculture.

Application of C-D Function in Indian Agriculture

Various attempts has been made so far to apply C-D function in Indian agriculture. Hanumantha Rao attempted to use it in old Hyderabad State comprising Telangana, Marathwada and Karnataka regions. Rajkrishna used it on Punjab State and recently Mohd. Shafi applied it on Uttar Pradesh. Besides Saran, V. Chenna Reddy, Bardhan and J.P. Singh have also attempted to use it in various states or regions.[14] Here we are introducing some main points of Hanumantha Rao's and Mohd. Shafi's study.

Hanumantha Rao's study (1953-54) is based on the data regarding gross output, inputs of land, labour and capital pertaining to 345 farms of the old Hyderabad State, comprising Telengana, Marathwada and Karnataka regions. The study comprises three stages: (i) it starts with simple input-output relationship by means of the ratio of output to individual inputs, such as, output per unit of land, labour and capital. In this stage, factor ratios such as land-labour, land-capital, and capital-labour are also examined. (ii) in the second stage study examines the elasticities of output with respect to each input and returns to scale by fitting Cobb-Douglas production function to input-output data. (iii) in the third stage, marginal productivity of these resources are analysed.

In the second stage, the estimated elasticities of output with respect to the inputs of land and labour are analysed. These elasticities are derived by fitting to the farm data C-D production function of the types: $Y = ax_1^{b_1} x_2b^2$, where "Y" is output which is dependent variable, "a" is constant, "X_1" and "X_2" are land and labour inputs which are independent variable and "b" coefficients are the elasticities indicates the per cent change in output associated with a 1 per cent increase in the output factor concerned while other factors are held constant.

The sum of these elasticities indicates the returns to scale. If these sum of elasticities is equal to one it would refer constant returns to scale if sum of elasticities is less or more than one, it would refer diminishing or increasing returns to scale. The estimates of elasticities show that all the elasticities are positive and less than one which indicates a decreasing marginal productivity of factor inputs.

Mohd. Shafi used C-D type of production function as: $Y_1 = A X_1 b$ $X_2 c X_3 d \ldots X_n y$. Taking logarithm of this equation, the same is written as:

$$\log Y_1 = \log A + b \log X_2 + c \log X_3 \ldots X_n.$$

The most important advantage of this type of function is that the coefficient of function are equal and the elasticities of production/productivity with respect to different inputs, and the function makes it possible for the principle of diminishing returns to operate within the scale.

His application of C-D production function in Uttar Pradesh revealed significant results among the different variables: irrigation by canals, irrigation by other sources and fertilizer inputs. C-D function here revealed the following sensitivities:

Keeping other input factor constant, 1 per cent change in respective variable will result in the following:

(a) 1 per cent change in irrigation by canal would bring a change in SUN[1] output as 0.016 per cent.

(b) 1 per cent change in irrigation by other sources would bring a change in SUN output as 0.022 per cent.

(c)) 1 per cent change in NPK consumption per 1000 hectares would bring a positive change of + 0.017 per cent in productivity index; and

(d)) 1 per cent change in agricultural workers 1000 hectares would bring a negative change of -0.99 per cent in productivity index.

As a remedial step, it has been suggested that agricultural labour should divert to some other industrial professions by creating useful job opportunities in the lower productivity zone. In case of fertilizer inputs, increase in irrigated area through such means as are suitable to the respective geographical conditions and irrigated area through canals calls for development of a dynamic decision model in the region concerned.[15]

REFERENCES

1. Based upon: Yotopoulas P.A., Nugent J.B., *Economics of Development: Empirical Investigation*, Harper & Row, N. York 1976 pp. 48-49; Ashok Rudra, *Indian Agricultural Economics: Myth and Realities*; Allied Publisher, 1982 pp. 258-61; Gupta R.K., *Economics of Development & Planning*, Atma Ram, 1977, p. 168; Sadhu A.N., Singh A, *Fundamentals of Agricultural Economics*, Himalaya, 1983 pp 68-70; Soni R.N., *Leading Issues In Agricultural Economics*, Shoban Lal Nagin Chand & Co. 1992 pp. (Chapter 21) pp. 315-323; Sampath R.K., *Nature And Measurement of Economic Efficiency In Indian Agriculture*, **Indian Journal of Agricultural Economics**, April-June 1979; Anderson J.R., Jodha N.S., *On Cobb-Douglas and Related Myths*, **Economic and Political Weekly**, June 30, 1973; Day A.K. Ashok Rudra, *A Test of Hypothesis of Rational Allocation under Cobb-Douglas Technology*, **Economic and Political Weekly**, Vol. II March 24, 1973.
2. Soni R.N., *Leading Issues in Agricultural Economics*, Shoban Lal Nagin Chand 1992, p. 318.
3. *Ibid.*, pp. 320-21.
4. *Ibid.*, p. 321.
5. *Ibid.*, pp. 322-23
6. See in details: Ashok Rudra, *Indian Agricultural Economics: Myths and Realities, op cit.*; Sampath R.K., *Nature and Measurement of Economic Efficiency in Indian Agriculture*, **Indian Journal of Agricultural Economics**, April-June 1979; Anderson J.R., Jodha N.S., "On Cobb-Douglas and Related Myths", **Economic and Political Weekly**, Vol. VIII, June 30, 1973; Day A.K. and Ashok Rudra", *A Test of Hypothesis of Rational Allocation under Cobb-Douglas Technology*, ***Economic and Political Weekly***, Vol. VII March 24, 1973.
7. Ashok Rudra, *Indian Agricultural Economics, op cit.*, p. 259.
8. Sampath R.K., *Nature and Measurement of Economic Efficiency in Indian Agriculture*, **Indian Journal of Agricultural Economics**, April-June 1979, p. 19.
9. Anderson J.R., Jodha N.S., *On Cobb-Douglas and Related Myths, op Cit.*PA.65.
10. Sampath R.K., *Nature and Measurement of Economic Efficiency in Indian Agriculture, op cit.*, p. 20.
11. *Ibid.*
12. Ashok Rudra, *Indian Agricultural Economics*: Myths & Realities *op cit.*, p. 255.
13. Gupta R.K., *Economics of Development & Planning*. Atma Ram, 1977 p. 168.
14. See. Hanumantha Rao CH. *Agricultural Production Functions, Cost and Returns to India*, Asia, 1965 pp 12-26; Raj Krishna, "*Some Production Function for Punjab*", **Indian Journal of Agricultural Economics**; 21, 1966

pp 87-97; Mohd. Shafi, *Agricultural Productivity and Regional Imbalances; A Study of Uttar-Pradesh Concept*, 1984 pp 244-257; Saran R, "Production Function Approach to the Measurement of Productivity in Agriculture", **Journal of the Indian Society of Agricultural Statistics,** 1965 pp 265-278; V. Chenna Reddy, *Production Function in South Indian Agriculture,* **Journal of Farm Economics,** 49, 1962 pp 816-820; Bardhan P.K., *Size, Productivity and Returns to Scale : An Analysis of Farm level Data in Indian* Agriculture", **Journal of the Political Economy,** 81, 1973 pp 1370-1386; *J.P. Singh, "Resource Use, Farm Size and Returns to Scale in a Backward Agriculture,* **Indian Journal of Agricultural Economics,** 30, 1975 pp. 32-46; Srivastavad and Borates, *Green Revolution for Northern Region — Impact of Selective Farm Mechanisation or Farm Employment,* (Mimeograph) Division of Agricultural Economics I.A.R.I., N.Delhi.

15. Mohd. Shafi, *Agricultural Productivity and Regional Imbalances, op cit.,* p. 253-257.

PART - III

CONSUMPTION ECONOMICS CONSUMPTION, DEMAND AND SUPPLY AND PRICE DETERMINATION OF AGRICULTURAL GOODS

(i) CONSUMPTION ECONOMICS

(ii) DEMAND ANALYSIS OF FARM PRODUCTS

(iii) DEMAND AND SUPPLY — PRICE DETERMINATION

(iv) PRICE POLICY

1

CONSUMPTION ECONOMICS

In the previous section (Part-II) we have focused our attention on the behaviour of producer. The production economics as explained in this part placed a great deal of emphasis to analyse how changes in economic conditions affect the actions of producers. This part focused the attention on the behaviour of consumers. The consumption economic conditions such as supply, demand and prices, etc – influence consumer's behaviour. Most consumers have little interest to know how does farmer produced the commodities; what they are producing and how the goods enter into the market? Consumer's are greatly concerned if farmers alter their production to cause the prices of some goods to rise. They are also concerned if the goods of their choice and taste are not available.

Producers expect that whatever they have produced and whatever they want to sell, have been consumed. Hence the income prospects of a farmer are being affected by consumer's demand. Consumer's purchases are the media through which they transmit knowledge to farmers in relation to the kind and amounts of products they want. Consumer's preferences and changes in demand are reflected to producer through changes in prices and quantities of goods purchased by the consumers. Agriculture produces all those commodities without which living of human being is impossible. Thus every human being is agricultural consumer. Our basic concern, therefore, is to analyse the question: Why consumers vary their purchases? This analysis will help us to understand the reasons for changes in the demand for farm products.[1]

Consumer's Preferences — Demand Analysis

Consumption of goods refer gain, utility and satisfaction. In purchasing goods, consumer, thus, attempt to buy those goods from which they get the greatest satisfaction in relation to the prices they paid for them. All consumers are limited in the amount of goods they purchase because their income is limited, preferences are different, tastes are varied and impact of price changes fluctuates. As a result, they make choices among various goods, which are influenced by income, prices, preferences and tastes.

The problem of choice in consumption is similar to that in production. In production, as we have seen in the previous part, the producer's choice of production alternatives depends on physical production relationship and relative prices. Consumer's decision is also based on relative prices as well as on preferences for various goods. In purchasing goods consumer buy some combinations of goods instead of others which they could also purchase. Nobody spends all his income on a single commodity. Instead, combinations of goods are purchased. When combinations are made, it refers the preferences for some goods against the other goods. In this process if a consumer substitutes one commodity for the other, he can usually find many combinations of two commodities which give him equal satisfaction. Here consumer is said to be indifferent to those combinations which are equally satisfactory.

Such consumer preferences can graphically be explained in following way.

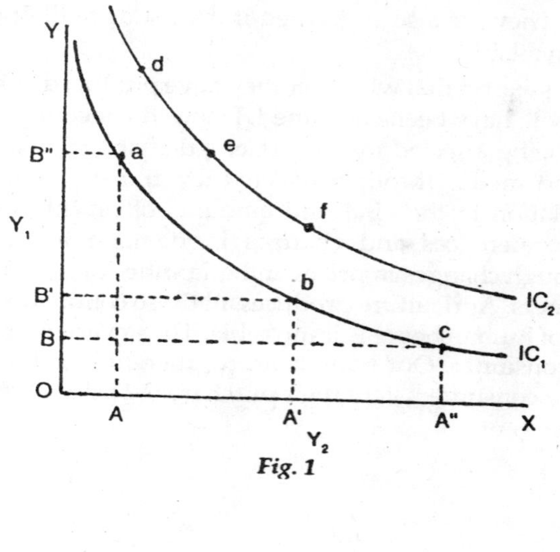

Fig. 1

Diagram shows two I C curves Y_1, and Y_2 with different combinations of commodities depicting equal satisfactions at various points a b c at IC_1 and d e f at IC_2. IC_2 gives higher level of satisfaction than IC_1. Each curve represents those combination of commodities to which consumer is indifferent.

These indifference curves are comparable to iso-product curves discussed in the previous part. We see that as there are different ways in which inputs are to be substituted in the production of commodities, there are different ways in which commodities are substituted for each other in consumption. Some commodities are to be substituted at constant rate in consumption. If this trend is found, then a consumer will be willing to trade a given number of one commodity for a given amount of the other. Under such circumstances, a consumer is usually willing to take only one of these commodity. However, most of commodities which the consumer purchase are not substituted at a constant rate.

Usually, if consumer takes more unit of one commodity he has to give up some units of the other one. That is, he can increase the units of one commodity at the cost of the other if he want to be remained indifferent between the two. Moreover, when consumer is increasing commodity of Y_1 for commodity Y_2 he will give up less and less commodity of Y_2 for each additional unit of Y_1. IC_1 shows it well. This means that IC should be convex to the origin.

Since consumers prefer more goods and services to less, they seek to attain the highest indifference curve possible, given the amount of money available for the purchase of goods. This fact that consumers prefer more of one good in preference to other, IC_s must have a negative slope. An upward-sloping IC would indicate that a consumer is indifferent to consuming more goods. An IC which lies above another, as has been shown by IC_2 in the diagram, represents a greater amount of satisfaction. These curve cannot intersect, because in doing so the intersection point will give equal satisfaction for both the curves which is not true. Consumer is getting higher satisfaction on IC_2 than the IC_1.

These curves refer the rate at which consumers are willing to trade one good for the other according to their preferences. Yet, the curves do not indicate which combination will be purchased, say 'a' or 'b' or 'c' in the diagram, unless we know something about prices of the two commodities Y_1 and Y_2. The combinations of goods which a consumer is willing to purchase depends upon two factors. One is the income of the consumer and the other is the prices of the commodities. If suppose consumer's income is Rs. 100/- and the price of Y_1 is Rs. 5/- and of Y_2 Rs. 10/- a consumer can approximately purchase 20 units of Y_1 and 10 units of Y_2 if he spend all his income on either Y_1 and Y_2. The price of Y_2 is twice as much as the price of Y_1. Thus a consumer can substitute the commodity in the market in the ratio of two to one. This has been explained in the following diagram.

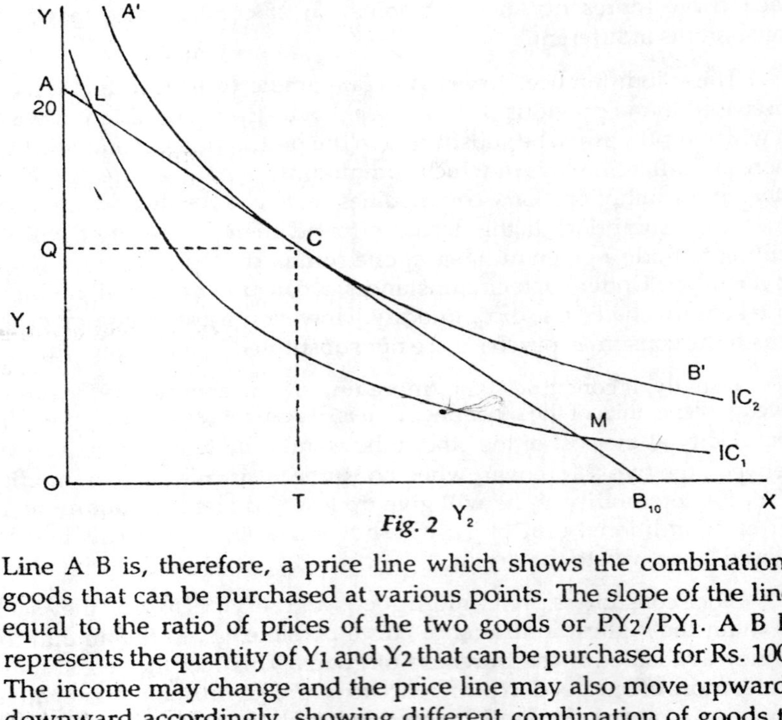

Fig. 2

Line A B is, therefore, a price line which shows the combination of goods that can be purchased at various points. The slope of the line is equal to the ratio of prices of the two goods or PY_2/PY_1. A B line represents the quantity of Y_1 and Y_2 that can be purchased for Rs. 100/-. The income may change and the price line may also move upward or downward accordingly, showing different combination of goods that can be purchased at the changed price line. So, there is price line for every amount of money available to spend, but all price lines are parallel. We want to know which combination of Y_1 and Y_2 commodity purchased with Rs. 100 provides best satisfaction. In diagram points L C and M presents such combinations. Among all, C lies on higher indifferent curve and, therefore, this will be preferred to point L and M. The consumer maximises satisfaction at C with OT amount of Y_2 and O Q amount of Y_1. This is the combination at which the rate of substitution of two goods is just equal to the rate at which the consumer can substitute the goods in the market. That is consumer gets maximum satisfaction where, $\Delta Y_1/\Delta Y_2$ · PY_2/PY_1.[2]

Changes in Income and Prices: Changes in income and prices affect the amount of goods purchased. When income increases or decreases, the consumption of some goods are either increased or decreased. If purchases of some goods do increase with increased income, the goods are said to be normal goods. On the other hand, if the quantity of goods purchased decreased when income increase, the goods are said to be inferior goods.

The effect of a change in the price of a good upon its consumption is a complex phenomenon. When prices change, it has two distinct effects upon an individual's behaviour. One is income effect and the other is substitution effect. A change in price of a commodity actually affects the purchasing power of income of a consumer and so affects the value of his income. Falling prices increases the value of money and rising prices reduces it. Similarly, a change in the price of a commodity in relation to other commodities changes the consumption pattern. If the prices of Y_1 falls in relation to other commodities, we expect more of Y_1 to be purchased, ignoring the income effect and vice versa. A decrease in price of a commodity, say 30%, increases 30% of his income as he has to spend now 30% less on that commodity. This extra 30% will be treated like any other increase in income. And it will lead the consumer to change his consumption on various goods.[3]

The effect of price change on normal goods and inferior goods are different. With a normal good, the income and substitution effects both operate in the same direction. If the price decreases, consumers will substitute this good for the other. The decrease in price, as we know, also increases the incomes. So the consumption of normal goods also increases with the increase in incomes. Thus, both the substitution and income effects cause an increase in consumption of normal goods when its prices decreases. And when price increase, both will also decrease.[4]

For an inferior good the change in prices brings opposite influence. When price decreases, the substitution effect causes an increase in purchases of the good as with normal goods. The price decrease results an increase in income. Since the good is inferior, purchases of the good are expected to decrease. Thus, whether a price decrease for an inferior good results in an increase or a decrease in purchases depends upon relative strength of the income and substitution effects. If the substitution effects is stronger, more of the goods will be purchased. And if the income effect is strong purchases will decreases.[5]

Following diagram illustrate these effects.

Diagram illustrates the effect of price change on quantities purchased. On IC_1, consumer gets maximum satisfaction at F combination of Y_2 and Y_1. Suppose the price of Y_2 falls more quantities of Y_2 can now be purchased for the same income. The decreasing slope of price line from A E to A B indicate the increased purchase as the slope of line has decreased from 2/1 to 1/1. As a result of new price ratio, the consumer now will get maximum satisfaction at Q on IC_2 where new price line A B is tangent to IC_2. The price decrease brings about a substitution of Y_2 for Y_1. The substitution effect can be shown by finding the combination of Y_1 and Y_2 which would give the same satisfaction at the new prices as combination F gave at the old prices. The substitution effect of the price decrease for Y_2 is shown by the shift of consumer from F to G.

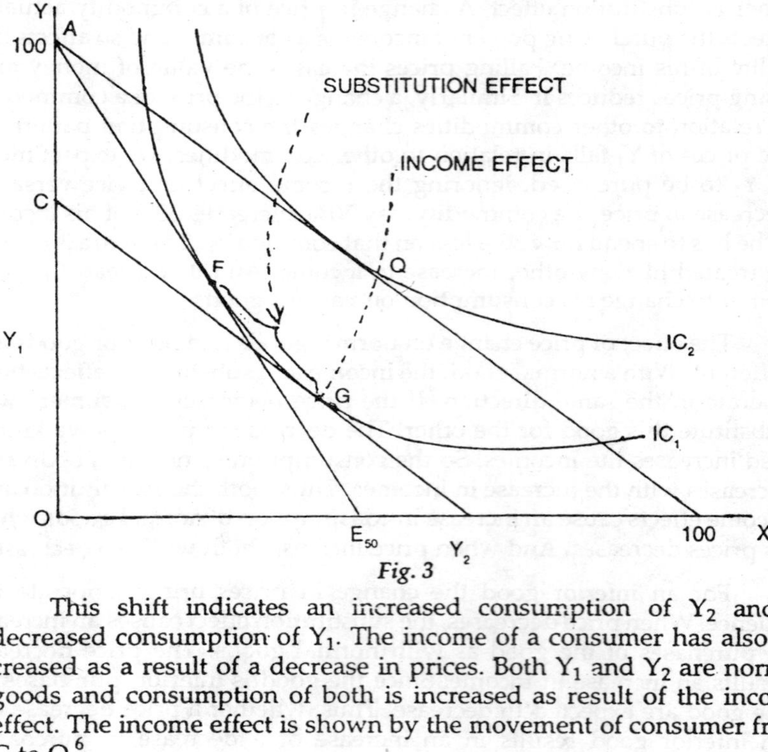

Fig. 3

This shift indicates an increased consumption of Y_2 and a decreased consumption of Y_1. The income of a consumer has also increased as a result of a decrease in prices. Both Y_1 and Y_2 are normal goods and consumption of both is increased as result of the income effect. The income effect is shown by the movement of consumer from G to Q.[6]

REFERENCES

1. Bishop C.E., Toussaint W.D., *Introduction To Agricultural Economics. op cit.* p. 181.
2. Bishop C.E., Toussaint W.D., *op. cit* pp. 183-84.
3. *Ibid.*, p. 185
4. *Ibid.*
5. *Ibid* p. 186
6. *Ibid* p. 187

2

DEMAND ANALYSIS OF FARM PRODUCTS

Consumer's preferences as have been discussed in the previous chapter show how consumer's preferences affect his demand for goods. Farmer is not interested how one individual behave, rather he is interested in the market demand for the products which he produce and the inputs which he use. Market demand of a commodity is the sum of all individual's demand and shows the aggregate relationship between the supplies of goods for the sale and the price paid for the various quantities. Thus "the amount of a commodity that households wish to purchase is called the quantity demanded of that commodity".[1]

There are four hypotheses about what determine the quantity of a commodity demanded by households:

(i) quantity demanded is influenced by the price of that commodity; (ii) quantity demanded is influenced by the size of income; (iii) quantity demanded is influenced by the price of other commodities; and (iv) quantity demanded is influenced by the households tastes. What we follows from the said hypotheses is that the amount of commodity a household is prepared to purchase is a "function of (i.e. depends upon) the price of goods in question, the price of all other goods, the household's income and its tastes".[2] This statement may be expressed in symbols what is called demand function:

$q_n^d = D(p_n, p_1, \ldots\ldots\ldots, p_{n-1}, Y, T)$.

Where q_n^d is the quantity that household demands of some commodity say "n", p_n is the price of this commodity, P_1, ... $\overline{P}_{n-1}$ is the shorthand expression for the prices of all commodities, Y is the. household's income and T is the tastes of the members of the family. What happens to the theory of demand if we consider all factors such as price, income and tastes are changing at once. Economist used a device. We assume that all except one of the factors in the right hand side are held constant. We then allow this one factor, say P_n or Y to vary and consider how the quantity-demanded q_n^d varies with it. We can apply this technique one by one on each factor and then consider the relation between quantity demanded and each of the variables on the right hand side of the demand function, taking them one at a time.[3]

Law of Demand, Demand Curve, and Elasticities of Demand

We observe in our daily life that the quantity demanded increases as the price of the commodity falls and it decreases as the price increases. Thus, there exists at any one time a definite relation between quantity demanded and price. And this relationship is, usually, an inverse relationship. Thus, other things remaining the same, the law of demand states that more will be demanded at a lower price and less when price is higher. Based on the law of demand we can construct a demand schedule for an agricultural commodity. An individual household demand schedule is a list of various quantities of commodity which an individual household purchases at different alternative prices. A market demand schedule can well be obtained by adding up all the demand schedules of the individuals households in the market. Following table shows the quantity of a vegetable that is demanded at different prices.

Price of a Vegetable per K.G.	*Quantity Demanded*
Rs. 25	1/2 kg.
Rs. 20	1.0 kg.
Rs. 12	1.5 kg.
Rs. 8	2.5 kg.
Rs. 5	3 kg.

We can plot the data on a graph with price on vertical axis and quantity on the horizontal one. This curve is called a demand curve. Its downward slope shows that the quantity demanded increases as the price falls.

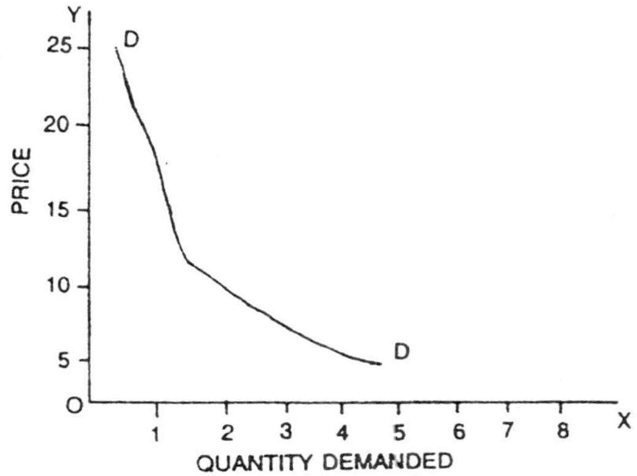

The demand curve that an individual farmer faces for his product is perfectly elastic. Since he is among the large number of producers, he is unable to influence the market price. In the market he is simply a price-taker. At the prevailing market price he can sell whatever quantity of produce he has produced.

In case of inferior goods, the demand curves may be perverse. Inferior goods, as has been explained earlier are those goods whose purchases decrease when income rises. For such goods the demand curve will only be perverse if they account for a significant proportion of the buyer's total expenditure. The purchases of staple goods comes under such category as they take higher proportion of the income of relatively poor population, leaving little scope for readjustment of their expenditure elsewhere.

Shift of Demand Curve

We must now consider the effect of a change income, prices and tastes on the demand curve.

It has been argued earlier that a rise in income will cause an increase in demand of most of commodities. Following hypothetical table explains this effect.

Price	*Original Demand*	*New Demand when income rises*
Rs. 25	1/2 kg.	1 kg.
Rs. 20	1 kg.	1.5 kg.
Rs. 12	1.5 kg.	2 kg.
Rs. 8	2.5 kg.	3 kg.
Rs. 5	3 kg.	3.5 kg.

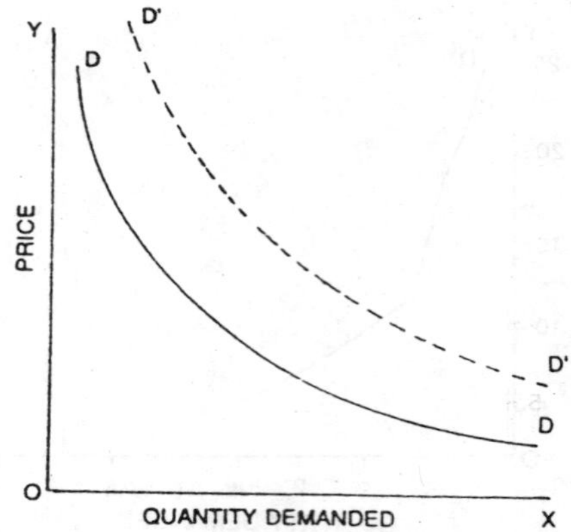

The original DD curve has been shifted to DD′ as income increases. This shift indicates an increase in the desire to purchase more vegetable at each price. At price Rs. 20 per kilogram the original demand was 1.5 kilogram. When income increases, the new demand is of 2 kilogram at the same price. A rise in income thus shifts the demand curve to the right, while a fall in price, it shifts to the left. In case of an inferior goods, a rise in income will cause a reduction in the quantity demanded at each market price, and the whole demand curve moves to the left.[4]

The effect on the demand curve of a change in price depends on whether the good, whose prices changes, is a complement or substitute. Take for example, the effect on the demand curve for gas (L.P.G.) stove. Gas prices and gas stove are complementary goods and a rise in gas price makes cooking with gas more expensive than previously. Thus a rise in the prices of gas leads to fall in the demand for L.P.G. stoves. Some household will replace their existing L.P.G. stove to Kerosene stove and some will buy a kerosene stove rather than L.P.G. stove. Now consider the effect of a rise in the price of kerosene stove. L.P.G. and kerosene stoves are substitutes for each other and when the price of kerosene and kerosene stove will rise, some households will buy L.P.G. stoves rather than kerosene stoves, and the demand for L.P.G. stoves will rise. Thus, a rise in price of a commodity complementary to X will shift the demand curve for X to the left, indicating that less X is demanded at each price. A rise in the prices of commodity that is substitute for X will shift the demand curve for X to the right, indicating that more X will be demanded at each price.[5]

The effect on the demand curve of a change in tastes of household indicates that at each price, more will be demanded if the taste is in favour of that commodity and less is demanded if the taste goes against it. Thus the whole curve either will move the right or towards the left.[6]

Movement and Shift of Curves: It is important to distinguish between a movement along a demand curve and a shift of the whole curve. A movement along a demand curve shows that different quantity of goods is being demanded because the prices has changed. A shift of a demand curve indicates that a different quantity of goods will be demanded at each possible price because something else, i.e. income, price of other commodity or the taste of consumer, has changed. When we speak of an increase or a decrease of demand, we refer to a shift of the whole curve, because we are here concerned with the whole functional relation between demand and price than with the particular quantity that is demanded at any one movement. When we refer to a movement along a curve we actually refer to a change in the quantity demanded, indicating a downward movement when price falls or an upward movement when price rises. A downward movement indicates that more quantity is demanded because of a fall in price and upward movement shows that less quantity is demanded because of a rise in price.[7]

Elasticity of Demand: Our demand analysis explains that lower prices increases the consumption of goods and services and higher prices reduce them. The downward sloping demand curve to the right proves it well. Consumer's decision as to how much to spend on a commodity at different prices is of great importance to the producers of that commodity. The law of demand simply shows the direction in which demand will move when the price changes. But it does not show by how much or to what extent a change in price will affect the quantities demanded. And this is an important aspect for the producer to know the responsiveness of consumers to price changes. Because, the degree of responsiveness determines the changes in total revenue resulting from changes in price, and producers profit is the difference between TR and TC. With some product, a change in price will bring about a proportionately large increase or decrease in the quantity demanded while with others the quantity demanded is only slightly responsive to price change. This responsiveness of consumers to change in price is known as "elasticity of demand". Thus, price elasticity of demand is the relative change in the quantity bought resulting from a given relative change in price. Let 'E' stand for elasticity. Then

$$EP = \frac{\text{relative change in quantity}}{\text{relative change in price}} = \frac{\frac{\Delta Q}{Q}}{\frac{\Delta P}{P}}$$

Where Q is quantity,

P is price

$\frac{\Delta Q}{Q}$ is relative change in quantity, and

$\frac{\Delta P}{P}$ is relative change in price.

The numerical value of E may vary from zero to infinity. If demand is completely unresponsive to the change in price, E will be equal to zero. Here demand is said to be completely inelastic. The demand is said to be relatively inelastic when the increase in quantity sold is proportionately smaller than the decrease in price. Here the value of E is greater than zero but less than one or (> 0 < 1). When the proportionate change in the quantity demanded is just equal to the proportionate change in its price, the case is of unit elasticity. Here the value of E is equal to one. When the proportionate change in the quantity demanded is more than the proportionate change in price, the demand is said to be elastic and the value of E is greater than one or E 1. Elasticity is called infinity when purchasers are prepared to buy all they can obtained at some price and none at all at an even slightly higher price. Thus, the range of price elasticity of demand from zero to infinity can be classified into the five categories.[8]

	Numerical Measure of Elasticity	*Description*	*Terminology*
1.	Zero (0)	Quantity demanded does not change as price changes	Completely inelastic
2.	Greater than zero less than one (> 0 < 1)	Quantity demanded changes by a smaller percentage change than does price	Inelastic
3.	One (E = 1)	Quantity demanded changes by exactly the same percentage as does price	Unit elasticity
4.	Greater than but less than infinity > 1 < ∞	Quantity demanded changes by a large percentage than does price.	Elastic
5.	Infinity (E = ∞)	Purchasers are prepared buy all at some price and none at all at an even slightly higher price	Perfectly elastic

These elasticities can be expressed in the following diagrams:

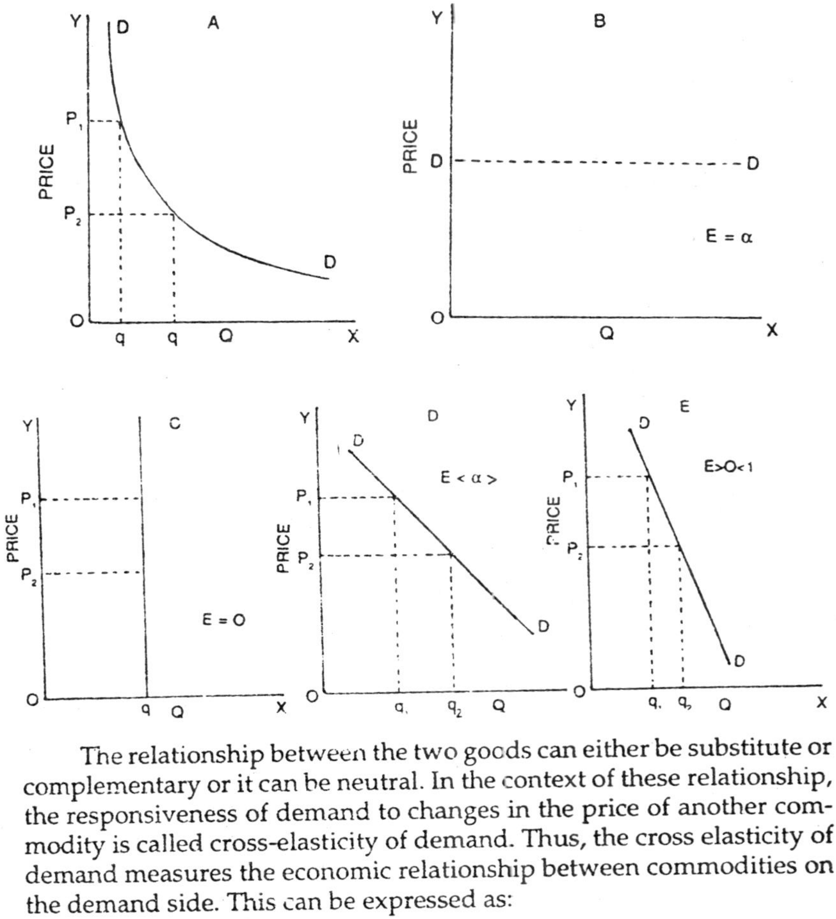

The relationship between the two goods can either be substitute or complementary or it can be neutral. In the context of these relationship, the responsiveness of demand to changes in the price of another commodity is called cross-elasticity of demand. Thus, the cross elasticity of demand measures the economic relationship between commodities on the demand side. This can be expressed as:

$$EO = \frac{\text{The percentage changes in the quantity purchased of X}}{\text{The percentage change in the price of Y}}$$

This fraction refers whether the two goods are related as substitutes or as complements. Cross-elasticity can vary from minus to plus infinity. Complementary goods have negative cross-elasticities and substitute goods will have positive cross elasticities. If X and Y, say bread and butter, are complements, a fall in the price of X is predicted to lead to an increase in the consumption of both X and Y. Thus the changes in the price of butter and the quantity of bread demanded will have opposite signs. If two commodities are substitutes, then a fall in the price of one is predicted to increase the quantity consumed but reduce the quantity of the other consumed. Thus the changes in the price of one and in the quantity of the other demanded will have the same sign. In this case the cross elasticity of demand will be infinity. If two goods are not substitutes at all, the value of cross-elasticity will be zero. The degree of substitutability between the two substitutable goods thus, refers that the cross-elasticity of demand will vary between two extremes — infinity and zero.[9]

Price Elasticity and Revenue: Consumer's decision as to how much to spend on a commodity at different prices is of great importance to the producers of that commodity. It is so because the responsiveness of the consumers to price changes, that is price elasticity of demand, determines the changes in total revenue resulting from changes in price. Producer's profit is, obviously, influenced by this change.

To illustrate this point, consider a straight-line demand curve such as A B in the following diagram:

In the segment of the demand curve A C, the percentage change in price is less than the percentage change in quantity. Thus the elasticity of demand is greater than unity and this segment of demand curve is elastic. In the lower segment C B demand is inelastic, because here the percentage change in price is greater than the percentage change in quantity. Since this demand curve is elastic in the upper segment and inelastic in the lower segment, there is a point between these two segments at which the elasticity of demand is unity. This point is the mid-point of the demand curve. At mid-point C the elasticity is unity.

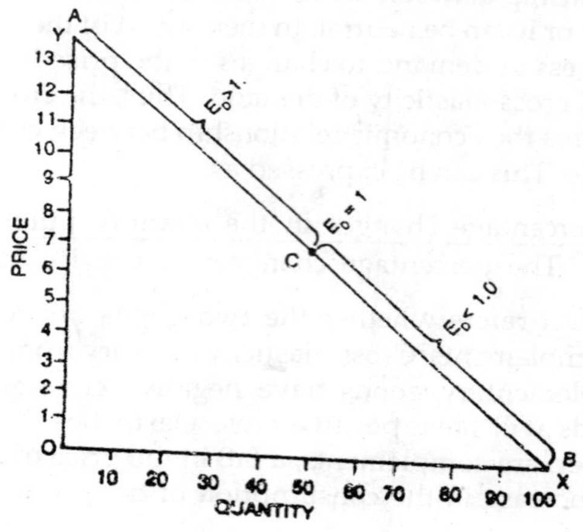

The important point to know is how these elasticities are related to total revenue. In the following diagram total revenue for various quantities of a commodity are shown as they correspond to demand curve.

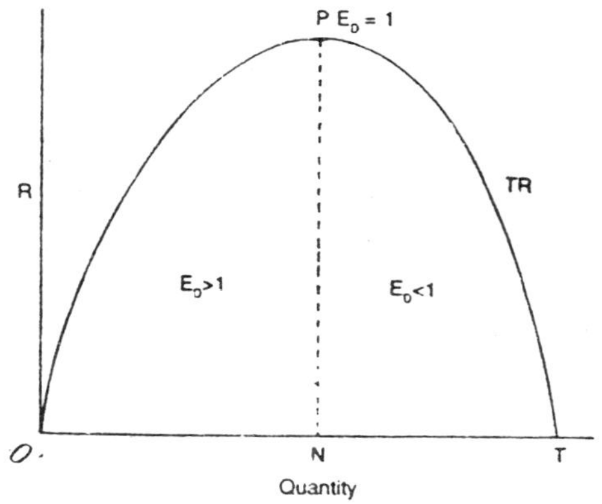

Total revenue increases as quantity increases from O to N. Total revenue is maximum at N quantity. From N to T the elasticity is less than one. Here percentage change in demand is less than the percentage change in prices. So revenue decreases from N onwards and becomes 0 at T. Thus, maximum total revenue from production of this commodity can be received if production is controlled at the output where elasticity of demand is unity. If a farm product has an elasticity of demand less than unity, farmer may receive greater total revenue if output is reduced. This is because here a given percentage decrease in quantity is accompanied by a greater percentage increase in price. Therefore, farmers in aggregate would also receive greater net revenue by restricting production.[10]

Income Elasticity of Demand: Farmers are concerned not only with the effect of price changes on quantity consumed but also with the effect of income changes on the consumption of their products. Income elasticity of demand for a commodity shows the extent to which a consumer's demand for that commodity changes as a result of a change in his income. It can be expressed as:

$$E_Y = \frac{\text{The percentage change in the quantity demanded}}{\text{The percentage change in Income}}$$

In other words, it is the respon~~veness of consumption relative to income changes. This can also be expressed as:

$$[(Q_2 - Q_1)/(Q_2 + Q_1)]\,[(I_2 + I_1)/\,(I_2 - I_1)]$$

Normally, we expect that as income increases, consumption of goods also increases. If goods are normal goods, income elasticity of demand is positive as an increase in income will bring about an increase in consumption. If, on the other hand, goods are inferior, an incrèase in income will bring about a decrease in consumption and income elasticity will be negative.

There is, of course, considerable variation in the income elasticity of demand for different food products. Income elasticity tends to be highest for the "productive foods" which are relatively rich in calories and contain a large amount of vitamins, proteins and minerals. Fruits, eggs, fish, meat, vegetables come under this category. Income elasticity is lowest for commodities like cereals and potatoes which may indeed be inferior goods. Industrial raw materials like rubber, wool, silk etc. may have rather high income elasticity.[11] Engle also put for this idea in a different way. He says that income increase, the percentage of incomes spent on food decreases. This idea is known as Engle's Law. He suggested that as income increases, a larger percentage of income would be spend on "luxuries" such as amusements and recreation of all types. Thus, while the income elasticity of demand for food is low, it is high in response to the expenditure on recreation etc. Studies done by the U.S. Department of Labour, Bureau of Labour Statistics, January 1957 — Employment and Earnings, U S D A's Study Agricultural Outlook Charts, 1956; Karl A Fox Study, "factors Affecting Farm Income, Farm Prices and Food Consumption, Agricultural Economic Research, July 1951 confirm this law.[12]

Over a period of years, changes have occurred in consumption patterns of population. Basically, these changes occur due to the changes in preferences and from changes in income People's preferences have been changed by education because it clarify the importance of different products in the diet. The increase in income also change the pattern of consumption. It has been observed that people prefer more protein than starch food. It refers that there is higher elasticity of demand for fruits, eggs, milk, butter, meat, vegetables than for cereals. This difference in income elasticities of demand indicate the direction to be followed by agricultural production in the future. If we all believe that incomes will continue to increase and shift to vegetables, eggs, meat and fruits and away from cereals and potatoes and fats, indicates that, in the long-run, it will pay farmers to increase such production relative to the products containing more fat and calories.

Supply Analysis: Supply of commodities refers that amount which producers are able and willing to offer for sale at a given price. The supply curve represents the maximum quantities of product which the firm is willing to produce for sale per unit of time at various product prices. Cost of production affect the quantity supplied. When a firm is unable to influence the price of its product, the most profitable level of output is that level where the price of the product is equal to the marginal cost. We also know that producers stop production when the price of the product is less than the average cost. Thus, when price is greater than average variable cost, the marginal cost curve is the supply curve for the firm.

Changes in Supply: There are numerous factors which influences the supply of agricultural commodities. Some of the important factors are as under:

(I) The supply of agricultural commodities depends upon the cost of its production. That is the price of the factors which are involved in its production. For example, the rise of the price of land will have a large effect on the cost of producing wheat, paddy etc. Thus, a rise in the price of factors of production will cause the supply of the product to decline and a fall in price may lead to an increase in supply.

(II) Supply of an agricultural commodity is also influenced by the price that commodity commands in the market. Higher the price of a commodity, other things remaining the same, the more profitable will be to increase its supply and vice versa.

(III) The supply of an agricultural commodity is also affected by the prices of other agricultural commodities. An increase in the price of other commodities will make the production of the commodity whose price has not increased relatively less attractive. Obviously, this leads to changes in cropping pattern in agriculture.

(IV) The state of technology and other improved methods influence the supply of commodities. Technology and other factors such as machines, improved tools, chemical fertilizers rainfall improved seeds etc. help in bringing down the cost of production and hence increases supply.

We may sum-up that the supply of agricultural commodity is a function of the price of that commodity, the price of all other agricultural commodities, the cost of production of the commodity — the prices of the factors of production — technology and natural factors. This can be expressed as:

$$q_n^s = f\,(P_n, P_1 - P_n, F_1 - F_m, G, T)$$

Where *qs* is the supply of agricultural commodity, 'n' and P_n is the price of that commodity, P_1 - Pn stands for prices of all other agricultural commodity, F_1 .... F_n denotes the price of factors of production, T is the state of technology and G stands for natural factors.[13]

There are two important factors which cause aggregate supply of a commodity to increase when its price increases. First, when price increases, it usually pays to increase output. Second when price increases, there is a tendency for new firms to enter the industry. It represents both the changes in output of firms in the industry and changes in output due to changes in number of firms.

The law of supply may be defined as the quantity of a commodity produced and offered for sale will increase as the price of the commodity rises and decreases as price falls. Based on this law, a hypothetical supply schedule for an agricultural commodity can be constructed. This schedule represents the relation between prices and the quantities that sellers are willing to sell in the market.

A Supply Schedule for Commodity 'A'

D	*Price Rs. per k.g.*	*Quantity Supplied*
1	5	10
2	10	20
3	15	40
4	20	60
5	25	80
6	30	100

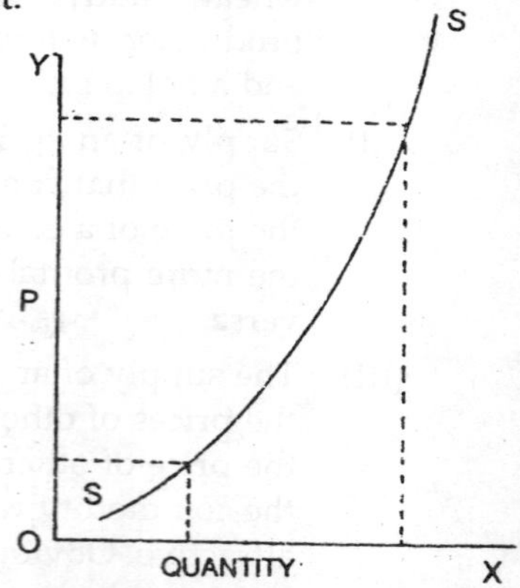

Supply Elasticity: To extent to which output changes in response to a change in price varies among commodities. The concept of elasticity refers the responsiveness of changes in quantity produced to changes in prices. It is a percentage change in quantity in response to a given percentage change in price. This can be expressed as:

$$E_s = \frac{\text{The percentage change in the quantity supplied}}{\text{The percentage change in the price}}$$

This can also be expressed as:

$$\frac{(Q_2 - Q_1)/(Q_2 + Q_1)}{(P_2 - P_1)/(P_2 + P_1)}$$

or inverting,

$$\left(\frac{Q_2 - Q_1}{Q_2 + Q_1}\right)\left(\frac{P_2 - P_1}{P_2 + P_1}\right)$$

Here elasticity is computed from two observations of prices and quantities. P_1 represents the price in one time period and Q_1 represents the quantity supplied at that price. P_2 is the price in another time period, and Q_2 is the quantity supplied at that price.[14] We, expect that as price increases, the quantity of farm commodities produced will also increase. That is under normal conditions, the elasticity of supply of farm product will be positive. In case where the supply is fixed, an increase in price will not increase the supply and the elasticity of supply is zero. That is, there is no change in quantity in response to change in price.

If elasticity is greater than one, supply is said to be elastic. If, on the other hand, quantity supplied responds relatively little to price changes, elasticity is less than one and is said to be inelastic. If the percentage change in quantity supplied is greater than the percentage change in price, the supply is said to be elastic.[15]

The elasticity of supply for many farm commodities is undoubtedly very high because the number of producers is large. A small rise in price leads to a large expansion in the number of producers, even though relatively small increases may be made in the production of each firm. This results in a highly elastic supply from the stand-point of the industry on a whole.[16] But in comparison to industrial product, the supply of agricultural product as a whole is much less elastic. According to Miss Cohen, during the world-wide depression of 1929-32 total world manufacturing production fell by 37 per cent while agricultural production only by 1 per cent.[17] In U.S.A. the price index of non-agricultural commodities fell by 38 per cent from 1929-32, but for agricultural produce, it fell by 54 per cent. During the same period, industrial production fell by 47 per cent, while agricultural production was actually higher in 1932 than in 1929.[18]

All supply decisions take time to implement. We may say that supply reacts with time lag. In other words, elasticity of supply may be different when prices rise and fall. This difference is due to the differences in the length of planning period. For example when price of a commodity increases relative to the prices of other commodities it may be necessary to purchase specialised inputs in order to expand production. In case of many agricultural commodities, this lag is of critical importance. The simplest possible time lag is one in which this year's price has no effect on this year's supply. Farmers while deciding about what crop to plant and how much to plant look to the existing market price. It means next year's supply depends on this year's price, while this year's supply is based on last year's price.[19]

Backward Bending or Perverse Supply

It has been confirmed that the supply curve of the produce of the small family farmer will be perverse. It has been proved for the small farmers in Asia and Africa, during the period of two great wars. It is based on the assumption that such farmer had a certain, rather low "target" or cash income and that, once this was attained, the farmer would only work as hard as was necessary to maintain it. If the price of this produce rose, he would produce less and enjoy more leisure. And if it fell, he will produce more in an attempt to enjoy the same income as before.

There are two types of perverse response of supply to price. First, supply of farm products may rise in response to price to a certain point, but after that it starts to decline though the price continues to rise. This has been expressed in the following diagram.

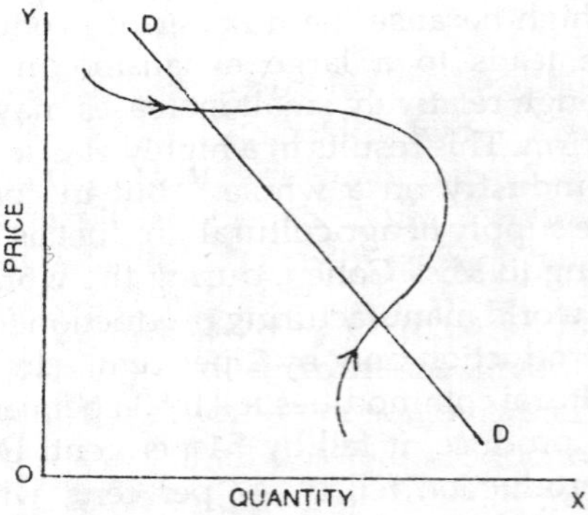

The situation seems to be irrational, if we take into account only price of the commodity as the sole determinant of its supply. But mostly, the prices of inputs used in the process of production, the prices of other agricultural commodities which can be produced as an alternative changes and hence it is just rational for the producers to reduce production of the first commodity and produce more of other commodities. Secondly, supply may not fall in response to a falling prices.[20]

REFERENCES

1. Lipsey R.G., *An Introduction To Positive Economic*, ELBS and Weiden Field & Nicolson 1975 (4th ed.) p. 74
2. *ibid., p.* 75.

3. *Ibid p.* 75.
4. *Ibid., p.* 84.
5. *Ibid.*
6. *Ibid.*
7. *Ibid., pp.* 84-85.
8. *Ibid., p.* 105; Sadhu A.N., Singh A, *Fundamentals to Agricultural Economics, op cit. pp.* 142-43.
9. Lipsey R G., *An Introduction To Positive Economics, op cit. pp.* 109-110; Sadhu A.N., Singh A, *op cit. p.* 143.
10. Bishop C.E., Toussaint W.D., *An Introduction to Agricultural Economics Analysis. op cit.*, p. 190-192.
11. Martin A., Economics of Agriculture, R.K.P., London 1958.
12. Bishop C.E., Toussaint W.D., *op cit.* pp. 194-97.
13. Sadhu A.N., Singh A., *op cit.* pp. 146-147.
14. Bishop C.E., Toussaint W.D. *Op cit.* pp. 164.
15. *Ibid.*, p. 16.
16. *Ibid.*
17. Cohen R, *The Economics of Agriculture,* Cambridge 1940, p. 112.
18. Mitchell B. *Depression Decade,* N. York 1947, Quoted by Martin A. *Economics And Agriculture,* R.K.P. London, 1958.
19. Sadhu and Singh. *op cit.* p. 148
20. *Ibid.*, pp. 149-50; Henderson J.M., Quandtr E., *Micro-Economic Theory: A Mathematical Approach.* McGraw Hill Ltd. 1971, p. 131.

3

DEMAND AND SUPPLY — PRICE DETERMINATION

Price determination is a process of balancing demand with supply. In this chapter we shall combine the demand and supply theories into a theory of determination of market prices.

Let us imagine a grain market where there are many buyers and sellers who want to buy and to sell commodities — wheat, rice, pulses etc. In a free market economy the prices are determined by the conditions of demand and supply and the function of the market price is to equate the two. In the short-run, in relation to agricultural commodities, the supply is given. The market supply schedule shows only the amounts the sellers would like to sell at different prices. The shape of the market supply schedule has been influenced by various factors such as perishability of the commodity, sellers price expectations, storage costs, sellers cash position etc. The short-run demand schedule is also influenced by buyers' expectations of future prices, availabilities of substitute goods and their prices, price elasticities of their demand and the level of income.

When quantity demanded equals quantity supplied we say that the market is in a state of equilibrium. When quantity demanded does not equal to the quantity supplied we say that market is in a state of disequilibrium. At equilibrium price the buyers are willing to purchase certain amount of commodity and sellers are also willing to sell exactly the same amount. Some buyers and sellers may remained dissatisfy since the equilibrium price is too high or too low for them.

Following figure shows how equilibrium price is determined in the short-period. D D and S S are on the demand and supply curves. The two curves intersects at point Q which shows OA quantity of goods which is sold at OP price.

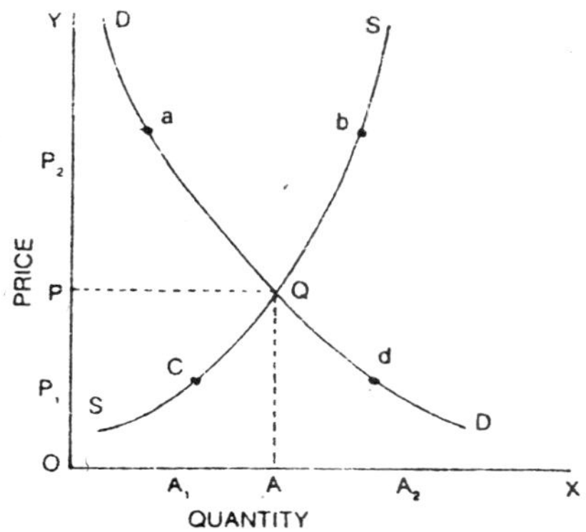

Fig. 1

At the price OP demand and supply are equal. The slope of demand curve is always negative while the slope of supply curve is positive. If the price rises from OP to OP_2 the quantity demanded reduces from OA to OA_1 while the quantity supplied is P_2b. The excess supply a b would force the price down. On the other hand, if prices fall to OP_1 demand will rise to OA_2 while the supply will reduce to P_1d. Here we will have excess demand d C which will force the price up. Hence, OP is the equilibrium price which balances demand and supply. At this price neither consumer nor producers have an incentive to contract, any further.

This short-term price-quantity combination model reproduce conditions in some agricultural markets at single points of time. But we know there are imperfections in agricultural markets and the peculiarities in the supply of agricultural products make this model of only limited use.

Changes in Demand and Supply: Changes may occur in both demand as well as supply. Price also changes accordingly. Price changes may brought about by shifts in either demand or supply curves or both.

If demand increases while the supply remains unchanged, a higher equilibrium price will be determined. In other case supply may increase or decrease while demand remains unchanged, the equilibrium price will either be determined on higher or lower level. Both case have been illustrated in separate diagrams as under:

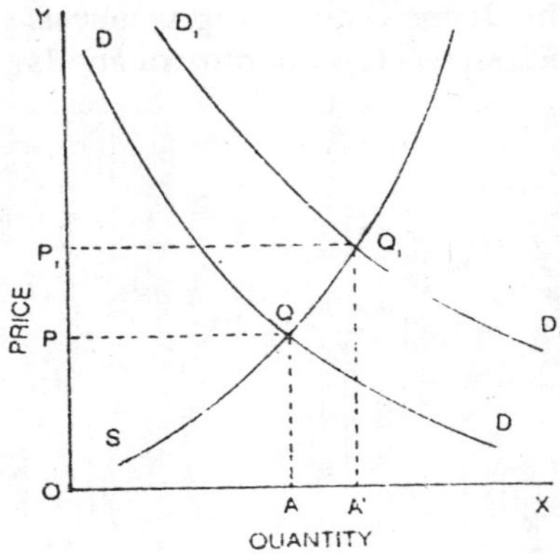

Fig. 2

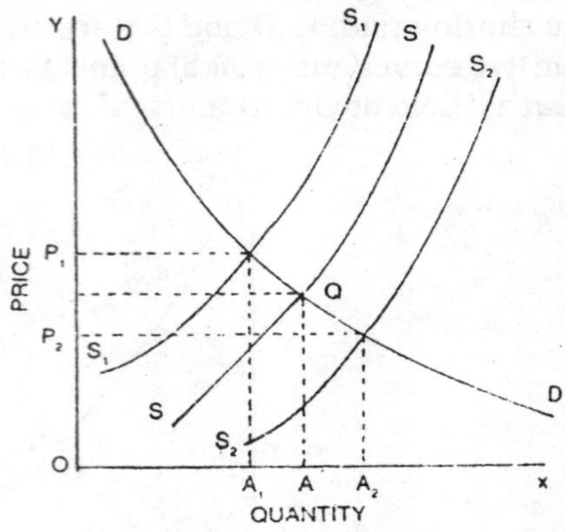

Fig. 3

Figure 1 shows changes in demand while supply remains unchanged. The demand curve shifts to the right from D D to D_1 D_1 indicating an increase in the demand. Under original market condition equilibrium price is OP and quantity supplied is OA. Under changed demand condition the new equilibrium price is OP_1 and the supply is OA_1. In figure 2 supply curve shifts to the right and left. When it shifts to the right (increases), the demand position remaining the same, price fall to OP_2 and when it shifts to the left (decrease), demand remaining constant, the price rises from OP to OP_1.

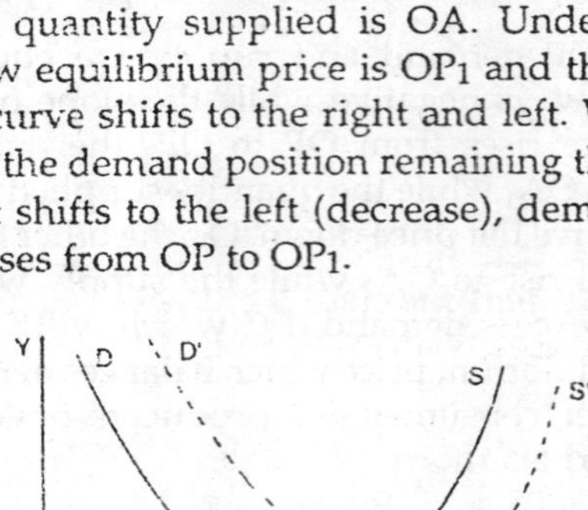

Fig. 4

When both the supply and the demand curves changes their position, as has been shown in the Fig – 3 the direction and the level of price changes are less certain than in the previous cases described above.[1]

Tax Incidence: What is the effect of taxes placed on the sale and purchase of commodities. Do such taxes leave prices unchanged or do they cause prices to rise? Does the producer pay the tax or is he able to pass it on the consumer through high prices ? If no tax is levied, sellers receive the whole market price for which the commodity is sold. If a tax is levied, then however, sellers will receive on each unit sold the market price of the commodity minus the amount of tax. If producers are to receive the same amount per unit as they were receiving prior to the tax, the market price will have to rise by the full amount of tax. If the willingness of sellers to supply the commodity is unchanged then, after a tax has been levied, every quantity supplied will be associated with a market price higher by the full amount of the tax than the one previously required.[2]

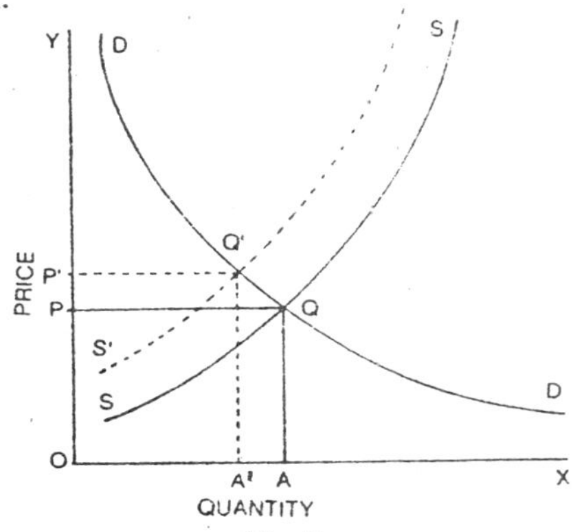

Fig. 5

The market equilibrium price is influenced by the tax. We know that the market price is determined by the supply as well as by the demand forces. In the above diagram (Fig. 4) we plot the demand curve and the pre-and post-tax supply curves.

The original equilibrium price is OP and the quantity supplied at this price is OA. If tax is imposed, the price will rise by the full amount of the tax and the quantity demanded would fall. There would be an excess of quantity supplied over quantity demanded. This would caused to price fall until it reached the equilibrium price where the new supply curve cut the demand curve. In the diagram the new equilibrium price is OP. This is the price that will be paid by customers. After deducting the tax, producer will receive less price. Thus, tax has the effect of raising the price paid by consumers and lowering the price received by producers.[3]

The influence of elasticity of demand and supply changes the situation. The situations have been explained in the following diagrams, namely (i) perfectly elastic demand curve, (ii) perfectly inelastic demand curve and (iii) two intermediate cases which is the combination of the previous two conditions.

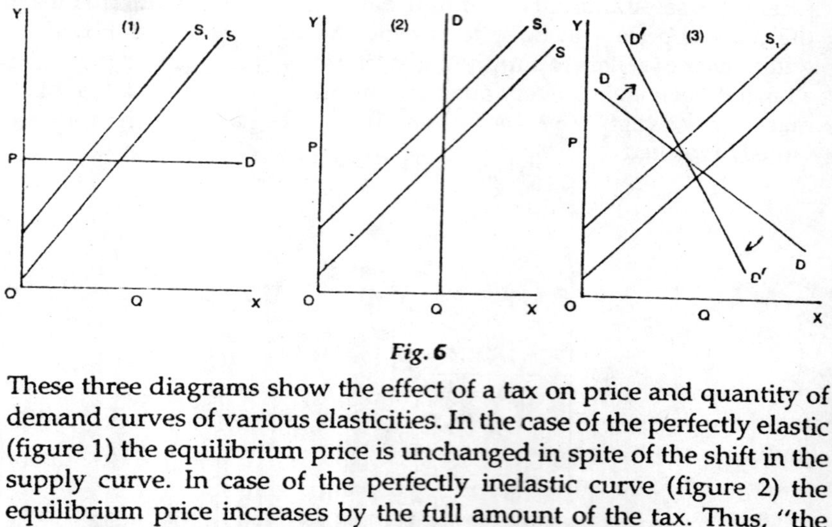

Fig. 6

These three diagrams show the effect of a tax on price and quantity of demand curves of various elasticities. In the case of the perfectly elastic (figure 1) the equilibrium price is unchanged in spite of the shift in the supply curve. In case of the perfectly inelastic curve (figure 2) the equilibrium price increases by the full amount of the tax. Thus, "the most elastic the demand for a commodity, the greater the rise in the price paid by the consumer and the less the fall in the price received by the producer as a result of the imposition of any given tax". This has been illustrated in the third diagram. Look at the original demand curve D D which intersects the original supply curve S S to determine the equilibrium price. Note the post-tax equilibrium price given by the intersection of the original demand curve with the new supply curve S_1 clearly, the steeper, and thus the more inelastic, the demand curve at the equilibrium point, the greater the rise in price paid by consumers and the smaller the fall in the price received by producers.[4]

The Equilibrium Price in Agriculture: As we have stated earlier the production of many agricultural goods is subject to large variations due to factors beyond human control such as lack or excess of rainfall, invasion of pests, floods and droughts and other natural calamities. These factors reduce the output to a level well below the planned level. Favourable conditions, on the other hand, can cause production to be well above the planned level. We may now analyse the effect of these unplanned fluctuation on the price of agricultural commodities and on the revenues earned by the farmers.

A supply curve shows a desired output and sales at each market price. If there are unplanned variations in output then actual production and sales will diverge from planned level. The supply curve shown in this

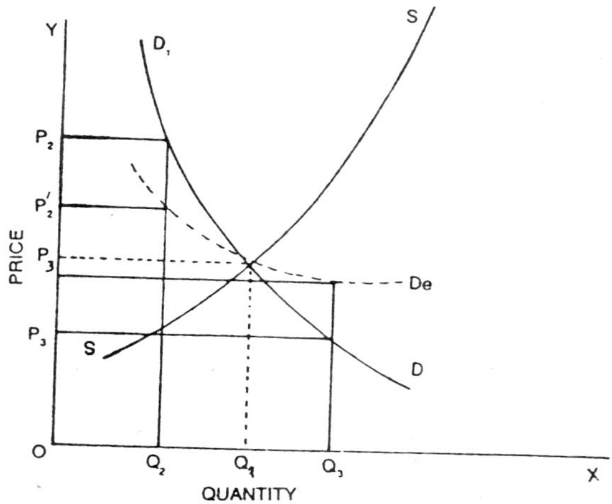

diagram illustrates the total quantity farmers desire to produce and offer for sale at various prices. If the price is P_1 the planned production would be Q_1, but actual production would vary around this planned amount due to factors beyond human control. Two demand curves are drawn; one is relatively elastic and the other is relatively inelastic over the production range Q_2 to Q_3. P_1 is the equilibrium price. But unplanned fluctuations in output will cause the actual price to fluctuate. If crop is poor due to insufficient rains, the production level falls from Q_1 to Q_2. The shortage will raise the price to P_2 in the case of demand curve D_1 and the price will be P_2 in the case of demand curve D_e. In each case the quantity demanded will be reduced to Q_2; a level at which it is equal to the available supply. If, on the other hand, conditions are favorable, actual production will exceed planned productions, a surplus will occur and price will fall. For example, when production is Q_3 price falls to P_3 in the case of D_1 curve and to P_3' in the case of D_e curve. Here again, in each case the fall in price increases the quantity demanded sufficiently to absorb the extra unplanned supply but the fall in price is larger when the demand is D_1 than when it is D_e. This leads to the conclusion that "unplanned fluctuations in output will cause price variations in the opposite direction to the output changes — the bigger the output the lower the price — and, for given output fluctuations, the price fluctuations will be larger the lower will be the elasticity — of demand for the product." [5]

If the commodities have an elasticity of demand greater than unity, then unplanned increase in supply raise farmers revenue while unplanned decrease lower them. If, on the other hand, the goods have an inelastic demand, consumer's total expenditure on the product and in return farmer's revenue both will raise P_2 when price rises and fall when price falls. Thus, good harvest will bring reductions in total farm revenue and bad harvests will bring increases in farm revenue. If the demand elasticity is unity, then farmers revenue would not vary as output and prices varied because every change in output would be met by an exactly compensating change in price so that total expenditure would remain constant.

The supply and demand response to price changes in agriculture, may thus, not be the same as visualised by the law of demand and supply. Agriculture produces mainly foodstuffs which are one of the main necessities of life. As a result the demand for all agricultural products, taken together, tends to be inelastic. Since human food needs in terms of capacity to eat is limited, they substitute better food for plain food when their income increase and they improve their standard of living. But beyond a certain point when their income increases, people start spending more on non-agricultural commodities. Similarly, when prices of agricultural commodities fall consumption of such goods will not expand, nor will it greatly reduce when prices rise. Accordingly, a low price elasticity indicates that consumers are not sensitive to changes in prices of food. This insensitivity arises due to two reasons: (i) food is an essential commodity and so when its price changes, it does not affect its quantity demanded and (ii) with a rise in standard of living, people spend relatively small fraction of their income on food which reduces the sensitivity of consumers to changes in the price of food. Because of the inelastic demand for farm products, it may be said that at any particular time any factor which increases the quantity of agricultural output will also reduces gross receipts. And similarly, any factor which reduces the quantity produced and marketed will also increases receipts of farmers. The aggregate agricultural production is also not very responsive to price changes. It is assumed that farmers are less responsive to price changes. In most cases, agriculture tends to use the same amount of factors of production especially land and labour, even when general level of prices is falling. Consequently, the output level remains almost stable notwithstanding the fluctuations in the general price level. Farmer's insensitivity to price changes has been influenced by various factors. Some of the important factors are: (i) the cost structure of agricultural output; (ii) subsistence farming; (iii) role of nature; (iv) small scale of farming; and (v) time element.[6]

Cobweb Behavior in Production: Agricultural output, as has been explained above, varies substantially over-time. These variations are mostly due to the factors beyond human control. Many changes in production also occurs due to the changes in relative prices and costs. In general, there are fairly definite cycles of production. If we analyse a definite period, say 30 or 50 years period, we will find a peak and trough about every 10 to 15 years. This cyclical behaviour is demonstrated by what is called the "cobweb" theorem of production. This is an elementary dynamic theory of price determination which is now going to be introduced in agricultural production.

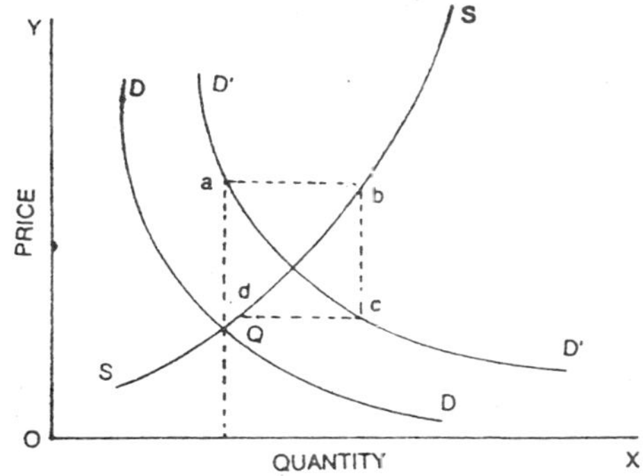

There are several conditions necessary for cobweb type of behaviour to result. According to this theorem, producers of a commodity expect the price in the next period of production to be the same as the current price and makes production plans accordingly. A cobweb type of behaviour is also influenced by the length of the production period. A commodity which has a short production period is usually subject to more violent fluctuations in production and prices than a commodity which has a long period of production. The cobweb theorem is most appropriate in the case of nonstorable goods.[7]

Diagram illustrates the cobweb behaviour. The equilibrium point is Q where the consumers are willing to purchase the same quantity that the produces are willing to supply. The original demand curve D D shows the maximum quantities of the good that consumers are willing to purchase at alternative prices. Suppose that the demand shifts to D′ D′ because consumers preferences change so that they are willing to buy more of the good at all prices. Now the consumers are willing to pay the price at 'a' for the same output for which they originally were willing to pay the price at Q. In planning their production, producers consider the current price at 'a' as the future price and make plans to increase their production to 'b' accordingly. When production is increased, it is necessary to take a lower price for the product than was anticipated. Consumers are now willing to pay a price equal to that at 'c' for the new output. In view of this, producers plan to decrease their production in the next time period to the amount at 'd'. This process will be continued. In some cases an equilibrium level of output is reached at the intersection of the supply curve and the new demand curve. In other cases, an equilibrium level is never reached and we have a continuous fluctuation in prices and production. [8]

REFERENCES

1. Sadhu and Singh *pp.* 150-53.
2. Lipsey G.R., *An Introduction to Positive Economics op cit.*pp. 122-123.
3. *Ibid.,* p. 124.
4. *Ibid.,* p. 25.
5. *Ibid.,* p. 127-28.
6. *Ibid., op. cit.* pp. 153-55.
7. Bishop C.E., & Toussaint W.D. *op cit.* p. 169.
8. *Ibid.,* p. 170.

4

PRICE-POLICY

As we have stated in the previous chapter that unplanned fluctuations in supply do occur frequently in agriculture. On demand side, many agricultural commodities the demand is quite inelastic. Moreover, agricultural development differs in different parts of the world. It may differ broadly on three fronts: (i) it may differ with respect to the demand outlook confronting the agriculture of a country; (ii) it may differ with respect to the product-pattern; and (iii) it may also differ to the resource potential available to it. Many countries of the Western Europe and America face problems created by the accumulation of surpluses. Many of the Asian and African countries face a wide gap between the growth of demand and the available supply. In many countries agriculture has a diversified product-mix. In many others, it has a single crop dominates the mix. For example India represents a picture of diversified product-mix while for Eastern countries rice is dominated the mix, rubber is dominated in Malaysia. The same characteristic is found in case of exports. In many countries few crops dominates the exports which are 50 to 90 per cent of the total. For example coffee, cocoa and bananas in several Latin American countries, cotton and few other in Egypt and Sudan, rice, rubber and tea in South Asia etc.[1]

In such diversities, the objective of price-policy must be radically different in different situation. Since situations cannot be discussed adequately, we focus our attention on the problem of excess demand countries.

Objectives: Historically the main objectives of agricultural price-policy have been price and income stabilization. As stated earlier, agricultural prices fluctuate violently and frequently under the free market mechanism which prove disadvantageous to both the producers as well as the consumers. In bumper crop prices fall too low which goes against the interest of the farmers. During bad crop year, prices rise steeply but farmers have little marketable surplus. The steep rise in price and scarcity of goods go against the interest of the consumers. The persistent imbalance between supply and demand causes violent fluctuations in consumer prices and affects the poor consumers. The two major aspects of the price-policy, therefore, are (i) to protect the interests of the farmers by removing or at least minimising the major uncertainties by assuring the farmers remunerative prices of their produce, and (ii) to protect the interest of the consumers, specially of the poor consumers, by assuring minimum supplies of food articles at reasonable prices.

Thus, the major objective of the agricultural price-policy is the price stability. In the developed countries like USA, Canada and Western Europe where in the process of economic growth the farm income have lagged behind non-farm income, the main objective of price-policy is to raise farm incomes so that their lower income could be brought about at the level of the non-farm income. In the under developed countries, however, the income oriented price-policy of the developed countries has not much direct relevance because here the problem is not of over-production. In these countries the objective of price-policy is to increase agricultural production by providing economic incentives to the farmers. The policy should, therefore, perform the following functions.[2]

(i) To accelerate the growth of agricultural production as a whole.

(ii) To stabilise prices in order to prevent fluctuations.

(iii) To bring about desired changes in production mix.

(iv) To increase the marketed surplus. And

(v) To ensure adequate supplies of foodgrains to the low income consumers at reasonable prices.

Under normal circumstances, allocation of resources and the consequent level of production is influenced by the prices of inputs as well as of outputs. Price manipulation can be used as one of the important instruments to give a particular desired direction to resource allocation. We know that in the initial stages, agricultural development contributes to the development of the industrial sector through supply of food products, agricultural raw material, the expanded market for the industrial sector and labour and capital. These contributions imply three important changes, namely: (i) increase in over all agricultural production; (ii) changes in the production pattern suitable for industrial development; and (iii) increased marketed surplus of foodgrains to meet the demand for food for labourers migrated to industrial sector.

Manipulation of prices of agricultural products as well as of inputs can help in achieving these objectives. Other measures which supplements the agricultural price-policy, specially these which enhanced physical productivity of various crops, will also be required for achieving these objectives.

These objectives are attached with reference to a developing economy where the agricultural sector helps the non-agricultural sector to grow. However, the objectives of agricultural price-policy change when the economy is sufficiently developed. Under changed situation, increase in agricultural production has no longer been the objectives of agricultural price-policy. It is the stability of income of the rural masses that becomes most important.

Price-Policy in Traditional Agriculture[3]

The agricultural price-policy which we are going to discuss here is that policy which is attached with those countries that are struggling to move on the development path. Agriculture in such countries passes through two stages: (i) in the traditional stages and (ii) in the technologically dynamic but low capital intensive stage. The effectiveness of agricultural price-policy in achieving the said goals will be different in both the stages.

Though higher prices and the resulted high profitability is considered an incentive for increasing agricultural production or for an increase in marketed surplus or for a change in the crop-mix, the response to higher prices is not expected to be very encouraging in traditional agriculture. Traditional agriculture is highly labour oriented as well as technologically stagnant sector. It is also assumed that either the industrial sector is almost non existent or if it exists, the demand of the agricultural sector for the goods and services from industrial sector is traditional and hence is inflexible. With these characteristics, it can be concluded that neither the aggregate agricultural production nor the marketed surplus will increase when the prices of agricultural product increase. In economic terminology, the traditional agriculture has a backward slopping supply curve with regard to both the aggregate production as well as the marketed surplus.

The only objective that can be fulfilled through manipulation of prices, in traditional agriculture, is that of changing the crop mix. A general impression is that with regard to substitution of crops in response to price changes, we expect good motivation and understanding on the part of the farmers. If something is to be sold in the market, why not to produce and sell that crop which brings in a better return? This has been confirmed by empirical research. Area under crops with low capital and labour intensive technology, shows a positive correlation with the prices of such crops. Thus traditional agriculture allows for a greater substitutability of crops than a modern agriculture.

Traditional agriculture has no specialised capital inputs committed to the production of certain specific crops. The only significant inputs in traditional agriculture are land and labour which are non-specific in character. Even the capital and technical inputs in traditional agriculture are quite flexible in use. Only the area devoted to crops in agriculture adds rigidity to the cropping pattern. These explanation clearly brings out the limitations of the manipulating prices in traditional agriculture. Where as objectives of increasing production and marketed surplus may necessitate a fall in prices due to the backward sloping supply curve, increase in the production of few crops will require an increase in the prices of these crops. Thus, the same price change will not achieve all the three objective mentioned above.

Price-policy in Non-Traditional Agriculture[4]

When agriculture enters into a technologically dynamic stage with low capital intensive techniques, price-policy proves to be quite effective in achieving all the three objectives described earlier. In developing agriculture, inputs are purchased from the industrial sector. These inputs help in expanding agricultural output. The dependence of the agricultural sector on the non-agricultural sector for the disposal of its surpluses encourages interaction between the two sectors and therefore, the demand of agricultural sector for the goods and services of non-agricultural sector change its traditional character. Under such situation, the prices of agricultural commodities will have nothing but a normal effect on production crops. Many studies carried out with reference to India show that response of agricultural production to price change has been positive.[5]

Some relevant points have to be noted with regard to the responsiveness of price-policy vis-a-vis its objectives, so far as the non-traditional agriculture is concerned.

First, the success of price-policy depends upon the price-elasticity of various crops which is different in a region for various crops as well as for the same crop in different regions. Many factors are responsible for these differences. Size of the farm, fertility of soil, irrigation facilities, proportion of area under crops, land tenure system, rain fall, level of technology, transport and communication, nature of crop—commercial crop or subsistence crop etc. Secondly, it may sometimes be difficult to achieve all the three objectives described above simultaneously with the same price-policy. This is specially concerned with the objectives of increasing aggregate agricultural production and the change in the composition of the crop mix. Aggregate production can be increased by an increase in absolute prices of all crops. But increases in the production of one crop in relation to other can be brought about only by a relative increase in the price of the given crop. If prices of various crops increase in equal proportions, there will be no change in relative prices and the composition of price mix may not change. This refers that though increase in the prices of all agricultural crops will help in increasing the aggregate production, such price change will only neutralise their impact on the composition of the price mix. Hence, for changes in the crop pattern, it is essential to change the prices of only few selected crops.

Thirdly, the agricultural price-policy is closely related with the development of non-agricultural sectors. This is simply because, the non-agricultural sector, in the initial stages of its development, depend on the agricultural sector. Higher agricultural prices, therefore, can affect the profitability and growth of non-agricultural sector adversely. The interest of the consumers of agricultural products need to be protected when the interest of the producers of agricultural products are to be promoted through a particular price-policy.[6]

"Negative" and "Positive" Price-policy:[7] We have explained above that the prices favorable to Agricultural Sector may work against the interests of the non-agricultural sector and vice-versa. This has been the major consideration in relation to the agricultural price-policy in various countries during the course of the development of their economies. Sometimes, the prices of agricultural products as well as of agricultural inputs have been so manipulated that the benefits of development of the agricultural sector were partly or wholly passed on the industrial sector. Such a policy changed the terms of trade against industries. On some other occasions, the price-policy have favoured the agricultural sector at the cost of the non-agricultural sector. These two types of price-policies are known as "positive" and "negative" price-policies.

In the context of the policy of accelerating economic growth, a "negative" agricultural price-policy has been adopted by a large number of countries in the early stages of their development. The main objectives of such a policy was to keep the prices of agricultural commodities — food and raw-materials — relatively low in comparison with the prices of non-agricultural products. The intention is to facilitate the growth of the industrial and tertiary sectors and to provide surpluses in form of savings to these sectors. In other words, the terms of trade were deliberately and purposively kept unfavourable for the agricultural sector. This was achieved by two ways.

One method is a compulsory sale or delivery of a portion of the agricultural output to the State at a very low price in comparison to the open-market price. There are some instances where agricultural output is also taxed away at zero-price. In such cases, the average price received by farmers per unit of total output has been lowered considerably. The second method is to keep the prices of industrial goods high. The goods include consumable article such as textile as well as farm inputs such as fertiliser machineries, pesticides etc. On the other hand, the prices of agricultural commodity were kept stable. This, once-again, provided relative advantage to industrial sector. One or both the methods have been used in varying degrees by different countries like the former USSR, Japan, U.K. and Argentina. In Japan during 1878-1907, agricultural taxes provided nearly 70 per cent of the public revenues.

In contrast to these negative agricultural price-policy, many countries today follow what may be termed as the "Positive Agricultural Price-policy". This policy insists on light taxes on agricultural sector as well as on providing fair prices for the goods produced by the farmers. It has been realised that unless the agricultural sector attains some critical "minimum rate of growth", it would not be possible to attain the general targets of economic growth and development. This is quite relevant for a number of reasons. Some important reasons are as under: (1) In most of the developing countries, agriculture continue to be the single most important sector from point of view of generating employment, income and exports; and (ii) the increasing demand for food due to increasing population and income can be met only through continuously growing agricultural production.

Experience of various countries has shown that negative price-policy will not lead to the desired minimum rate of growth of the agricultural sector. As a result many countries have shifted from negative to positive agricultural price-policy. In the former USSR for example the State has successively increased the purchase prices of agricultural commodities since 1951. Similarly in a number of East European countries, such as Rumania, Bulgaria or East Germany. Compulsory deliveries to the State have been reduced and prices of agricultural commodities have been considerably raised. At the same time, minimum prices of farm products have been guaranteed in a number of countries in Asia, Africa, Eastern Europe and Latin America.

Price Fixation:[8] In order to provide sufficient incentives to farmers to increase production, agricultural prices have been considered one of the important tools. Many criteria for fixation of prices for agricultural commodities were evolved. At present, the prices are fixed on the basis of one or more of the following criteria.

(i) Cost of Production Approach

(ii) Ruling Price Approach

(iii) Parity Prices Approach

Cost of Production Approach: There are two important criteria of calculating cost of production. One criteria is calculating the average cost with the help of cost accounting technique. Another criteria is the budgeting technique. In this approach the cost of recommended farm practices and their average yields are taken into account to estimate the cost per unit of output.

The cost of production approach for determining administered prices is helpful to protect the producer against any loss due to an unexpected fall in prices. There are, however, many problems in calculating the average cost. One problem is assigning appropriate values to family labour and management input in calculating the cost of production. Moreover, the concept of an average cost per unit of output is nebulous in view of the wide variations in agro-climatic conditions and farm practices. In this way, it may be said that the variability of cost between different farms is very high.

Further, a price-policy aimed at increasing production cannot be based on average cost of production, because much of the increase in agricultural production has been due to the increases in the conventional and non-conventional inputs. The rate at which the cultivators take up the use of such additional input is a function of financial returns. He is, thus, more concerned with the marginal rather than the average cost and returns. He should increase the use of inputs to the point where the value of the marginal product equals the marginal cost.

One more factor is important. This criteria considers only the supply side and totally ignores the influence of demand in the determination of prices. Thus, the criterion of cost of production is not considered a very sound approach for policy decisions.

Ruling Price Approach: This approach requires that prices be linked to a moving average of market prices in the recent past. The advantage of this approach is that it takes into consideration the effect of demand trends while the cost-approach ignores it. This approach co-ordinates the demand as well as supply growth over a relevant time-period. In the event of an excess supply out-look, demand effect should influence the price fixation via the moving average of market price. However, in an economy, where the prices have been kept deliberately low in the past, the moving average may not properly reflect the market trends. Moreover, the prevailing prices, often fail to provide necessary incentives for an increase in production on long-term basis.

Parity Approach: Parity approach refers the relationship of the administered farm prices with some index of prices paid by the farmers. It stabilise inter-relationship between agricultural and non-agricultural products as well as among those of different agricultural products. We have already pointed out that if the objectives is to provide the primary producers with appropriate incentive to produce more and better, a positive-price-policy for agricultural products has to be followed. This means that not only the parity between prices of agricultural and non-agricultural products be maintained but also that prices be made favourable to the agricultural sector. This implies that the price-policy should aim at changing the terms of trade in favour of agriculture. This objectives can be achieved if parity ratio are used as a basis of fixing prices of farm products. Parity ratio may be estimated in a number of ways. Some are as under.

(a) Parity between prices of all agricultural commodities and all non-agricultural commodities. This is calculated as:

$$\frac{\text{Price Index of agricultural commodities}}{\text{Price Index of all manufactured commodities}} \times 100$$

Here the purchases made by the farmers for manufactured commodities consists of agricultural inputs as well as consumer goods. The parity ratio calculated in the manner does not distinguish between protection given to the farmer as a producer and as a consumer. This method is, therefore, useful only when we want to know the movement of terms of trade between the agricultural and manufacturing sectors.

(b) Parity between prices received for the farm products and prices paid for farm inputs. This is calculated as:

$$\frac{\text{Price Index of all agricultural commodities}}{\text{Price Index of farm inputs}} \times 100$$

This method is useful when the objectives is to protect the interests of the farmer as a producer. A rising parity ratio will indicate favourable movement of the terms of trade for the farming sector.

(c) Parity between prices of individual agricultural commodities and general agricultural prices. This is calculated as:

$$\frac{\text{Price Index of all individual agricultural commodities}}{\text{Price Index of all agricultural commodities}} \times 100$$

This approach is useful for bringing about adjustment in crop-mix for the purpose of achieving planned targets of production in respect of certain crops. Parity ratio should be made favourable for those crops whose production is required to be increased.

Parity approach discussed above obviously delinks the administered prices from the cost of production. Sometime, this can create disincentives for the producers. As we have already pointed out that non of the above approach is free from weaknesses. As such the price fixing authorities do not base their decisions totally on one approach. These approaches provides only the guidelines. The decision-makers may not only take help from these guidelines, but may also consider many more factors while fixing agricultural prices.

Price-policy for Agricultural Inputs:[9] Positive price-policy for the agricultural products is useful in order to encourage the adoption of improved technology and the consequent growth of agricultural output. Some economists argue that this objective can better be achieved through subsidizing the farmer's purchase of inputs rather than through guarantees of minimum prices of agricultural commodities. This point-of-view is supported by the following logic.

The increase in production prices does not necessarily mean that the farmer will too improve their method of cultivation. The income generated by the increased price may increase their consumption. This means the expected capital formation in agriculture may not proceed in the desired direction. If this happens then the public expenditure for the support of agricultural prices may not be fruitful. On the other hand, if inputs are subsidised, prices of the inputs are kept low, peasants adopted an improved method of cultivation, Government expenditure will be incurred only to the extent of the subsidisation. Here the benefits of the Government expenditure will be distributed in proportion of the improved inputs used.

The desirability of protecting the urban consumers against rising prices is also equally important. It may be argued that the input subsidization may keep the food and raw-material prices from rising and hence may reduce or eliminate the need for providing price relief for the industrial or urban population. In this sense also, inputs price subsidisation appears cheaper than guarantee of minimum prices of agricultural commodities.

Although, the arguments in favour of input price subsidies do have some validity, it is not a complete substitute for product price guarantees. In fact, product price guarantee may be needed in addition to input subsidies because some output response cannot be obtained from the input subsidies. There are various reasons.

Firstly, farmers in less developed countries are not very responsive to changes in input prices in the initial stages of development. This is so because many of them are not familiar with these inputs. So in the early stages of development, raising product prices appears to be a better method of increasing the growth of agricultural output. Even after the farmers have been familiar with improved inputs, guaranteed product prices which also ensure coverage of the cost of using these inputs, will still be needed. Here the rate of absorption of improved inputs is certainly be low in the absence of such guarantee.

Secondly, product price guarantees encourage the better use of conventional as well as non-conventional (new/improved) inputs, whereas input price subsidies encourage the use of only the purchased new inputs such as fertilizers, pesticides, irrigation, water, machinery and equipment which account for a small part of the total cost of production.

Thirdly, farmers need insurance against downward rather than upward fluctuation in the prices of purchased inputs. The fear of a downward trend in prices is enhanced if production is expected to increase due to increased use of improved inputs. Any policy to encourage the use of modern technology must, therefore, accompanied by a policy of minimum support prices for farm outputs.

Fourthly, input price subsidies are ineffective in crop-mix adjustment. Only product price guarantees can be effective in including the changes in output of specific crops.

These views conclude that both input price subsidisation and guarantee of minimum remunerative crop prices are, in general, complementary rather than competitive to each other.

Agricultural Price-policy and the Consumer[10]

This aspect of agricultural price-policy is difficult as well as complicated because it imply a balance of conflicting interests between million of consumers on the one hand and the farmers on the other. If increasing the prices of agricultural output is considered as an inducement to agricultural growth, we should also consider the fact that agriculturers produces consumer goods whose purchase covers the bulk of expenditure of low income consumers. If the prices of agricultural produce increases and so the cost of living also increase, the demand for high wages will adversely affect the industrial profits and capital formation. This implies that a policy of providing price incentive to the farm products must be accompanied by controlling and regulating increases in food prices for the consumers.

Urban rationing may be the only way to keep the prices under control. Buffer stock and its release is another way of keeping the prices under check. Under this policy Government may import grains and purchase the grains from the farmers at home. The purchases at home can be made at or above the minimum guaranteed prices. The buffer stocks so acquired are released for distribution in urban areas on fixed retail price. These prices must be lower than the open-market prices. For this reason the retail price fixed by the Government is usually termed as 'fair price". This price relief may be given either to all classes of urban consumers or only to the low-income consumer. This is essentially a welfare price which operates within two important constraints. These are: (I) availability of stocks and (II) the capacity of the exchequer to finance the subsidy.

Concluding Remarks: Two important conclusions may be drawn from the discussions on agricultural price-policy.

First, a minimum support price for a crop is essential to ensure increase in its output and marketable surplus; and

Secondly, a ceiling price is also necessary to ensure the protection of the interest of the consumers, specially poor urban consumers.

The basic of the price-policy as has been stated earlier is to enhance agricultural production. But price-policy alone cannot attain this objective. Some other measures along with an appropriate price-policy will be an effective way of achieving this objective. Some important supporting measures are as under:

(i) A sufficient human and material resources be allocated to research so that some new varieties and improved production practices could be introduced. This will induce cost reducing technological change in agriculture. This will also provide substantial incentive to farmers to use more inputs and thereby increase agricultural production. Many new varieties of wheat, rice, cotton, vegetable specially potatoes have already been introduced in India and efforts are underway to bring about improvements in other products.

(ii) Technological change leads to an increase in the demand for inputs such as fertilizers, machinery, water or irrigation equipment credit etc. These must be readily available to the farmers. Hence to produce these inputs at home or import them must be undertaken. Only production aspect of these inputs is not important, but the distribution side is also very essential. Setting up of an effective organisation is, therefore, needed to be introduced. An ineffective supply front will make the efforts of increasing production sluggish in spite of high prices.

(iii) A smooth low cost transport system is also important. An adequate farm to market roads and link roads are essential to make the market organisation strong. An efficient marketing system will narrow the gap between the prices received by the producers and those paid by the consumers. Hence, no price-policy can be successful in achieving its objectives if the market organisation is poor and inefficient. These supporting measures are relevant for the effective use of price-policy.

Agricultural Price-policy in India[11]

During the last four decades India's agricultural price-policy has moved through two distinct phases. Upto 1965 Government adopted an "ad hoc" type policy showing hectic activity in years of poor crops and complete complacency in the years of good crops. In early sixties Jha Committee was set-up on foodgrain prices which witnessed the beginning of the more stable and meaningful price-policy. Jha Committee recommended the following guidelines for fixing prices of agricultural commodities.

(i) Prices should give incentives for the adoption of improved technology and maximisation of production.

(ii) Prices should encourage optimum utilisation of land.

(iii) Prices should aim at ensuring a balance between demand and supply for various crops.

(iv) The impact of the prices on export and imports of the crop concerned should be kept in view.

(v) The effect of the over-all price-policy on the other sectors of the economy specially with reference to wages, cost of living, industrial cost structure etc should be kept in view.

(vi) Agricultural price-policy should cover as many crops as possible so that a balanced and integrated price structure could be evolved.

(vii) The committee also recommended that efforts should be made to reduce the cost of production through supply of subsidised inputs.[12]

The Agricultural Price Commission (APC) was set up in 1965. The commission follows the guidelines recommended by the Jha Committee and recommends minimum/procurement prices for various crops. The main objective was to evolve a balanced and integrated price structure in the perspective of overall needs of the economy and with due regard to the interest of the producer and the consumer.[13] The major function of APC are as under:

(i) To advise the Government on the price-policy of agricultural commodities, particularly paddy, wheat, jowar, bajra, maize, gram and pulses.

(ii) To recommend measures to make price policy effective.

(iii) To suggest measures to reduce costs of marketing and recommend fair price margins for different stages of marketing.

(iv) To advise the Government on any problem relating to agricultural prices and production.[14]

The APC while deciding the price-policy takes into consideration a comprehensive overview of the entire structure of the economy of that commodity. That is (i) its demand and supply situation, (ii) cost of cultivation, (iii) export potential, (iv) the level of the administered prices for competing crops so that a measure of inter-crop price parity is achieved, (v) changes in input prices, (vi) effect of the price fixed on the industrial cost-structure, (vii) its effect on cost of living, (viii) input-output price parity in relation to raw-material and finished product prices and prices received and prices paid by the farmers, and (ix) projection of the trend in demand, supply and prices observed in case of a commodity in the past into the future.[15]

Among all factors stated above, the cost of production is considered to be the most important for price fixation if we have to ensure that the price fixed serves as an incentive for maximisation of production and for the widest adoption of improved technology. For the cost analysis the commission depends upon the data collected through various farm management studies, and the data collected by the Directorate of Economics and Statistics. It also takes into consideration the cost of cultivation estimates provided by the State Governments and other recognised institutions.[16]

The cost "C" concept is the basis of fixing the minimum prices for crops in India. This concept includes: (i) value of hired human labour,

(ii) value of hired and owned bullock labour, (iii) hired machinery charges, (iv) value of owned machine labour, (v) value of seeds, manure, fertilisers, irrigation charges; (vi) value of insecticides, pesticides, (vii) value of depreciation of implements and farm buildings, and (viii) land revenue, cesses and other taxes, interest on working capital, miscellaneous expenses like charges paid to the artisans, rent paid for the leased-in-land, imputed rental value of owned land, imputed interest on owned fixed capital and imputed value of family labour.[17]

During the short period of National Front Government some changes were introduced in the procedure followed for fixing the prices of agricultural commodities. One important change was that while determining the total cost of production of a crop, minimum wages fixed for the agricultural labour or the wages actually paid, whichever was higher, would be taken into consideration. Earlier, only the wages actually paid were included in the cost of production. The other important change announced was that the floor prices fixed for a crop would be revised upwards at the start of marketing season so that the inflationary impact could be neutralise during the period following the announcement of the prices.[18]

The commission generally takes the average cost of production and adds certain margin of profit in order to determine the minimum price of the crop. In this regard the National Front Government has also introduced a change. It declared that 10 per cent of the total cost of production would be taken as the payment for management/entrepreneurial function of the farmers and added to the cost of production of determining the minimum price of crop.[19]

Although agricultural price-policy during all the plans has been production incentive-oriented, the Sixth Plan gave a fresh change in the outlook. The plan realises that: (1) the modern agriculture increasingly involve the use of costly inputs and hence assured minimum price becomes a necessary underpinning for sustained agricultural production. (ii) the price-policy is an important tool for facilitating crop planning. This aspect has not so far received adequate attention in the country; and (iii) price-policy can be geared towards ensuring that the relevant income levels of the farming community are not eroded by continuing unfavourable terms of trade between agricultural and non-agricultural sector.

The following table shows the minimum support/procurement prices fixed by the Government for major crops produced in India for the last few years.

Minimum Support/Procurement Prices of Some Major Crops/Commodities

(Rs. Per Quintal)

Crops/Commodity	*Year of Marketing*						
	1984-85	85-86	86-87	87-88	88-89	89-90	90-91
Wheat (Procurement Price)	152	157	162	166	173	183	215
Paddy (Procurement Price)	137	142	142	150	160	185	205
Coarse Grains (Procurement Price)	130	130	132	135	145	165	180
Barley (Minimum Support Price)	124	130	132	135	135	145	180
Gram (Minimum Support Price)	240	-	260	280	290	325	420
Mustard (Minimum Support Price)	360	385	400	415	430	460	575
Groundnut (Minimum Support Price)	340	350	370	390	430	500	580
Sun Flower Seed (Minimum Support Price)	325	335	350	390	450	530	600
Soyabean (Minimum Support Price)	410	425	430	440	500	570	620
Cotton (F 414/H-777)	535	535	540	550	600	690	750
Sugar Can (Statutory Minimum Price)	14.00	16.50	17.00	18.50	19.50	22.00	23.00
Twte (W-5 Grade Ex-Assm) (Statutory Minimum Price)	195	215	225	240	240	295	375
VFC Tobacco (F-2) (Black Soil) (Statutory Minimum Price)	1115	1115	1115	1125	1175	1250	1325

Source: Soni R.N., Leading Issues In Agricultural Economics op.cit. p. 118.

Evaluation of Agricultural Price-Policy

Agricultural Price-policy in India is designed by the Agricultural Price Commission (APC) which after taking into consideration the cost factor of production fixes procurement and minimum support prices of different agricultural commodities. Procurement prices are those at which the Government procures surplus grains from the farmers and support prices are those at which the Government is bound to purchase the surplus if prices fall below the minimum level. However, the effectiveness of these prices depends upon the level of implementation of the policies. If the level of implementation is below the expectation, a gap will be created between the actual procurement price and the effective market prices. This will affect adversely the market arrivals. Hence, effective implementation of the policies is essential to minimise the gap between the procurement price and the market price and the resultant undesirable fluctuations in agricultural prices may also be avoided.

The other important precaution which has to be kept in view is that the benefits should reach to all sections of farms population. It has been noticed as well as studied that the benefits accrue more to large and rich farmers than to small and marginal farmers. Large farmers have better access to improved inputs and they generate more marketable surplus in comparison to small farmers who do not enjoy that access to modern inputs. The procurement system is such where the small farmers usually remained untouched. The Government operates through private commission agents and she does not enter the open market. It has also been noticed that the rich and prosper farmers hold their stock and sell it at a higher price sometime later in the open-market. This benefit does not accrue to small farmers who are economically under pressure of cash and hence, compel to sell their surplus through procurement channel only. Strong regular measures are, therefore, needed so that incentives are provided to both large and small farmers.

An agricultural price-policy should also provide adequate safeguards to the consumers, specially middle class and poor urban consumers and the best way to do so is through proper public distribution system. The base of fair-price shop should be widened. They should include all the major crops, pulses and other essential items of daily use. The present system does not fulfil the most essential demand of the vulnerable sections of the society. Sales are often inadequate; sometimes the quantity is inadequate and they too are distributed quite late; mainly rice and wheat of bad quality are covered ignoring inferior grains which forms the food of the poor and also does not cover all the rural poor population.

The agricultural price-policy has been ineffective for creating incentive to producers and safeguarding the interest of the consumers. It has also failed to protect the interest of the rural poor such as marginal farmers and landless labourers. High procurement prices have enhanced the holding power of large farmers which in turn, becomes a distributing factor to further rise in procurement prices. Hence, procurement prices have been inflationary and makes thing hard for the poor whose bulk of earning go to the purchase of foodgrains. Since they do not possesses marketable surplus they could benefit from the enhanced procurement price. Thus, the agricultural price-policy has to be reoriented in meaningful way covering two important aspects: (i) production incentives to all, and (ii) consumers protection of all level.

REFERENCES

1. Raj Krishna, *Agricultural Price-policy And Economic Development*, In Southworth H.M., Johnston B.F., *Agricultural and Economic Growth*, (Edi.) Cornell University Press 1970, Chapter 13.
2. Kaur R., *Agricultural Price-policy In Economic Development*, Kalyani, Delhi. 1975.
3. See — Mellor J.W., "*Agriculture Price-policy in the Contest of Economic Development*", **American Journal of Agricultural Economics**, 51 (5), 1959; Soni R.N. *Leading Issues in Agricultural Economics*, Shobhanlal Naginchand & Co., 1992. pp. 104-6.
4. See reference 37.
5. See Krishna Raj, *Agricultural Price-policy And Economic Development*, In Southworth H.M., Johnston B.F., *Agricultural And Economic Growth (Edi.)* 1967, Cornell University Press — Ithaca; Dharam Narain, *Impact of Price Movements on Area Under Selected Crops In India, 1900-39*, Cambridge University Press 1965; Maji C.C., Jha D And Venkataramanan L.S., *Dynamic Supply & Demand Models For Better Estimations & Projection: An Econometric Study. For Major Foodgrains In The Punjab Region*, Indian Journal of Agricultural Economics, Jan-March 1971; World Bank, "Some Aspects of Wheat and Rice Price-policy In India, **World Bank Staff Working Paper No. 381**, 1980, Tyagi D.S., *Farmer's Response to Agricultural Prices in India*, Heritage, Delhi, 1974; Cumming J.T., ***Supply Responsiveness of Indian Farmers In the Post-Independent Period: Major-Cereals and Cash Crops, India Journal of Agricultural Economics***, Jan—March, 1975; Madhavan M.C., *Average Response of Indian Farmers: A Case Study of Tamil Nadu*, **Indian Journal of Agricultural Economics**, Jan—March, 1972.

6. Soni R.N., *Leading Issues in Agricultural Economics, op cit.* pp. 106-107.
7. Krishna-Raj, *Agricultural Price-policy and Economic Development,* In Southworth H.M., Joshnston B.F., ***Agricultural and Economic Growth*** *(Edi.) op cit.*
8. Soni R.N., *Leading Issues In Agricultural Economic, op cit.* pp. 110-112.
9. *Op cit.* pp. 112-113.

   Ibid., pp. 114-115.
10. Singh A, Sadhu A.N., *Agricultural Problems In India,* Himalaya 1986 pp. 291-98; Soni R.N., *Leading Issues In Agricultural Economics, op cit.* pp. 116-118.
11. Soni R.N., *Leading Issues In Agricultural Economic, op cit.* p. 116.
12. Singh A. & Sadhu A.N., *Agricultural Problem In India, op cit.* p. 292.
13. *Ibid.*
14. Kohlan A.S., *Role of Positive Price-policy in Indian Agriculture Yojna,* Feb 16th 1980; Soni R.N., *Leading Issues in Agricultural Economics, op cit.* p. 116; Singh A. and Sadhu A.N., *Agricultural problems In India, op cit.* p. 293.
15. *Ibid.,* p. 117.
16. *Ibid.,*

PART - IV

SOME IMPORTANT ISSUES IN INDIAN AGRICULTURE

(i) Agriculture in Five Year Plans : An Assessment of Achievements and Failures

(ii) A Note on "Green-Revolution"

(iii) Farm-size, Production and Productivity Debate

(iv) Land-Reform : Some Important Dimensions

(v) Marketed and Marketable Surplus

(vi) Farm-Mechanisation

(vii) Agricultural Labour

(viii) Rural Credit

Appendix - A :

Variability in Credit-Deposit Ratio : Towards an Explanation of Performance of Public Sector Banks.

(ix) Agriculture Tax.

Appendix - B :

India Agricultural Tax : An Analysis of "Under-Tax Hypothes."

(x) Micro and Macro Dimensions of Economic Reforms in India.

Appendix - C :

Dunkel Negotiations : Impact on Agricultural Sector.

Bibliography.

Index

1

AGRICULTURE IN INDIAN PLAN & AN ASSESSMENT OF ACHIEVEMENTS AND FAILURES

In India, the importance of agriculture arises out of the position the agrarian sector occupies in the overall economic growth of the country. Agriculture, being the largest sector of the economy plays a crucial role in the country's economic development by providing food and raw material, employment to a large proportion of population, capital for its own development and surpluses for national development.

To understand the vital and catalytic importance of agronomy in the over-all economic development of India, the following indicators in brief are most essential.

(i) Agriculture in India contributes maximum national income and employment. During 1950-51 — 1960-61 the share of agriculture to national income has been about 50 per cent. 1970-71 — 1980-81, it has been near 40 per cent. During eighties, its share has been substantially declined. It has been 32 per cent to 38 per cent. Besides, agriculture also provides a livelihood to about three quarter of the population.

(ii) Agriculture sustains many industries with the supply of raw material. Among such industries some industries of national and international repute are textile, sugar, leather, tobacco, jute, tea and coffee and rubber. Besides, many other industries such as food-processing industries, oil industry, various chemical industries, colour and paints, silk and wool, vegetable oil etc. depend upon the raw material provided by this sector alone.

(iii) Indian agricultural sector plays an important role in foreign exchange earning. The main agricultural export commodities are tea, coffee, tobacco, sugar and sugar product, leather goods, fruits, raw wool, spices, etc. Due to increase in the domestic production of wheat, rice and cotton the imports of these commodities has been considerably declined. As a result the agricultural sector emerged as a net earner of foreign exchange which is needed for capital imports essential for the non-agricultural sector.

(iv) Variations in agricultural output level play a key role in the state of the national economy. Rural consumption of industrial goods is nearly three times of urban consumption.[1] It shows a direct relationship between agricultural production and income and demand for industrial goods. Agricultural performance also influences total demand via Government savings and public investment. A rise in agricultural production results in increased Government savings both as a result of increasing revenues and reduction in Government expenditure like drought relief.

The interdependence between agriculture and industry has become stronger. Isher-Ahluwalia and Rangarajan have drawn attention towards three important linkages that have developed between the agricultural sector and the industrial sector over the last four decades. These are:

(i) production linkage which refers interdependence for productive inputs — supply of agricultural raw material such as cotton, jute, silk, wool, sugarcane etc. to agro-based industries and supply of fertilisers, machinery, electricity and pesticides etc. by industry to agriculture. Recently agriculture's dependence on industry has increased at a faster rate than the dependence of industry on agriculture. This is because of the fast-moving modernisation of agricultural sector.

(ii) there is strong demand-linkage between the two sector. The impact of urban income and industrialisation on the demand for food and raw material is generally recognised. Equally important is the impact of rural income on industrial consumption goods such as foot-wear, clothing, sugar, bicycle, motor-cycles, scooter, construction-material etc.

(ii) saving and investment linkage is also quite important. The relative terms of trade between the two sectors not only influence the level of private saving and investment, but also reflects into Government savings and investment.[2]

We can conclude that agriculture in India occupies a central place in the national economy and hence a strong foundation of agriculture is an essential condition for a stable and rapid socio-economic development. Furthermore, it has the potential of becoming a leading sector in development. In any scheme of planned economic development, therefore, measures aimed at the development of the agricultural sector hold a position of basic importance. In this section, we propose to examine how for the planners in India recognisd this role of agriculture in India's economic development in terms of allocation of resources for the agricultural sector, the strategies adopted, the targets fixed and the policies followed to achieve these targets.

While planning for the development of agriculture, Planning Commission has laid down the following broad objectives.[3]

(i) Increase in agricultural production and productivity through extensive and intensive cultivation method.

(ii) Reduction in the pressure of population on land and shift the surplus labour to non-agricultural sector, preferably in rural and semi-urban areas.

(iii) Increase in employment opportunities in the agricultural sector and provide opportunities for increasing the income of the poorer sections in the village.

(iv) Reduction in income inequalities in rural areas through agrarian reform and distributing the surplus land among the small and marginal farmers.

Among all the four main objectives, only the first one, that is, the objective of increasing production and productivity has been practiced while the other objectives have been virtually neglected.

The relative importance of agriculture in the Five-Year Plans can be evaluated on the basis of the allocation of expenditure on various heads of agriculture and rural development. The following table gives the allocation of expenditure on major heads of agriculture and rural development.

Allocation of Actual Expenditure on Agriculture Under the Plans (Rs. in crores)

Major Heads	*Five Year Plans*						
	Ist Plan	*IInd Plan*	*IIIrd Plan*	*IVth Plan*	*Vth Plan*	*VIth Plan*	*VIIth Plan*
1. Agriculture and Allied Activities	290 (15%)	549 (11.8%)	1089 (12.7%)	2320 (14.7%)	4865 (12%)	15201 (14%)	22793 (12.6%)
2. Irrigation and Flood Control	434 (22%)	430 (9.2%)	665 (7.8%)	1354 (8.6%)	3877 (10%)	10930 (10%)	16979 (4.9%)
Total	724 (37%)	979 (21%)	1754 (26.5%)	3674 (23.3%)	8742 (22%)	22769 (24%)	39772 (22%)

The table shows that except in the First Plan the relative share of agriculture in the Plan in general has been on the low side. If agriculture in India contributes about 40 per cent to the national product and provides employment to near 70 per cent of the population, then the above allocation of around one-fifth of the planned outlay has been altogether considered inadequate.

Besides, agricultural development also requires the creation of social capital in the form of tube-wells, canals, reservoirs, dams etc. for irrigation, flood control, and soil-conservation. These provisions require huge amount of capital. The investment on irrigation and flood-control, as the table shows, has not been very impressive during the entire planning period.[4]

As against this, there is an opposite view. It is argued that India like other less developed countries suffers from a structural disequilibrium as disproportionately large part of the labour force is engaged in agriculture. Hence, for a balanced structural development, it is necessary that the non-agricultural sectors should be transferred to the non-agricultural sector. This requires relatively heavier planned allocations to these new sectors. A lower allocation to agricultural sector is, therefore, justified.[5]

No doubt, the above view has its own merit. Yet, a balance needs to be struck between the requirement of agricultural development and that of structural change in the economy. Indian agriculture, heavily based on rains, faces uncertainties. It has been estimated that the total irrigation potential in the country has risen from 23 million hectares in the pre-planned period to barely 67.0 million hectares at the beginning of the Seventh Plan. This slow development raised a question mark

General Phase: The main thrust during the two plan period (1950-61) has been to create a suitable atmosphere for the farmers to invest in agriculture and increase the productivity. Two important measures have been adopted. One was the land reforms and the other was the introduction of integrated development programme for rural areas. The land reforms measure comprise of (i) abolition of intermediaries, (ii) tenancy reforms for regulating the rent system, security of tenure and grant of ownership rights to cultivator etc. (iii) ceiling on agricultural holdings (iv) consolidation of holdings and (v) co-operative farming. The implementation aspect of land-reform measures have been weak and severely criticised. The measures whose sole purpose was to bring about an institutional change in the rural society have been half-heartedly carried out and hence failed to bear the desired results.

The integrated development approach was introduced with the intention of all round development of rural areas, where the active participation of the rural community has been encouraged. Community Development Programme (CDP) and Block Development Programme (BDP) were introduced in 1950. The programme was implemented through National Extension Service (N.E.S.) Blocks. Each block comprises about 100 villages and three such blocks formed a C.D. project. By the end of Second Five Year Plan, there were 3100 NES Blocks covering about one half of Indian village. [12]

Intensive Development Phase (1961-66): This strategy covers the Third Plan period. The heavy imports of foodgrains and the continuous poor performance of agricultural production due to droughts and unfavourable climatic conditions, compelled us to adopt an effective long-term policy of getting self-sufficiency in foodgrains. To achieve this objective two main programmes were introduced. One was the Intensive Agricultural District Programme (IADP) and the other was the establishment of Agricultural Prices Commission (APC).

IADP was the beginning of the intensive phase and initially was introduced in selected districts. It is also popularly known as "Package Programme" as it comprises a package of improved practices such as the use of improved and better seeds, better implements and machinery, fertilisers and pesticides etc. to increase food production. These programmes demonstrated their superiority over the traditional programmes. In 1964, another similar programme was introduced and that was Intensive Agricultural Area Programme (IAAP). This programme concentrated the efforts in selected blocks, aimed at progressively increasing the production of main crops—wheat and rice.

Another important element of the strategy in this phase was the establishment of Agricultural Price Commission (APC) in 1965 to assure remunerative prices of agricultural commodities to the farmers. Its main function was to advise the Government on the fixation of support prices of agricultural commodities. In 1985 it was redesigned as Agricultural Costs and Prices Commission (ACPC).[13]

Specialised Phase (1966 onwards)

This phase is the beginning of the NEW AGRICULTURAL STRATEGY. The NAS aimed at higher yields of main crops such as wheat, paddy, maize etc. and increased crop intensity. The popular name of this phase is "GREEN-REVOLUTION". A detailed discussion on Green-Revolution has been made in a separate chapter. Some important elements of this phase are as under: (i) Adoption of High Yielding Varieties (HYVs), (ii) Adoption of multiple cropping system to bring about new crop rotations and increased cropping intensity. This is possible when a short duration varieties of various food crops, oilseeds and vegetables will be introduced, (iii) Introduction of modern farm practices which involves greater use of modern farm inputs like fertilizers, pesticides and farm machinery which provide good support to HYVs of different crops, (iv) Assured irrigation which aimed to provide adequate and assured irrigation facilities. For this a National Grid System has been developed to ensure adequate water supply to water deficit areas, (v) Establishment of regulated markets and improvements in marketing practices through standardisation of weights and measures, gradation of products, provisions of information regarding market prices to farmers etc. It also involves efforts to strengthen to co-operative marketing structure, (vi) Government adopted the support prices which provided incentive prices for main agricultural commodities to arrest and correct the violent fluctuations in farm prices and to encourage the farmers to adopt seed fertilizer technology, and (vii) Apart from all such programme, two special programmes — Small Farmers and Agricultural Labourers Development Agency (SFALDA) were also launched during the Fourth Plan Period. The main objective was to ensure a fair deal to the relatively weaker sections among the farming community. Here the emphasis was to provide adequate institutional credit and subsidised inputs to these farmers.[14]

During Seventh Plan period the main agricultural strategy was to widen the base of agricultural growth and concerted effort for modernisation. The main elements were: (i) Extension of new technology, particular breakthrough in dry land farming, (ii) Special rice production programme in eastern region, (iii) National oilseed development programme, (iv) National water shed development programme for rain fed agriculture, (v) Greater attention to increase the production of commercial and export-based crops, (vi) Development of social forestry, and (vii) Appropriate price and procurement policies for crops. These efforts are considered essential to accelerate the growth of agricultural output, reduce violent fluctuations in output and to correct inter-regional, inter-crop and inter-class disparities.[15]

Agricultural Development During the Plans : A Review

Accelerated growth in agricultural production has been one of the principal aims of the Government from the beginning of the plans. This aim has been further strengthened in recent years in view of the increasing pressure of population on land and the increasing cost of importing food and raw-material from abroad. The growth of agricultural production can be reviewed by dividing the entire plan period into two distinct phases: The Pre-Green Revolution Period and the Post-Green-Revolution Period. The Green Revolution in India started around 1966-67. Hence the period covered by the first three Plans may be called as pre-green-revolution period and from Fourth Five Year Plan onwards, the post green-revolution period. The progress of agricultural production in these two phases can be reviewed in terms of: (i) increase in the areas under cultivation, and (ii) increase in the yield per hectare. Comparable data on agricultural production area and productivity is available both in absolute figures and in the form of index numbers compiled by the Government of India. We shall here make use of these data to portray the growth of agricultural production during pre and post green-revolution period.

Pre-Green-Revolution Period: Agricultural output data, as given in various Economic Surveys, shows that although the growth of output has not been very impressive during 1950-51 to 1965-66, yet the trend is clearly upward in respect of both foodgrains and non-food crops. Following table gives the detailed accounts of food and non-food production trend during the pre-green revolution period.

Table shows that the average level of output in the early sixties is much higher than the average level of output in the early fifties. Further, on point-to-point basis, the average rate of growth of output has been 2.2 per cent per annum for foodgrains, 3.2 per cent for non-foodgrains and 2.6 per cent for all agricultural commodities between 1950-51 and 1965-66. This rate of growth has little significance if we do not compare it with the rate of growth of population. Such comparison will determine the per capita availability of food and if we ignore the growing population merely average rate of growth of foodgrains fails to illustrate the growing per capita availability of food and if we ignore the growing population merely average rate of growth of foodgrains fails to illustrate the growing per capita availability of foodgrains. A rough estimate shows that during the period under consideration while average rate of growth of foodgrains has been 2.2 per cent, the rate of population growth has also been nearly the same. It means, despite showing an increasing trend, agricultural sector could not ensure an increased per capita availability of foodgrains.

Pre-Green-Revolution Production Trends
(1950-51 — 1965-66)

Year	*Foodgrain production (m.ts)*	*Index Of Agricultural output (1949-50=100)*		
		Foodgrains	*Non-Foodgrains*	*All Agricultural Commodities*
1950-51	54.9	90.5	105.9	95.6
1955-56	59.2	115.3	119.9	116.8
1956-57	72.3	120.8	131.5	124.3
1957-58	66.5	109.2	129.5	115.9
1958-59	78.7	130.6	139.4	133.5
1959-60	76.7	127.9	135.0	130.3
1060-61	82.0	137.1	152.6	142.2
1961-62	82.7	140.3	153.9	144.8
1962-63	80.2	133.6	151.6	139.6
1963-64	80.6	136.5	156.5	143.1
1964-65	89.0	150.2	175.4	158.5
1965-66	72.0	120.9	156.4	132.7

Source: GOI, Economic Survey — 1967-68 Table 1.5 — 1.6 *pp* A-8 and A-9.

An increase in agricultural production can be reviewed on the basis of an increase in area under cultivation and an increase in the productivity. Productivity has been estimated from two angles — land productivity and labour productivity.

The area under cultivation can be increased by the reclamation of uncultivated or water logged and waste lands or through adoption of such practices as double-cropping and multiple-cropping. During 1950-51 to 1965-66, the index number of area under agricultural crops went up from 78.2 to 96.1 (1969-70 = 100). On an average, the area under crops has increased at an annual rate of 1.31 per cent. The area under foodgrains increased by 1.07 per cent and under non-foodgrains 2.31 per cent. These estimates clearly show that the rate of growth of the area under non-foodgrains has been higher than the rate of growth of the area foodgrains.[16]

On per-hectare-yield basis, estimates show that per hectare output of all foodgrains went up from 552 kg. to 710 kg over the period of two Plans but declined to 629 kg by the end of the Third Plan. The overall growth has been about 14 per cent. Among the foodgrains the highest increase in yield per hectare was of maize (about 84 per cent), followed by 29 and 26.2 per cent increase in the yield of rice and wheat respectively. Among the non-foodgrains, cotton registered highest increase — 18 per cent over the period under consideration. Next was the Jute which showed an increase of 13.1 per cent between 1950-51 — 1960-61. Thus, with the exception of maize, no other foodgrains and non-foodgrains could show an appreciable increase.[17]

Not only is productivity per hectare low in land, the average productivity per worker engaged in agriculture is also very low. Labour productivity in India in 1965 was only 2.2 tonnes of wheat while it was 123.5 tonnes for USA, 125.8 tonnes for Australia, 57.3 tonnes for U.K., 115.2 tonnes for Canada, 49.6 tonnes for Germany and 42.9 tonnes for Argentina.[18]

Thus, the pre-green revolution period 1950-51 — 1965-66 was not marked by spectacular changes in Indian agriculture from quantitative or qualitative point of view. However, it can be realised that the pre-independence stagnation was certainly broken. Some institutional changes were made and some progress was also achieved in the supply of agricultural inputs such as irrigation and fertilizers. The use of chemical fertilizers has been increased by 700 per cent during the first three plans. But such substantial increase was constrained by lack of adequate irrigation facilities. These facilities grew only by 48 per cent during this period. In 1965-66 only 17 per cent of the area under cultivation was receiving irrigation. Despite all such draw-backs no one can deny the fact that the production trend has been upward. It was actually a period of preparation for launching the Green-Revolution.[19]

The Post-Revolution Period

Two years 1965-66 and 1966-67 witnessed the worst droughts and agricultural production naturally slumped. During this period some technical breakthrough became possible. Mexican wheat varieties developed by Prof. Norman Borland of Mexico were imported into the country and quickly adopted to Indian conditions. These varieties were considered to be relatively high yielding and were successfully experimented in number of countries. As a result of these HYV, production of wheat per hectare rose to the high level of 5,000 to 6,000 kg in Mexico in 1965. Taiwan also recorded similar increase. These HYV seeds required proper irrigation facilities and extensive use of fertilizers, pesticides and insecticides. Obviously, they had to be adopted in the form of package programme. This seed-fertilizers — water package is commonly known as "Green-Revolution."

This new agricultural strategy was put into practice for the first time in India in Kharif season of 1966 and was termed High-Yielding Varieties Programme (HYVP). Initially it was introduced in a total area of 1.89 million hectare. At the end of Fourth Five Year Plan the coverage was estimated to be 9.2 million hectare. In 1989-90 the total area under HYVP was 63.8 million hectare. This is almost 35 per cent of gross cropped area.[20]

The new technical breakthrough was initially confined to wheat production. Later on, some other crops like paddy, maize and bajra were also included. The most conspicuous result of such revolution has been a sharp decline in the imports of foodgrains in 1970, specially the stoppage of PL-480 imports of wheat from USA. During 1970-80 India became the net exporter of small quantities of foodgrains.

The Post-Green Revolution period has thus, witnessed a sharp change in the level of output of agricultural sector. Following indicators are important to be examined.

Trends in Agricultural Production: Following table shows the trends in agricultural production. The new technology package started bearing fruits from 1971-72 onwards.

Table depicts that the output of both food and non-foodgrains has fluctuated even during post-green revolution period. A smooth upward movement in output is lacking which indicates that Indian agricultural is still dependent upon the favourable weather conditions. Point-to-point comparison shows that the output of foodgrains and all agricultural commodities grew at an annual average rate of 2.7, 2.4 and 2.6 per cent respectively. If we compare these growth rate with the growth rate of pre-green revolution period, the rates turns-out to be higher for foodgrains, lower for non-foodgrains and same for all agricultural commodities. It gives an impression that in quantitative terms, the impact of the Green-Revolution has been mainly on food-out put, specially wheat.

Following figure depicts the trends in the yield per hectare of principal crops during the Post-Green-Revolution period.

Index Numbers of Agricultural Production (1970-92)

Year	*Foodgrains*	*Non-Foodgrains* (Base Year 1969-70 = 100)	*All agricultural commodities*
1970-71	112.9	108.6	111.5
1975-76	172.2	120.5	125.1
1980-81	137.5	130.5	135.3
1982-83	135.8	141.1	137.5
1983-84	161.1	146.3	156.4
1984-85	154.3	155.3	154.6
1985-86	161.9	150.9	158.4
1986-87	154.0	149.2	152.5
1987-88	149.8	154.5	151.3
1988-89	182.5	184.8	183.2
1989-90	183.4	194.5	187.0
1990-91	189.4	196.9	191.8
1991-92	181.4	197.6	186.6

Source : GOI Economic Survey 1988-89, 1990-91, 1991-92, 1992-93 (Base for the year 1991-92 is 1969-70 = 100)

Index Number of Yields of Principal Crops (1969-70 = 100)

	70-71	*75-76*	*80-81*	*85-86*	*86-87*	*87-88*	*88-89*	*89-90*	*90-91*
Foodgrains	110.7	121.1	132.2	153.9	147.4	152.2	174.0	176.1	180.7
Cereal	110.4	118.8	129.3	149.6	142.8	146.0	167.0	186.0	191.6
Rice	105.8	116.9	126.3	147.1	139.4	138.9	160.1	165.4	166.0
Wheat	115.0	124.1	143.4	180.0	168.6	176.1	197.4	186.6	200.0
Coarse-Cereal	117.0	120.1	120.2	114.1	116.8	123.6	142.9	160.4	157.7
Pulses	101.9	103.7	92.8	107.0	99.3	101.8	117.7	108.4	113.4
Grains	98.0	104.3	97.2	109.6	95.9	92.9	111.3	96.2	103.5
Non-Food-grains	104.3	114.4	116.8	137.9	143.0	149.4	158.4	164.4	162.9
Oilseeds	114.0	123.1	109.5	122.8	128.4	131.9	172.2	163.0	165.3
Cotton	87.0	112.4	124.5	161.1	138.2	137.4	165.6	206.3	183.4
Jute	96.4	111.0	101.1	138.3	133.3	120.9	141.3	152.0	145.9

Source : Economic Survey 1991-92 *p*.5-15

Figure shows that yield per hectare of all commodities increased from 109.4 in 1970-71 to 141.3 in 1987-88. The increase was about 29 per cent. During the pre-Green-Revolution period the increase was only 14 per cent. The increase in yield has been much higher for wheat than for rice. The increase for wheat was 52.6 per cent while for rice it was 32.0 per cent. It was only 26.2 and 29.0 per cent during pre-Green-Revolution period. Thus, the increase in yields of all foodgrains as well as of wheat during post-Green-Revolution period. For Coarse-Cereals, the increase in yields has been only marginal, that is 2 per cent.

As regards non-foodgrains the yield per hectare during 1970-71 to 1990-91 increased from 104.8 to 162.9 points. The increase in yield was by about 42 per cent. Cotton shows the highest increase of 96.4 per cent. The increase in yield of jute is 51.3 and of oilseed 49.5 per cent respectively. In comparison to the pre-Green-Revolution period the increase in case of cotton has been five times more. The increase in the yield of cotton in the pre-Green-Revolution period was 18 per cent while during post-Green-Revolution period it was 96.4 per cent. In case of jute and oilseed the post-Green-Revolution period shows more favourable trend in comparison to pre-Green-Revolutionperiod. A comparative compound rate of growth of foodgrains and non-foodgrains is given in the following table covering pre and post-Green-Revolution period.

All-India Compound Growth Rate of Production — Selected Crops

(% per annum)

Crops	*Pre-green-revolution Period 1949-50-1964-65*	*Post-green-revolution Period 1970-71-1988-89.*
Foodgrains	**2.93**	**2.79**
Rice	3.49	2.84
Wheat	3.99	4.82
Coarse Grain	2.23	0.41
Pulses	1.39	1.04
Non-foodgrain	**3.54**	**2.56**
Cotton	4.56	1.75
Oilseeds	3.11	1.92
Groundnut	4.33	1.19
Sugarcane	4.26	2.74
All Crops	3.13	2.68

Source: The Economic Times, Nov. 15, 1990 *p*.13

140.4 million tonnes in 1987-88 increase was 21.3 per cent. Yet on peak to peak basis annual compound rate of foodgrains production works out to be 2.2 per cent between 1983-84 and 1988-89 which is a modest performance. In 1990-91, the foodgrains production touched the level of 176.2 million tonnes. One thing that emerges clearly from these trends is that though foodgrains production targets has often remained below targets, it has made a rapid stride. The rise in production from a meagre 51 million tonnes in 1950-51 to 176.2 million tonnes in 1990-91 may not be called a modest performance. Among the foodgrains, wheat production rose rapidly during the post-green revolution period. However, the matter of concern is that production of non-foodgrains crops such as jute, cotton, oilseed etc. has all remained much below the targets.

(iv) The Need and the Potential Front: An assessment of our achievements and needs is another important criteria of evaluating performance. India has been one of those developing countries which, despite rapid increase in foodgrains production, have a high food import bills to provide minimum level of subsistence to its growing population. Furthermore, domestic production of commercial crops has never been sufficient to meet the domestic needs to keep the industries running. The rate of growth of agricultural output and of population is almost equal which indicates that agricultural production is nearly stagnant and if this trend continues, the rate of agricultural production may significantly fall below the demographic growth rate.

On potential front, the unutilised potential of the existing technology is substantially higher than the potential actually utilised. That is, on available technology, crop production is far below the optimum. This is realised by demonstrations and operational research projects on farmers fields. A wide-gap is realised between the average yields obtained under national demonstration projects and the existing crop yields obtained under identical conditions in various States. This gap is denoted by the ratio of average yields under national demonstration projects to the existing crop yields. That is the ratio of achievable to achieved yields. For rice, this ratio for the year 1978-70 (the latest year for which the rate is available) was 1.48 in Punjab, 1.75 in Tamil Nadu 1.44 in Karnataka, 2.20 in U.P., 3.50 in Bihar, 3.32 in Orissa and 2.94 in Gujarat. For wheat it was 1.49 in Punjab, 2.76 in U.P., 3.98 in Bihar, 2.04 in Haryana 1.97 in West Bengal and 2.40 in M.P. Thus Bihar shows the highest gap between the achievable and achieved yields. Next comes Orissa. The gap is also quite wide in U.P., M.P., Gujarat, and Haryana.[24]

(v) Criteria of Regional Imbalances: Post-Green-Revolution period has witnessed that only States such as Punjab, Haryana, Andhra Pradesh, Western part of U.P. and Tamil Nadu which have better irrigation facilities have gained the maximum benefits of the new farm technology. Obviously, these States were able to achieve higher rates of growth in agricultural production than the other States. The States of the Eastern and North-East region have shown the lowest growth rate. There are two main reasons. One is socio-cultural and the other is geographical. These regions accounted for a very high proportion of tribals who lived in isolation and resisted the use of modern farming practices. Geographically, most part of these regions consist of highly terrain which have made the infrastructural development deficient and costly. Besides, the States Governments have also neglected to pay adequate attention to the development of such areas because the tribals were not keen in pressing their economic problems, nor they were strong enough to build a political lobby to secure adequate funds for agricultural development.[25]

Agriculture in India has shown a remarkable progress during post-Green-Revolution period. The package approach adopted since the mid-sixties has opened up entirely new dimensions of growth in the agricultural sector and has raised a large segment of the agrarian economy from its subsistence character. Under the impulse of new technology the farmers is responding to market incentives and fluctuation and is thus participating in a more meaningful manner in the economic development of the country.

FOOTNOTES AND REFERENCES

1. Chakarvarty S., "*Reflections on the Growth Process in The Indian Economy*" Administrative Staff College of India, Hyderabad, (Address) 1974.
2. Ahluwalia I.J., and Rangarajan C., *Interdependence of Agriculture and Industry : A Study of Indian Experience*, in R.K. Sinha (Ed). *Economic Development since Independence*. Deep & Deep, N. Delhi. 1988.
3. Janeja ML., Myer R.M., *Economics of Development of Planning*, Shobhanlal Naginchand & Co. 1991. p. 190.
4. *Ibid.*, pp. 190-91
5. *Ibid.*, p. 191.
6. M.L. Dantwala, *Strategy of Agricultural Development Since Independent*. In M.L. Dantwala and others: *Indian Agricultural Development Since Independence*, Oxford and IBH, N. Delhi 1986 p. 3.
7. M.L. Dantwala, *Agricultural Policy in India Since Independence*, in C.H. Shah (ed.) *Agricultural Development of India; Policy & Problem*, Orient Longman, Bombay 1979 p. 6.

8. Kumar A. Ganesh, *Falling Agricultural, Investment and its Consequences*, Economic & Political Weekly, October 17, no. 42, 1992 p. 2307-2312.
9. *Ibid.*, p. 2307.
10. *Ibid.*, p. 2307
11. *Ibid.*, p. 2312.
12. Taneja M.L., Myer R.M., Economics of Development Planning, op. cit., pp. 192-93.
13. *Ibid.*, p. 193
14. *Ibid.*
15. *Ibid.*, pp. 194-95.
16. GOI, Economic Survey.
17. GOI, *Six-Five Year Plan and Economic Survey 1982-83.*
18. Kulshrestha S.N. and Tiwari D.D., *Agriculture in India-Problems & Prospects*, in Uppal J.S. (Ed.) *India's Economic Problems.*, New Delhi, 1987 Table 5.12, p. 10.
19. Taneja M.L., Myer R.M., *Economics of Development & Planning, Op. Cit.*, p. 197.
20. GOI, Economic Survey.
21. GOI, Economic Survey 1988-89 p. 5-21 Table 1.14.
22. Sen S.K., *Growth and Instability in Indian Agriculture, Agricultural Situation In India*, June 1967.
23. Dantwala ML, *From Stagnation to Growth*, Indian Economic Journal, Oct-Dec., 1970.
24. Dhingra I.C., A Text Book of Indian Economy, Sultan Chand & Son, 1990, p. 199.
25. *Ibid.*

2

A NOTE ON GREEN REVOLUTION

"Green Revolution" has been identified with technological break-through — seed-fertilizer-irrigation-mechanisation — in Indian agricultural. Since HYVs of seeds have been introduced alongwith chemical fertilisers, pesticides, adequate irrigation and machines, the package could also be termed as biological-mechanical revolution. It implies a well-marked improvement in agricultural production in a short period as well as a sustenance of a higher level of agricultural production over a fairly long-period of time.

Production & Productivity Assessment: Green Revolution which started in India during mid sixties has different views in regards to its extent and depth. Even Minhas who raised various doubts about the extent of the revolution admits that a transformation has occurred in Indian agriculture.[1] R.W. Cummings and S.K. Ray also hailed this transformation as Green Revolution.[2] Those who admits that the technological changes in agriculture have brought about certain quantitative changes claim the following merits.[3]

(i) Unfavourable weather conditions have been responsible for fluctuations in agricultural output. However, since the green revolution, the magnitude of these fluctuations has narrowed considerably.

(ii) The new technology has opened a process of modernisation of Indian Agriculture and has substantially increased its production capacity.

(iii) The impact of the green revolution can be assessed by a sharp increase in investments in irrigation and increased purchases of modern inputs like fertilizers, pesticides, irrigation equipments and machinery.

(iv) The inter-class disparities which have arisen in the wake of the green revolution may be corrected with the help of effective and appropriate policy measures, because the application of the new technology is neutral to scale.

(v) The new dwarf plants can grow and mature even under cloudy skies which cuts down the cropping period. This had made multiple cropping possible. This means that the per acre yields can be raised many fold.

The basic approach of "Green Revolution" has been to tackle the entire agricultural problems in totality and to find out the ways and means to bring about significant improvement in the agricultural productivity. As a result of the adoption of new agricultural strategy foodgrains output increased substantially from 81.0 million tonnes in the Third Plan to 103.0 million tonnes in the Fourth Plan and further to 133.1 million tonnes in 1981-82, 145 million tonnes in 1987-88, 172.7 million tonnes in 1989-90 and 176.2 million tonnes in 1990-91 HYVP was initially restricted to only five crops namely wheat, rice, jowar, bajra and maize. Non-foodgrains were excluded from the ambit of the new strategy. Even in foodgrains only wheat output has shown a substantial increase from 11.1 million tonnes in the Third Plan to 23.4 million tonnes in the Fourth-Plan, 29.8 million tonnes in the Fifth Plan to 41.2 million tonnes in the Sixth Plan and 54.5 million tonnes upto 1990-91 (All figures are in annual average). The overall contribution of wheat to total foodgrains, has increased from 13 per cent in 1950-51 to 30.4 per cent in 1989-90. On production index side, whereas the index of foodgrains production of India (1969-70=100) increased from 75.8 in 1965-66 to 182.7 in 1988-89, and further 189.4 in 1990-91 the index of wheat production increased from 57.6 in 1965-66 to 29.1 in 1988-89 and further 302.0 in 1990-91. On the basis of productivity, while the yield per hectare of all foodgrains increased from 710 kgs in 1960-61 to 858 kgs in 1971-72 and 1,327 kgs in 1988-89, the yield of wheat rose from 851 kgs to 1,380 kgs and further 2,241 kgs over the same period. It shows that the main focus of the green-revolution has been on wheat only.[4]

The production of rice has shown comparatively slow growth. The average annual production of rice increased from 35.1 million tonnes in the Third Plan to 41.8 million tonnes in the Fourth Plan, 47.3 million tonnes in Fifth Plan and further 54.5 million tonnes is in the Sixth Plan. In 1985-86, the level of output was 63.8 million tonnes. In next two years 1986-87 and 87-88, the production fell considerably due to drought. But the year 1988-89 showed a record production of 70.7 million tonnes. This trend was maintained in the year 1989-90 when rice production touched the level of 72.8 million tonnes.[5]

Contrary to the production trends of wheat and rice, the production of the coarse cereals — jowar, bajra and maize — continued to be static or moved very slowly upwards. The production of pulses also remained static. The performance of major oilseeds was also dismal. The total production increased from 8.3 million tonnes in Fourth Plan to 8.9 million tonnes in the Fifth Plan (annual average). Thus, the production increased only by 7.2 per cent in a period of five years. During the next five years ending 1984-85 the average production increased upto 11.4 million tonnes, the increase was 28.1 per cent. During the last two years of the Seventh Plan 1989-90-91, a substantial increase has been witnessed. The production of oilseeds touched a record level of 17.9 million tonnes in 1988-89 and slightly lower 17.2 million tonnes in 1989-90. A major part of this increase come from groundnut, rapeseed/mustard, castorseed and sesamum. However, it is quite relevant to point out that such increased level of oilseed production has been entirely inadequate to meet the domestic demand. As a result, imports of major edible oil constituted almost one half of the total edible oil obtain from domestic source for a number of years. Within a short period of six years (1984-85—89-90) the country had to spend more than Rs. 4,000 crores on the imports of edible oils[6].

This brief statement shows that, except in the case of wheat, progress in other crops has not been satisfactory. It is only in case of wheat that the growth rate of production is higher in the green-revolution period, as compared to pre-green-revolution period. In the early phase of green-revolution many economist had noted these trends and termed green-revolution as wheat-revolution. In support of this view, some conclusion drawn by R. Thamarajakshi can be presented.[7] The study presented estimates of growth rates in demand vis-a-vis production for some major crops over the period 1967-68 to 1983-84. While the growth in demand of wheat has been 3.09 per cent per annum, the growth in production has been considerably higher at 5.77 per cent per annum. In case of rice, while the demand was 2.75 per cent per annum, the growth in production was 2.27 per cent per annum. For all other crops, the study revealed, there were substantial gaps in the demand

and supply. For instance, production of pulses grew at a rate of merely 0.35 per cent per annum against 3.38 per cent per annum increase in demand over the same period. Production of vegetable oil increased by 1.35 per cent per annum against a 3.51 per cent increase in demand.

One more study compares the productivity in the farms which have adopted the new agricultural strategy extensively and the farms which are still following the traditional technology. This study was made by Punjab University in collaboration with the Haryana Government.[8] In this study, it has been revealed that both the large as well as small farms have adopted the new agricultural strategy. In small farms only few have adopted this strategy. Study reveals that the output per acre in the relatively larger farms has been less than the output per acre in the smaller farms. However, the output per acre in the large progressive farms compares favourably with the output per acre in the small non-progressive farms. As a matter of fact, the trend that the output per acre in a big farm is less than that in small farm is reversed by the adoption of the new agricultural strategy.

The failure of green revolution is further supported if we measure per capita availability of foodgrain, pulses, and other essential food items and the general level of calories and protein consumed per individual. It has been estimated that cereals consumption per capita per day increased from 354.08 grammes in 1951-55 to 400, 420 grammes in 1961-65. But during 1961-65 - 71-75 the consumption was almost constant - 400.92 grammes per day. Pulses shows a constant reduction from 64.66 grammes in 1951-56 to 60.68 grammes in 1961-65 and further 45.50 grammes in 1971-76. Thus, green-revolution failed to improve the consumption level. The so-called green-revolution, according to K.N. Raj "has failed to raise the overall rate of growth of agricultural output in the country above the level achieved in the 15 years prior to 1965. It certainly helped to increase very significantly the output of few crops such as wheat, bajra and maize within a short period... In any case, the output of even the few crops which had recorded sharp spurts towards the late sixties is not growing so rapidly any more".[9]

Number of factors are responsible for such failure. (i) The new seed-fertilizer-water technology has influenced only a limited number of commodities such as wheat, rice, maize and jowar and even that in few States such as Punjab, Haryana and Western U.P. (ii) Expansion in output of crops such as wheat has been at the expense of other crops such as pulses, cotton and groundnut because the area under cultivation has been competed away from them. (iii) Fertilizer application which is an important component of the new technology has been found to be subject to diminishing returns. (iv) Under new technology a number of inputs are complementary in the sense that their joint application yields a much greater volume of output. However, the non-availability of any one input such. as irrigation limits the use of other inputs.

In the second phase, however, the green-revolution has spread to other crops also. Most of the important crops registered substantial increase during this period. Jute, cotton, sugarcane etc. have also included in the revolutionary processes. The production of jute has been increased by 16.3 per cent in 1987-88 over 1969-70, sugarcane 65 per cent and cotton 14.8 per cent during the same period.[10]

Imbalances: The new agricultural technology represents a breakthrough in traditional agriculture. It has certainly changed the outlook of farmers who looked upon agriculture as a way of life, mostly a subsistence way of life. Its effects on the level of output and productivity of important food and commercial crops has been analysed in the previous part. However, green-revolution is not an unmixed blessing. It has generated some serious problems too. One of the problem widely discussed is imbalances and wide disparity in income distribution.

The green-revolution has generated imbalances in the economy because it has benefitted mainly those areas which already had the irrigation facilities. The farmers of these areas are already economically better off in comparison to the farmers of those areas who were depended upon the rains for cultivation. If such well-off farmers will get more facilities in term of fertilizers, HYV seeds, pesticides credit and machines, a disparity will certainly be generated between them and those who are unable to take such benefits. For example areas comprising Punjab, Haryana, and Western U.P. have made remarkable progress in agricultural output and productivity. But the areas like Eastern part of U.P., Rajasthan, Orissa farmers have not been able to reap the benefits of new technology due to take of assured/controlled water supply.

This imbalance can also be analysed in different angle. HYVP was initiated on a small area of 1.89 million hectare in 1966-1967 and even upto 1989-90 it covers only 63.8 million hectares which is only around 35 per cent of the gross cropped area. Obviously, the benefits of new-technology remained concentrated in this area only. Further, since green-revolution remained limited to wheat only, its benefit actually concentrated in the 20.84 million hectares of the area under wheat which represented only about 12 per cent of the gross cropped area. Again, within the area under wheat in HYVP, only regions having assured water supply and package of other inputs derived benefits from the new technology. The regional imbalance is quite clear from the fact that while the combined share of Northern States (Punjab, Haryana and Western U.P.) in total foodgrain production increased from 29.5 per cent in 1970-71 to 1972-73 to 37.1 per cent during 1986-87 to 1988-89, the Western States of Gujarat, and Maharashtra registered a small increase from 7.9 per cent to 8.6 per cent. All other States show a decline.[11]

The inter-regional imbalances as a consequence of green-revolution is well-established. Some economist also referred towards the widening disparities in the distribution of income. Some micro level studies reveal that inter-personal inequalities have increased in the green-revolution period. Some other studies indicate that they have considerably narrowed down. Some other economist also hold the view that the new technology has been "neutral" in the sense that the pattern of inequalities has remained unaffected. The studies such as of Francine R. Frankel, G.R. Saini and Pranab Bardhan reveal that large farmers in comparison to small farmers have benefitted the most from green revolution. Contrary, the studies of J.R. Westley, Usha Nagpal and George Blyn come to this conclusion that inequalities have narrow down as small farmers have also benefitted considerably from the green-revolution.

Actually such conclusions are quite natural. The adoption of new technology involves substantial investment on package inputs which were beyond the means of majority of this country's small and marginal farmers. Only rich farmers can afford the expensive new technology. It has been pointed out that under traditional cropping system, the small farmers were not much at disadvantage state because productivity per acre on small farms in comparison to large one is more. The adoption of the new capital intensive technology shifted the productivity per acre in favour of rich and big farmers. Further, the big farmers have also greater risk-bearing capacity and thus are in better position to use these new technologies. Obviously, the advantage got reflected in the distribution of benefits from new technology in the regions where they are adopted. Co-operative societies by granting major proportion of loans to the rich farmers, further help in accentuating inequalities.

The studies made by Usha Nagpal and George Blyn reveals that disparities between rich and poor small farmers, instead of increasing, have actually narrowed down. Nagpal's study of Palanpur Village of District Moradabad indicates that during 1964-65 and 1974-75 the share of small farmers in the value of the total crop increased from 29 per cent, while the share of rich farmers fell from 36 to 15 per cent. Blyn after reviewing the findings observed that "the real income from family sources increased relatively more for families with smaller holdings, thereby reducing income inequality".[12]

G.S. Bhalla and G.K. Chadha[13] in their study of the effect of green-revolution on the small and marginal farmers came to this conclusion that "the advent of the green-revolution in Punjab has brought overall prosperity to its peasantry". But in case of small and marginal farmers the study revealed that "about one-third of the marginal farmers (tilling less than 2.5 acres of land) are living below the poverty line. It is equally disturbing that about 24.0 per cent of small farmers (tilling between 2.5 and 5.0 acres of land) are also living below the poverty line.

Shrinking Employment and Income Opportunities: Green-revolution embarks three changes, namely biological, chemical and mechanical. The biological and chemical changes influences the agricultural productivity. The introduction of HYV seeds and fertilisers represent this changes. The mechanical changes refer the introduction of better implements which generally displace human and animal labour. Thus, while the biological and chemical changes are labour absorbing, mechanical changes are labour saving.

All three changes have been introduced in areas where green-revolution has started. There is an evidence that while the use of biological and chemical inputs as well as the multiple cropping system have increased the demand for labour, the use of machinery has reduced this demand specially during the sowing and harvesting seasons. On big farms where the landless workers generally works, due to introduction of machines, no employment opportunities are found. But this issue is debatable. P.K. Bardhan in his study Land, Labour and Rural Poverty concluded that the average daily earnings in agricultural operations by men belonging to agricultural labour households during the years 1964-65 and 1974-75 had declined by 12 per cent in real terms for the whole of rural India. At the State level wages declined in all the States, except in Punjab, Haryana, U.P. and Jammu & Kashmir.[14] Deepak Lal in his study "Agricultural Growth, Real Wages And The Rural Poor India", reveals that the condition of rural poor households had improved between 1956-57 and 1970-71. In a later study he admits that gains have been very little.[15] Some other studies such as Bhalla and Chadha, A.V. Jose support this point of view.[16]

C.H. Hanumantha Rao brings out the favourable as well as unfavourable effect of new technology on employment. He says that "if the Green-Revolution is regarded as a package consisting of HYV and fertilisers, its contribution to employment has been substantial. Also, tube-well seems to have contributed significantly to the employment of labour... the highest labour co-efficient relates to operated area followed by HYV and irrigation". But the effect of machanisation on employment is negative. He reveals that "the net employment of tractor use may turn out to be negative when tractorisation of farm operations is complete. A harvest combine would displace farm labour on a large-scale while its land augmenting effect would be negligible."[17] Martin H. Billings and Arjan Singh have attempted to quantify the labour displacement effect in the wheat growing areas of Punjab with different degrees of mechanisation. They revealed that as against 5.5 per cent displacement of labour in 1968-69 labour displacement would be of the order of 17.4 per cent in 1983-84. About 55 per cent of the total labour displace is expected to be caused by tractors and pump-sets and 37 per cent by threshers and reapers.[18]

The capital-intensive technique of new agricultural strategy are supported to be labour intensive. The frequent applications of water, fertilizers, insecticides, pesticides weeding, double cropping, large volumes of transportation, marketing, food processing and dairy development may lead to increased employment and increased income among the small farmers and landless labourers. This is also expected that agricultural growth is highly correlated with the growth of allied and other subsidiary activities and hence may increase employment. For instance, the development of dairy activities, fisheries, bee-keeping horticulture and various cottage and rural industries tend to grow faster in areas of high agricultural growth. Thus the net effect on employment of the labour-intensive aspects of the new-technology and the labour displacing effects of machanisation is a matter of controversy.[19] In case of labour-displacing effect of machanisation it is also argued that only animal power is displaced, not human labour.

Srivastava D. and Shayam Borate's study: Green-revolution in Northern-Region-Impact of Selective Farm Mechanisation on Farm Employment based on Alipur Block of the Union Territory of Delhi reveals: "It is very interesting to note that the extent of mechanisation did not significantly influences the utilisation of labour on farms." They further states, "though for each individual operation, the use of machinery displaces labour; taking cropping pattern as a whole, the use of machinery did not, in the study show any significant influence on the annual utilisation of labour. Thus, the green-revolution and the consequent emergence of the new cropping pattern did not displace labour even after selective mechanisation".[20] Such conclusion indicates that the danger of displacing labour can be removed by adopting new cropping pattern.

Such micro-level studies and their conclusions confirms two important points. One is that the green-revolution has both the negative as well as positive impacts on increasing employment and the income of the poor. If new agricultural strategy in form of HVP, fertiliser, water etc. has employment increasing potentiality, the mechanical aspect has labour-displacing potential if not balanced by multiple-cropping system. In view of this all out efforts must be made to create alternative employment opportunities within and outside the crop enterprises, so as to absorb the farm family surplus labour. M.S. Gurupadaswamy, a former Minister of State for Food and Agriculture has timely warned: "if new openings for their productive involvement in alternative occupations are not created simultaneously (with the new agricultural strategy), unemployment or under-employment of agricultural labour might land us in a situation which might become explosive both politically and economically.

Penetration of Capitalism: The capital-intensive package approach of new agricultural strategy necessitated heavy investments which, as has been discussed earlier, are beyond the capacity of small and marginal farmers. In India, there are about 81 million farm households and only 6 per cent of the big farmers accounts for 40 per cent of the land. Naturally, they are making heavy investment in the installation of tube-wells, pumping sets, fertilizers, machineries and on other land development programmes. Consequently, the new agricultural strategy is encouraging the growth of capitalist farming in India. This revolution is lacking in spread effects and thus is fostering an "enclave-type" development in Indian agriculture. It has led to concentrate the wealth in the hands of the top 10 per cent of the rural population.[21]

Ashok Rudra, Majid and Talib conducted a survey of the Punjab farmers to analyse the development of capitalist farming. Their definition of capitalist is that where at least 20 acres of land is engaged in farming. The survey revealed that the total number of farms above 20 acres was 67,000 covering 26 lakhs acre of cultivated area. A further break-up of big farms reveals that farm-size group 20-25 acres of land expanded only by 4 per cent whereas those of the size group 100-150 acres increased by 40 per cent. It shows that the "gentlemen" farming has grown more fastly during post-green-revolution period. They have taken agriculture as an industry and find investment quite profitable. Such progressive capitalist farmers command 8.5 per cent of the total number of farms and over 27 per cent of the cultivated area. It is this group of farmers who are able to invest on modern inputs, land improvements and other allied activities.

U. Thant, a former U.N. Secretary General observed: "There are many observers who contend that if left to market forces, the green-revolution is likely to benefit primarily those farmers who are already engaged in commercial production rather than subsistence farmers, and among commercial farmers, big ones more than small producers".

Thus, green-revolution has helped to develop a capitalist culture within the agricultural sector which in turn has widened the disparities among the rich and the poor farmers as well as enhanced the inequalities. V.K.R.V. Rao has rightly pointed out that "the so-called green-revolution which helped the country to raise its output of foodgrains has also been accompanied by a widening of the range of inequality in rural incomes, the loss of their status as tenants by a number of small farmers and the emergence of social and economic tensions in the countryside... The challenge which Indian agriculture faces is not only of production but also that of distribution; and in our anxiety to concentrate on production problems, we should not forget the human and social implications of agricultural development.[22]

Concluding Remarks: The good and the bad effects of new-agricultural technology (green-revolutions) may be examined and analysed from various angles. But nobody can deny that it has changed the attitudes of farmers in areas where it is practised. Increase in productivity in these areas has enhanced the status of agriculture from a low level subsistence activity to commercialised activity. Wolf Ladejinsky has rightly pointed out that "where the ingredients for the new technology are available, no farmer denies their effectiveness. The desire for better farming method and a better standard of living is growing not only among the relatively small number of the affluent using the new technology, but also among countless farmers still from the outside looking in".[23] The need is to extend the new strategy in as many districts as possible along with more coverage of crops, both food and non-food. Much attention should also be given to small and subsistence peasant class through effective implementation of land-reform measures, cooperative societies, credit facilities etc. We have succeed in spreading the green-revolution in many more districts. The area under HYVP increased from 1.89 million hectares in 1966-67 to 63.84 million hectares in 1989-90. The consumption of fertilizers has also substantially increased from merely 2.9 lakh tonnes in 1960-61 to 122 lakh tonnes in 1989-90. Tractors per lakh hectare of gross cropped area increased from 34 in 1965-66 to 234 in 1978-79. Tube-wells which were only 80,000 by the end of the Third Plan, reached to the figure of 719,000 in 1973-74 and that too were only private tube-wells. Similarly the number of power and oil-engine operated irrigation pump-set has also substantially increase. These remarkable figure shows a structural change which is brought about by this new agricultural strategy. But despite all such facts, the overall situation is still not very satisfactory. Though the foodgrain production has registered significant increase in recent years, the population is likely to touch the 1 billion mark by 2001 and the demand for foodgrain will rise to 220 million tonnes. However, the maximum production recorded so far is 172.7 million tonnes 1989-90. Over the period of 40 years (1950-51 to 1989-90) we could increase the output from 51 to 173 million tonnes. The increase is only 122 million tonnes in 40 years. Is it possible for us to increase the output by 50 million tonnes in about a decade time?

FOOTNOTES AND REFERENCES

1. Minhas B.S., *Planning and the Poor*, S. Chand & Co., N. Delhi 1974.
2. Cummings R.W., Ray S.K., *"The New Agricultural Strategy"*. ***Economic and Political Weekly,*** 29th March, 1969.
3. Shetty S.L., *"Structural Retrogression in the Indian Economy since the mid-sixties"*, ***Economic and Political Weekly,*** Annual Number 1978 p.189 and Sudhir Sen, **Reaping the Green-Revolution** 1975 p.p. 5-17.
4. See GOI, Sixth Five Year Plan (Annexure 9.2) p.140; Economic-Survey 1988-89 p. 5-14-15. For 1960-61 and 1971-72 figures see Economic Survey 1980-81 p. 77.
5. *Ibid.*
6. Misra S.K., Puri V.K. *Indian Economy: Its Development Experience* (9th ed.) (Himalaya) 1991 p. 504.
7. Thamarajakshi R, *"Agricultural Growth, Rural Development and Employment Generation"*, Economic & Political Weekly March 25, 1989.
8. Das Gupta A.K., *Agriculture and Economic Development in India*, Associated Publishing House, 1973, pp. 32-34.
9. Quoted by S.L. Shetty, *"Structural Retrogression in Indian Economy Since the Mid Sixties"* op. cit p. 191.
10. GOI, Economic Survey 1988-89 p. 5-12.
11. The Economic Times Nov. 15, 1990.
12. See, Saini GR., *Green-Revolution And The Distribution of Farm Incomes,* **Economic & Political Weekly**, March 27, 1976; Bardhan P.K., *Inequality of Farm Incomes: A study of four Districts"*, **Economic And Political Weekly,** Annual Number 1974; Usha Nagpal, *Share of Small Farm Sector In Agriculture: A Case Study of Village Palanpur in Western U.P.*, Agriculture Economic Research Centre, Delhi University, 1979; Srivastava U, Grown R.W. and Heady E.O., **Green-Revolution and Farm Income Distribution", Economic and Political Weekly,** December 25, 1971; Francine R.F. *"India's Green-Revolution-Economic Gains & Political Costs* (Bombay 1971); Westley J.R., **Agriculture and Equitable Growth: The Case of Punjab-Haryana** (Ph.D Dissertation submitted to American University-Washington DC) 1983 quoted by Misra & Puri — Indian Economy op.cit; George Blyn, *"The Green-Revolution Revisited"*, *Economic Development And Cultural Change,* Vol. 31, July 1983.

13. Bhall G.S and Chadha G.K., *"Green-Revolution and the Small Peasant — A Study of Income Distribution In Punjab Agriculture"*, **Economic And Political Weekly**, May 15, 25. 1982.

14. Bardhan P.K., *Land, Labour & Rural Poverty* — Delhi, 1984, p. 189.

15. Deepak Lal., *Trends in Real Wages in Rural India 1880-1980* In Srinivasan T.N. And Bardhan P.K., **Rural Poverty In South Asia** (Ed.) N. Delhi 1988 p.290.

16. Jose A.V., *"Agricultural Wages In India,* **"Economic & Political Weekly,** June 25, 1988.

17. Hanumantha Rao C. H. *"Technological Change and Distribution of Gaires in Indian Agriculture* 1975 p. 121.

18. As quoted by Ruddar Dutt, K.P.M. Sundaram, *Indian Economy,* (20th ed). 1982 p. 517.

19. Ashok Rudra, "Organisation of Agriculture for Rural Development. The Indian Case". In Dharam Ghai (ed.) Agrarian Systems And Rural Development (Macmillan) 1987 p. 94.

20. Dru Srivastava and Shayam Borate, *"Green-Revolution in Northern Regions. Impact of Selective Farm Machanisation on Farm Employment."*Division of Agricultural Economics I.A.R. Study (Memeograph) N. Delhi.

21. Ashok Rudra, *"Big Farmers of Punjab"*, **Economic and Political Weekly,** December 27, 1969.

22. Rao V.K.R.V.: **"New Challenges Before Indian Agriculture"** Pense Memorial Lecture April 1974.

23. Ladejinsky Wolf, *"How Green In India's Green-Revolution"*, **Economic & Political Weekly,** December 29, 1973 .A-134.

3

FARM-SIZE, PRODUCTION AND PRODUCTIVITY DEBATE

The relationship between farm-size, production and productivity is a debatable subject among the economists. The main point of discussion is the determination of the appropriate size of the farm because the size of the operating unit as in the case of industries, decides the level of income. In industry, we have an optimum size of the unit which has the lowest average cost of production per unit. In agriculture too we have a size of operational unit which, under given conditions, would yield the best result to the farmers. The advantages of large and small farms have been debated since a long time. Some economists advocate large-scale farming for efficient use of resources, a satisfactory income to the farmers and food to the consumers at reasonable rates. But some economists equally and strongly advocate small-scale farming on the ground of social justice. Poverty in agriculture is closely related with the size of farms. More than 80 per cent of farm-families live on under-sized and inadequate units. Since the income is dependent on the size of farms the dominance of small holding is mainly responsible for poor peasantry in developing countries. Thus the size of operational unit is a vital element in determining the level of output, the earning capacity of the farmers and the efficiency of a farm unit.

Farm-Size and Productivity Controversy [1]

The relationship between the farm-size and productivity is not clear among the economists. While some hold the view that there is an inverse relationship between the farm-size and productivity (productivity declines as farm-size increases) others argue that no such relationship exists. Some economists also argue that such relationship is positive. That is as farm-size increases productivity also increases. A group of economists hold the view that productivity is neural as between the different farm-sizes. Some economists adopted a mid-way. They argue that inverse relationship holds over" certain range of size" and not over "all ranges of size". Thus in relation to farm-size and productivity we have different views. The most interesting part of the debate is that all have used Farm Management Survey data and reached on different conclusions.

This debate was started by A.K. Sen by producing two papers, namely "An Aspect of Indian Agriculture" Economic Weekly (Annual Number) February 1962 and "Size of Holdings and Productivity", Economic Weekly (Annual Number) February 1964. By using Farm Management Survey data he reached on a conclusion that an inverse relationship between the size of the farms and productivity is existed in India. As the size of holding increases productivity declines. This conclusion implies that productivity is higher on small rather than on large farms.

Many other economists Deepak Mazumdar, A.M. Khusro, G.R. Saini and C.H. Hanumantha Rao also analysed the data and reached on the same conclusions. Deepak Mazumdar wrote: "The data presented by the Farm Management Surveys in India have added another example to a phenomenon observed in many parts of the underdeveloped world, viz, that in peasant agriculture, as the size of the farm decreases the output per acre increases".[2] Khusro also support the view and observed that "as farm-size (average) expands, gross output per acre declines".[3] G.R. Saini whose observation is based on the disaggregated farm management data wrote that "by and large, inverse relationship between farm-size and productivity is a confirmed phenomenon in Indian agriculture and its statistical validity is adequately established by an analysis of disaggregated data".[4] C.H. Hanumantha Rao also support this thesis. He wrote: "In all the districts studied, the percentage of cultivated to uncultivated area as well as the cultivated area cropped more than once decreased sharply with increase in the size of holdings".[5]

Sen explains the inverse relationship between farm-size and productivity in terms of low opportunity cost of family labour in a labour surplus economy and the resultant variations in the input of human labour over different size classes of farms which range from essentially family-labour based small farms to large farms employing relatively greater proportion of wage labour. He explains his view-point with the help of a diagram:

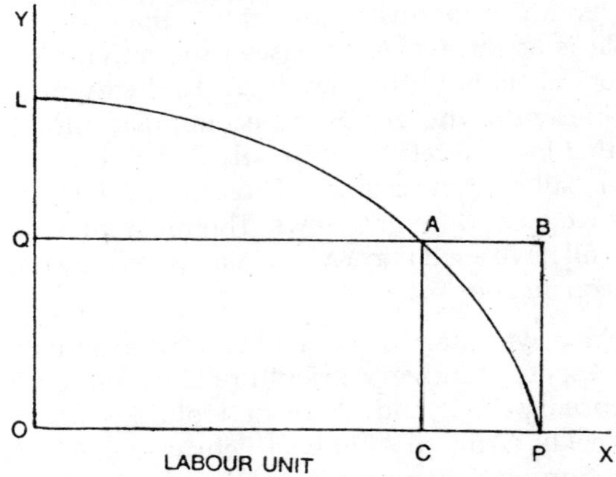

In this diagram the curve L P presents schedule of net marginal product of labour used to a given acre of land. If the cultivation is family based and further if the per acre supply of labour in the family equals or exceeds OP we can expect that OP amount of labour will be applied, provided labour has no outside opportunity of employment and again there is no significant disutility of work in the relevant range of effort. If the wage rate is O Q, a wage-based farm will restrict labour input to O C. It is that level of labour input where marginal productivity is equal to the wages paid to the labour. Hence, we find that land-labour ratio is higher on small farms as compared to large farms. The greater intensity of labour on small farms keeps their productivity higher than the large farms.

According to Khusro, Jagdish Bhagwati and Hanumantha Rao, the productivity of small farms as compared to large farms is higher because "as farm-size expands, the proportion of bad and indifferent land to total land increases, thus, in turn accounting for the decrease in per acre output and farm income.[6] Sen, Krishna Bhardwaj, Khusro, Deepak Mazumdar, Usha Rani all are agree that the need of the small farmers insist them to put their best effort to survive. The poor peasant family dependent on a small piece of land for subsistence will be forced to exert itself to the utmost or else it will be wiped out. It will also try to improve the quality of land leave fallow as little land as possible and try to cultivate as many crops as possible. Thus, small farmers make more intensive use of their inputs and provide better and more efficient management. Hanumantha Rao explains the same view-point with a different angle. He says that productivity on small farms may be higher due to the fact that large farmers give more preference to leisure as they are not faced with economic compulsion as is the case with small farmers.

Sen's explanation is based on certain assumptions. He assumes that there are no outside opportunities for family labourand its opportunity cost is zero. If, at the ruling wage rate, the outside employment opportunity exists, the family member will not extend the application of their labour beyond the point where the marginal productivity of their labour is equal to the ruling wage rate. In this context, Sen examines various possibilities. In the event of large-scale persistence of unemployment, the marginal opportunity cost of labour will be zero and the farmer will continue to employ his labour to the point where its marginal productivity is reduced to zero. But this is an extreme case. General unemployment is not found to the extend to render the marginal productivity zero. He believes that there is always some possibility of finding employment elsewhere. Hence, the marginal opportunity cost is never zero but it is always less than one. He argued that the probability of getting employment elsewhere is, in normal circumstances, less than one and hence productivity per acre on large farms will be less than the productivity on small farms. Large farms will not employ labour beyond the point where the marginal productivity is equal to wage rate. While the small farms using mostly family labour will keep on using it to a considerably more extent. In fact, they will keep on employing it to the point where marginal productivity is equal to the opportunity cost.[7]

Though Khusro is not denying with the hypothesis of inverse relationship, he does not agree with the above assumptions. He criticises Sen on the following grounds.[8]

(i) The assumption of non-existence of outside opportunities for family labour is not true.

(ii) Sen's explanation may be valid when we compare productivity in smaller farms — say a 3-acre family farm and a 10-acre wage based farm. However, we compare large wage-based farms, the argument may no longer hold. For example, let us consider a 15-acre farm and a 50-acre farm. Family-labour on both these farms is likely to be negligible and their dependence on hired labour heavy. Hence it may not be argued that output per acre on 15-acre farm is more than to 50-acre farm because it uses comparatively more family labour.

(iii) Sen also assumes homogeneity of quality between family labour and hired labour. This is not true since in Indian agriculture, a unit of family labour does more or better work than a unit of hired labour. Accordingly, the product for the former will be larger even if same quantities of labour are employed in both the cases.

(iv) The explanation is concluded in terms of diminishing product of labour alone as more and more of it is applied to a single acre of land. Small farmers can use indivisible factors say, a pair of bullocks, more intensively and obtain a large per acre output.

Deepak Mazumdar, Krishna Bhardwaj and Usha Rani support this last point. They put forward the argument that small farmers make more intensive use for their input as compared to large farmers because they are faced with compulsion of providing for themselves and their families from whatever small holdings they have. Contrary, the large farmers are not faced with any such compulsion and consequently do not use their inputs as intensively as small farmers.

Critics of Inverse-Relation Hypothesis

The above inverse-relationship hypothesis developed, explained and tested by leading economist has been vehemently opposed and criticised by Ashok Rudra, A.P. Rao, R.K. Patel, Rajvir Singh and Krishna Bhardwaj. Ashok Rudra joined the debate in 1968 with two articles entitled: "Farm-Size and Yield per Acre" and "More on Returns To Scale In Indian Agriculture" appeared in Economic and Political Weekly's Special Number July 1968 and October 1968. He argued that while such inverse relationship between farm-size and productivity may exist in certain areas, it is not a universal phenomenon and, hence, cannot be said to operate in all parts of the country. His main findings are best summed up in his own words as under: "We may emphasize that we never expressed the view that the inverse relationship was not to be observed in any circumstances in Indian agriculture, our view was that such a relationship could not be regarded as a universally valid law operating in Indian agriculture, and that there were indications in the Farm Management Survey Data themselves that in certain areas yield per acre, instead of declining with increase in size, might actually be increasing. Also, that in certain cases where an inverse relationship could be recognized to hold it might do so among the smallest size class of farmers but not among others. It was our view that in many areas, one could not possibly observe any systemic pattern of dependence between yield per acre and farm side".[9] If we compare this conclusions with the various statements and explanations given by the supporters of the inverse-relationship hypothesis. One important point clearly emerges and that is whereas Sen, Khusro, Mazumdar, Hanumantha

Rao, Saini and others indulge in generalization of the whole economy based on some regional data, Ashok Rudra seems to be more cautious and vigilant in drawing conclusions.

A.P. Rao,[10] Krishna Bhardwaj[11] and Usha Rani[12] the supporters of Ashok Rudra are also cautious in their conclusions. They also expressed their doubts about the hypothesis of inverse relationship between farm-size and productivity. A.P. Rao's study is based on disaggregated data and a logarithmic linear function is fitted to farm-level data belonging to the same village. He concludes: "Contrary to the Findings of Farm-Management Studies, according to the present study productivity remained constant over all the holding sizes in all the villages, which indicates that holding size has no effect on productivity".

Krishna Bhardwaj carried out tests on grouped data and fitted logarithmic straight lines to data pertaining to the earlier round of Farm Management Surveys. She reached to the conclusion that: (1) inverse relation while not supported invariably, is not rejected either and (2) there is no systematic and significant relation between the per acre yield (in physical unit) of individual crops and the size of holding. Usha Rani is also quite cautious and conditional in her analysis and conclude that "yield per acre remains constant over different size groups of farms".

Some studies[13] have also brought out evidence against the inverse relationship but the number of such studies are few. But the relevance of such studies is because they prove that the universality of the inverse relationship is not acceptable. The introduction of new agricultural strategy too, does not support the inverse relationship hypothesis. Rajiv Singh and R.K. Patel's study in Meerut district of U.P. conclude from their regression analysis that "in the context of new technology, there is no indication of decrease in output per hectare with an increase in farm-size and, therefore, the hypothesis of inverse relationship is rejected in the area under study". Their explanation is that as farm technology undergoes a change, large farmers take greater interest in using land more intensively with modern inputs at proper time in the wake of higher profitability offered by the new technology.

A Negotiation: The above discussion presents a confusing picture regarding the farm-size and productivity relation. The amazing part of the controversy is that from the same set of data different economists have drawn different conclusions applying different statistical techniques. However, the main rivals in the debate A.K.Sen and Ashok Rudra have attempted a synthesis of their views. Both have now come to agree that:

(a) The inverse relation may hold in certain parts of the country at certain time but not everywhere and not at all times;

(b) Even when the inverse relationship holds, it may hold in certain ranges but not in other and in most cases it is noticeable only for small size classes;

(c) The inverse relationship is more frequently confirmed than rejected but it would be a mistake to take it to be an empirical generalisation for Indian agriculture as a whole.[14]

The controversy regarding the inverse relationship between farm-size and productivity is not simply an academic discussion but is of fundamental significance from the point of view of economic policy. The farm-size and productivity raise many issues. Important one are the choice between: (i) small family-based "peasant farms"; (ii) large-hired labour-based "capitalist farms" and (iii) large farms with cooperative type of organisations. Policy implications will differ depending on whether we treat the inverse relationship as an indication of higher efficiency of small farms or regard it as reflecting conditions of distress of small farms. If we accept the former position then we would advocate that land should be transferred from larger and middle farmers to small farmer either through sales or tenancy as recommended by C.H. Hanumantha Rao or, one could argue like V.M. Dandekar that capitalist form of wage-labour organisation will lead to inefficient aggregate output and peasant family system based on family labour is more suitable. By and large it may be accepted that small farms of economic size are more efficient than large size farms. Promoting large farms would make small size farms weak in their competition against large farms and may create distress among them and may even lead to the disposal of small holdings in distress. This will certainly swell the already large army of landless labourers in this country.

FOOTNOTES AND REFERENCES

1. Some important participants in this debate are : A. K. Sen, A. M. Khusro, C. H. Hanumantha Rao, Krishna Bharadwaj, G. R. Saini, Ashok Rudra, Deepak Mazumdar and A. P. Rao. Their views spread over a number of papers have appeared in number of journals, the most important being the Economic and Political Weekly. On this issue a comprehensive bibliography has been prepared by G. R. Saini, *Farm-Size, Resource Efficiency and Income Distribution* (New Delhi 1979).
2. Deepak Mazumdar, *"On the Economics of Relative Efficiency of Small Farmers"*, **Economic Weekly**, (Special Number) 1963.
3. Khusro A.M., *"Economics of Land Reforms and Farm-Size in India"*, McMillan (India) 1973, 106.

4. Saini G. R., *"Farm-size, Resource use, Efficiency and Income Distribution"*. Allied, New Delhi 1979. This idea had been explained earlier in his articles : Farm-size, Productivity and Return to Scale. **Economic Weekly,** June 28, 1969; *"Holding size, Productivity and Some Related Aspects of Indian Agriculture"*. **Economic and Political Weekly**, June 26, 1971.
5. Hanumantha Rao C. H., *"Alternative Explanations of the Inverse Relationship between Farm-size and output per acre in India"*, **Indian Economic Review**; Vol. I. October, 1966.
6. Khusro A.M., *"Returns to Scale in Indian Agriculture"*, In A.M. Khusro (Ed.) Readings in Agricultural Economics — Calcutta 1968. pp. 140-41.
7. Sen A.K., *"Size of Holdings and Productivity"*, The Economic Weekly, Feb. 16, 1964 pp. 223-26.
8. Khusro A.M., *"Returns to Scale in Indian Agriculture"*, *Op. Cit.* pp. 139-40.
9. Ashok Rudra, **Indian Agriculture Economics,** New Delhi 1982 pp. 150-151.
10. Rao A.P., *Size of Holding and Productivity*, **Economic and Political Weekly**, Nov. 11, 1967.
11. Krishna Bhardwaj, *"Notes on Farm-Size and Productivity"*, **Economic and Political Weekly,** March 30, 1974.
12. Usha Rani, *'Size of Farm and Productivity"*, *Economic and Political Weekly,* June 26. 1971.
13. See Rajiv Singh & R. K. Patel : *"Return to Scale, Farm-Size and Productivity in Meerut District,* **Indian Journal of Agricultural Economics,** Vol. XXVIII - April-June 1973.
14. Ashok Rudra and A. K. Sen, *"Farm-Size and Labour Use : Analysis and Economic & Political Weekly,* Annual Number, February 1980.

4

LAND REFORMS: SOME IMPORTANT DIMENSIONS

Among all the issues the modern world is confronted with, none are more important than those arise out of man's relations with the natural resources and here again, with land, in particular. For ages, the use and the holding of land has been of greatest importance for every economic system. Land has always been given the highest esteem and importance and with rising pressure of population on land, its supply remaining constant, it will continue to be a precious and scarce commodity in the rural environment.

Concept & Scope: The agrarian system under which cultivators work is of key importance in determining the pace of agricultural development. Agrarian structure which refers to the manner in which man-land relations and governed covers the way in which land is held and cultivated and the rights and privileges enjoyed by the different categories of people who have access to land. Hence, the pattern of ownership of land has to be just and rational to secure growth with social justice. And the tenure system should be such which could ensure to the cultivator fair regard for his efforts, promote individual virtues of self-help, self-reliance, thrift and independence and at the same time could develop the social virtues of tolerance, public spiritedness, cooperation and mutual working for common good.[1]

Land reform programme is an integrated programme of measures designed to eliminate obstacles to economic and social development arising out of defects in the existing agrarian structure. The main objective of such land reform measures is to remove the impediments to agricultural developments as arise from the agrarian structure and to eliminate exploitation and social injustice within the agrarian system so as to ensure equality of tenurial status and opportunity to all. In other words land reform measures make the property relations favourable to the tillers of the soil and raise the size of the units of cultivation to make them operationally viable. Hence these measures encompass two type of structural changes. One is related to agrarian relations and the other to the size of the unit of cultivation.

The agrarian structure in most developing countries is neither favourable to the status of the farmer nor it suits to the investment. In an overwhelming number of cases, the size of the unit of cultivation is too below the minimum required for progressive agriculture. The redistribution of the ownership from view point of social justice and reorganisation of operational holdings from the view point of optimum utilisation of land are needed. The purpose is two fold: (a) to remove terms and conditions of land ownerships of poor peasantry class so that their exploitation could be stopped; and (b) to make more rational use of scarce land resource with a view to make it most economical for cultivations.

These structural changes in the agrarian system can occur in two ways: (1) as a result of direct intervention in the system and (ii) as a result of the spontaneous operation of socio-economic processes; changes occur directly.

Changes brought about in the agrarian system through direct intervention are characterised as land-reforms. Zamindari abolition, consolidation of holdings, determination of rent and ownership, fixation of ceilings of the holdings are the example of such direct intervention of the Government through legislation. Some direct action may also be taken by the non-Government agencies." "Bhoodan" and "Gram-Dan" movement by Acharya Vinoba Bhave is an example of non-Government direct action. Sometimes such action is also taken by the people themselves. Naxalites movement is an example of such direct action taken by the public. Thus direct changes may be occurred either by the Government agencies through legislation or by the non-Government agencies through persuasion or by the public itself through force. These may be characterised land-reform from the "above", land-reform by persuasion and land-reform from the "below" (by public revolution).[2]

As against these direct intervention, changes in agrarian structure may also occur indirectly. These changes occur "in response to spontaneous operation of socio-economic process". For example with the introduction of new agricultural strategy, various socio-economic changes may occur in agrarian life. A capitalist life of farming may emerge and the cultivator may become wage-labourer hired by the capitalist landlord. This change is called "induced" change which emerges out of the changed situation.

To sum up, the concept of land reform includes changes in the agrarian structure that are deliberate and are associated with the direct intervention of the Government or non-Government agencies. These changes are basically concerned with the agrarian relations and the size of the cultivation. These reforms have been considered as "standard prescription" to remove some "specific barrier" for agricultural development and to "create a new climate" for its expansion and growth. These actions are generally called as "surgical measures" to remove an obstacle. But actually they are not "surgical measures". Instead, they are "preventive medicine".[3]

Components of Land-Reforms: The concept of land-reform has the following components :

(i) Abolition of intermediaries.

(ii) Tenancy reforms which include (a) regulation of rent; (b) security of tenure for tenants, and (c) conferment of ownership on them.

(iii) Ceiling on land holdings.

(iv) Consolidation of holdings and prevention of sub-division and fragmentation, and

(v) Organisation of cooperative farms.

These components fulfil two objectives: (a) greater equality; and (b) efficiency of resource use. Greater equality may be achieved: (i) through equity among land holding which implies reducing income disparities between rich and poor—marginal farmers by redistributing the land from the former to the latter farmers; and (ii) through improving equity between farmers as a whole whatever their tenure status may be. Efficiency of resource use objective is debatable. The redistribution of land on efficiency criteria can only be built if the marginal returns over inputs vary over different sizes of holding. Many studies prove that a smaller average size of holdings and a lower concentration of land ownership were associated with an increase in output per hectare.

The measures which are taken under the garb of land reforms may have many facets. Firstly the most obvious change is one in the status of the various classes of the rural population in respect of land. Secondly a change may also occur in the general pattern of distribution of land in farming units. This change would mean redistribution of land by breaking down large centrally operated estates into a number of smaller farms. Thirdly, the measures may improve the condition of life of the rural people without changing the status of the farmer or existing distribution of land. Measures intended to reform existing condition of tenancy — increasing the security of tenant–cultivator and measures which limit or prevent the alienation of agricultural land to non-agriculturist, changes in law of inheritance to prevent undue sub-division and fragmentation — come under this category.

Economics of Land-Reforms

Land, the first requisite of agricultural production, is a scarce factor because its supply is limited and fixed and cannot be increased with rising demand. In India nearly 3 per cent has been added to gross sown area in 1970's. But with population growing at the rate of 2.2 per cent per annum, per capita real income by about 12.5 per cent and per capita income by a far greater 99.5 per cent in a decade, the demand for land is bound to rise faster than its supply.

Rising rent is not burdensome if the productivity per hectare also increases pari-passu. But in most of the Third World Countries including India productivity has not kept pace with time and as a result rent as a percentage of value of gross produce has been increasing and is reported to have reached levels as high as one half to two third of the value of produce, sufficient to throw the most well organised enterprises in the world out of business. Khusro has depicted the problem in the following diagram.

Diagram shows that with the passing of time, the successive supply curve of land St_1, St_2 and St_3 shift right wards or down wards to some extent but the successive demand curve Dt_1, Dt_2 and Dt_3 right word or upward at a faster rate. As a result rent increases from R_1 to R_2 and R_3. At the highest rent R_3 most of the small tenants cannot hope to lease in any land while others lease in less than before. High-rent, thus, has tendency to reduce the size and of course in many cases below the minimum and commercially feasible size.

The aggregate macro demand curve for land Dt_3 shown on the right hand side of the break in X axis is made up of various individual demand curves shown on the left-hand side of the break. These micro-demand curves represent demand for land-use by numerous small and low-income tenants (ds) and some large or high-income tenants (di). At the time t_2 when micro demand for land is Dt_2 and rent R_2 would have

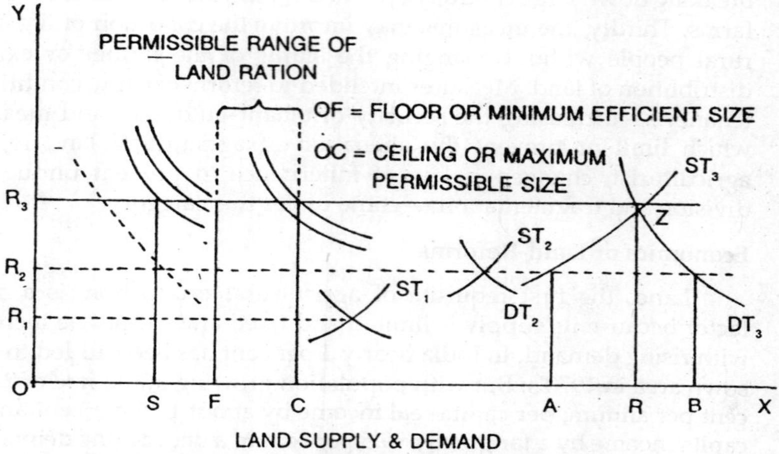

Fig. 4.1 Land Supply and Demand

been a minimum economical feasible holdings. But at time t_3 when micro-demand for land has risen to Dt_3 and rent to R_3 the small tenant's demand curve will be dt_3. At this prevailing rent he can only afford to lease-in OS land which is of-course less than economically feasible holding OF. The main implication of such a high increase in rent would be that small tenants would turn wage labourers and give rise to a tendency towards the proletarianization of the peasantry.

In order to save this situation if rents are controlled by Government's intervention the problem will not be solved. The equilibrium between demand & supply may not be established. Because, if supply of land could be quickly augmented and rent is controlled by some legislation, it would widened the supply and demand gap. Actually the situation will further be aggravated. In diagram if equilibrium rent is OR_3 demand and supply both are equal to OE hectares. But if rent is controlled at OR_2 then at this rent, supply would shrink to OA while demand increases to OB. A B would be the land hunger or unsatisfied demand. Hence, more price (rent) control will not solve the problems. Along with rent control, the most important is to ration out the use of agricultural land. Land reforms policy, thus, attempts to introduce price control (rent control) and ration the use as well as ownership of land through tenancy and ceiling measures.

With this type of land reforms the tenants could acquire, firstly, and economically feasible minimum of land with no fear of eviction and secondly they have to pay controlled rent to the land-owner. On macro-side of the diagram, rent will be reduced to OR_2 and it will prevent the withdrawal of land by land-owners and the reduction of aggregate supply in the lease market to OA. It will also prevent the increase in demand from OE to OB by putting a ceiling on land.

On the micro-side, if a small tenant's holding at the high rent OR^3 had fallen to OS hectares which is less than a sensible minimum OF, the land reform will provide: (i) a permanent right on OS to the tenants, (ii) a check on further decline in the size of his holding, (iii) rent will be reduced from OR_3 per hectare to OR_2 per hectare and (iv) he can purchase away some land from the land-lord — some acreage — say SF at less than the market price. This would, thus, guarantee the tenants an economically feasible minimum of land. This may be achieved if a ceiling is fixed on large holdings at OC.[5]

Land Reforms and Agricultural Productivity

Since, land reforms provide greater incentive to producers and help in more efficient farm management, it is, sometimes, asserted that land reforms and agricultural productivity and output both are directly related. If agricultural output has to be increased by intensive means, land must belong to the cultivators itself. With the help of the following diagram Khusro has explained the relationship between land reforms and agricultural productivity.

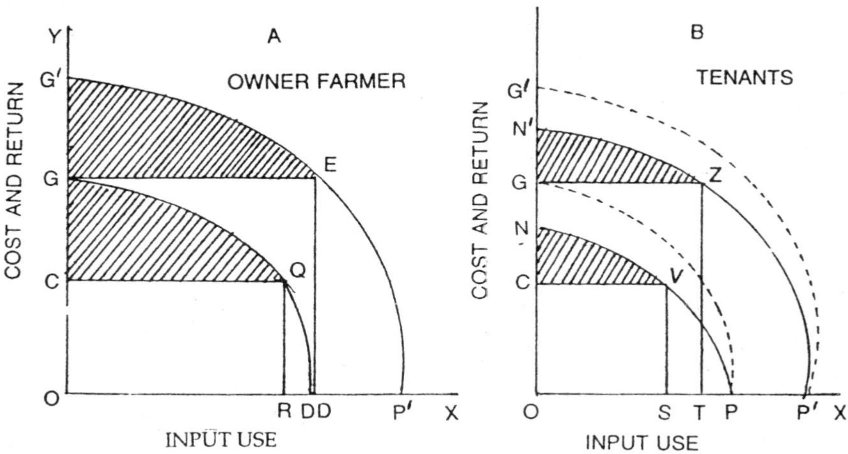

Fig. 4.2

We have two diagrams. Diagram 'A' shows owner farmer farm and 'B' as tenant-farmer farm. Both have equal acres of land. Inputs are assumed to be combined in fixed proportions in a package of practices with costs OC per unit of package-input. As the farmers apply more and more inputs along with X-axis, marginal gross product would fall along with GP curve owing to fixed factor land. The owner farmer would stop using more inputs at DR when the marginal productivity is equal to marginal cost of input. His total cost would be OC QR and total profit CGQ.

Tenant-farmer, (Fig. B) on the other hand, has similar cost and gross product situation but has to pay his landlord rent as a fixed percentage to produce. Applying the principle of equating marginal net produce to marginal cost, his total cost would be OCVS and his profit net of rent CNV.

Let us know suppose that both these farmers are offered a package programme for better inputs and high production. Due to this application of better inputs, cost of production would rise from OC to OG. The marginal gross product curve would also shift from GP to G' P'. The owner farmer will now use OD units of inputs, his total cost would be OGED and his profit is GG' E which is greater than the previous profit. This greater profit will induce him to go ahead with the new agricultural techniques.

Tenant-farmer's gross product, on the other hand, will also rise. This curve will rise to OG' P', but net of rent would only be ON' P'. To maximise his returns, he will use OT units of inputs where his marginal net product equals marginal cost. After the introduction of new package of agricultural inputs his profit would be GN'Z which is lower than his previous profit CNV. Thus, tenant farmer has no incentive to go in for new package of agricultural practices. Tenancy-reforms hence, plays an important role in improving productivity of agriculture.[6]

Land Reforms and Agricultural Development: The world-wide emphasis on the effective implementation of land reform measures is based upon the insights and belief that the tenurial systems are blocking agricultural development in developing countries. In these countries, the overwhelming majority of the people live by agriculture and the essential condition of economic growth and the improvements of the standard of living of the masses rest on raising agricultural productivity. It is believed that so long the system of tenant farming prevails no improvement could be expected in agricultural output. The negative effects of tenancy system on agricultural development are viewed in the following manner.

(i) Tenancy system generates an absentee landlordism in the system which do not help in increasing agricultural productivity. When the landlord does not live in his estate and is merely extracting the rents and spending the amount in city, their existence has no economic justification.

(ii) Insecurity of tenure is another important deterrent to any kind of long-term improvement by the tenant, particularly to investment in immobile equipment and land improvement such as irrigation etc. This is true when the landlord has an unqualified right to enhance the rent and evict the tenant. The high risk of increasing rent and eviction induce the tenant to take little interest in maintaining the fertility of the soil by good manuring or otherwise. Contrary, he would like to extract from the land all that he can before he is compelled to leave the land. Such continuous neglect of land may substantially reduce the agricultural productivity and production.

(iii) The impact of high rent and low-productivity of land on farmer is that they are necessarily poor. Neither they save enough to afford any improvement nor are able to borrow in order to carry out an improvement in the land. This can be happened only when the return is both certain and profitable by a wide margin.

(iv) Tenants society is traditional and rarely possess an entrepreneurial spirit. Even where the landlord provides nothing but land, he is likely to interfere with the management of his farm and his interference may sometimes work against technological progress.

These potential defects of tenancy system have resulted in two-fold adverse effects : (i) from economic point-of-view the system either fail to induce the full use of land or tend to its exploitation, and (ii) from the social and political point-of-view it creates instability since it restrict both economic and individual liberty of tenant farmers.[7] The similar opinion has been expressed in ECAFE paper. It said that "in a number of countries of the region, defective land tenure system stultify the farmer's initiative for the improvement of production and the impact of economic plan".[8]

Land reform measures introduced by the Governments are to change the property relations in agriculture and help in fostering the economic development in many ways. These measures seek to change the owner-tenant relationship in favour of tenants. Firstly, they try to regulate the tenure of lease so that tenant could feel secure and be motivated to contribute his own or borrowed capital and his family labour towards the improvement of land. It also helps the tenant to keep a major portion of produce for himself. The ultimate objective is to abolish tenancy altogether by enabling tenants, on easy terms, to become the owner of land themselves.

An ideal land reform measures are an integrated programme of reforms designed to eliminate obstacles to economic and social development arising out of defects in the agrarian structure. This becomes an important measure to increase agricultural production and productivity. A UNO report explains the relationship between agrarian reforms and agricultural development in the following manner.[9]

Land Reforms and Agricultural Production: Agricultural production can be increased on the basis of two types of incentives provides to farmers. First, a farmer should be encouraged to work hard and could pay better attention towards supervision. And secondly, he should be encouraged to make use of resources necessary for efficient agriculture. These incentives could be guaranteed to the farmer if agrarian structure is so change that he is made convinced of getting full benefits from his labour and investment. Abolition of intermediaries, tenancy reforms, consolidation of holding, determination of ceiling, redistribution of land and introduction of cooperative farmings are such sources of incentives that would promote a feeling of self-reliance and progressive living on the part of the individual. The major impact of such measures is on agricultural productivity and output as they provide greater incentive to operators and to more efficient farm management.

Land Reforms and Employment: In a defective agrarian structure where an acute misallocation of land labour resources exists, larger-scale unemployment and under-employment of labour also exists. Land reform measures not simply alter the distribution of wealth and income to improve technological level of agricultural sector or to release productive energies, but also with specific reference to rural employment problems. These reforms may increase employment by effecting a change in the size of farm operating units. Some empirical evidence is available to show that output per acre increase as size of farms diminishes and that the small farms have greater potential for labour absorption than large farms. Data for India, Chile, Taiwan, Peru and Mexico prove it well.[11] Land reforms can also enhance the capacity of agriculture to absorb more labourers as it give more tenure security and the incentive resulting in the intensification of cultivation practices. Japan is an example where more labour is employed in agriculture by intensive land use practices including double and triple cropping until the industrial sector was large enough to relieve the pressure on land.[12]

Impact on Purchasing Power: Successful land reform measures often achieve a considerable improvement of the cultivator's economic position through the combined impact of: (1) redistributing the existing gross returns of agriculture to the benefits of cultivator; and (2) increasing gross returns of agriculture through increased production. Either method should have the result of increasing the purchasing power of cultivator. But while increased farm incomes due to greater production create additional purchasing power, increased incomes through merely redistribution of the agricultural income only transfer potential purchasing power from one hand to another. Since propensity to consume among poor cultivators is high, an increase in the purchasing power of cultivator will be of great benefit to develop secondary and tertiary industries.

So far as expenditure on agricultural equipments are concerned, it is said that the small farmers may lack the capacity to buy and to use the more expensive and heavy machines. Thus, the breaking up of large estates may cause a diminution in demand for tractors and other heavy power driven machines, but it will also stimulate the demand for hand tools and animal drawn machines. A well conceived and efficiently applied agrarian reform programme which increases the real income of the farmers will help in speedy industrial development.

Impact on Savings and Investment: The tenurial conditions influence the volume of capital available for productive investment. Agrarian reforms generally aim at redistribution of income through either redistributing the land by changing tenant farmers into owner cultivators or by regulating the rents. Redistribution of income not only transfers the income but also the saving capacity. An adequate and organised tenure system provides security of tenure and of investments which in turn increases the efficiency of cultivator and hence saving and investment. In the initial stages saving may go down considerably due to higher propensity to consume among poor farmers, but in the long run, however, due to higher agricultural productivity and output, higher incomes of tenants will make possible larger savings and capital formation. Thus, we find that the relationship between land reforms and investment, savings and capital formation may not be direct, yet potentials of land reforms for capital formation in agricultural sector is great if they are properly planned and executed.

In view of the above few important dimensions of the impact of land reforms on economic development it may be concluded that these measures contribute significantly to the economic development of a country. However, it is not easy to demonstrate from recent quantitative information how great a contribution land reform has made to economic development. Distribution of land more equitably is not enough. Small holdings cultivated by new owners without adequate resources and technical skill create new obstacles. Hence, land reforms in itself is not a solution. Instead such programme should be followed by a series of institutional and technical reforms to make agriculture more efficient and productive. Provision of credit and capital for infrastructural facilities, technical guidance and training, adequate supplies of inputs will help to make land reform measures more effective. Further more, land reforms as an aid to agricultural development have some other limitations as well. For instance no amount of land reforms may remove the obstacles of unfavourable soil and climatic conditions. These obstacles can be overcome only by technical improvements, research, training and education. Similarly, land reform measures will not help to solve the problem of pressure of population on land and of economic defects such as lack of organised markets for agricultural products or satisfactory supplies of agricultural inputs. These problems can be solved by diversification of the economy as a whole in the course of over all economic development. Thus, land reform measures as discussed above are merely a part of package programme for rural development. Agricultural production and productivity, level of income and the standard of living of the rural masses and their employment will certainly be affected if such measures are properly executed. But they show their own limitations. There are various other institutional and technical factors which do not come under the preview of land reform measures, but they are equally important for improving agricultural condition.

Land Reforms During Plans: In India land reforms measures were introduced in 1952 during the First Plan period. The national land policy was enunciated during this plan which declared that "the future of land ownership and cultivation was a fundamental issue of national development". The land-laws aimed at bringing the peasant and State into direct contact. In the areas where Zamindari system was prevailed, the new laws provided for abolition of the intermediaries. In areas where Royotwari system was functioning, the laws aimed at providing protection to the tenants, actual tiller of the land.

Laws were legislated to abolish intermediaries and to regulate the distribution of land. Emphasis was laid on making the tiller the real owner of land in order to provide incentive to farmers to modernise agriculture and raise agricultural productivity. The following principal measures of land reforms have been implemented in fulfillment of this objectives.

(i) Abolition of intermediaries.

(ii) Provision of security to tenants with the ultimate objectives of conferring ownership rights on them.

(iii) Imposition of land ceiling on agricultural holdings and distribution of surplus land to landless agricultural workers as well as small land holders;

(iv) Preparation and maintenance of land records; and

(v) Consolidation of agricultural land holdings.

The second and the Third Five Year Plan's main objective in regards to land reforms were to remove such impediments to agricultural production as arose from the agrarian structure and to create conditions for evolving an agrarian economy with high level of efficiency and productivity. The Fourth Plan reviewed the existing land reforms and acknowledged that there were many gaps between objectives and legislations and between the laws and their implementation. The Plan noted that there had been considerable leasing out of land and in view of the insecurity of the informal tenancies neither the tenants and share croppers nor the land owners were willing to invest in land to improve production. The Plan, therefore, recommended that: (i) all tenancies be declared non-resumable; (ii) resumption cases be finalised early; (iii) voluntary surrenders be regulated; (iv) complete security of the tenants in their homestead lands be assumed; (v) legislation for security of tenants and sub-tenants be properly implemented and (vi) penalties for wrongful eviction be provided in law.[13]

In 1970 a Central Land Reforms Committee was constituted to consider all aspect of the question relating to ceiling on holdings. The recommendation of the committee were considered in Chief Minister's conference on ceiling on agricultural holdings held in July 1972. By consensus the policy on ceiling was formulated and national guidelines were thereafter laid down which are still effective.

The Draft Fifth Five Year Plan analysed the situation and concluded that "the laws for the abolition of intermediaries have been implemented fairly efficiently which in the field of tenancy reforms and ceilings on holdings, legislation has fallen short of desired objectives and the implementation of enacted laws has been inadequate." The Plan, therefore, recommended certain immediate steps. These included: (i) speedy and effective implementation of measures recommendation in the earlier plans within a firm time-bound programme; (ii) prompt enactment and implementation of ceiling provisions by the States as recommended in the Chief Minister's Conference to bring about uniformity; (iii) redesigning the programme of consolidation of holding which should be made effective after ensuring security of tenure; (iv) up-dating records of tenancies and their maintenance; (v) gearing up of the administrative machinery and making beneficiaries familiar with the provision of laws. The Plan has also made certain policy recommendation with respect to personal cultivation, leasing out, distribution of surplus land, consolidation of lands of the new allottees into compact blocks and jurisdiction of laws in the matter of implementation of land reforms measures.[14]

The Sixth Plan noticed that more equitable distribution of land through land reforms measures has not taken place because the will to implement this policy has been sadly lacking. The Plan, therefore, recommended that the ceiling legislation should need to be enforced more vigorously so that the distribution of surplus land could be completed during the five year period. The Plan also emphasised the importance of tenancy reform. It declares that "land should belong to the tiller and except for categories subject to disabilities, occupancy rights should be conferred on tenants and share croppers. As the first step, the indefinite right of resumption, wherever it exist, should be extinguished. At the same time, steps should be taken to record the interests of tenants and share-croppers in the land records. Without this, the protection available under the tenancy laws will not accrue". For better implementation of reform measures plan suggested the setting up of village committee.[15]

Seventh Plan treated land-reforms measures as an intrinsic part of the anti-poverty strategy. In those States where laws have not been enacted for the right of tenants and regulation of rent, the States will be asked to take appropriate steps to enact such laws during the plan-period. In order to expedite the process quick survey be organised for recording and registration of tenants with maximum involvement of the local community and institution.[16]

Some Controversial Issues : Among all the land reform measures, the most controversial one has been ceiling on holdings. Abolition of intermediaries has been welcomed by everybody, except the intermediaries themselves. Security of tenure to the tenant too, did not face any significant opposition on social and economic grounds. Ceiling on holding of course, has been a subject matter of heated discussions.

Arguments in Favour of Ceiling:[17] Ceiling on holding is favoured on the ground that small farms are efficiently managed than the large farms. The reason behind this argument is that agriculture needs effective supervision by the farmer and even require "On the spot" decisions in many cases. This is possible only when the size of the farms is small.

Employment argument is another strong point which goes in favour of ceiling on holdings. It has been pointed out that small farms are more labour-oriented. This is because of two reasons. Firstly, on small farms the use of machines is generally limited. And secondly, farmers generally use the labour of his own family. He employs outside labour only when the family labour is in short supply such family labour is treated as free labour and it is used upto the point where its marginal productivity is equal to zero. The use of hired labour, on the other hand, is stopped as soon as its marginal productivity becomes equal to its wage. The bigger farmers who depends upon hired labour will thus employ relatively less labour. Greater use of more labour on small farms with maximum use of their efficiency will also lead to more productivity per hectare on such farms than the bigger farms.

It is also argued that ceiling on holdings will also bring about a better distribution of income among the majority of people. Ceiling on land holding is the way to improve the income distribution by redistributing the source of income themselves. It will also encourage self-cultivation and discourage absentee landlordism.

It is also pointed out that ceiling on holdings will help in the formation of cooperative farming societies. The new class of small owners may be persuaded and even compelled to form cooperative farming societies.

Arguments Against the Ceiling: Various strong points put forth against the ceiling. Firstly, the economies of scale cannot be achieved on small farms. Large farms enjoy such scale like marketing, financial and managerial economies. Large farmer can not only save from their own income but also get financial assistance from the outside on more favourable terms. Similarly, they also enjoy the lowered marketing costs of produce and avoid the exploitation by the marketing functionaries. Various development activities like digging a well, installing a tube well, drainage, fencing etc. are not remunerative on small farms. Such activities are suitable to only large farms. Even some improved crop practices like crop rotation etc. cannot be adopted on small farms. Thus, small farms are not conductive to agricultural development.

Secondly, it has been pointed out that marketable surplus will go down if the large farm are divided into small farms. Domestic requirements for various crops are met out of the production on the farms. It is the surplus that is marketed. If a large farm is split into small farms this would imply that more families asserting a prior claim on the amount produced and as a result the level of marketed surplus will go down. It is also possible that the families which acquire ownership rights on land, may increase their consumption of agricultural products after such a change. Here again the surplus available for the market will obviously go down.

Thirdly, it has been argued that a considerable portion of large farms is engaged in the production of industrial raw materials like cotton, sugarcane, oilseed etc. When these farms are divided into small farms, major portion will be devoted to produce foodgrains to meet domestic requirement. This will be an indication of shift of cropping pattern against industrial raw materials, which would mean an adverse effect on the growth of industrial sector.

Fourthly, it is also pointed out that small farms are, generally, off the market. As such the usual market forces of demand and supply have no effect on the resource utilisation on such farms.

Some Controversies at the Empirical Level

The above argument far and against the ceiling on holdings can be put forth by any academician irrespective of country where such change was proposed. However, some other arguments are related with the situation prevailing in India.

In India the unjust concentration of land in different hand has been made the basis for ceiling. The data provided by the National Sample Survey (8th round) and the figures supplied by the census of holdings are the two main sources of the information. According to NSS report 6 per cent of population held 40 per cent of the land and 3/4th of the population held 16 per cent of the land of these 1/4th had no land at all. Again 53 per cent of the population had farms less than five acres in area. N.K. Kurian provide more detailed information about the operational holdings and area operated by size classes.

The table shows that the average size of holding (Col. 7) is very small in India. It was merely 1.7 hectares in 1985-86. If we regard holding of size less than a hectare as uneconomic then it would be clear from Col. 4 of the table that as much as 58.1 per cent of holdings have to be categorised as uneconomic-concentration of holdings in a few hands is not only unjust from social and economic point of view but also can have political repercussions. A rising tide of landless people with highly disparate ownership pattern can lead to a political explosion.

There are some other views which goes against ceiling in the existing Indian agricultural conditions. First Five Year Plan was quoted which said, "If it were the sole object of policy to reduce the holdings of the large owners with a view to providing for the landless or for

Number of Operational Holdings and Area Operated by Size-Classes — All India (1985-86)

Category	*Size of Holding (Hectares)*	*No. of Holding*	*%*	*Total area operated (Million Hectares)*	*%*	*Average area operated per holding (Hectares)*
(1)	(2)	(3)	(4)	(5)	(6)	(7)
1. Marginal	0 - 1.0	56.8	58.1	21.6	13.2	0.4
2. Small	1.0 - 2.0	17.9	18.3	25.5	15.6	1.4
3. Semi-medium	2.0 - 4.0	13.3	13.6	36.6	22.3	2.8
4. Medium	4.0 - 10	7.9	8.1	47.0	28.7	5.9
5. Large	10 and above	1.9	2.0	33.2	20.2	17.2
Total		97.8	100	163.9	100	1.7

Source: Kurian N.K., "Employment Potential in Rural India", **Economic and Political Weekly** Dec. 1990 Table 1, 2 and 3 p. A-179.

increasing the farms of those who have uneconomic fragments, the facts at present available suggested that these aims are not likely to achieve any substantial measure of success". According Mahalanobis' estimate if ceiling was placed at twenty acres per family, then every landless family would be able to get only two acres of land. It was also argued that in a developing economy it was unjust to put a ceiling on the prosperity of people in the agricultural sector while leaving non-agricultural sector unaffected.

Another view-point has been expressed by S. Lal Singh in relation to size-holding. He says "since, there is hardly any other occupation except farming in rural areas..., it means that no one and not even the highest family in the rural areas comprising 85 per cent of the main population under normal conditions should aspire to possess landed property worth more than Rs. 20,000 to Rs. 30,000... and an income Rs. 36 1/2 to Rs. 54 1/2 per month per person (inclusive of their personal labour) with which to meet all wardly expenses so that the highest agricultural family is to be brought to the level of a low grade Government official or that of a small shopkeeper, if not a mere peddler or hawker... as members of their families jointly can expect to earn ten rupees or so per day. There is nothing to prevent a man in the urban areas owning properties, worth crores and earning lakhs"[18]. This argument, however is not accepted because ceiling is concerned with the land area and not with the income. If the land owner worked hard and produced more, the Government will not take away his surplus income. But the income is taxed in the urban areas.

Implementation of Land-Reforms in India: A Critical Evaluation

Land reform legislations in India can be broadly divided into two phases. The first phase was during fifties and the second one was during seventies. During the first phase the legislation mainly covers the provisions regarding abolition of intermediaries, security of tenures, ceiling on holdings and the grant of ownership of land to tenants and other landless workers. During seventies, the legislation covered mainly the ceiling on holdings. In various States, lower ceilings were fixed according to the directive of the Fifth Year Plan.

As a result of these measures, 17.3 crores acres of land were acquired from the intermediaries and till April 1988, about 29.3 lakh hectares had been declared as surplus land which was available for the allotment to landless workers. Out of the available surplus land about 8.5 lakh hectares had been allotted. Under the tenancy reforms, sixty-seven lakh tenants has been granted ownership rights in respect of 56 lakh hectares of land by April 1988. These estimates do not reflect how much land is still in the illegal possession of the intermediaries or in other words how much land has been illegally saved from being declared as a surplus. Hence, there is an ample reason to believe that the land reform laws have, by and large, been evaded. Achievement in the field are much less than what has been expected and indicated on papers.[19] Many reasons were responsible for the poor implementation of these reforms. These may be classified into following categories.

(i) Loopholes in the land reform legislation.

(ii) Strong vested interests — opposition of the land owner.

(iii) Lack of social consciousness among the beneficiaries.

(iv) Inefficiency and partiality of the administrative machinery.

(v) Lack of political will.

Land reforms in India were started with great enthusiasm, but soon the vitality of this enthusiasm was lost. No doubt, land reforms were conceived broadly in a proper perspective, but due to severe loopholes, they have brought little to the rural people. M.L. Dantwala has rightly observed: "by and large land reforms in India enacted so far and those contemplated in the near future... are in the right direction; and yet due to the lack of implementation the actual results are far from satisfactory".[20] Mahalanobis Committee after making a statistical analysis of NSS data came to the conclusion that "in general our finding is that both ownership and operational holdings are very concentrated. Also, there is no appreciable reduction in inequality between 1953-54 and 1959-60, in spite of the fact that a good deal of land reform measures had been enacted during the period".[21]

The basic purpose of the ceiling legislation was to ration out the most scarce yet the basic asset land for the benefit of those who are the real cultivators such as landless labourers, share-croppers or small holders. This is possible only when a limit on the possession of land is imposed on big land holders. But the legislation shows various loopholes. And as a result evasion is possible even within a legal provisions. First, the range of ceiling has been kept too large. In Andhra Pradesh this range was 27 to 324 acres, in Rajasthan from 27 to 216 acres, in Maharashtra from 20-80 acres, in Punjab 27 to 100 acres, in Karnataka 27 to 216 acres and in Gujarat it was 27 to 100 acres.[22] Due to this wide range very little surplus land could be acquired after the imposition of ceiling. Although the Fifth, Sixth and Seventh Five Year Plans, as has been explained earlier, realise some weaknesses of ceiling legislation and recommend some effective measures accordingly, the ineffectiveness of the legislation still persists.

Second, the definition of "family" on which ceiling has been imposed is also not clear. The definition of family include husband, wife and three minor children. For instance, if a ceiling of 15 acres has been provided for a family having two major children along with two minor children, then the total land that can be held by this family will be 45 acres. That is 15 acres for the family with three minor children and 15 acres for each major children. This is unjust. A more justified way is to treat major children as the part of the family and provide an additional 3 acres land to each major child, subject to maximum of twice the ceiling. Here this family should have 21 acres of land (15 acres plus 6 acres) instead of 45 acres.[23]

Third, ceiling legislation also provides a number of exemptions. For example sugarcane farms, orchards, grazing land, land for charitable and religious trusts and cattle breeding etc. has been exempted from this law. These concessions were used by the vested landlord interests to evade ceilings on holdings.

Like ceiling legislation, tenancy legislation for the security of tenure, its fixation and condition also shows various loopholes. The implementation of such laws without bringing about proper redistribution of ownership of land will provide no solution of the problem. Since tenancy legislation is not comprehensive it failed to grasp the inter-dependence of fixation of ceiling on rents and security of occupancy rights. Myrdal has rightly pointed out that "in the absence of limits on rents, all rules about security of tenure can be nullified; the landlord can simply raise the rent beyond the tenants capacity to pay and then legally evict him for non-payment. By the same token, legislation on maximum rentals is meaningless if not buttressed by security of tenancy".[24] Furthermore, legislation aimed to provide security to a majority of tenants and left out the majority of sharecroppers who presented the more vulnerable section of the Indian peasantry.

Lack of uniformity in the execution policies of land reform measures is another defect. In the matter of regulation of rent, for instance, the variation exists between 20 to 50 per cent of the gross produce. In some States there is no provision for bringing the farmers into direct contact with the States or for an optional ownership right of purchase except in respect of surplus land vesting in Government. A report of the survey of Tanjore district observed that "Tanjore... is a district with one of the nation's worst land tenure systems... some 20 per cent of the tenant held oral leases which deprives them of any legally enforceable tenurial status. Although the tenure system prescribes that the owner shall not be entitled to more than 40 per cent of the produce as rent... that the landowner often appropriates 50 to 60 per cent of the crop or more".[25]

We have discussed the various measures of land reforms introduced in India and have also pointed out the reasons for its poor implementation. The loopholes prevail in the legislation shows how the instrument of implementing land reforms have turned out to be an instrument of subverting land-reforms. The relations between politicians, administrators and large land owner have brought the rich peasant power into the limelight. This power dominates State Government, regional and local administrators and serve as the principal instrument of land grabbing and as a strong impediment in the implementation of land reforms.[26] The report of the Task Force on Agrarian Relations released by the Planning Commission and headed by the P.S. Appu has rightly pointed out that the lack of political will, absence of pressure from below because the poor peasants and agricultural workers are passive, unorganised and articulate, lukewarm and often apathetic attitude of the bureaucracy, absence of upto date land records and legal hurdles in the way of implementation of land reform are some important reasons for the poor implementation of land reforms in India."[27]

The ceiling legislation in the post-1971 phase has been considerably improved and put on a more or less uniform basis throughout the country. The ceiling limits have also been considerably reduced and the long list of the exempted categories of land have been substantially cut. Measures to control benami transfers have also been provided for. The ceiling is applicable to family of 5 consisting of husband, wife and three minor children. The best category of land with assured water supply and capable of yielding at least two crops a year has a ceiling within the range of 10 to 18 acres (4.05 to 7.28 hectares) taking into account the fertility of the soil and other conditions. The land having assured irrigation only for one crop in a year, the ceiling does not exceed 27 acres (20.93 hectares). For all other categories, ceiling has been placed at 54 acres. In special category like desert and hilly areas, ceiling may be further raised with the consultation of Government of India. Since the inception of the land ceiling programme a total of 73.34 lakh acres have been declared surplus under prerevised and revised ceiling laws of this 56.90 lakh acres have been taken possession of and 43.54 lakh acres have been distributed to 31.84 lakh persons. This cleanly shows that there is still a considerable gap between the declaration and possession of surplus land and the actual distribution to poor farmers. The full potential of land distribution has not been realised both in terms of covering the entire surplus the may be available and distribution of the already identified.[28]

In order to make land reforms a success some more effective measures will have to be taken in the light of the Task Force Committee's recommendations on agrarian relations. Reassessment of ceiling of surplus land will have to be done by the States, specially in the command and newly irrigated areas. It shall have to be objective in character and will have to be backed up by strong political will, competitive and strong administrative machinery and a general social acceptability. All efforts will fail unless we mean it and pursue it with honesty of purpose. No doubt, land reform policies in India are steps in the right direction but the purposiveness of these policies has been adversely affected by poor implementation, defective legislation and lack of strong political will. Furthermore, land reform measures and more specially land ownership is just one of the component, though an important one, of the package required for higher production. Unless, the beneficiaries of land reform, namely, the tenants and the new owner created as a result of tenancy reform and settlements of land, are provided with adequate agricultural credit, physical input and other essential services and facilities. It could not yield the expected result.[29]

FOOTNOTES AND REFERENCES

1. U.N.O., *Inter relationship between Agricultural Reform and Agricultural Development*, 1953.
2. Joshi P.C., Land Reforms in India (Allied) 1976 p. 87.
3. Roup P.M., *The contribution of land reforms to agricultural development — An Analytical Frame work*, **Economic Development and Cultural Change** Vol. XII October 1963 p. 21; Warrier D., *Land reforms in Principles & Practice*, Oxford 1969 p.13; UNO, *Inter-relationship between Agricultural reform and Agricultural Development* 1953.
4. Based on Khusro A.M., *The Economics of Land-Reforms* and Farm-size in India, Macmillan 1973.
5. *Ibid*.p.29 ; Sadhu & Singh, *Fundamentals of Agricultural Economics* 1991, Pp. 229-30.
6. Khusro A.M., Reading's in Agricultural Economic (Edi) Allied 1968 pp.; Sadhu & Singh, Fundamentals of Agricultural Economics, *Op. Cit.* 1991, pp. 231.
7. Thomas E., An Introduction to Agricultural Economics, Thomas Nelson. N. York p. 156.
8. U.N. Economic Bulletin for Asia and for East, Vol. XI No. 1 June 1960.
9. UNO, "Inter-relationship between Agrarian Reforms and Agricultural Development", 1953.
10. I.L.O., "Agrarian Reforms with Particular Reference to Employment and Social Aspects", Geneva, 1964 p. 38.
11. See Khusro A.M., *"Returns to Scale in Indian agriculture" Op. Cit.* Sen A.K., *An Aspect of Indian Agriculture"* And "Size of Holding And Productivity, **The Economic Weekly,** *Op. Cit.* Mazumdar D., *"On the Economics of Relative Efficiency of Small Farmers"*, **The Economic Weekly**, Special number July 1963; Kanel D., Size of Farm and Economic Development," **Indian Journal of Economics**, Vol. 22, 1967 p. 29
12. Dorner P., *"Land reforms and Economics Development"*, England 1972 p.17.
13. Singh A. and Sadhu A.N., *"Agricultural Problems in India, Op. Cit.*, p. 127-28.
14. Ibid. p. 128.
15. *Ibid.* p. 129.
16. *Ibid.*
17. See Hanumantha Rao C.H., *"Ceiling on Agricultural Land holding* — Its Economic Rationale", **Economic and Political Weekly**, June 24, 1972; Rao V.M., Two Prospective on Redistribution of Land, "**Economic & Political Weekly**, March 30, 1974; Bandhyopadhyay D., Land Reforms in India: An Analysis, **Economic & Political Weekly** June 21-28 1986.
18. Quoted by R.N. Soni, Leading Issues in Agricultural Economics *Op. Cit.* pp. 431-32.
19. R.N. Soni, Leading Issues in Agricultural Economics, *Op. Cit.* p. 433.

20. Report of the Tokyo Seminar on "**Problems of Economic Growth**" Congress for Cultural Freedom$. p. 2.
21. Mahalanobi's Committee Report of the Distribution of Income and levels of Living (Part-I) 1964 pp. 20-21.
22. Economic Times, March 31, 1975.
23. Rudar Dutt, Indian Economy — Chapter on Land Reforms.
24. Myrdal G., Asian Drama Vol. II p. 324.
25. Quoted by Raj. K.N. "Same Current Hypotheses", Mainstream Oct. 10 1964 p. 12.
26. Joshi P.C., "Land Reform Implementation and Role of Administrator", **Economic and Political Weekly**, Sep. 30, 1978 p A-82.
27. GOI, Planning Commission "Report of Task Force on Agrarian Relations," 1973 pp. 9-10.
28. Singh A., Dadhu A.N., "Agricultural Problems in India", (Himalaya) 1986 pp 133-35.
29. GOI, Fourth Five Year Plan — Draft outline pp. 131-132.

5
MARKETED AND SURPLUS

In the introductory part we have explained the role and the significance of agricultural surpluses in the process of economic development. In fact, it is not the level of agricultural output but the level of surplus it generates that plays a central role in the development of predominantly agricultural economies. For a rapid and stable rate of growth it is therefore, not enough to increase agricultural production, even more important is to increase simultaneously the marketable surplus.

Marketable and Marketed Surplus: Marketable surplus refers to the potential surplus available for disposal with the farmer left after his genuine requirements of family consumption, payment of wages in kind, feed, seed and wastage etc, have been met. Marketed surplus on the other hand, represents only that portion of marketable surplus which is actually marketed and is placed at the disposal of non-farming rural and urban consumers. Under commercial agriculture which is motivated by profit consideration, the whole output is put on the market and the producer meets his consumption requirement through purchases from the market. But in case of food crops, the farmer may sell only the surplus over and above his own needs. Marketable surplus of agricultural products, hence, refers to the amount which a farmer can sell in the market. Marketed surplus, on the other hand, refers that part

* Take the reference from p. 243 at the end of Chapter VI (Form — Mechanisation).

of marketable surplus which is actually sell in the market. In this way, Marketed surplus, in a given year, may be equal or less or more than the marketable surplus depending upon the external factors operating on the market economy. However, marketed surplus may generally be expected to be less than marketable surplus, as the farmers who have the surplus may usually not dispose of his entire output. Due to some speculative practices in relation to price and the level of output, the selling amount of the farmers may be less than the amount they can actually sell. This is particularly true in case of big farmers.

In some circumstances, marketed surplus may be more than marketable surplus, This is possible when the farmers are compelled by circumstances to sale. For instance the output of a farmer is just sufficient for his own requirements, but his cash commitments to the money lenders or to co-operative credit societies or his tax obligation or his social or religious obligation may force him to sell part of his output even when his own subsistence needs do not allow him to do so. In such circumstances, the actual marketed surplus may be more than the potential marketable surplus. And here the concepts of real and forced surplus may clearly be distinguished.

Marketable Surplus and Economic Development

For an under-developed economy, a continuous rise in marketed surplus is considered a pre-condition for achieving as rapid rate of industrialisation. The economists like M. Dobb, W.H. Nicholls and W.W. Rostow all agree that if marketed surplus does not increase along with the increase in production, it may be proved a fundamental limiting factor on the tempo of development.[1]

The crucial role of marketed surplus in developing economies may be explained as under:

(a) A continuous increase in the marketed surplus helps in releasing labour force from agriculture to non-agricultural sector without affecting adversely the level of output.

(b) It helps in raising the income of the farmers which in turn, stimulates the demand for industrial products in the rural sector. The expansion of the market of industrial goods in the rural sector raises the profit of the capitalists and their savings. Hence marketed surplus contributes to capital formation in the non-agricultural sector.

(c) It also helps in increasing the exports and hence helps in importing capital goods and other essential raw materials for rapid industrial development.

(d) It contributes to an improvement of the standard of living in the agricultural sector by the expansion of the market for the industrial goods.

(e) It also contributes to the capital formation in the agricultural sector through providing the requisites of agricultural production.

Price mechanism is said to be the most important means of effecting the transfer of agricultural surpluses. A high degree of monetisation of the rural sector and the transfer of the subsistence sector into market-oriented economy would effectively help in transferring of agricultural surplus. Moreover, the steps such as the collection of land revenue and fertiliser and irrigation charges in kind may also help the State Government to procure sufficient amount of farm products. The establishment of more regulated markets may also contribute in maintaining a fairly steady and uniform flow of marketable surpluses. Such markets promote fair market practices and protect the incentive of the farmers. A well defined price policy in the form of minimum support prices; maintenance of parity between the prices of agricultural products and those of other commodities etc. may attract sufficient amount of marketable surpluses. And, therefore, price policy also plays an important role in increasing the marketed surpluses. A better and cheap transport system also encourages the flow of surpluses from rural areas to urban areas. Thus these are some important means through which agricultural surplus may be effectively transferred from rural to urban areas.

Factors for Determining the Level of Marketable Surplus

Experience shows that the amount of marketable surplus differs from region to region, holding to holding and even crop to crop in the same region. Main factors which determine the level of marketable surplus in an economy are as under:

Firstly, marketable surplus is the function of the level of output. A steady and sustained rise in the level of output depends upon the improvement in the level of production through a permanent change in the productivity. In this connection, intensity of cropping is an important determinant of marketable surplus. Higher intensity of cropping refers that more area has been sown more than once. Similarly lower intensity shows that lesser area has been sown more than once. Thus, high intensity of cropping leads to higher production which in turn leads to large margin of marketable surplus.

Secondly, the size of farm is another important factor of influencing the level of marketable surplus. It has been studied that the bulk of the agricultural surplus is being supplied by the medium and big farm. The small farms being a subsistence farms hardly have a surplus of output for sale. Dharam Narain's empirical study for the year 1950-51 revealed that the marketed surplus as a proportion of the value of the produce decline upto 10-15 acre size group and it steadily increased afterwards.[2] Thus the size of farm and the level of marketable surplus shows a strong positive correlation. The larger the size of the farm, the larger will be the marketable surplus and vice versa. Many other empirical studies also support this conclusion.[3]

Although all such studies support the contention that size of holding and the level of marketable surpluses are positively correlated. But there are some other empirical studies which prove that the proportion of marketable surplus may be higher on small farms in comparison to large holdings. Some studies in Madras and Kerala shows that in five villages out of ten, the small farmers marketed surplus is higher than the big farmers.[4]

On this point the land redistribution with the intention of more social justice came in direct conflict with increasing marketable surpluses. Here, land reforms can influence the marketable surplus in two ways. Firstly marketable surplus which is available with the big farmers (landlords) should be placed in the hands of larger number of smaller units. And secondly, the small farmers who were previously not in a position to meet their requirements from their total produce would now consume or at least retain more with them.[5] Thirdly another important factor affecting the level of marketable surplus is the level of consumption of the producers. Food habits of the producers of Punjab show that about 70 per cent of rice produced in Punjab is sold out in the market as it is not the chief diet of Punjab farmers, while only 9.4 per cent of total wheat produced is marketed because wheat is the main food of Punjab.[6]

Fourthly, process of food commodities in the market is another very influential factor for determining the level of marketed surplus.

In this connection two important views have been expressed. One hypotheses is developed by Mathur and Ezchiel who claim an inverse relationship between price and marketable surplus. They claim that since the cash requirements of farmers are given and almost fixed, marketed portion will also be fixed on a given price level. If cash requirement is inelastic, the farmer will sell less when prices are high and more when prices are low. Their findings are based on macro-level arguments. The second hypothesis is developed by the Ministry of Food and Agriculture. In its micro-level study on the enquiry into the Pace and Pattern of Market Arrivals of Foodgrains 1958-59 it explains that the farmers have become highly price conscious.[7] This hypothesis arrives at the conclusion that the market arrivals in the current season are very much affected by the changes in the market behaviour of growers. "Their experience of last year's high prices as well the relatively lower prices prevailing in the current season", as the report says, "have induced the growers to currently withhold stocks of wheat from the market in expectation of realising higher prices in the later months."

Fifthly, the nature of crops grown also contributes in determining the level of marketable surplus. A common experience shows that the level of marketed surplus of Foodgrains would be lower than that of non-foodgrain as the former is consumed by the producers while the latter is not consumed.

Sixthly, the financial status of the producer is also an influential factor for the market arrivals. Market arrivals shows the economic status of a producer. Larger the a farmer's demand for cash for the payment of varied socio-economic obligations—land revenue, debt payment, purchase of agricultural inputs, industrial goods and livestock and expenses of social function—the greater is their incentive to sell higher proportion of their produce in the market and vice versa.

And lastly, the healthy market condition also affects the market arrivals. Deficient storage; capacity lack of transport system, unorganised and uncertain market conditions, prevalence of large number of intermediaries., bargaining and unhealthy speculative tendencies may affect adversely the marketable surpluses.

Measurement of Marketed Surplus: A precise data about the size and the level of the marketed surplus is quite significant for planning and policy purposes as it helps in projecting the future development activities in the various sectors. Measurement is required not only from the regulated market but also from unregulated and unorganised markets. But there are various difficulties in measuring marketed surplus in India. Some important problems are as under:

(a) One serious obstacle in getting reliable information on marketed surplus is that a large proportion of the farmers sell out considerable part of their output at the time of their harvest to meet their immediate cash requirement and later on when they require foodgrain for their consumption they purchase back from the markets. Hence foodgrain released by the farmers do not represent the real marketable surplus.

(b) Most of the small and marginal farmers make local sales of their produce which while estimating the marketable surplus are generally not recorded. Moreover, arrivals are not separated by year of production from both the previous and the current crops year, estimates of marketable surplus will be inflated. Further large quantities of the product move from one market to another for sale and resale and in this way transactions are accorded twice. If so happens, the figures of marketed surplus would get inflated.[8]

(c) Another important problem of estimating marketed surplus is realised in anticipating the part of produce which is kept a side as seed, feed etc. The estimates have to be ex-ante under the assumption that such requirement in the coming year will be more or less the same to the quantity used in the current year.

Reliable information about the marketed surplus in India is quite inadequate. However, attempts have been made by some economists to measure marketed surpluses in India. Among them Dharam Narain estimates of 1950-51, Patnaik estimates of 1960-61 and Ashok Gulati estimates of 1971-72 are quite relevant. The findings of these estimates are given below:

Holding Size (Acres)	*Dharam Narain Estimates (1950-51)*	*Patnaik Estimates (1960-61)*	*Gulati Estimates (1970-71)*
	(Marketed surplus as % of the total output)		
0-5	34%	23%	26%
5-10	27%	27%	45%
10-15	23%	31%	52%
15-20	30%	36%	55%
20-25	32%	45%	60%
25-30	40%	49%	64%
30-above	47%	58%	78%

Source: Gulati A, Indian Economic Almanac December 1980.

In all three studies, the ratio of marketed surplus had been rising with a rise in operational holdings. It was quite high for the richest cultivator (78 per cent in 1971). This shows the economic dominance of the rich farmers. Dharam Narain estimates of 1950-51 follows a U-shaped pattern of marketed surplus with respect to size of operational holdings. That is, the surplus ratio is high with small holdings. It declines over the holdings groups. And thereafter it steadily increased. An interesting conclusion of this study is that small cultivator (upto 0-10 acres) contributes about 47 per cent of the total marketed produce and this is again confirmed by the Ashok Gulati's estimate in 1971. This usual high share of the small cultivator is characterised by V.K.R.V. Rao as "distress surplus." It is "distress" in the sense that the fixed commitment of farmers of the lower groups (such as payment of land revenue. tax, debt etc.) might compel them to dispose of a large portion of their produce.

Dharam Narain study brought about another aspect of the problem and that is negative response of marketed surplus to price change. It also implies that marketed surplus also have a negative income effect for a given change in price. Since small farmers have a fixed money requirement, a rise in price compel them to reduce his "distress" sales and sell smaller quantity of his produce and vice versa.

The other two studies, namely Patnaik and Gulati in 1960 and 1971, there is no U-shaped pattern of marketed surplus in respect to size-holdings. In these studies the pattern is a steady rise in marketed surplus ratio to output. This pattern shows that with larger size holdings, marketed surplus ratio also increases.

All such studies lead to one basic conclusion that the ratio of marketed surplus to total output in India is very poor. An aggregate estimates shows that this ratio vary between 25 to 33 per cent.[9] According to a Report of foundation, "By for the largest portion, – over 75 per cent – of India foodgrain production is never marketed .... The total marketable surplus represent less than 25 per cent of total foodgrain production in an average year."[10] According to very liberal estimate, this surplus never exceeds from one third of the total produce.

There have been various reasons for such low marketable surplus in India. Some important reasons are: (a) uncertain level of output, (b) dominance of subsistence cultivators, (c) small size of holdings (d) family size of a farmer, (e) consumption habits, (f) unorganised and defective marketing system, and (g) prevalent of tendency to hoarding.

These drawbacks may be removed through various steps taken by the Government. Among them some important steps are: (a) the measures that can induce to consume less and sell more of the output. One method is to increase the demand for manufactured articles. Such demand will induce farmers to sell more of their foodgrains. (b) A proper price policy may also help in bringing increasing quantities of foodgrains to the market. In this respect price should neither be fixed so high that could generate inflationary pressure nor should it be so low that could discourage the producer. The most suitable way is that Government should provide cheap agricultural inputs to the farmers with a fixed procurement price. (c) The payment of loans to cooperative credit societies and banks may also be made in kinds. In this way marketed surplus may be increased. (d) taxes may also be used to restrict consumption and increase marketable surplus. An increase in land tax and tax on agriculture may force the farmers to sell more of their surplus grain in the market.

FOOTNOTES AND REFERENCES

* Material is based on the following books: Sadhu & Singh *Op. Cit.*; Ruddar Dutt, K.P.M. Sundaram, Indian Economy, S. Chand & Co. 1982; A.N. Agarwal, Indian Agriculture Vikas 1983.

1. M. Dobb, "On Economic Theory and Socialism", p. 152; W.H. Nicholls, "An Agricultural Surplus as a Factor in Economic Development", The Journal of Political Economy, Vol. 71 Feb 1973; W.W. Rostow "The Stages of Economic Growth", (London) 1960.
2. Dharam Narain, Distribution of the Marketable Surplus of Agricultural Produce by the size of level of holding in India 1950-51. (Asia) N. Delhi.
3. For examples see: Village Survey conducted by the Agro-Economic Research Centre (Visvabharat University). See in the Agricultural Situation in India Jan 1960; Betul Community Development Block Survey (Madhay Pradesh) (See "Indian Journal of Agricultural Economics Vol. XVI, 1961; Vyas V.S. and Maharaja M.H., Factors Affecting Marketable Surplus and Marketed Supplies" Artha-Vikas Vol. 2 Jan 1, 1966; Misra B and Sinha S.P., "A study of problems of marketable surplus of foodgrains in a village Bihar", Indian Journal of Agricultural Economic, Vol. XVI, 1961.
4. See: The Indian Journal of Agricultural Economics (Conference Number) (January to March) 1961.
5. Bansil P.C., "Problems of Marketable Surplus in India, Indian Journal of Agricultural Economics Vol. XVI, 1961.
6. Kahlon A.S., Reed C.E., "Problems of Marketable Surplus in Indian Agriculture", The Indian Journal of Agricultural Economics Vol. XVI 1961.
7. See: Mathur P.N. and Ezchiel H., "Marketable Surplus of food and price fluctuation in a Developing Economy", KYKLOS 1961; GOI, Ministry of Food and Agriculture, "Report on the Enquiry into the pace and pattern of market arrivals of foodgrains 1958-59." 1959.
8. Kahlon A.S., Read C.E., *Op. Cit.*
9. See: Dharam Narain Study *Op. Cit.*, Estimates of Directorate of Marketing and Inspection; Estimate of Indian Council of Agricultural Research; GOI, Ministry of Food and Agriculture, "Report on India's food crisis and steps to meet it.
10. GOI, Ministry of Food & Agriculture, "Report on India's food crisis and steps to meet it.

6

FARM-MECHANISATION

In India, traditional techniques of production with crude and primitive implements and tools are still continued to be adopted on a large scale in agriculture. These tools and implements require human and animal labour for their operation. In other words they require biological sources of energy. As against this, Western countries mainly use mechanical sources of energy, that is, tractors, harvester, pump set, threshers etc. In India also in some States such as Punjab, Haryana and western U.P. large farmers have now started adopting agricultural machinery on a substantial scales. But from the point of view of the nation as a whole the level of mechanisation is not very satisfactory. It has been estimated that agricultural sector uses 44 million horse-power energy out of which 25 per cent is generated by human labour, 64 per cent by animals and only 4.1 per cent by mechanical and electrical sources.[1]

Mechanisation simply refers the introduction of machines for carrying out farm operation. In other words, it refers a transformation from biological sources of energy to mechanised sources of energy. Whereas such transformation has been considered by some quarters as a basic and essential condition for modernisation of rural sector, certain parts have vehemently opposed it on the grounds that it encourages unemployment by displacing farm labour and renders animal power useless.

Mechanisation may be either partial or complete. When machines are used along with traditional implements, mechanisation is called partial. On the other hand, when all farm operation are mechanised and animal labour is completely displaced and human labour requirement is reduced to minimum, mechanisation is called total mechanisation. In developing nations like India where labour is abundant and capital is scarce, partial mechanisation has been accomplished.

Progress of Mechanisation in India: During the first two Plans the progress of mechanisation in India has been quite slow. It is the introduction of new agricultural technology since the Third Plan which gave it a big boost-up. Thus, while the number of wooden ploughs remained stagnant over the entire planning period, (1961-71) the use of iron ploughs has been doubled during the said period. There has been only 7 tractors per lakh hectares of gross cropped area in 1950-51. The number rose to 34 in 1965-66, 166 in 1975-76 and further 234 in 1978-79. Similarly the number of oil engines per lakh hectares of gross cropped area was only 62 in 1950-51. The number rose to 295 in 1965-66 and again to 1074 in 1974. The number of irrigation pump-sets with electricity operated tube-well was only 16 per lakh hectare in 1950-51. This number increased to 326 per lakh hectare in 1965-66, 1617 per lakh hectare in 1975-76 and again 2308 in 1978-79. The consumption of power per thousand hectares of gross cropped area increased from 1.5 KW in 1950-51 to 12.2 KWh in 1965-66, 50 KWh in 1975-76 and further 76.9 KWh in 1978-79.[2]

Some important trends of the progress of farm mechanisation has been explained in the following table.

Trend of Progress in Farm Mechanisation (1951-78)

	Per one lakh hectare of cropped land.			*Consumption of Electricity (KWh.) per hectare of cropped area*
Year	Tractor	Oil Engine	Elect. Pumps.	
1951	7	62	20	1.5
1956	14	84	32	2.1
1961	20	151	105	5.5
1966	34	303	267	12.2
1970	72	*N.A*	829	23.0
1975	147	1038	1416	50.0
1978	213	N.A	1555	N.A

Source: Commerce (Annual Number) 1979 p. 274.

Farm Mechanisation—An Issue: The main discussion around the subject is the prospect of labour-displacement that mechanisation is supposed to cause. The vast surplus labour in the Indian economy, mostly located in rural areas, and the scarcity of capital tends to use human and animal power more than mechanical power. Rapid mechanisation will certainly displace human and animal power and will aggravate unemployment problem.

The supporters of farm mechanisation argue that it helps in reducing the cost of output, increasing economic surplus, enhancing productivity of land and per capita productivity of labour employed on land, changing the structure of agriculture from primitive and traditional type to modern and commercial type and in changing the outlook of farmers towards their day-to-day life, economic behaviour and social status.

Mechanisation and Production: Mechanisation increases the speed of work and the time is saved. This has led to many people to argue that mechanisation leads to large increase in agricultural production. Here we must calculate the contribution of labour displacing machines in increasing agricultural production. Moreover, we must also enquire whether increased agricultural production is due to mechanisation or increased capital investment. This is a firm opinion that farm mechanisation not only increases the efficiency of operations but also leads to increase in productivity. A survey in India also proves that productivity per hectare and per labour employed is higher in mechanised farms as compared to non-mechanised farms. But here the credit goes to HYV seeds and fertilisers which along with mechanisation has increased the productivity. The fact is that the contribution of mechanisation is much less than what generally appears in surface. Raj Krishna also points out that if the effects of fertilisers and cropping intensity on productivity is subtracted from the effect of mechanisation, the actual contribution of machines turns out to be negative.[3] However, by reducing time of the agricultural operations, mechanisation can certainly help in increasing productivity. For example, the use of tractor in sandy area of Rajasthan where rainfall is deficient the sowing period after rainfall can considerably be reduced and this can help in increasing agricultural production.

Mechanisation and Reduction in Costs: The second important argument in favour of mechanisation is that it helps in reducing the costs of production in agriculture. In developed countries of the West, mechanisation have helped in keeping the cost of output low and the basic reason is that in all such countries biological source of energy (human & animal labour) is costlier than mechanical sources of energy (machines & fuel). As C.H. Hanumantha Rao has rightly pointed out that "technical progress and industrial development contribute .... to increasing the ease with which capital can be substituted for labour and also to reducing the cost of machines and fuel. In the other hand, economic development and the growth of per capita income raise the cost of biological sources of energy by increasing the demand for labour in the non-agricultural sector."[4] He showed a trend of the rising prices of the biological and mechanical sources of energy in U.S.A. The price index of farm machinery has been doubled between 1940 and 1956 from 153 to 330. But the cost index of labour to farmers during the same period has increased more than three times from 129 to 536.[5]

This problem is more complex in India. Apparently due to abundant labour supply the impression is that labour is the cheaper factor of production. But Rao does not support this view. In his opinion the cause of increasing use of tractors in Punjab and Haryana is due to the fact that tractor is relatively cheaper input. According to Rao, rapidly increasing population has substantially increased the food prices and this in turn, has increased the wages for the labour (both in form of cash and kind). He analysed the data during the period 1961-1968 and finds that where as the money wages of labours and bullock prices rose faster than the prices of agricultural commodities in many regions the rate of mechanisation has also been quite rapid. The prices of tractors and tractor fuel seem to have increased by not more than 50 per cent, while in comparison to it, the rise in the prices of agricultural commodities has been 100 per cent. It is also argued that the operational costs of traditional agriculture are also likely to be greater than the cost of mechanised agriculture. This is because that while tractors and other machines use fuel energy only when they are in operation, the biological sources of energy (human being and animals) requires feeding all the year owned whether on work or not on work.[6]

A.S. Kahlon and S.R. Verma's study, however, supports the view that the improved techniques reduce the costs. According to this study, reduction in costs is quite sizable. The study is based on the use of improved implements operated with the help of bullocks. On one case it is the wooden plough that has been replaced by the disc-harrow. In the other case the bullock drawn seed-cum-fertiliser drill is introduced. In both the cases costs have been droped sharply. Following tables explains their case.

Table A
Comparative Cost and Output of Different Bullock-Drawn Equipments for Seed-Bed

Pre-Operation

Equipment	*Output acres per day*	*Cost of Operation (Rs. per hectare)*
Bullock drawn wooden plough	0.5	400 – 450
Disch-arrow	2	240 – 270

Table: Comparative Performance of Indigenous and Improved Seed Equipment

Method	*Output (acre per day)*	*Cost of operation (Rupees per hectare)*
Bullock drawn Kera	.5 – .6	30 – 35
Pora Bullock drawn seed-cum fertiliser drill	1.5 – 2	15 – 20

Source: Kahlon A.S. and Verma S.R., "Merchandising Punjab Agriculture—Situation & Need", *Agricultural Situation in India*, Feb. 1979 p. 695.

Mechanisation and Labour Productivity: The supporter of mechanisation also argue that the increasing use of machines improve labour productivity. As machines are introduced, less labour is required to obtain the same level of output. In this respect the examples of USA and USSR are before us. In U.S.A. whereas in 1830 320 man-hours of labour were required to produce 100 bushels of wheat, in 1900 only 108 man-hours and in 1947 only 47 man-hours were sufficient for the same amount to produce. Similarly in U.S.S.R. mechanisation on collective farms has resulted a substantial increase in labour productivity. According to a study, labour productivity on farms was three times during 1960's as compared to the pre-revolution days.[7] However, the substantial improvement in labour productivity may not be claimed only due to mechanisation. There are various other factors which are equally important in improving the labour productivity. But it cannot be denied that mechanisation has helped in labour-saving on land and such released labour was made available to use in other areas of economic activity. In developing countries, the transfer of surplus labour from agriculture to nonagricultural sector will also help to make them more productive. Moreover, the available resources of power from all living and mechanical sources are proved insufficient to meet the peak labour loads. It also become over-abundant in the slack period.

Mechanisation, therefore, helps to meet these peak power needs with better land preparations and higher cropping intensity. It would lead to substantially bigger harvests which, in turn, require more labour during post-harvest slack period for threshing, storage, transport and trade etc.[8]

Mechanisation, Size of Holding and Land Productivity: It has been estimated that in India about 7 million hectares of fertile land are affected by alkalinity and salinity. As a result, it shows a very low yield. The development of such land including its levelling and shaping, reclamation of such land and better utilisation of water, fertiliser and other inputs on it is difficult without mechanisation.

Besides, for an effective and optimum use of the modern inputs such as HYV seeds, chemical fertilisers, machines, spray etc. mechanisation seems to be essential. Land reform resources like consolidation of holding, surplus land distribution and cooperative forming etc. have helped to improve the size of holdings. Thus, in future, without mechanisation the improvement of land productivity would become a difficult task.

Mechanisation, Farm Income and Economic Surplus:[9] Use of machines in farms increases the income of farmers. It is observed that the traditional and primitive methods of farming make it a subsistence occupation and the introduction of machines and other modern implements change the very nature of traditional agriculture and transform it into commercial occupation. Under this change decisions regarding production and investment are taken on the basis of price trends and this in turn, increases the farm income.

It is said that larger the surplus in an industry greater will be the level of capital formation and potentialities of economic development. Traditional agriculture produces meagre surplus. This limits the capacity of the farmer to invest and as a result agriculture remains backward. Obviously under these circumstances agriculture is unable to provide investible resources to the other sector of the economy. Introduction of machines in farms leads to generate more surplus in agricultural sector. The surplus generated with the help of mechanisation is not only enough to induce development of agriculture but also help in carrying out basic changes in the structure of industrial development and creation of infrastructure.

It is also observed that by the introduction of machines working condition of the farmers also changes. Farmer instead of doing very hard manual labour, can enjoy more leisure time and work under more agreeable circumstances. It changes the moral outlook of the farmers and they become more sensitive to changes in their socio-economic environment as well as factors affecting their general well-being.[10]

Concluding Remarks: The aforesaid views of the supporters of mechanisation are based on the advantages of large-scale production made possible by the machines. Machines work fastly and accurately and hence the introduction of machines are time-saving and economical. It also increases the production and productivity of land and labour, generates the surpluses and relieved man of much of the heavy work. By the use of machines, huge plots of land can be ploughed; large crop can harvest huge amounts of produce can be taken to the market. All these operations can be taken without any loss of time. As a result, the cost of production can be reduced substantially. Machines will create employment opportunities in non-agricultural sector such as industry, transport and trade etc. and then the unproductive surplus labour in agriculture will become productive. Mechanisation will also increase the income of the farmers by transferring the traditional agriculture into commercial agriculture, changes the outlook of the farmers and provide more leisure.

CASE AGAINST MECHANISATION[11]

The supporter's views on mechanisation, no doubt, have some validity in the context of the need to raise production as fast as possible within the shortest possible time. But the arguments against mechanisation are also quite convincing.

Firstly, mechanisation has no scope in India because of the extremely small size of holding — between 3 and 12 acres. According to 1971 census about 70 per cent of the 70.5 million holdings in the country are below two hectares and are held by small marginal farmers. The average size of holding is sufficiently large in Western countries. In Canada for example the size was 145 hectare in 1961. It was 122 hectares in USA in 1959, and was 124 hectares in Mexico in 1960. Machines can be used profitably only when the size of farm is sufficiently large. In Indian case full scale mechanisation is not possible on such small holdings. Not only this, even the small holdings are split into tiny plots scattered all over the village. Moreover, Indian farmer uses tractors of 35 h.p. and above considering the size of an average Indian farm, these tractors are too big and uneconomical in terms of fuel consumption. A small tractor of 20 horse-power to 25 horse-power would be an answer for the most of the problems of Indian farms. Japan presents a good example of small holding and mechanisation. The mechanisation suits the small holding where small machines were introduced for small-holdings.

The second serious objection on mechanisation is that it displaces labour. According to one estimate if complete mechanisation is introduced it is possible to cultivate the existing area of land with only 3 to 4 million persons. Millions of farmers will be thrown out of agriculture and will have to be provided alternative sources of employment. If the absorptive capacity of non-agricultural sector is low, unemployment problem will become more serious. Actually in labour abundant economy, the introduction of machines are a luxury. According to C.H. Hanumantha Rao estimate tractorisation displaces 20-30 per cent of the total human labour days per cropped acre on account of tillage and transportation. Other machines like threshers and harvesters also promotes unemployment. A mechanical thresher, according to Rao, displaces amount 15 per cent labour and harvester combine around 25 per cent in addition to that displaced by mechanical threshers.[12] This would make it clear that mechanisation will certainly displace labour on a large scale and if the released labour is not absorbed properly in other sectors, it would create a serious unemployment problem.

Lack of trained personnel is another important point which goes against mechanisation. It is a known fact that our farmers are illiterate and lack the necessary technical knowledge to adopt mechanisation on a large scale. There is also lack of trained personnel for repairing and servicing the machines. However, these points may be called a hurdle than an argument against mechanisation. With changing time, the rural environment is also changing and the young rural generation is coming up with sufficient education, training and technical knowledge.

Fourthly it is also argued that farm machinery will require fuel in form of petrol, diesel and kerosene oil. The production of these extremely valuable commodities in India is somewhat limited at present, and therefore, mechanisation would generate greater pressure on the foreign exchange position of the country. With a steep rise in the price of petrol and diesel the whole question of the economics of mechanisation versus that of traditional agricultural techniques has again become an open debate.

Fifthly, mechanisation widen inter-personal and inter regional inequalities. It helps in increasing in-equalities in inter-personal income level between large and small farmers. Similarly, certain agriculturally better-endowed regions in terms of physical resources and entrepreneurial ability like Punjab, Haryana and Western parts of U.P., deltaic rice-belt of Tamil Nadu and Andhra Pradesh have adopted mechanisation to a much larger extent as compared to other regions. Hence, the development of disparities among the regions or within the regions are quite obvious.

Lastly, mechanisation assist in the maximisation of production per worker while the land which is the scarce factor is not assisted with the aim of maximising its output. In a country like India where land, in relation to labour is scarce the problem is that of making the maximum use of that scarce factor. In Indian agriculture increasing productivity of land is more important than increasing labour productivity.

Conclusion: Both views have some validity. It is true that complete mechanisation is not possible in India as is being adopted in other Western countries. At the same time it is also wrong to agree that there is no scope at all for mechanisation in labour-surplus developing country like India. The real approach should be to adopt selective mechanisation. As the Sixth Five Year Plan stated: "Unrestricted mechanisation of agricultural operation will not, however, be in the interest of our country as it severely worsens the rural unemployment problem. As such a policy of selective mechanisation will be adopted".

In Indian case we are adopting four techniques: (1) traditional techniques which were primarily based on the use of plough – wooden and iron and animal labour. In such case neither fertiliser nor HYV seeds are used; (2) land augmenting techniques which continue to employ the traditional implements but makes ample use of fertilisers irrigation and HYV seeds; (3) use of machines by displacing biological source of energy (human and animal labour). This is known as labour substituting technique; and (4) a mixed technique of land augmenting and labour substituting. Large farmers of Punjab, Haryana, Western U.P., Tamil Nadu and Andhra Pradesh are adopting this techniques an increasing scale.

These are the four options available to the Indian farmers to select an appropriate technique, keeping in mind the socio-economic situation of the country. Actually not one technique is appropriate. Each techniques has some favourable and unfavourable points. Thus that technique can be considered appropriate in India which could help in increasing agricultural output and demand for labour without accentuating economic inequalities. This view leads to concentrate on expanding irrigation facilities and increasing the supply of fertilisers and HYV Seeds to farmers.[13]

FOOTNOTES AND REFERENCES

1. Desai SSM, Israney S.M., Rairikar B.R., Gopakumar K, Development Issues of the Indian Economy, (Himalaya) 1979-80 *p.* 171.
2. Omedt G, Capitalist Agriculture and Rural classes in India, *Economic & Political Weekly*, Vol. XVI, December 26, 1981 (Table I) *p.* A-143.
3. See Seminar on Dynamic of Rural Development (Delhi).

4. Hanumantha Rao C.H., Farm Mechanisation in C.H. Shah (Ed.) Agricultural Development of India. Policy & Problem (Bombay) 1979, *p*. 393.
5. *Ibid.*
6. *Ibid., p*. 297.
7. U.S. Department of Agriculture (Bureau of Agricultural Economic) "The farm cost situation", Sep. 1946 *p*. 28.
8. Desai S.S.M., Israne S.M., Raisikar B.R., Gopakumar K., "Development Issue of the Indian Economy" *Op. Cit. p*. 173.
9. Misra S.K., Puri V.K. Indian Economy (Himalaya) 1983 *pp*. 451-52.
10. See C.H. Hanumantha Rao, "Farm Mechanisation", *Op. Cit*. 293-94.
11. See Misra S.K., Puri V.K. Indian Economy, (Himalaya) 1983 *p* 455-56; Desai SSM, Israney S.M., Raisikar B.R., Gopakumar K, Development Issues of the Indian Economy *pp*. 173; Rudar Dutt Sundaran KPM, Indian Economy (S. Chand) 1983 *pp* 405-6; Agarwal A.N. Indian Agriculture (2nd Ed.) Vikàs 1983 *pp* 331-336.
12. C.H. Hanumantha Rao, "Farm Mechanisation", *op.cit. pp* 301-302.
13. Misra S.K., Puri V.K., "Indian Economy", *op.cit p*. 457 -58.

7
AGRICULTURAL-LABOUR

Farm workers have always been considered the most neglected class in Indian rural structure. Their employment is irregular and hence income is low and uncertain. Since they are generally unskilled illiterate and untrained they have no alternative employment opportunities within and outside of the rural sector. A large number of agricultural workers belong to scheduled caste and scheduled tribes and hence they are socially oppressed class. These workers are scattered all over the country and therefore, due to the aforesaid factors, they are completely unorganised and are unable to fight for their rights. Consequently, they have also very poor bargaining power as compared to industrial workers who generally use strike and negotiations as a weapons of bargaining. The wages of farm workers are also comparatively very low because of the vast number of workers. Their productivity is also low due to out-dated mode of cultivation and of low bargaining power. Because of all these reasons, their socio-economic status has failed to improve even after more than three decades of planning.

The first Agricultural Labour Enquiry Commission of 1950-51 define agricultural labour as those who were engaged in raising crops on payment of wages. This definition is considered incomplete on the ground that a large number of workers do not work against payment of wages all the year round. Accordingly, the committee improved the definition by saying that those people should be regarded as agricultural worker who worked for 50 per cent more days on payment of wages. This definition widened the scope. Now those people also included under the category of agricultural workers who possesses some land or were rural artisans but who worked for 50 per cent or more days on the land of others against payment of wages.

The second Agricultural Labour Enquiry Committee of 1956-57 again widened the view of agricultural workers. It include all those workers who were engaged in allied activities like animal husbandry, dairy, piggery, fisheries and poultry etc. The committee also explains the concept of labour household. If, according to committee, 50 per cent or more of its income is derived as wages for work rendered in agriculture only, then it could be classified as agricultural labour household. This change over from "work" to "income" seems to be more scientific. But even this is not without flaws. This may be happened that the head of the household work in an unorganised sector on a temporary basis or he may find job in some public construction programme whereas other members remain in the village and work in agriculture against payment of wages. In this way, household is an agricultural labour household even its head derives a major portion of income from other occupations.

In 1961 census all those workers were included in the category of agricultural workers who worked on the farms of others and received payment either in money or kind or both. The 1971 census excluded those people for whom working on the farms of others was a secondary occupation.

This brief analysis shows that the experts are not agreed upon the definition of agricultural labour. The working definition is sufficient to understand the concept. That is, all those persons who derive a major part of their income as payment of labour done on the farms of others, can be designated as agricultural labour. The term "agriculture labour" refers all persons who are hired for carrying on different agricultural operations either on permanent or temporary basis. The agricultural labourers may own some land which they cultivate or they may not own any land. A very few agricultural labourers own their piece of land which is not sufficient to maintain their subsistence living. As a result, they are forced to work as labourer on other's farms even they cultivate their own lands.'

Classification of Farm Labour: The Indian census figures indicate an increasing tendency of landless agricultural workers. Their absolute number has been increasing even after the three decades of planning.

The agricultural labourers in India have been classified as: (a) landless agricultural labourers who are attached to landlords; (b) landless agricultural labourers who are independent and work for others as and when employed by landlords; (c) Small cultivators working most of the time on the fields belonging to other landlords; (d) Cultivators who have economic holding but who have one or more of their sons or family members working on bigger landowner's farms to earn additional income as their own farms is insufficient to support large family.

Among all four categories, the position of the first group of worker is most deplorable. They are slaves who work for the landlords and provide all sorts of services mostly free or on some nominal payment in kind. When the landlords sells his land, they are automatically transferred to the new landowner.

The second and the third group of agricultural workers also constitute important sections of total agricultural labour in India. The socio-economic status of these three group is very poor and while discussing the agricultural labourers in India, attention is focused mainly on these three group.[2]

Growth of Farm Labour: Farm labour force constitutes a sizeable portion of India's total labour force. According to 1961 census, there were 31.5 million farm labourers in the country. They were 16.6 per cent of the total labour force and 23 per cent of the labour force in the agricultural sector. According to 1971 census, the number of agricultural labourer has been increased from 31.5 million to 45.5 million. The increase was 38 per cent to the total agricultural work force. This increase in the number of farm labour has been followed by a decrease in the number of cultivator from 99.22 million in 1961 to 78.1 million in 1971. This shows the extent of poverty in the rural sector.[3]

According to the All India Debt and Investment Survey 1971-72, 14.6 per cent agricultural workers were landless. 1974-75, Rural Labour Enquiry showed that there were 25.5 per cent agricultural labour families and 5 per cent were other rural labour families. Out of these, about 50 per cent were landless, while the other 50 per cent had small holdings three-fourth of them less than 1.5 acres. The same enquiry also pointed out that in 1964-65 the number of agricultural household were 5.7 million which rose to 10.2 million in 1974-75. The increase was 78.6 per cent in a single decade. As against this the number of all rural households increased only by 16.6 per cent. This also shows the extent of poverty of agricultural workers.[4]

There are number of factors responsible for the continuous and rapid increase in the number of agricultural labourers in India. These are: (a) rapidly growing population on limited land resource; (b) Eviction of small owner-cultivators by landlords and making them a landless labourers; (c) the process of sub-division and fragmentation of holdings which has rendered a large number of holdings uneconomic. Farmers who work on these tiny holdings find it difficult to make both end meet. Consequently, they are forced to work on the farms of other landlords to supplement their income; (d) increase in indebtedness of small farmers is also responsible for increasing the number of agricultural workers. The malpractices of money lenders and mahajans such as, charging exorbitant rate of interest, manipulating accounts, etc. are responsible to make them agricultural labourers; and (e) the development of capitalist agriculture. During the last three decades, capitalist agriculture has received a big boost.

Abolition of intermediaries, technological development, cheap cooperative and institutional credit, expansion of marketing facilities and the pricing policy of the Government has created a favourable condition for the development of capitalist agriculture. The farmers have turned into entrepreneurs and have adopted capitalist farming on a large scale. They began to attract agricultural workers from far off places.

Measures Taken by the Government: Since independence Government has shown awareness of the problems of agricultural workers and all plan documents have suggested ways and means to improve their conditions. Some of the important steps taken so far as under:

(a) The fixation of minimum wages is one of the important such steps. The Minimum Wages Act was passed in 1948 and since then necessity of applying it has been constantly felt. The first plan advocated that this Act should be enforced in the first instance in those areas where the rural wages were extremely low. However, because of the number of difficulties, it was not found possible to fix minimum wages upto 1974. The main problems were low productivity of agricultural workers, small size of holdings, determination of wages by traditional methods, and opposition to any changes from the landlords, lack of organised workers force, excessive labour supply from some areas, and prevalence of widely different conditions of employment etc. But due to the improvements in overall agricultural condition, the prosperity of farmers has induced agricultural workers to demand more wages. Besides, land reform measures, price policy, and marketing etc, also increased the aspiration of agricultural labours. In such changing environment, Government initiated a number of steps to fix minimum wage for agricultural workers. At present except Jammu and Kashmir, Nagaland and Sikkim, legislation have been passed in all States for fixing minimum wages. But on account of practical difficulties and excessive supply of labour, benefits from these legislation have been very limited.[5] (b) Indian constitution declared that the institution of slavery in any forms has been abolished. Though institution of slavery was abolished, it continued in one or the other form. In rural areas it is continued in form of bonded labour in 17 out of 22 States. The Central Government in a notification issued in October 1975 abolished bonded labour practice. Later on a legislation was passed, known as the Bonded Labour System (Abolition) Act 1976. Under this act the bonded labour system was abolished and every bonded labour was freed and discharged from any obligation to render bonded labour. As a result, 1,20,946 bonded labourers were identified and freed in various parts of country upto December 1980. In this respect the estimates are varied. Different State Governments have reported a total of 1.20 lakh bonded labourers. The 32nd round of the NSS puts the figures at 3.5 lakhs. Gandhi Peace Foundation and National Labour Institute has estimated the figure as high as 22 lakh. All such estimates show that a large number of bonded labourers are yet to be liberated.[6] (c) The distribution of land to landless workers is another important step in this direction. This step has been taken to improve their economic condition. The First Plan provision was of Rs. 1.5 crores for the resettlement of landless labourers on newly reclaimed land as well as cultivatable wasteland. In 1957, the National Development Council proposed that lands obtained by enforcing ceilings, Bhoodan and Gramdan etc. should be primarily devoted to the settlement of landless labourers. This proposal was made because of the past experience of the First Plan in which only 1 crore expenditure was made on such scheme. And out of it two third went to the only two districts (Lakhimpur Kheri and Pilibhit) of Uttar Pradesh and one third on the central mechanised farm of Bhopal. A few small schemes were under taken in Andhra Pradesh. Mysore and Madras. During Third Plan Rs. 8 crores was provided under the Central plan and Rs. 4 crores under the State Plans for resettlement of landless labourers. Here priority in the distribution of land is accorded to the landless labourer belonging to Scheduled Castes and Scheduled Tribes. It has been estimated that approximately 70 lakhs hectares of land has been distributed among landless labourers so far. However, most of such distributed land is not fit for cultivation. The hunger for land is no doubt satisfied, but it has not been able to improve their economic conditions.[7]

Besides, some other important steps to improve the socio-economic conditions of agricultural workers are: (a) rural workers programmes; (b) development of small scale and cottage industries; (c) liquidation of rural indebtedness; (d) provision of housing sites and (e) development of special agencies for farmers development such as Small

Farmers Development Agency (SFDA) and Marginal Farmers and Agricultural Labourers Development Agency (MFALA). The other development programmes such as Intensive Area Development Programme (IADP) with its twin strategies of HYVP and multiple cropping programme (MCP) has been found to have created a more intensive and continuous demand for labour. Such programmes have created additional employment opportunities for seasonal labourers.

Thus, it is quite evident from the above analysis that agricultural workers and their socio-economic conditions demand more serious attention of the Government. It is very deep rooted and complex problem which requires some drastic steps to over come. Though some measures are taken in the right direction yet they have failed to have a significant impact. It is necessary to consider that the programmes introduced by the Government should be spread overall regions of the country and should not concentrate in one or two selected areas or States. For this an increased outlay is the basic requirement which should be met by the Government. The development programme of agricultural workers should be closely linked up with rural development programmes and development of alternative avenues of employment. Unless this happens on a sufficiently large scale, measures to help agricultural workers cann ,t be expected to yield much.

REFERENCES

1. See. Misra S.K., Puri V.K., Indian Economy, (Himalaya) 1983 pp. 424-425; Desai S.M., Israney S.M., Rairikar B.R., Gopakumar K., *Development Issues of the Indian Economy*, (Himalaya) 1979-80. pp. 149-50.
2. *Ibid.*
3. *Ibid.*, pp. 526-527 and p. 151.
4. *Ibid.*, See also Das Gupta A.K., *Agriculture and Economic Development of India* (Associated Publishing House) 1973 pp. 16-17, 26-28, 32-34, 49-50 chapter 4 and 5.
5. *Ibid.* (Misra, Puri, Desai and others) p. 532-33, 154-55.
6. *Ibid.* (Misra and Puri) p. 533.
7. *Ibid.* p. 534.

8
RURAL CREDIT

Agriculture is an industry and like other industries it requires capital. Due to the peculiar characteristics of agriculture, specially its uncertainties, seasonality, low returns, and limited scope for employment, a large number of cultivators cannot manage the needed finance and tend to borrow money from different sources. For stimulating the tempo of agricultural production an adequate and timely credit is, therefore, essential.

Like any productive activity, agriculture needs financing for its various production processes such as improvement of land, purchase of inputs, sale of output, development of agriculture and even for the payment of previous debt. The uncertainty and low-productivity also compelled the marginal farmers to borrow money for various non-productive purposes such as consumption, marriages and other social obligations. These financial requirements are there even in the case of agriculture run on traditional lines. But these are much more in relation to agriculture which is in the process of modernisation. Farm production technology being advocated at present is sophisticated in nature. Besides, it is highly input and labour intensive. It is also inter-dependent on several interrelated practices each one of which has to be applied rationally in time and in the manner recommended by the specialist. Thus, scientific crop planning has created an unprecedented upsurge in the demand of various inputs such as high-yielding varieties of seed, chemical fertilizers, pesticides, irrigation, tractors, threshers and various other machines and equipments etc. This in turn has increased heavy demand for credit.

Agricultural Credit and Agricultural Development

Studies show a strong positive relationship between agricultural growth and availability of credit. Broadly, credit in agricultural sector may be divided into short-term loans to meet the input expenses and medium and long-term loans to facilitate the development of fixed farm assets such as land. The short-term loans or crop-loans is expected to bridge the gap in the short or long-term resources of the borrowers. This gap arises in relation to static or dynamic production function. Under a static functioning the level of input use per hectare of cropped area being constant, the year to year variation in the amount of credit reflects the changes in input prices. Under a situation of diminishing returns, however, increasing input use is required to maintain the same level of output. The supply of credit related to static production conditions will not contribute to increase in output, although the withdrawal of it might lead to a decline in output. Under dynamic functions, credit requirements would rise from year to year even if input prices remain constant. The growth in credit under such dynamic conditions would lead to increased output. Similarly, the investment credit too would lead to an improvement in the production potential of the farms through the process of net capital formation.

The lesson of universal agrarian history from Rome to Scotland is that an essential of agriculture is credit. Neither the condition of the country nor the nature of land tenures nor the position of agriculture affects one great fact that framers must borrow.[1] Agricultural credit, thus, in a practical sense, is a nucleus of the system of farm operation. It provides flow to the system averting ruins which would have occurred due to the lack of monetary capacity of a farmers. Adequate and timely credit to the farmer is, therefore, vital and indispensable for the rehabilitation and progress of agriculture. In poor countries, agriculture assumes even more importance. Farmer's inability or least limited ability to save does not allow him to finance his pursuits and raise better production from his farms. Agricultural credit through institutional channels is the only way to break agricultural stagnation in such situations. Private funding agencies play a limited role keeping in view the larger public interest.

Estimates of Credit Requirements: The credit requirement of a farmer vary from crop to crop, season to season and from region to region. Further, there is no agency which provides adequate statistical information regarding individual credit needs. These two factors make it difficult to estimate the aggregate requirements of agriculture sector.

However, economists have attempted to formulate the model applicable at the micro level to estimate the credit requirement of a farmer. According to Singh & Gupta[2] short term credit requirements of a farmer can be estimated by taking into consideration the area under cultivation and capital inputs in a given farm. The equation is as under:

$$Y_i = R_{ij}^{m} = 1\ P_{ij} \times ij$$

where : Y_i = Credit requirement;

$R^{m}{}_{ij}$ = Proportion of credit to capital inputs on i th farm;

P_{ij} = Capital input per acre in the ith farm;

X_{ij} = Area under ith crop on Jth farm;

Singh and Gupta have taken the value of

R_i = 0.50 small farms.

R_i = 0.45 medium farms.

R_i = 0.40 large farms.

Credit requirements for a block would, therefore, be estimated as:

$$C = \frac{A_{tk}}{A_{si} = 1} n_i y_i$$

Where C = credit requirement

Atk = Total cultivated area in a block

Asi = Sample holdings

n = Number of holdings

The credit requirement of a farmer is functionally related with the cost of exogeneous inputs like fertilizers, seed, pesticides, irrigation etc, its requirements can be calculated by using regression equations of the following type:

$$Y = A\, x_1^{\,b}\ X_2^{b2}\ x_3^{b3}\ X_4^{b4} \ \ldots\ldots\ x_n^{bn}$$

$$C = Bi\, Xi\ B_2 X_2\ B_3X_3\ B_4\ X_4 \ldots\ldots\ Bn\ Xn$$

where Y = total returns from crop

X_1 = investment on irrigation

X_2 = investment on cattle

X_3 = investment on fertilizers

X_4 = area cultivated

C = amount of credit required

and b_1, b_2, b_3, b_4 ... and b_n and $B_1...B_n$ are respective regression co-efficients.

This micro model, however, is not suitable for estimating total credit requirements for agriculture as a whole since regression coefficients vary from region to region. The total requirements of credit is not easy to be ascertained. A farmer needs credit for diverse purposes which include both production and consumption. Further, quite often there is no clear line of demarcation between production and consumption itself. Where a farmer borrow to pay for his family labour during the period the crop getting ready, it is difficult to classify this loan as production loan or consumption loan. However some attempts have been made to estimate the credit estimates of the agrarian sector. The latest one is made by the working group of the Planning Commission. One group has estimated agricultural credit requirements at Rs. 30,000 crores during the Seventh Plan period 1985-90. A more recent-estimate put this figure at Rs. 75,000 crores for the next decades.[3]

Sources of Agricultural Finance: Agricultural credit is supplied by several agencies. These can be grouped under two main categories: (1) Private sources or non-institutional sources and (ii) institutional sources.

Private or non-institutional agencies which supply credit to farmers and other rural people include professional money lenders, agricultural money lenders, land-lords, commission agents and friends and relatives. Traditionally, these agencies have played an important role in meeting the credit requirements of villagers. Most of the money advanced by them used to be spent on house-hold consumption and social and religious ceremonies and very little on production activities.

The interest rates were very high usually ranging from 24 per cent to 60 per cent per annum. The incidence of indebtedness was also very high because such loans were highly exploitive by nature and most of the rural poor were never get rid of the ever expanding spiral of such loans. According to the All India Rural Credit Survey Committee Report (1951-52) non-institutional sources supplied 92.7 per cent of the total rural credit advanced in 1951-52. It shows the intensity of the problem. However, there has been a marked decline in the share of non-institutional credit in the total rural credit advanced over the period of 1961-62, 70-71, 80-81 and 1990-91, partly due to the growing competition among the institutional sources and partly to various agrarian reforms implemented since independence. But non-institutional agencies are still important source of rural credit.

Decision of Credit

Credit is an asset for all those farmers who have limited capital. The efficient use of credit may increase farm efficiency and the income and the standard of living of the farmers. Contrary, the unproductive use of credit may bring doom to the farmers and in the process he may even lose his land and savings. The decision to borrow the money, thus, means success or failure and hence it is most important farm management decision. The questions: when to borrow? what to offer for security? and what should be the length and repayment schedule of loans etc. are some important elements of such management decision.

The credit management decision basically depends upon added-return-added cost principle. On any one farm, the productivity of land, the amount of capital owned, the health and age of the farmer and the level of management determine the amount of credit that can safely be borrowed. Moreover, all farmers are also subject to varying degree of uncertainty which introduces an element of risk. The safe amount to borrow, therefore, varies from farmer to farmer, area to area and from period to period.

At the micro level an individual farmer will decide to invest if the net present value of that investment is greater than zero. The net present value of an investment (NPV1) can be calculated on cost-series, on the one hand, and income series, on the other. This can be expressed as

$$NPV1 = \sum_{c=1}^{n} \frac{Yi}{(1-r)^{i}} - C$$

Where C = initial capital cost of investment

Y_i = net cash flow at the end of year *i* where the benefit of the investment is spread over "n" years.

This formula calculates NPV1 of a self-financed investment. But when investment is made by the farmer out of a loan whose repayment is spread over later years, this formula requires a slight modification. The capital cost in this case will be equal to the aggregate present value of all the investments of principal and interest payments to be made over "n" years by the farmers. The present value of the capital cost incurred at a number of periods is arrived at by summing over the discounted values of principal and interest components of costs in each period. Thus the equation become:

$$C = \sum_{c=1}^{n} \frac{ci}{(1+x)^{i}}$$

The modified formula of NPVI, thus, can be expressed as

$$NPV1 = \sum_{c=1}^{n} \frac{Yc}{(1+r)^{i}} - \sum_{c=1}^{n} \frac{Ci}{(1+r)^{i}}$$

$C = P_i + P_{i,}$ P_i refers to the annual instalment towards repayment of principal and 1 to annual interest payment.[4]

The institutional sources of rural credit include the government, the Reserve Bank of India, the National Bank of Agriculture and Rural Development (NABARD), Land Development Bank, Commercial Banks, Co-operative Banks, Regional Rural Bank (RRBs), Co-operative Credit Societies, Farmer's Service Societies, Large Area Multipurpose Societies, various corporations, foundations, etc.

Among all the non-institutional sources, money-lender has been the main supplier of short and medium-term credit to the farmers. Two types of money-lenders are found in rural areas: (1) Professional money-lenders whose main function or the only function is to grant loans to the farmers, and (ii) agricultural money-lenders, who combine money-lending with farming. In most of the under-developed countries money-lender is the biggest contributor of farm-credit. All India Rural Credit Review Committee and RBI Bulletin showed that in 1951-52, the share of this agency in India stood as high as 90.9 per cent of the total credit. Its share gradually declined. In 1961-62 it was 67.4 per cent, in 1970-71, 68.4 per cent and in 1981-82 it was 38.8 per cent. This preponderance of the money-lenders in the arrangement for agricultural credit is, however, no guarantee that they too satisfies the essential requirements of a good agricultural credit system more than the other agencies. Contrary, they satisfy none of the tests of a good credit system. But there are some important features which attract most of the farmers and make it more popular. These are:

(i) Money-lender's credit can be utilised for productive as well as unproductive purposes;

(ii) He may not insist on tangible security for his loans. He knows the borrower intimately or has some hold over him;

(iii) The loans advanced are seldom related to the purpose and he is not particular about deciding the duration of the loans;

(iv) He is available at service at any-time-day and night;

(v) He adopts a somewhat flexible attitude towards execution of documents and the security to be obtained.

But these attractions are not because of his satisfying the tests of a sound agricultural credit agency, but because alternative agencies have not been able to build up their organisation to replace the money-lender.

This widely prevalent profession in rural India has not helped agriculture to grow, it has over the years held peasants to ransom. It is generally carried on at extortionate terms, at compound rate of interest, and employing land, bullocks, cattle, house, utensils, farm implements, and even the peasant and members of his family as collateral which gives rise to illegal bonded labour. Further, the resources at the command of each individual money-lender also prove inadequate to meet the demands for credit for modern agriculture.

Major Sources of Agriculture Credit (per cent)

Institutional Sources	*1951*	*1961*	*1971*	*1981*
	7.2	17.3	29.2	61.2
i. Government	3.7	6.6	6.7	4.0
ii. Co-operative Societies/Banks	3.5	10.4	20.7	28.6
iii. Commercial Banks	–	0.3	2.2	28.6
iv. Insurance	–	–	0.1	0.3
v. Provident Fund	–	–	0.1	0.3
Non-Institutional Sources	92.8	82.7	70.8	38.8
i. Land-lords	3.5	1.1	8.6	4.0
ii. Money-lenders	25.2	47.0	23.1	8.6
iii. Professional Money Lenders	46.4	13.0	13.8	8.3
iv. Traders	5.1	7.5	8.7	3.4
v. Relatives/Friends	11.5	5.8	13.8	9.0
vi. Others	1.1	7.5	2.8	5.5
	100	100	100	100

Institutional agencies have, lately, made a dent in the agricultural finance situation. Efforts to build up the institutional financing system for agriculture commenced with the adoption of the Co-operative Credit Societies Act in 1904. Co-operatives were nurtured as the primary institutions to relieve farmers from traditional burden of debts and to promote thrift. They assumed an increasingly larger role in the agricultural sector both in the matter of quantitative expansion and diversity of functions, although credit continued to be other main function. The banking system also made certain pioneering efforts in this regard was inadequate till the nationalisation of 14 scheduled commercial banks in 1969. Since then, the commercial banks have taken a growing interest in financing agriculture. A brief statement of the growth of non-institutional and institutional credit agencies is given as under.

Table shows that massive expansion has taken place in the rural credit sector. The institutional sources have gradually increased their participation from a meagre 7.2 per cent contribution in 1951 to 61.2 per cent in 1981. The two major sources of institutional credit, co-operative credit societies/co-operative banks and commercial banks in combined increased their share from 3.5 per cent in 1951 to an impressive 56.6 per cent in 1981. Commercial banks alone have shown a substantial increase in its share during 1971 and 1981. In 1971 its share was merely 2.2 per cent which rose to 28 per cent in 1981. This was the direct result of the rapid expansion of bank branches in rural areas after nationalisation of 14 commercial banks in 1969. In fact the steep decline in the importance of non-institutional sources in rural credit from 70.8 per cent in 1970 to 38.6 per cent in 1981 was mainly due to the steep rise in the participation of banks in rural credit. Following table shows the share of participation of banks in rural credit.

		June 1969	*April 1981*
(i)	Share of Rural Branches in Total Number of Branches	22.2	49.0
(ii)	Share of Rural Deposits in Total Deposit	3.1	11.0
(iii)	Share of Rural Credit to Total Bank Credit	1.5	9.4
(iv)	Share of Agricultural Credit to Total Bank Credit	5.2	14.4
(v)	Rural Credit Deposit Ratio	37.2	57.0

The non-institutional agencies have been the traditional source of loans in the agrarian economy. Among these, the most important has been the village money-lender. His method of business is very simple. He generally lends on the basis of personal security and adjust his terms to the borrower's needs provided that a sufficient high rate of interest is paid for the loan. The rate of interest is high by all standards, and accounts are manipulated frequently without the knowledge of borrower. The explanation lies in the fact that money-lender is the "only basis of thrift in a desert of improvidence" and the needs of the borrowers cannot wait. Loans are also available on the mortgage of crops or valuables from traders and their agents. The traders usually advance loans before the sowing season on the understanding that the crops will be sold to them. In such cases they not only change high rate of interest, but also pay an unusually low price for crops. Here the money-lending and trading function are combined.

A Profile of Institutional Agencies – A Multi-Agency Approach: The institutional agencies have lately made a dent in the agricultural finance. The first effort was made in 1904 when the Co-operative Credit Societies Act was passed. Co-operatives were the primary institutions to relieve farmers from the traditional burden of debt. They were considered the most influential institution in the matter of quantitative expansion and diversity of functions. The banking system also made certain pioneering efforts in this efforts but progress made by them was inadequate till the nationalisation of banks in 1969. Co-operative Societies and Commercial Banks taken together have been proved the most effective institutional agencies to fulfil the farmer's need. Seventh Five Year Plan provides some relevant information about these two agencies.

	Institutional Agencies	*Advances in 1984-85*	*Level to be reached in 1989-90*
(i)	**Co-operatives**		
	Short-term	2,500	55,400
	Medium-term	250	500
	Long-term	500	1,030
(ii)	**Commercial Bank Including RRBs**		
	Short-term	1,110	2,500
	Term loans	1,450	3,000
	Total	5,810	12,570

Source : GOI, Seventh Five Year Plan 1985-90

It was observed that the Co-operative Societies alone would not be in a position, despite their increased coverage since 1950, to meet the increasing requirement of credit. The nationalisation of commercial banks was seen as an opportunity to bring these banks in a big way in the areas of agricultural finance. During pre-nationalisation period, there was an exclusive dependence on the co-operatives to distribute credits; commercial banks were more or less ineffective. Since 1970, India came to practice what has been called as the multi-agency approach in rural credit.

The multi-agency approach came to be adopted as the overall national policy as no single complex financial institution has the necessary organisational structure or financial strength to cater the total requirements of Indian agriculture. In the wake of this policy, commercial banks began to participate in agricultural finance as equal partners of co-operatives. Not only this, two new institutions — Regional Rural Banks (RRBs) and the Farmer's Service Societies (FSS) – were also established during this period. Thus, since 1970 India has a multi-agency system in which a number of institutions are functioning to serve the financial needs of the farmers. Among these institutions we have co-operative societies, commercial banks, regional rural banks and farmer's service societies at the grassroots level. These are supported by central co-operative banks and regional offices of commercial banks and RRBs at the district level. RBI and NABARD support them at the national level.

Co-operatives: The co-operative credit structure in India is divided into two parts. One provides short-term and medium-term loans, whereas the second provides long-term loans. The short and the medium term loans has 3-tier structure with the State Co-operative-Banks at the apex, central co-operative banks at the district level and primary agricultural societies (also known as multi-purpose co-operative societies and Farmers Service Societies) at the village level. Long-term loans are provided by the State Co-operative Land Development Banks and Primary Co-operative Land Development Banks.

The role and the importance of co-operatives in providing rural credit has been explained in the World Economic Conference held in Geneva in 1927. A special resolution of the Conference defined their role in these words: "The increase in agricultural production is intimately bound up with the organisation of agricultural credit which will place at the disposal of the agriculturist the necessary capital on favourable terms. The first condition surmounting these difficulties in the organisation of the credit institution in those countries where they do not exist and their development where they are already in existence. The best form of institution appears to be the co-operative credit society operating by means of resources which the very fact of association enables it to procure and no increase with or without the assistance of the public authorities".

In 1954, the Rural Credit Survey Committee stated: "Today more than ever before, there is every reason for an institutional system of rural credit to be based on a co-operative association in the village."[5]

Primary Agricultural Credit Society (PACS)

PACS are mainly responsible for the agricultural co-operative movement in India. They were established in India after the enactment of the Co-operative Societies Act in 1904. The movement was basically aimed at institutionalise efforts to relieve farmers from the traditional burdens of debt and promote thrift. Gradually they played a more positive role as compared to their earlier characteristic of merely preventing exploitation by money-lenders. There was not only a steady quantitative expansion in the numbers but also a growing diversity in the functions. Following the recommendation of All India Rural Credit Survey —1951-54, large sized multi-purpose societies known as Service Co-operatives came to be organised. These multi-purpose societies are expected to provide credit to its members, promote savings, supply farm requisites and arrange for the marketing of surplus farm produce. Multi-purpose Co-operative Societies, however, never became a reality on the national scale, because too much emphasis has been laid only on the credit aspect and other services has been neglected.

During 1950-51 and 1960, there was a distinct emphasis on the quantitative growth of the PACS. The PACS had more than doubled during this decade. But the quantitative expansion had an adverse effect on the quantitative standard of the movement. Patel Committee in 1961 on taccavi loans and co-operative credit drew the attention of the Government to this undesirable growth. Since then the Government undertook to reorganise the PACS by amalgamating the very small ones with the viable ones. In this way, the second phase which began with 1960-61, the quantitative expansion of co-operative societies has stopped. As a result all PACS acquire a viable character. Upto 1987-88, their number stands at a little over 89,000.[6]

Though the absolute number of such societies had been declining since 1960-61, the coverage of these societies has been increasing from 75 per cent of all villages in 1960-61 to 97 per cent in 1987-88. The membership of the co-operative societies too has been increasing very fast from 44.08 lakh in 1950-51 to 170.41 lakhs in 1960-61, 309.63 lakh in 1970-71 and a little over 725 lakhs in 1987-88.

Another important indicator of the progress of PACS has been a substantial increase in either paid-up capital from Rs. 7.61 crores in 1950-51 to Rs. 365.74 crores in 1985-86. Similarly, the working capital has increased from Rs. 37.25 crores in 1986-87. The deposits and loans advanced by PACS have been increased at an encouraging rate. Following table explain this phenomenon.

Deposits and Loans of PACS
(1950-51 — 1986-87)

(Rs. in Crores)

Years	*1950-51*	*1960-61*	*1970-71*	*1980-81*	*1986-87*
Deposits	4.28	14.50	69.46	266.0	709
Loans	22.90	202.72	577.88	1656.0	3149

Source: RBI Report on Trend & Progress of Banking in India 1987-88. p. 156.

Although loans advanced by the societies have been increasing as has shown in the lakhs, yet they were behind the estimated requirements of the order of Rs. 5,540 crore.[7] The figures of Rs. 3,149 crores looks very inadequate. It means the PACS are hardly in a position to meet a little over one-half of the requirements of the agrarian sector. Further, due to the adoption of modern techniques the credit requirement of agricultural sector would all along be increasing at a faster rate to meet the demand of new agricultural technology. The PACs would have to gear up for a bigger role.

Central Co-operative Banks (CCB) : In the 3-tier credit structure, the PACs derive their finance from the central co-operative banks which operate at the district level. At present, there are 353 central co-operative banks with a membership of about 8 lakhs. Their working capital amount to Rs. 10,221 crores. The total loans advanced by these banks upto 1986-87 amounts to Rs. 6,393 crores.[8]

State Co-operative Banks (SCB): At the top of co-operative credit structure are the state co-operative banks which are 29 at present. Their membership is 36 thousand with a share capital of Rs. 64 crores and a working capital of Rs. 6,239 crores. The SCB had advanced loans value at Rs. 7,278 crores during 1986-87.

Co-operative and Long-term Loans: Long-term loans in the co-operative structure has been provided by Land Development Banks (LDBs). These were aimed to fill the gap in the rural credit sector and to create institutional arrangement for credit services to the farmers who were exploited by the money lenders. It was actually a production oriented system of lending. It is a widespread and well-knit structure today with 19 central land development banks and 848 primary land development banks. They provide long-term credit for various agricultural development purposes. Following table provides an information about the growth of these banks.

L.D.Bs — 1950-51 To 1986-87

(Rs. in Crores)

Year	*1950-51*	*1960-61*	*1970-71*	*1980-81*	*1986-87*
Loan Advanced	1.38	11.62	170.36	426.0	552
Loan Outstanding	6.59	37.74	636.16	2047.0	2,829

Source: Indian Agricultural in Brief & RBI: Report on Trend and Progress of Banking in India 1987-88.

These banks provide loans for a variety of purposes like minor irrigation, farm mechanisation through tractors, power tillers etc. land reclamation and horticulture. Banks have diversified lending for other equally important productive purposes which are subsidiary to agriculture. The emphasis is not on raising production but also on helping farmers to supplement their income by taking up other subsidiary occupations. These banks are also the most important institutions for implementing various agricultural development projects financed by the World Bank Group.

Weaknesses of Co-operative Credit

In spite of its important role in providing agricultural credit co-operative credit suffers from various weaknesses.

Firstly, co-operative credit, in many parts of the world, has been flowing mainly towards large cultivators and the marginal and small farmers have been deprived of in having access to co-operative credit both for current inputs and viable investment. During 1985-86, for example, out of the total credit of Rs. 3,140 crores disbursed by the PACSs borrowers with ownership holding upto 1 hectare received Rs. 454 crores (14.47 per cent) and those with holding between 1 and 2 hectares received Rs. 598 crores (18.77 per cent), tenant cultivators and agricultural labourers received only Rs. 99 crores. Further, in 1987-88, farmers having holding less than 2 hectares received 35.06 per cent of total loans advanced by PACSs while owners of holdings more than 2 hectares received 59.6 per cent. The share of tenants, share-croppers and landless labourers who are poorest and hence the most needy, was only 4.8 per cent.[9]

Secondly, a large number of primary agricultural credit societies are neither viable nor even potentially viable and must be regarded as inadequate and unsatisfactory agencies for dispensing production-oriented credit. It has been estimated that about 15 per cent of the total number of 353 of central co-operative banks in the country have been defined as weak. They are weak in the sense that they have bad and doubtful debts, accumulated losses and overdues over three years which have exceeded to 50 per cent of their owned funds (paid up share capital and reserves). It has also been estimated that only 61 per cent of the primary agricultural credit societies are working at a profit and only 40 per cent of them have full-time paid secretaries.

Thirdly, coordination between the authorities and agencies in charge of co-operative credit and those of supplies, extension etc. under agricultural programmes has been inadequate.

Fourthly, co-operative credit has frequently fallen short of standard of timeliness, adequacy and dependability. This is due to paucity of resources, lack of eligibility, time consuming and cumbersome procedure, poor quality of management and general efficiency of working methods.

Fifthly, co-operative credit societies have shown an undue dependence on external sources of finance, among which the more important are borrowings. RBI, NABARD provide very large financial support. As a result borrowings of co-operative have substantially increased. Further, a good part of the share capital of many co-operatives also comes from the Government. This dependence has to be reduced because (i) it adversely affects the autonomy of co-operative, and (ii) it adds to the inflationary pressures in the economy.

Sixthly, co-operative societies have been faced with the problem of recovery of loans and advances. The overdues of co-operative societies are large and growing. Overdues was 5.2 per cent in State Co-operative Banks, 24.9 per cent in State Co-operative Banks and 33.5 per cent in district credit co-operative branches and 33.5 per cent in PACSs in decade ago. In 1985-86, these dues were 8.8 per cent, 35.9 per cent, 45.2 per cent. The defective lending policies pursued by the co-operatives, the apathy of the managements in taking quick action against defaulting members and the absence of a favourable climate has been the main factors for such growing overdues.

Commercial Banks: Until the introduction of social control in 1968 and nationalisation of major 14 commercial banks in 1969, the official policy was to give fillip to co-operative system as the best suited channel for institutional credit for agricultural and rural development. The involvement of commercial banks in agricultural financing was negligible. It was only 0.9 per cent in 1951-52 and further only 0.7 per cent in 1961-62. The main reason for such insignificant participation of commercial banks in rural credit distribution was the economic factors. Since commercial banks were private sector industry, they put more emphasis on credit-worthiness of work, person, place, region and state.

The subsistence nature of agriculture, its unorganised, individualistic functioning and heavy dependence on monsoon make it uncertain, risky and unreliable venture. As against it, the industrial sector is relatively more organised and less dependent on nature. Consequently, it is economically strong and reliable sector. Commercial banks being a private sector industry to avoid risk and uncertainty to maintain high project which agricultural sector could not guarantee. The industrial sector can show its credit-worthiness. The concentration of banking activities in urban centres, cities, commercial and industrial pockets was mainly due to this reason. The negligence of other risk-prone sectors such as agricultural, education, small-scale industries, self-professionals and artisan-class was quite obvious.

As a remedial step to this state of affairs 14 major commercial banks were nationalised in 1969. This was followed by nationalisation of 6 more banks in 1980. After nationalisation, the banks opened a large number of branches in rural areas and have substantially increased their advances in these areas. In June 1969, out of the total of 8,252 branches of commercial banks, 1,832 or 22.2 per cent were in rural areas. In June 1992, the total number of branches increased to 60,649 of which 34,470 or 56.8 per cent were in rural areas. The trend clearly shows that while the total number of bank branches increased by seven times, the total number of rural branches increased by eighteen times. The share of priority sector in bank credit which was only 14.9 per cent in June 1969, rose to 40.4 per cent in March 1990.

The number of accounts in agriculture direct finance was 160 thousand in June 1969. It rose to 19,735 thousand in March 1991. In case of indirect finance the number of accounts were merely 4 thousand in 1969. In 1991, the number increased to 564 thousand. Similarly, the amount outstanding in relation to direct finance to agriculture was Rs. 40.31 crores in June 1969. This figure rose to Rs. 15,739 crores in March 1991. In case of indirect finance the figure rose from Rs. 12,212 crores in June 1969 to Rs. 1,132 crores in March 1991. On percentage basis direct finance contribution to total advances increased from 1.3 in June 1969 to 14.6 in March 1991.

The trend of progress shows that commercial banks, after nationalisation, have played an important role in providing rural credit. The objective of branch expansion programme has been fulfilled and now emphasis should be given to consolidate the rural credit facilities. A necessary infrastructure has already been built-up. For instance bank's operational base in rural areas has been widened and there is distinct bias for rural centres in the branch licensing policy of the Reserve Bank. Liberal refinancing facilities have been provided by RBI and NABARD to the banks for lending to agriculture. Area specific credit plans have been prepared under the lead bank scheme. Credit Guarantee Corporation of India (CGCI) was established in 1971. It was later on merged into Deposit Insurance Corporation and now called DICGC.

Despite remarkable achievements of commercial banks in the field of rural credit their operation and the performance have been criticised on various grounds. Some important and leading issues are as under.

Firstly, the prime objective of bank nationalisation was increased credit flow to weaker sections and rural areas. The expansion of banking facilities in under-banked and unbanked areas was the first step. In two decades banks have achieved this objective. But it has created various problems. One problem in relation to rapid expansion of branches has been the deterioration of quality of scheme preparation, particularly under the anti-poverty programme. Another important problem has been realised in form of rising operational cost of rural branches. Opening of a large number of branches in rural areas which do not have adequate business potential rise in establishment and operational cost which has adversely affected the profitability of banks. All the branches operating in the rural areas are not viable units. The decreasing deposits and increasing overdues prove it well.

Secondly, the recovery position of the commercial banks is also bad. Upto June 1986 the overdues of commercial banks amounted Rs. 1,744 crores which was 43 per cent of demand. More than 53 per cent of overdues were more than three years old. This is an alarming situation which needed a corrective action. Seventh Plan has correctly warned: "If this trend is not reversed and banks are reduced to institutions providing grants rather than recycling scarce resources to get the maximum benefits for the country as a whole, the banking system will be unable to provide more credit to meet the growing needs of the farmers".[12]

Thirdly, commercial banks have failed to fill the gap in the availability of credit not covered by the co-operatives. Instead, they have served those areas which were already well-served by the co-operatives, e.g., Southern and Western region, Punjab and Haryana. The proper geographical spread of bank branches is also absent. It is found that more than one bank operates in the same area resulting in unhealthy competition between one commercial bank and the other.

Fourthly, there are regional and State-wise imbalances in the credit disbursed by the banks. A detailed analysis of credit-deposit ratio-C/D ratio is given in the Appendix-A. The analysis shows that although the C/D-ratio is improving, yet the imbalances are still exist.

Fifthly, the problem of coordination is another serious problem which hampers the effective implementation of credit schemes. The problem of coordination is not only between one commercial bank and another but also between commercial banks and co-operative credit structure and between banks and Government department.

A review of the working of the commercial banks in the field of rural credit shows that the commercial banks have been helping the farmers in promoting dry farming, purchasing agricultural machinery and other inputs, dairying, lift irrigation and electrification of tube-well etc. Despite the increasing role of commercial banks in rural finance, it has been found that the non-institutional credit—landlords, money-lenders, sahukars, relatives etc — still accounts 40 per cent of total rural credit. The commercial banks have still to cover too much to establish themselves as an important agency of rural finance. The small and marginal farmers have not much benefitted from these banks. Most of these credit has flowed to the rich farmers. Many backward areas still remain unattended and many branches are non-viable units. Mounting overdues, non-profitability, declining deposits, and increasing operational cost are some serious problems which have made their performance poor.

To make banking institution an effective source of rural finance various new schemes such as the Lead Bank Scheme (LBS), Village Adoption Scheme (VAS), Service Area Plan (SAP), Intensive Centre Scheme (ICS) and Regional Rural Bank Scheme (RRBS) were introduced. A brief introduction of all such schemes is given below.

The Lead Bank Scheme: This scheme was started in December 1969. The scheme applies to such districts which are identified as "under-banked". One of the banks functioning in the under-banked district is assigned the role of the "lead-banks". This lead-bank is expected not only to provide more banking facilities to agriculture and other priority sectors in the districts but also helps in its overall development. This bank has a district consultative committee consisting of the representatives of (i) the State Government, (ii) the scheduled banks and (iii) other financial institutions working in the district. The consultative committee decides various financial schemes in relation to the development of agricultural and other priority sectors.

Village Adoption Scheme: In order to approach the unbanked areas of the district, a techno-economic survey of the area under the jurisdiction of the lead bank was conducted. The lead banks were then asked to select a needy village or a cluster of villages and extend need-based credit facilities to all the viable and potentially viable farmers.

Service Area Plan: This scheme focused on micro level credit planning. Under this plan, the entire responsibility of assessing and meeting the credit needs of all the approximately 6 lakhs villages in the country are assigned to the branches of commercial banks and the co-operative banks. Fifteen to twenty villages are assigned to each bank. This approach aims to coordinate the commercial banks credit and co-operative credit to serve the area.

Intensive Centre Scheme: This scheme is introduced by the State Bank of India. Under this scheme State Bank selected compact area (mostly backward area) where the financial needs of all the aspects of its economy are looked after.

Regional Rural Banks (RRBs): These banks were established in 1975 on the recommendation of "The Working Group of Rural Banks". The aim was to supplement the efforts of the Commercial Banks and the Co-operative Credit Societies in extending credit to weaker sections of the rural community, small and marginal farmers, landless labourers, artisans and other rural residents of small and poor means.

The intention was to develop better coordination among banks and co-operatives. Further, an atmosphere of local feel and familiarity with the rural problems which the co-operatives possess and the degree of business organisation and the modern outlook which the commercial banks had, could be combined with a view to reach the rural poor more extensively. The commercial banks with the predominantly urban culture are not suited for rural people. Hence the staff of RRBs was to be recruited from the neighbouring areas and as such would have better understanding of the local problems. The co-operative sector, on the other hand, is no doubt familiar with the local problems yet it does not possess the professional competence needed for developing steadily growing secondary and tertiary sectors of the rural economy. RRBs is considered the ideal combination of both — co-operatives and banks.

In 1975, 5 RRBs were initially set up whose number later rose to 196. The number of branches rose from 17 to 14,525 over the period of 1975 to 1992. The number of district covered from 12 to 380 over the period of 1975 to September 1990. Deposits with RRBs which were Rs. 20 lakhs in 1975 rose to Rs. 4,429 crores and at end of March 1992. This shows a commendable expansion in the operation of RRBs.[13]

Besides the commendable expansion of banks, their qualitative aspect is more significant. These banks have played an important role in mobilising rural savings as they are more close to the farmers and hence paid specific attention to the credit needs of the rural poor. Aggregate advances to the weaker sections accounted for more than 90 per cent of the total direct advances of RRBs. More than 90 per cent of branches of these banks are operating in unbanked rural areas.

A study by T.K. Velayudham and V. Sankaranarayanan[14] highlights various problems in relation to the functioning of these banks. These problems may be grouped as organisational problems, management problems, non-viability and problems of recovery.

Organisational problems have arisen from the concept as well as structure of RRBs. Earlier on the authorised capital of every RRB, was Rs.1 crore and issued capital was Rs. 25 lakhs. The authorised capital later increased to Rs. 5 crores and the issued capital to Rs. 1 crore. The multi-agency control has contributed a lack of uniformity in the functioning of RRBs. Further, it has resulted in lack of support from State Government and lack of proper monitoring by sponsor banks. The restricted area of operation and restricted target group are another constraint in relation to effective functioning of these banks. The process of recruitment and training of RRB staff has also not received adequate attention. The trend of urban biased recruitment of staff is prevailing and this has not developed any confidence in the rural poor. It has also been realised that the unplanned and unwidely growth of these banks under pressure from the State Bank created numerous problems in the control and management of these banks.[15]

Since the RRBs are district level banks, the sponsor banks have been deputed only middle-management staff to run them. Such staff finds it difficult to take independent decisions in a new environment. In addition, meetings of the board of directors of RRBs are not held regularly and various new official directors do not show much interest in the working of these banks. Moreover, the functioning of RRBs is also not uniform in all the States/districts.[16]

The study also shows that a large number of RRBs are running on loss year after year and this has rendered them non-viable. The accumulated losses has been estimated to Rs. 550 crores. Various factors are responsible for such losses. Firstly, these banks are confined to lend to only weaker sections where the interest rate on loans is the lowest in the banking system. Secondly, low margins with high cost of servicing a large number of small accounts added to the losses. Further, opening RRBs branches year after year has also added to the over-head costs without proportional increase in income.

Recovery position of RRBs is also very bad. The overdues as percentage of loans outstanding at the end of March 1992 was 32 per cent. The high incidence of overdues is attributed to a number of internal and external factors. Internal factors include defective loaning policies, weak monitoring and supervision, apathy towards recovery, failure to link loan with development and to ensure effective utilisation of loan. Among the external factors, political interference, droughts and floods, lack of legal and administrative support from the State Government are some leading factors.

National Bank for Agriculture and Rural Development (NABARD)

The most important development in the field of institutional rural credit is the setting up of the National Bank for Agriculture and Rural Development (NABARD) in July 1982. This bank was established on the lines of the Industrial Development Bank of India. A committee called "Committee to Review Arrangements for Institutional Credit for Agriculture and Rural Development (CRAFICARD) recommended that a new apex bank called National Bank for Agriculture and Rural Development should be set up for "providing undivided attention, forceful direction and pointed focus" to the credit problem arising out of the integrated approach to rural development. Accordingly it took over from Reserve Bank all the functions that were performed in the field of rural credit. NABARD is an apex organisation in respect of all matters relating to policy, planning and operational aspects, concerning the flow of credit for the development of agriculture, rural industries, handicrafts and other allied activities in the rural areas. It is a single integrated agency for meeting the credit needs of all type of agricultural and rural development. In short, it has taken over the entire operations of the Agricultural Refinance and Development Corporation (ARDC) as well as the refinance functions from RBI in relation to State Co-operatives and RRBs. The authorised share capital of NABARD is Rs. 500 crores and paid-up capital is Rs. 100 crores.

Functions: The main functions of NABARD are as follows:

(i) It works as an apex body for development policy, planning and operational matters relating to credit for agriculture, allied activities, rural industries and rural artisans and other rural development activities.

(ii) Training, research and consultancy relating to credit for agricultural development.

(iii) Co-ordination and monitoring of all agricultural and rural development activities with a view to tying them up with planned development activities in the rural sector.

(iv) Refinance – short, medium and long-term – the co-operatives and RRBs including marketing and distribution.

(v) Refinance to commercial banks against term lending and short-term accommodation for special purposes.

(vi) Direct lending through consortium arrangement in special cases.

(vii) Inspection of co-operative banks and RRBs.

Performance: NABARD was established in July 1982 and it is difficult to judge its performance in the short span of one decade. It must be remembered that NABARD does not deal directly with the farmers, it grants assistance to them only through co-operative banks, commercial banks and RRBs.

In the field of short-term assistance to institutions, NABARD sanctioned short-term credit limits amounting to Rs. 3,015 crores in 1990-91 for financing seasonal agricultural operations. It also granted short-term credit limit of Rs. 621 crores during the same year for purposes other than seasonal agricultural operations.

Purpose-Wise Lending by NABARD in 1989-90

Areas	*No. of schemes sanctioned*	*Commitments (Rs. crores)*	*Disbursement (Rs. crores)*
Minor Irrigation	5174	578	498
Land Development	86	36	11
Farm-Mechanisation	–	262	225
Plantation/Horticulture	1133	171	97
Poultry	1058	99	58
Sheep/Goat/Piggery	165	10	10
Fisheries	317	28	21
Dairy	894	107	75
Forestry	64	18	17
Storage/Market yards	26	9	13
IRDP	–	511	549
NFS	–	78	62
Others	294	77	66
Total	9211	2039	1702

NABARD sanctioned medium-term credit limits amounting Rs. 10 crores in 1990 for approved agricultural purposes. Assistance of Rs. 161

crores was also sanctioned in 1990-91, to commercial banks to convert short-term agricultural loans granted to farmers affected by droughts, floods or other natural calamities into medium-term loans.

In case of long-term refinance assistance under various schemes is concerned NABARD sanctioned 10,650 schemes in 1990-91 involving commitment of Rs. 2,119 crores. Disbursement of loan was Rs. 1,902 crores. The number of schemes sanctioned upto end of March 1991 was 89,513 with commitments and disbursements amounting Rs. 18,299 and Rs. 14,310 crores respectively. Largest number of schemes sanctioned were in the field of minor irrigation followed by farm mechanisation. The purpose-wise lending by NABARD in 1989-90 is given in the following table.

NABARD has adopted a policy of developing and promoting agricultural investments in the less developed and under-banked States. The disbursement in these States stood at Rs. 821 crores during 1990-91 which was 43.2 per cent of the total disbursements of all India level.

NABARD also provides assistance to the non-farm sector with a view to promoting integrated rural development. Finance is thus provided to small-scale industries, cottage and village industrial co-operative societies. For meeting their working in block capital requirement. Short-term credit is also provided to production and marketing activities of co-operative sugar mills, handloom weavers and rural artisan members of the village level co-operatives.

Financial assistance to 87 RRBs was sanctioned by NABARD till 1990-91 from its Research and Development Fund for setting up/strengthening their Technical, Monitoring and Evaluation (TME) cells. NABARD also sanctioned financial assistance from its Research & Development fund to various institutions for undertaking research seminars/conferences/symposia studies.

Evaluation of Performance: Agriculture in India is entering into dynamic phase. In this shape technological innovations and its application requires increasing amount of production and investment credit. The major policy in the sphere of agricultural credit is, therefore, its progressive institutionalisation for rural development programmes with a larger flow of funds to assist weaker sections and less developed regions. The basic objectives of the credit policy has been to set up provision of timely and adequate credit to farmers, particularly to small and marginal farmers.

Khusro Committee evaluated the performance of NABARD. Among the three main functions – refinance, institutional development and inspection of client banks, Committee says that the refinance function has attracted relatively more attention and resources over the year. Its intention of providing credit to agriculture, small-scale and cottage industries and bringing about prosperity to rural areas has not been matched by action. Moreover, it is also realised that a major chunk of its personnel is stationed at the head office, regional offices and sub-offices. It has only 176 district level officers. A study done by V. Krishnadevan rightly pointed out, "it is somewhat strange that an agency dealing with agricultural finance and which is supposed to be in touch with grassroots realities, houses a significant number of its employees in cities"[17]

The success of NABARD can be measured by the transformation it can bring about in the rural credit system so as to shape it into an effective instrument for the welfare of the poorer sections. A major problem today is the lack of healthy credit delivery motivation at the field level for sustaining rural credit on a continuous basis. Despite making efforts, NABARD has not been able to strengthen co-operatives as the management control vests in the State Government. Moreover, the acute shortages of resources may hamper the future functioning of NABARD. It has been estimated that if it has to achieve a growth rate of 15 per cent in 8th Plan period, it would require additional resources worth of Rs. 2,500 crores. In the absence of such resources NABARD will have to face hard times.[18]

Multi-Agency Approach: A Review

The multi-agency approach as has been described and analysed here came to be adopted as the overall national policy because no single complex financial institution has the necessary organisational structure or financial strength to cater the total requirements of Indian agriculture and rural development. Co-operatives, Commercial Banks, Regional Rural Banks, Farmers Service Societies, Lead Banks and over the above NABARD have their defined role and function to serve the financial needs of the Indian peasantry. Among these institutions, co-operative societies, commercial banks, RRBs, and Farmers Service Societies are operating at the grassroots level and regional offices and commercial banks and RRBs at the district level. RBI and NABARD are serving at the national level.

The multi-agency approach to agriculture has given rise to some problems in the efficient disbursement of rural credit. In order to review the working of the various financial agencies and the problems they face the RBI constituted a Working Group in August 1975 under the chairmanship of C.E. Kamath. Following problems of multi-agenc approach were identified by the Committee.

(i) The existence of a number of agencies retailing credit in a common area of operation and disbursing credit in an un-coordinated manner resulted in multiple financing, over-financing, under financing, financial indiscipline and diversion of scarce resources to unproductive purposes.

(ii) Multi-agencies have failed to formulate and develop meaningful agricultural credit programmes on an area approach basis. Further, this approach has developed a needless competition among the commercial banks and also among the commercial banks and co-operatives, resulting in an avoidable waste of expenditure.

(iii) This approach has aggravated the problem of recovery of loans. Recovery of loans in a situation where more than one agency may have claims on the same income/security became complicated because in this situation the borrower will try to play one agency against other.

(iv) Problems have also arisen due to different systems, procedures and policies. Banks function on banking principles, backed by large resources, professional management and organisation. Co-operative, on the other hand, works on the basis of support by the members, limited reserves and State patronage. In disbursing loans, adopting security norms, service and supervision charges, recovery procedures these two systems, agencies differ with each other; and

(v) Besides the problems associated with the multi-agency approach, the reviews of the working of the institutional credit system have also revealed a lacunae in the procedure and organisation of the system in the country. Lack of coordination among various agencies has created lot of problems in effective implementation of the policies.

FOOTNOTES and REFERENCES

1. Nicholson F.A.: Report Regarding the Possibility of Introducing Land and Agricultural Banks into the Madras Presidency, p. 46.
2. Singh and Gupta L.C., "Estimates of Credit Requirement", *Indian Journal of Agricultural Economics*, Vol. xxvi in Sharma D.P., Rural Economy of India, Vikas Delhi : See also Sadhu A.N., Amerjit Singh, Fundamentals of Agricultural Economics, op. cit. pp. 297-98; Agricultural Problems in India, pp. 212-213 & pp. 221-222.
3. Economic Times Dec. 27, 1984 and February 20, 1988.
4. Mukhopadhyay A, "Net present value of loan Financed Investment for Irrigation Development and Repayment Capacity of Farmers—A Case

Study in Punjab. *Indian Journal of Agricultural Economics* Oct.-Dec. 1971; Sadhu A.N., Singh A, Fundamentals of Agricultural Economics Op. Cit. (1991) P. 307.

5. RBI, Rural Credit Survey Report, Vol I pp. 163-64.
6. R.B.I. Report on Trend and Progress of Banking in India 1987-88, p. 156.
7. GOI, Seventh Five Year Plan Vol II p. 26.
8. RBI Report on Trend and Progress of Banking in India 1987-88 p. 155.
9. RBI, Report on Currency and Finance 1990-91, Vol. II Statement 46 P. 79.
10. For the detail analysis of the objectives of nationalisation of banks and its success and failures see S.A.R. Bilgrami, "Public Sector Banking, Growth: Regional Growth Analysis", Deep & Deep (Delhi) 1982.
11. For statistical figures see GOI, Economic Survey 1992-93 Tables 4.5, 4.6, p.560-61.
12. GOI, Seventh Five Year Plan, p.17.
13. GOI, Economic Survey 1992-93; RBI, Report on Currency & Finance (Various issues); Misra S.K., Puri V.K., Indian Economy, Himalaya 1993 p. 512.)
14. Velayudham T.K., Sankaranaryanan V. "Regional Rural Banks and Rural Credit: Some Issues" Economics & Political Weekly, September. 22, 1990, pp. 215a-61.
15. Misra S.K. Puri V.K. Indian Economy op cit p. 512.
16. *Ibid* p. 513.
17. Krishnandevan V, "NABARD – Promises To Keep" The Economic Times July 30, 1992 p. 9.
18. *Ibid.*

APPENDIX 'A'

VARIABILITY IN CREDIT-DEPOSIT RATIO: TOWARDS AN EXPLANATION OF THE PERFORMANCE OF PUBLIC-SECTOR BANKS*

A serious drawback that caused great concern in the growth of pre-nationalisation banking sector in India was the sharp variation in credit-deposit ratio (C/D-ratio) among the regions and the States/U.T. This ratio envisages the proportion of the credit sanctioned by the banks in a region or State to the deposit collected in that region or State. It, thus, helps to investigate the extent to which a region or State has been benefitted out of their deposits. Pre-nationalisation studies and the data available indicate serious imbalances in the ratio which confirm that banks are mobilising resources from certain areas and lending them elsewhere, thus, aggravating inter-regional and inter-State imbalances in terms of generating income and employment opportunities. The economic injustice caused by the wide variations in C/D ratio among the regions and the States can be corrected and the policy of balanced regional development can be implemented when banks are under public control.[1] We, therefore, propose to investigate and analyse to what extent banking growth under public sector has succeeded in reducing the wide variations in credit-deposit ratio among the regions and the States during 1969–92.

I

The pre-nationalisation trend of bank lending was more security rather than welfare based. The lending policy has been true to the dictum: "where enterprise leads, finance follows". Consequently, the economically weaker-sections, high-risk bearing activities such as farming, small-scale and household industries, low-profit ventures such as small business, trade education, professionals, self-employed activities, and artisans all were deprive of bank's lending facilities. The inflow of money in form of deposits was most welcomed and encouraged from all segments of the society while the outflow of money in form of credit was restrictive, selective and was based on credit-worthiness of the borrower. The emergence of wide-variations in C/D ratio and the resulted inter-regional, inter-State and inter-sectoral imbalances in terms of income and employment opportunities and of overall economic growth was quite obvious. If sharp variations have been found, it is indication that certain regions or States are gaining more than others in terms of credit-flow.

In this paper an attempt is made to study the inter-regional and inter-State variability in credit-deposit ratio. The trend visualised will help us to reach on certain conclusions.

Technique adopted is as under.

(i) Six regions and twenty six States/UT have been studied at two points of time 1969 and 1992.

(ii) The regional and State-wise C/D ratio have been estimated at given points of time and compared with the national C/D ratio. This will

* Appeared in "FINANCE INDIA", MARCH 1995

help us to examine the pattern of the movement of regions/States above and below the national average.

(iii) C/D ratio ranges have been formed and the shifting trends of the regions and the States among these ranges have been analysed to establish their favourable or unfavourable movement.

A balanced and a just bank lending policy will be that where the gap between the very low and substantially high C/D-ratio is minimised. If the very low level C/D-ratio regions/States are showing an upward trend and the substantially high C/D-ratio regions/States, a downward move, the trend may be called a favourable one because the process will lead to minimise the disparity. Contrary, the disparities will be widened and the trend will unfavourable.

Our regional C/D-ratio estimates 1969–1992 (Table-I) reveal that in June 1969, one month before the nationalisation of 14 commercial banks, while the C/D-ratio for the banking system as a whole – national C/D-ratio – was 77.87 per cent, the variation was wide enough with the Southern region having 107.69 per cent at the top and North-Eastern region having only 32.81 per cent at the bottom. Thus, while the Southern region was 29.82 per cent above the national level, the North-Eastern region was 45.06 per cent below that level.

Three out of six regions, namely, Southern (107.69), Eastern (90.50 per cent) and Western (83.27 per cent) were above the national level and the other three, namely, North-Eastern (32.81 per cent), Central (48.78 per cent) and Northern region(58.0 per cent) were below the national level. Their percentage variation range above and below the national level was 5.4 per cent – 29.82 per cent and 19.87 per cent – 47.06 per cent respectively.

In 1992, after more than two decades, some positive trends can be realised. On the basis of the declined national C/D-ratio in 1992 (59.98 per cent), one region, namely, Southern is found fairly above the national level with the C/D-ratio 80.01%. Western region with the C/D-ratio 60.62 per cent is slightly above the national level. Hence, it is better to call it at par. On percentage basis the Southern region is 20.03 per cent while the Western region is merely 0.64 per cent higher than the national level. The other four regions – Northern (57.40 per cent), Central (49.50 per cent), Eastern (48.26 per cent) and North-Eastern (44.95 per cent) remained below the national level. Their C/D-ratio variation range below the national level has been 2.58 per cent – 15.03 per cent respectively.

Two important conclusions may be drawn. (i) In 1992, in comparison to 1969, the number of regions above the national level has been reduced and equally the number below the national average has been increased. And (ii) the wide variation in C/D-ratio in relation to national level has been substantially minimised. The last column of the table I shows this minimising trends. The North-Eastern region which was 45.06 per cent below the national level in 1969 remained below the national in 1992 as well, but the level come down from 45.06 per cent to merely 15.03 per cent. It shows that the region, in comparison to 1969, closer to national level in 1992. Southern region, on the other hand, which was 29.82 per cent above the national level in 1969 showed an appreciable reduction and come down to the level of 20.03 per cent above the national level in 1992. Although, the region remained above the national level at both points of time, the trend showed that this region too, in comparison to 1969, in approaching nearer to the national level. The some trend has been realised in all the above and below the national level regions in 1992 in comparison to 1969. All regions above the national level shows a downward trend while the regions below the national level, an upward trend. This is a clear indication that since 1969 the regions are coming closer to the national level and their wide variation has been substantially minimised. The bar-diagram based on table I support this positive trend.

II

State-wise C/D-ratio variations have been estimated in Table-2, 3, 4A and 4B. Table-2 estimates C/D-ratio of 26 States/ U.T. at two points of time, 1969 and 1992. In 1969, 6 out of 26 States/U.T. or 23 per cent of the total were above the national level and 20 or 77 per cent of the total, were below the national level. The C/D-ratio variation was wide enough where Chandigarh was at the top with having C/D-ratio 185.61 per cent and Tripura at the bottom with having C/D-ratio only 4.25 per cent. Here I exclude "all-others" category of States as it presents a combination of various tiny States/U.T. The C/D-ratio variation range of 6 States/U.T. above the national level has been 93.67 per cent to 185.6 per cent and 20 States/U.T. below the national level 3 per cent to 76.17 per cent.

In relation to national level, the variation range was also quite sharp. Chandigarh which was at the top was 107.73 per cent above the national level and the bottom State Tripura has 73.62 per cent below the national level. The variation range of all 6 States/U.T. above the national level has been 15.8 per cent to 107.73 per cent above the national base and of 20 States/U.T below the national level 1.7 per cent to 73.62 per cent.

In 1992, the over-all situation has been appreciably improved. 9 out of 26 States/U.T. or 34.4 per cent of the total have been found above the national level and 17 or 65.4 per cent below the national level. The percentage of States/U.T. above the national level has, thus, improved from 23 per cent in 1969 to 34.4 per cent in 1992 and of States/U.T. below the national level declined from 77 per cent in 1969 to 65.4 per cent in 1992.

The C/D-ratio variation among the States/U.T. which have been realised wide enough in 1969, now shows an appreciable reduction in 1992. Tamil Nadu has been at the top with having 97.09 per cent C/D-ratio and Meghalya at the bottom with having only 19.60 per cent C/D-ratio. Among the 9 above national level States/U.T. the C/D-ratio variation range has been 97.09 per cent to 63.2 per cent and among the 17 below the national level States/U.T., it has been 56.54 per cent to 19.6 per cent. Thus, in comparison to 1969, the C/D-ratio variation range among the States/U.T. has been considerably reduced. The variation gap of 6 and 9 above the national level States/U.T. has been reduced from 91.3 per cent to 34.09 per cent or 57.84 per cent during 1969 and 1992. The variation gap of 20 and 17 below the national level, on the other hand, has been shrinked from

71.92 per cent to 36.94 per cent or 34.98 per cent during the same years. Following table based on Table-3 presents this trend in a summary form.

Table-A
C/D-Ratio Variation Gap of Above and Below the National Level States

	No. of States/UT	*C/D-Ratio Range*		*Variation Gap*
1969 :	Above National Level = 6	185.6 – 93.07	91.93	)
				) – 57.84
1992 :	Above National Level = 9	97.09 – 63.2	34.09	)
1969	Below National Level = 20	76.17 – 4.25	71.92	)
				) – 34.98
1992 :	Below National Level = 17	56.54 – 19.6	36.94	)

By classifying the C/D-ratio range into various categories, as shown in table 4–A and 4–B, the variation trend become more clear. Table 4–A presents changes in C/D-ratio among the top and bottom level States/U.T. in 1992 in comparison to 1969. All 5 top level States/U.T. (above 100% C/D-ratio) shows a declining trend. Their C/D-ratio decline from 119.95 per cent to 20.5 per cent. Here Chandigarh was at the top whose C/D-ratio shows a highest decline and Andhra Pradesh the lowest.

On the other hand, all 5 bottom level States/U.T. (C/D-ratio upto 15%) show a rapid increase. Their C/D-ratio increases between 57.54 per cent to 18.79 per cent. Manipur was at the top with having 57.54 per cent increase and the group of tiny States/U.T. in combined (All others) the lowest, 18.79 per cent.

The other 16 States/U.T. falling under the category of 75%-100%, 50%-74% and 25%-49% (Table 4–B) C/D-ratio range gives a mixed picture. Two States/U.T. come under the range of 75%-100% C/D-ratio. Here Pondicherry shows a rapid decline (45.3%) and Karnataka a slight improvement of 2.04 per cent. 50%-74% C/D-ratio range covers 5 States/U.T., out of which Kerala shows a 14.97 per cent decline while the others, namely, Delhi, Madhaya Pradesh, Rajashthan and Orissa show an improvement. Here Orissa shows a highest improvement of 40.33 per cent and Delhi, the lowest of 1.57 per cent.

9 States/U.T. come under the range of 25%-49%. 3 out of 9 show a declining trend while the remaining 6, an improvement. Goa D.D. shows the highest decline of 10.26 per cent and Uttar Pradesh, the lowest 1.5 per cent. Punjab, on the other hand, shows highest improvement of 15.07 per cent and Himachal Pradesh the lowest 5.13 per cent.

Thus, all the 16 States/U.T. falling under the C/D-ratio range of 25%-100% gives a mixed trend. 5 out of 16 shows a declining trend and the remaining 11, an improvement. The C/D-ratio declining range of 5 States/U.T. has been 1.5 per cent to 45.3 per cent and of increasing range 1.57 per cent to 40.33 per cent. This trend also leads to a conclusion that most of the States/U.T. having poor C/D-ratio range n 1969 have shown an improvement in their C/D-ratio in 1992. Out of 14 such States/U.T. (C/D-ratio range between 25% to 74%) 4 shows a declining trend and 10 an improvement. C/D-ratio range and number of States/U.T. falling in each ranges is given in the following table.

Table-B
C/D-RAtio Range And Number Of States/U.T.

C/D-Range %	*No. of States/U.T. in 1969*	*No. of States/U.T. in 1992*
.01 – 0.25 –	5	2
0.26 – 0.50 –	10	11
0.51 – 0.75 –	4	9
0.76 – 1.00 –	3	4
1.01 – 1.25 –	2	–
1.26 – 1.50 –	1	–
1.51 – 1.75 –	–	–
1.75 – 2.00 –	1	–
	26	26

Table indicates that in 1969 States/U.T. are spreaded over a wide range started from 0.01–0.25 the lowest/poorest to 1.76–2.00 the highest. In 1992, the spreading trend shows a rapid shrink. Now all the 26 States/U.T. remained in the range of 0.01–1.0 That is no States come under the range of 1.01 to 2.0 (above 100 per cent) while in 1969 4 states/U.T. fall under this range.

The number of States/U.T. falling the poorest range also shows a marked improvement. In 1969, 5 States/U.T. fall under the poorest C/D-ratio range 01–0.25. In 1992 only 2 states come under this range. In 1992, 20 States/U.T. concentrate in the C/D range 0.26–0.75. In 1969, the same number of States were spreaded over the C/D-ratio range of 0.26–1.50. This trend shows that in 1992, in comparison to 1969, more States/U.T. have come closer to higher C/D-ratio range. This is a clear sign of minimising the disparities among the States.

The C/D range given in the Table 4–A and 4–B are named as "Surplus C/D-ratio Range" (Above 100%), Optimum/Near Optimum Range (80%-100%), Moderate Range (51%-79%), Low-Deficit Range (25%-50%) and Highest-Deficit Range (1%-24%). Table 5 provides an information about the shifting position of States/U.T. falling under each category. Chandigarh, Tamil Nadu, West Bengal, Maharashtra and Andhra Pradesh all were under "Surplus" C/D-ratio range. Their rank status substantially fell. Chandigarh came down to moderate range, Tamil Nadu to Optimum, West Bengal to low-deficit, Maharashtra to moderate and Andhra Pradesh come down to optimum.

Among all these States, West Bengal presents an extreme case. It was a surplus State in 1969, but in 1992 it became a low-deficit State.

Manipur, Nagaland, Jammu & Kashmir, Tripura and all others were high-deficit States/U.T. in 1969. In 1992, all the States/U.T. except "all-other" show an improvement in their rank position. Manipur which was a high-deficit State in 1969 became a moderate State in 1992. Nagaland, Jammu & Kashmir and Triputra have improved their rank status from high-deficit to low-deficit. The rank position of "all-others" remained unaltered.

Among 9 low-deficit States only 2 States, namely, Gujarat and Harayana could improve their rank status. Both ranked from low-deficit status to moderate rank status. The other 6 States/U.T., namely U.P., Goa D.D., Assam Bihar, Himachal Pradesh and Punjab could not improve their status. They claimed in the low-deficit range in 1969 and 1992. Meghalaya presents an extreme case. It was under low-deficit range, but in 1992, it further came down to high-deficit range.

III

The regional and State-wise study of credit-deposit ratio variation in 1969 and 1992 presented above, thus, leads to the following conclusions :

(i) Our regional analysis shows that in 1992, in comparison to 1969, not only the number of regions above the national level has been reduced, but the C/D-ratio variation range has also been considerably reduced. It refers that most of the regions are approaching towards the national level and their disparities which were quite wide in 1969, have been substantially reduced in 1992.

(ii) States/U.T. also follow the same trend. Study reveals that not only the number of States/U.T. below the national level has been reduced or the number of States/U.T. above the national level has been increased, but the C/D-ratio variation range has also been substantially reduced in 1992 in comparison to 1969. A detailed analysis of C/D-ratio variation range (Table 3, 4–A and 4–B) grouping the States/U.T. into various range explains that all top and bottom level States/U.T. show a positive or favourable trend. 5 top level States/U.T. show a declining trend while the other 5 bottom level States/U.T. an improvement. Among all the remaining 16 middle-range States/U.T. (C/D-ratio range 25%-100%), 11 States/U.T. indicate a positive trend. Their C/D-ratio show an improvement. 5 States/U.T. show an unfavourable trend as their C/D-ratio, instead of showing improvement, show a decline. Thus, out of 26 States/U.T. 21 have shown improvement in their C/D-ratio.

(iii) Some exceptional cases are also found. Few States such as Meghalya, Uttar Pradesh and Goa D.D. were considerably poor states in terms of their C/D-ratios. Their C/D-ratio were 28.4, 45.59 and 40.42 per cent in 1969. Their position has been deteriorated in 1992 as their C/D-ratios have been further reduced to 19.6, 44.09

and 30.16 per cent. Pondicherry is again an exceptional case. It was substantially at high range (93.67%) in 1969. But in 1992, it shows a sharp decline and reaches at the level of 48.37 per cent.

(iv) There are some States/U.T. where very sharp changes have occurred. Chandigarth which was at the top in 1969 with having 185.61% C/D% C/D-ratio reached at the level of 65.66% C/D-ratio in 1992, showing 119.95% reduction. Manipur, Nagaland and Tripura, on the other hand, shows a very sharp improvement. They were very poor in terms of C/D-ratio but entered into middle range in 1992. Orissa also shows very appreciable improvement. Here C/D-ratio was only 49.5% in 1969. It increased to 89.83%, near optimum, in 1992.

(v) Most of the States/U.T., have shown not only an improvement in their C/D-ratio, but their variation range have also been reduced. Table 3, 4A and 4B, the bar-diagram and the table-B on page 9 all describe this trend. This trend shows that most of the States/U.T. have reached nearer to the national level in 1992 while they were quite away from that level in 1992 while they were quite away from the level in 1969. It further indicates that the wide disparities which have been shown in 1969, have been reduced in 1992.

These conclusions indicate that the public sector banking growth during the two decades have succeeded in minimising the disparities and if this trend strengthens, the widening disparities among regions and the states will further be sharply declined.

Table 1

REGIONAL IMBALANCES IN CREDIT-DEPOSIT RATIO

Regions	*C/d Ratio (%)*		*Var in 1992 Over*	*Var in National*	*Relation Average*
	1969	*1992*	*1969 (%)*	*1969*	*1992*
1 NORTHERN REGION	58	57.4	-0.6	–19.87	–2.58
2 NORTH EAASTERN REGION	32.81	44.95	12.14	–45.06	–15.03
3 EASTERN REGION	90.5	48.26	–42.24	12.63	–11.72
4 CENTRAL REGION	48.78	49.5	0.72	–29.09	–10.48
5 WESTERN REGION	83.27	60.62	–22.65	5.4	0.64
6 SOUTHERN REGION	107.69	80.01	–27.01	29.82	20.03
ALL INDIA	77.87	59.98	–17.89		

Source : GOI, Economic Survey, 1992-93.

Table 2

State Wise Credit Deposit Ratios: 1969-92

(Rs. in Crores)

STATES/UT'S	DEPOSITS		CREDIT		C/D RATIO (%)	
	1969	1992	1969	1992	1969	1992
ANDHRA PRADESH	121.11	10920	122.09	8905	100.8	82.3
ASSAM	33.2	2234	12.85	1079	38.7	48.29
BIHAR	168.67	9219	52.05	3518	30.85	38.16
GUJARAT	401.31	13457	194.89	7218	48.56	53.63
HARYANA	48.78	4119	23.15	2307	47.45	0.56
HIMACHAL PRADESH	12.38	1496	3.49	503	28.19	33.62
J & K	17.95	896	0.86	277	4.79	30.92
KARNATAKA	187.79	9705	143.04	7591	76.17	78.21
KERALA	116.79	7084	76.95	3607	65.88	50.91
MADHYA PRADESH	107.43	8014	63.14	5065	58.77	63.20
MAHARASHTRA	902.67	38900	911.79	25040	101	64.37
MANIPUR	1.06	106	0.15	76	14.15	71.69
MEGHALAYA	8.87	357	2.52	70	28.4	19.6

NAGALAND	1.07	214	0.06	87	5.6	40.65
ORISSA	29.49	2185	14.6	1963	49.5	89.83
PUNJAB	185	41	10865	50.29	4578	27.12
RAJASTHAN	73.73	5298	38.2	2996	51.81	56.54
TAMIL NADU	233.48	12862	311.32	12488	133.3	97.09
TRIPURA	3.76	255	0.16	111	4.25	43.52
UTTAR PRADESH	337.15	20291	153.74	8948	45.59	44.09
W. BENGAL	456.45	18159	525.8	8788	115.19	48.39
CHANDIGARH	34.55	1570	64.13	1031	185.6	65.66
DELHI	359.8	18195	244.9	12670	68.16	69.63
GOA D & D	48.68	1694	19.68	511	40.42	30.16
PONDICHERY	5.06	339	4.74	164	93.67	48.37
ALL OTHERS*	0.33	468	0.01	102	3	21.79
ALL INDIA	3896.97	199531	3034.6	119603	77.87	59.98

* Include Andaman & Nicobar Islands, Arunachal Pradesh, Dadra & Nagar Haveli, Lakshadweep, Mizoram & Sikkim.

Source : Economic Survey, 1992-93, p. 5-62

Table 3

State Wise Variation in Credit-Deposit Ratio (1969-1992)

1969			1992		
STATES/UT'S	*C/D RATIO*	*VAR. IN RELATION TO NL. AV.*	*STATES/UT'S*	*C/D RATIO*	*VAR. IN RELATION TO NL. AV.*
NATIONAL LEVEL		77.87	NATIONAL LEVEL		59.98
ABOVE NATIONAL LEVEL			ABOVE NATIONAL LEVEL		
1 CHANDIGARH	185.6	107.73	1 TAMIL NADU	97.09	37.11
2 TAMIL NADU	133.3	55.43	2 ORISSA	89.83	29.85
3 W. BENGAL	115.19	37.32	3 ANDHRA PRADESH	82.3	22.32
4 MAHARASHTRA	101	23.13	4 KARNATAKA	78.21	18.23
5 ANDHRA PRADESH	100	22.13	5 MANIPUR	71.69	11.71
6 PONDICHERRY	93.67	15.8	6 DELHI	69.63	9.65
BELOW NATIONAL LEVEL			7 CHANDIGARH	65.66	5.68
7 KARNATAKA	76.17	–1.7	8 MAHARASHTRA	64.37	4.39
8 DELHI	68.06	–9.8	9 MADHYA PRADESH	63.2	3.22

9	KERALA	65.88	–11.99	BELOW NATIONAL LEVEL			
10	MADHYA PRADESH	58.77	–19.1	10	RAJASTHAN	56.54	–3.44
11	RAJASTHAN	51.81	–26.06	11	HARYANA	56	–3.98
12	ORISSA	49.5	–28.37	12	GUJARAT	53.63	–6.62
13	GUJARAT	48.56	–29.31	13	KERALA	50.91	–9.07
14	HARYANA	47.45	–30.32	14	W. BENGAL	48.39	–11.59
15	UTTAR PRADESH	45.59	–32.28	15	PONDICHERRY	48.37	–11.61
16	GOA D & D	40.42	–37.45	16	ASSAM	48.29	–11.69
17	ASSAM	38.7	–39.17	17	UTTAR PRADESH	44.09	–15.89
18	BIHAR	30.85	–47.02	18	TRIPURA	43.52	–16.46
19	HIMACHAL PRADESH	28.19	–49.68	19	PUNJAB	42.13	–17.85
20	MEGHALAYA	28.19	–49.73	20	NAGALAND	40.65	–19.33
21	PUNJAB	27.12	50.75	21	BIHAR	38.16	–21.82
22	MANIPUR	14.15	–63.72	22	HIMACHAL PRADESH	33.62	–26.36
23	NAGALAND	5.6	–72.27	23	J & K	30.91	–29.07
24	J & K	4.79	–73.08	24	GOA D & D	30.16	29.82
25	TRIPURA	4.25	–73.62	25	ALL OTHERS	21.79	–38.19
26	ALL OTHERS	3	–74.87	26	MEGHALAYA	19.6	–40.38

Source: Computed from Table (1)

Table 4–A
Changing C/D Ratio's
Among the top and bottom level States

STATES/UT'S	*C/D RATIO'S*			*RANKS*	
	1969	1992	CHANGING POSITION	1969	1992
TOP LEVEL STATES ABOVE 100%					
1 CHANDIGARH	185.61	65.66	–119.95	1	3
2 TAMIL NADU	133.33	97.09	–36.24	2	1
3 W. BENGAL	115.19	48.39	–66.8	3	5
4 MAHARASHTRA	101	64.37	–36.63	4	4
5 ANDHRA PRADESH	100.8	80.3	–20.5	5	2
BOTTOM LEVEL STATES/UT'S UP TO 15%					
1 MANIPUR	14.15	71.69	57.54	1	1
2 NAGALAND	5.6	40.65	35.05	2	3
3 J & K	4.79	30.91	26.12	3	4
4 TRIPURA	4.25	43.52	39.27	4	2
5 ALL OTHERS	3	21.79	18.79	5	5

Table 4–B
Changing Position of States/UT's in Relation to C/D Ratio's

C/D RATIO RANGE AND STATES	*C/D RATIO*		*CHANGING POSITION*	*RANKS*	
	1969	1992		1969	1992
75% – 100%					
1 PONDICHERY	93.67	48.37	–45.3	1	2
2 KARNATAKA	76.17	78.21	2.04	2	1
50% – 74%					
1 DELHI	68.06	69.63	1.57	1	2
2 KERALA	65.88	50.91	–14.97	2	5
3 MADHYA PRADESH	58.77	63.2	4.43	3	3
4 RAJASTHAN	51.81	56.54	4.73	4	4
5 ORISSA	49.5	89.83	40.33	5	1
25% – 49%					
1 GUJRAT	48.56	53.83	5.27	1	2
2 HARYANA	47.45	56	8.44	2	1

3 UTTAR PRADESH	45.59	44.09	–1.50	3	4
4 GOA D & D	40.42	30.16	–10.26	4	8
5 ASSAM	38.7	48.29	9.59	5	3
6 BIHAR	30.85	38.16	7.31	6	6
7 HIMACHAL P.	28.19	33.32	5.13	7	7
8 MEGHALAYA	28.4	19.60	–8.8	8	9
9 PUNJAB	27.12	42.13	15.07	9	5

Table 5
Shifting Trends of Some States/UT's 1969–1992

C/D RATIO RANGE	*RANK STATUS* 1969	1992
SURPLUS C/D RATIO RANGE		
CHANDIGARH	S	M
TAMIL NADU	S	O
W. BENGAL	S	L.D
MAHARASHTRA	S	M
ANDHRA P.	S	O
HIGH DEFICIT C/D RATIO RANGE		
MANIPUR	H.D	M
NAGALAND	H.D	L.D
J & K	H.D	L.D
TRIPURA	H.D	L.D
ALL OTHERS		
LOW DEFICIT C/D RATIO RANGE		
GUJRAT	L.D	M
HARYANA	L.D	M
U.P.	L.D	L.D
GOD D & D	L.D	L.D
ASSAM	L.D	L.D
BIHAR	L.D	L.D
HIMACHAL P.	L.D	L.D
MEGHALAYA	L.D	H.D
PUNJAB	L.D	L.D

1. Surplus C/D Ratio Range [S] above 100%
2. Optimum/Near Optimum Range [O] 80–100%
3. Moderate range [M] 51–79%
4. Low Deficit Range [L.D] 25–50%
5. High Deficit Range [H.D] 1–24%

1. The Banker, July 1969, p.366.

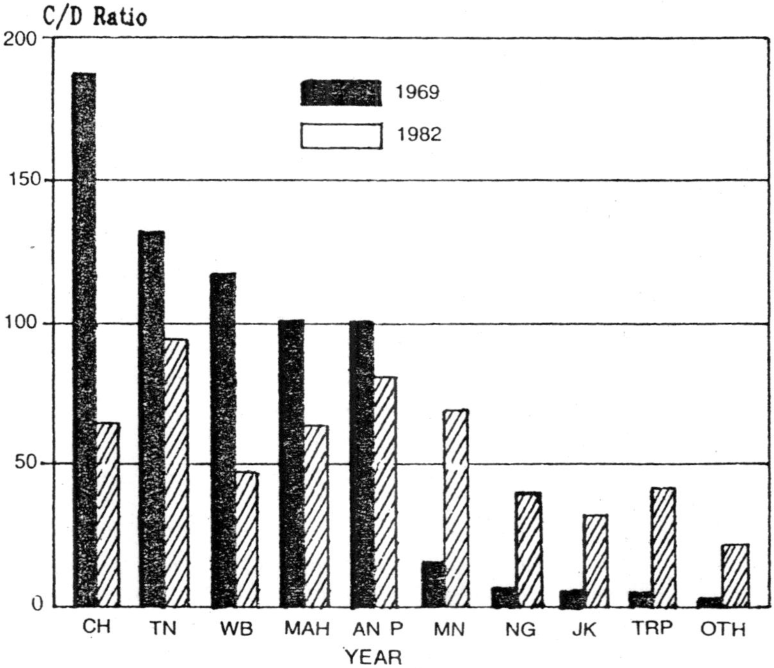

Fig.1 Changing C/D Ratios: Top & Bottom Level States

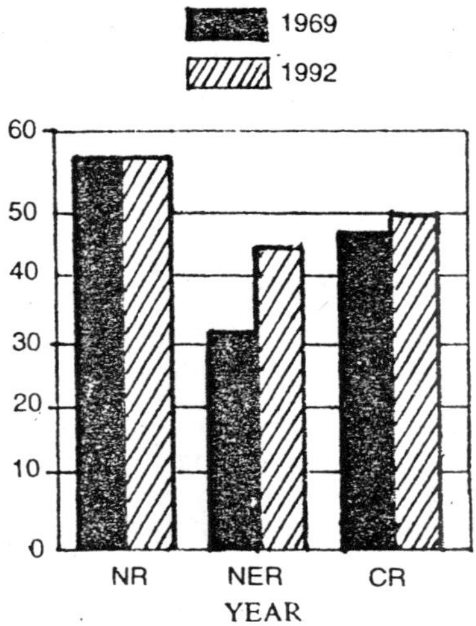

Fig.2 C/D Ratios among above the Average Regions

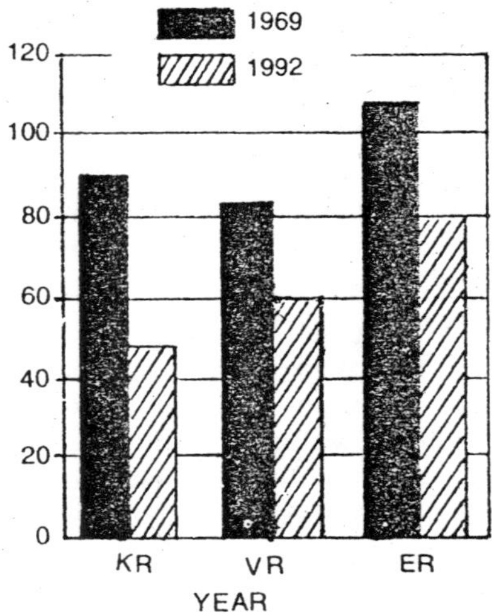

Fig.3 C/D Ratios among below the Average Regions

9
AGRICULTURAL TAX

In a developing economy like India agriculture bear a substantial portion of the cost of economic development. During the process of development, it has to supply larger food surplus and raw materials to other sectors of the economy. It also has to supply increasing proportion of the manpower. The economic development with subsistence cultivation create a shortage of foodgrains and other raw materials and thus, push up the prices. But the rise in price may not always call for the increased production and increased supply of agricultural commodities, specially of foodgrains. In fact a rise in price may actually lead to a decline in produciion. To increase the agricultural surplus, it is, therefore, suggested that taxes should be introduced in this sector. As Kaldor suggested: "The taxation of agriculture has a critical role to play in the acceleration of economic development since it is only the imposition of compulsory levies in the agricultural sector itself which enlarges the supply of savings for economic development". Thus, on the ground of raising marketable surplus, agricultural taxation has been made essential.

The other important reason of suggesting agricultural tax is that India's economic development plans have necessitated mobilisation of increasing volumes of domestic sources. We know, sources of capital for economic development are foreign aid, foreign commercial investment and domestic saving. No country would like to depend for a long period on foreign aid and foreign commercial investment. And therefore it is argued that "greater the extent to which a low income country chooses not to receive or cannot receive foreign aid and foreign commercial investment, the greater the extent to which it must draw upon its own resources, chiefly from the dominant agricultural sector"[2]. But Indian plans, in spite of reducing foreign aid and foreign capital investment, has suffered from inadequate domestic resources. Domestic resources for financing our plans were 73 per cent in the First Plan which declined to 56 per cent in the second and with a slight improvement of 59 per cent in the Third Plan. The basic reason of inadequate domestic resources is the failure of mobilising savings from agriculture sector. It has been argued that when the Government is investing increasingly larger amounts on agricultural development plans. Why should not a substantial portion of the resulted increase in income of the farmers be taxed. This is particularly true in the case of the large farmers whose income, have substantially increased as a direct consequence of the process of economic growth.

Some Considerations in Relation to Agricultural Taxation[3]

Both the level as well as the form of agricultural tax are influenced by the following consideration.

Firstly increased taxation on a static level of output is more burdensome than increased taxation on a rising income base. Secondly, agricultural taxation for local purposes will generally be considered less burdensome than taxation for distant national purposes. Thirdly, taxation of unemployed resources is more palatable than taxation of existing income. Taxation of local under employed resources will generally be more feasible when they are turned to such uses as local public work as the development of such complex avoids the problems of moving labour to more distant sites. Moreover, local use also allow the employment of seasonally under employed labour. Substantial use of local labour will also be feasible where the local people appreciate the nature of the project and the benefits will be given to the local people.

Fourthly, administrative aspect of the tax must be easy. Tax policy, therefore, must be developed with special attention to the administrative resources of low income countries. This consideration also influences the choice of taxes levied on agriculture and adds local responsibility in collection and use of taxes.

And finally, care must be taken in relation to "Political unpopularity", political opposition and the resulted evasion. All such reaction will raise the administrative problems.

Indian Agricultural Tax Structure: Agricultural taxation includes all those which are paid by agriculturist directly and also those which are paid by them indirectly. Direct taxes on agriculture consist mainly of land revenue, surcharges on land revenue, taxes on crops and agricultural income tax. As consumers, farmers may be paying indirectly the excise duty, the sales tax, the import duty the motor vehicle tax etc. These are indirect taxes which agriculturists pay.

The most important tax on agricultural land is land revenue. It is the oldest tax among all taxes. Land revenue is levied and collected by the State Government. This tax is assessed on the basis of net assets or on the value of net produce or in some cases it is also left to the judgement of the assessing officers. In 1951-52, Rs. 52 crores has been collected. The amount has gone up to Rs. 97 crore in 1960-61, Rs. 113 crores in 1970-71 and again Rs. 166 crores in 1980-81. But on percentage basis, land tax shows a gradual declines due to the introduction and extension of many new levies. According to a R.B.I. estimates, in 1951-52 land revenue accounted for 17 per cent of the total state tax revenue. This contribution declined to 9.6 per cent in 1960-61 and further only 1.7 per cent in 1980-81.[4] This tax is being abolished completely and partially in many States.

Agriculture income tax is also levied and collected by the States. Bihar was the first State which levied this tax in 1938. Some other States which have levied agricultural income tax are Assam, W. Bengal, Rajasthan, U.P., M.P., Kerala, Tamil Nadu, Karnataka and Orissa. The rate of agricultural income tax have been generally lower than those applicable to the urban income tax. It plays a very insignificant role. In 1951-52 its percentage share in total State tax revenue was 1.1 per cent. In 1960-61, its share was only 1.0 and in 1980-81 still less than 1 per cent (0.8 per cent).[5] Among all the States which levied and collected agricultural income tax, only three, namely Karnataka, Tamil Nadu and West Bengal, accounted for the bulk of the revenue from this tax.

Direct taxes as a whole on agriculture account for about 11 per cent of the total revenue of all State taxes and duties. This tax ranges between 3-25 per cent among all States.

Some important indirect taxes are tax on transfer of property — in form of stamps and registration excise duties, general sales tax, import duties, entertainment tax, electricity duties, motor vehicle tax etc.

Agriculture Tax Burden and Incidence:[6] In recent years attempts have been made to measure gross as well as net burden and incidence of agricultural taxes on that basis, it has been proved whether Indian agriculture is over-taxed or under-taxed.

According to E.T. Mathew's estimate the per capita gross burden of agricultural taxation in 1958-59 was Rs. 14-52 which accounted for 6.8 per cent of the per capita income in the agricultural sector.

The net per capita burden of agricultural taxation had been estimated to be Rs. 6.88 or 3.2 per cent per capita income in the agricultural sector. On the other hand, the per capita gross burden of non-agricultural taxation during the same year was Rs. 46 or 9.2 per cent of the per capita income. And similarly the per capita net burden was 7.2 per cent of the per capita income. Thus, in absolute as well as in relative sense and even on the basis of the need for additional resources for economic development agriculture is under-taxed.

V.P. Gandhi provides some more clarity. According to Gandhi, in 1951-52 agricultural sector contributed Rs. 200 crores in form of direct and indirect taxes, where as the non-agricultural sector contribute Rs. 450 crores. Thus, the ratio between agricultural and non-agricultural sector in contributing direct and indirect taxes was 44:56. In 1968-69 this gap again widened. During this year agriculture was contributing over Rs. 900 crores and non-agricultural sector Rs. 2,700 crores. Now the ratio for the two sector was 33:67. It leads to the conclusion that during the planning period, the average tax in the agricultural sector, instead of rising has actually declined.

The estimates of average and marginal tax rates also prove that agricultural sector is under-taxed, per capita taxes on incomes are showing an increase in both the agricultural and non-agricultural sectors. The ratio of taxes to per capita income has also shown an increasing tendency in both the sectors from 3.8 to 6.5 per cent in the agricultural sector and from 9.5 to 19.1 per cent in the non-agricultural sector. But the fact that the agricultural sector is contributing 6.5 per cent of its income which is only one third of the ratio of income contributed by the non-agricultural sector.

The estimates of marginal rates of tax provide some more relevant information. Marginal rate of tax refers additional taxation during a given period out of the additional income during the same period. Gandhi estimated that during 1950-51 and 1960-61 the additional income which accrued to the agricultural sector was Rs. 1717 crores, but the additional tax was only Rs. 198 crores. The marginal tax rate was only 11.5 per cent. On the other hand, during the same period, additional income of the non-agricultural sector was Rs. 2,420 crores and the additional tax Rs. 499 crores. Here the marginal rate of taxation was 20.6 per cent. It is thus, clear that the marginal rate of taxation for non-agricultural sector is substantially higher than agricultural sector.

The comparative analysis of the marginal tax burden of the upper and lower income groups in agricultural and non-agricultural sector shows that 7 per cent burden in agricultural sector falls on upper classes. This means that the marginal burden of the lower classes is essentially higher. In the non-agricultural sector the marginal burden borne by the upper class is 13 per cent. It means that the lower income group in the non-agricultural sector bears a marginal burden of about 23 to 24 per cent which is comparatively higher than the burden of lower income group of the agricultural sector.

Thus, the analysis of the burden of agricultural taxation leads to the following basic conclusion: (1) agricultural sector bear less tax burden than the non-agricultural sector; (2) The lower income groups bear high burden than the upper income group in both the sectors and (3) on the basis of the above two conclusions it may be said that there is a great scope for an increase in agricultural taxation, specially upon the high income groups.

Agricultural Taxation — A Controversy: Those who have firm conviction that agricultural sector should be taxed expressed their arguments in the context of development expenditure, contribution of agricultural sector in resource mobilisation for development, defence needs, social and economic justice and equality, tax burden and in respect of over all dimension of taxation and its rate of growth. Their strong argument is that agricultural has not been contributing anything in form of taxes to economic development while their economic welfare, due to the continuous expenditure made by the Government for their development, has been consistently rising. Morarji Desai stated in his budget speech that "those who benefit by the substantial investments in agriculture, including research, irrigation facilities, fertiliser, plants, rural electrification, credit facilities and the support price should contribute a part of their prosperity towards the cost of development in general. This is all the more so when the benefits of improved technology cannot yet be shared by the majority of our farmers, particularly in dry regions where fertilisers and new seeds are not easy to apply. If the benefits of the new agricultural technology are to be carried progressively to a growing proportion of our farmers, the resources needed for this purpose should come at least in part from the beneficiaries of the progress."[7]

But apart from such strong support a powerful lobby has all along opposed every move to raise additional resources from agricultural sector in form of taxes. Firstly, the dominance of poor peasantry class, their uneconomical size of holdings and the resulted meagre output, income and the very poor standard of living do not allow to put extra burden in form of taxes. A substantially higher percentage of farmers are below the poverty line and their living conditions are miserably poor. It would, therefore, be more wise step to encourage them with all possible ways.

Secondly, commercialisation of agriculture in terms of modern or scientific farming has no-doubt started, but it has not yet reached on the stage which could transfer uneconomic, fragmented and sub-divided small holdings of the million of peasants into an economic holdings. Therefore, it may not be in the interest of the nation to tax the revenue of the developing commercial sector of the agriculture. Agricultural tax will discourage the process of shift from peasant economy into market economy.

Thirdly, a good part of untaxed income of the big farmers is certainly being invested in the accumulation of farm capital or in financing the scientific inputs. Any additional tax will certainly affect adversely their resources for development finance.

Agricultural sector is already paying indirect taxes of all sorts and in this way, its contribution to the revenues of States is steadily growing along with the growing income and expenditure. Thus, there is no need of introducing any other tax for this sector.

Raj Committee's Recommendations for Additional Agricultural Taxes

Various proposals for additional agricultural tax have been made by official organisations (such as Planning Commission) and economists. These proposals have three main objectives: (a) to secure larger investible and marketable surplus for agriculture; (b) to provide an incentive to raise agricultural output and (c) to introduce an element of progression in agricultural taxation so that it may become more equitable.

For the attainment of these objectives, Planning Commission suggested the introduction of a progressive surcharge on land revenues and surcharge on livestock. Some economists suggested that the land revenue should be raised and progression should be introduced. Others had suggested that the regressive type land tax should be eliminated and it should be replaced by a progressive agricultural income tax.

Since agricultural tax is a State subject, the imposition of additional taxation has always been a source of conflict between the Centre and the State. The Chief Ministers' Conference on Resource Mobilisation in October 1971 recommended the appointment of an expert committee to examine the Centre's proposal to link or merge income tax with agricultural income tax. Accordingly, the Central Government appointed the Committee on Taxation of Agricultural Wealth and Income, under the Chairmanship of K.N. Raj in Feb, 1972. The main objective was to examine the question of taxation of agricultural wealth and income from all aspects. The committee submitted its reports in October, 1972. Its main recommendations are: (a) a progressive agricultural holding tax (AHT) should be imposed on agriculturist who have no other assessable income; (b) in case of assessees having non-agricultural taxable income, income from agriculture should be included in the total income for the purposes of calculating income tax; (c) income from livestock, fisheries, poultry, dairy farming etc., should be subject to tax; (d) an integrated taxation of agricultural property through wealth tax should be introduced and finally (e) capital gain tax on transfer of agricultural lands should be imposed.[8]

Among all the recommendation, the most controversial is agricultural holding tax (AHT). The basic criticism against AHT relates to its procedure for the computation of the rateable value of agricultural holdings. The steps are: (a) a thorough survey of the soil with regards to its nature, quality, suitability to the various crops, irrigation requirements for different crops etc.; (b) a thorough survey of the climatic conditions in different district tract; (c) division of the country into soil climatically homogeneous tracts; (d) crop wise production for the past 10 years for each district/tract and crop-wise prices for the last three years; (e) preparation of farm management studies in each soil climatic district/tract and (f) actual assessment of the operational holdings. All such procedures involve very heavy cost. Besides, it is also pointed out that the committee has not given proper thought to the administrative difficulties in collecting the relevant data.

According to C.H. Hanumantha Rao, the calculation of norms of productivity on the basis of the 10 years yield is wrong as this would definitely understate the income of the large farmers under conditions of rapid technological development. He also criticised that "since the case for taxing rental incomes is even stronger than the taxation of farm business income, the committee's recombination in this respect if accepted, would introduce a fresh element of inequality in fact perversity in the system of agricultural taxation in India"[9]. The lack of proper record of occupational holdings, incorrect reporting of aggregate holdings of families, deliberate misreporting of crop patterns, problems of benami holdings and benami transfer holdings are some other problems in the way of implementing AHT. But these criticism as K. N. Raj has points out may be dismissed on the ground that they are not particular to A.H.T. but are common to any form of direct taxation.

been turned down by the Chief Minister of State. However, Government accepted Raj Committee's proposals to integrate agricultural and non-agricultural incomes for calculating income tax. Thus, the problem of mobilising additional resources from agricultural sector for the purpose of development is yet to be solved satisfactorily.

FOOTNOTES AND REFERENCES

1. This portion is based upon N. Kaldor, "The Role of Taxation in Economic Development" (paper presented at the International Congress on Economic Development Vienna 1962; Mathew E.T., "Agricultural Taxation and Economic Development; Gandhi V.P., Tax Burden on Indian Agriculture, Mellor J.W., The Economic of Agricultural Development (Vora) (Cambridge 1966-1969 pp. 83-95; Raj Krishna, Inter-sectoral Equity and Agricultural Taxation, In D.N. Dwivedi, Readings in Indian Public Finance (Edi.) Chanakya Publication, Delhi 1981; Raj Committee "Report on the Committee on Taxation of Agricultural Wealth and Income; K.N. Raj", Direct Taxation of Agriculture, Mainstream March 31, 1973; Economic and Political Weekly November 25 and December 30, 1972; Economic Times (The Economic Research Bureau) April 2, 1969; Lewis S.R., "Agricultural Taxation in a Developing Economy" In Southworth H.M., Johnston B.F. (Ed.) Agricultural Development and Economic Growth, Carnell University Press, 1970, pp. 453-486. Sahota, 1961 Khan N.A., "Resource Mobilisation from Agriculture and Economic Development in India", Economic Development and Cultural Change, October 1963.
2. Mellor J.W., The Economics of Agricultural Development (Vora) 1969 p. 84.
3. Based on Mellor J.W.: The Economic of Agricultural Development. *Op. Cit.* pp. 86-88.
4. RBI Reserve Bank of India Bulletin.
5. *Ibid.*
6. See Gandhi V.P., Tax Burden on Indian Agriculture (Chapter 3-5); Mathew E.T., Agricultural Taxation and Economic Development; The Economic Times (The Economic Research Bureau) *Op. Cit.* 2, 1969.
7. See Budget Speech of the Finance Minister in Parliament, Feb. 28, 1969.
8. GOI, Report of the Committee on Taxation of Agricultural Wealth and Income (Raj Committee).
9. See Economic and Political Weekly (November 25, 1972)
10. See Mainstream (Ramaswami Memorial Lecture) March 31, 1973.
11. Economic and Political Weekly December 30, 1972.
12. Economic and Political Weekly May 21, 1968.

APPENDIX 'B'
INDIAN AGRICULTURAL TAX : AN ANALYSIS OF "UNDER-TAXED" HYPOTHESIS

In Indian fiscal structure, agricultural taxation has always been a debatable subject. A well established notion is that the agricultural sectors, is "under-taxed" and hence, it violates the cannon of equity and justice. Various studies, committees and Government agencies unanimously support this opinion and suggest that agriculture sector must have to bear more tax burden. Controversies arise when suggestions are made in relation to increase more tax burden. The present paper aims to analyse the basic components of "under-taxed" hypothesis as well as the issues raised on increasing agricultural tax burden.

Basic Components of "Under-Taxed" Hypothesis: The "under-taxed" hypothesis has been developed on two basic grounds. Firstly, agriculture since the beginning of Plans has been contributing less in comparison to other sectors fastly increasing aggregate development expenditures. And secondly, it bears-substantially less tax burden in relation to other sectors in absolute as well as in the average and the marginal terms. In both cases, it violates the principle of equity and justice in the sense that while its taxable capacity has been considerably increased, its contribution in comparison to other sectors remained static. As a result, it wided inter-sectoral imbalances.

Indian Plans show that Government has invested large amount of money — roughly 15 to 23 per cent of the total plan outlay — on agriculture and rural development programmes. As a result, agricultural performance in terms of production, productivity and income has been substantially improved. Again, the general high level of agricultural prices, particularly of commercial crops, the introduction of special rural development programmes such as IADP, IRDP, HYVP, NREP, FFW, DRDA, TRYSEM and RLEGP,[1] the provision of subsidies, concessions and direct participation of the Government in the distribution and management have helped Indian agriculture not only to move out of subsistence to commercial farmings, but have also guaranteed security against uncertainties. As a result, the number or rich farmers has been increasing rapidly and the general rural environment has become more protected and safe. But despite all such concerted efforts and the resulted remarkable achievements in agricultural development, the contribution of agriculture in form of direct taxes (land revenue and agricultural income tax) have almost remained static since 1950-51 — below 2 per cent of the income from agriculture (Table I). It has been estimated that between 1960-61 and 1970-71 while the proportion of income and corporation tax to the national income from sources other than agriculture has risen from 4.1 per cent to 4.6 per cent, the proportion of land revenue and agricultural income tax to national income derived from agriculture has declined from 1.63 to .85 per cent.[2]

Morarji Desai in his budget speech pointed out that "those who benefit by the substantial investment in agriculture should contribute a part of their prosperity towards the cost of development in general of the benefits of the new agricultural technology are to be carried progressively to a growing proportion of our farmers, the resources needed for their purpose should come at least in part from the beneficiaries of the progress."[3]

Indian Five Year Plans also support these views.[4] Planning Commission visualised that "the agricultural production and income have risen considerably due partly to large public sector investment in agricultural research, extension, irrigation, credit, fertilisers etc. under successive plans. The level of agricultural taxation, however, continues to be relatively low. Direct tax receipts from agriculture, chiefly land revenue and agricultural income tax, continues only about 7 per cent of the net domestic product from agriculture. A major share of higher agricultural incomes remain untaxed while similar urban income are subject to substantial taxation". The plan, therefore, suggested "progressive taxation of these income at rates comparable to those payable by non-farm earners to secure horizontal equality as between the taxation of agriculturists and non-agriculturists and to reduce the disparity between the less affluent and more affluent sector of the rural community itself."[5]

The views expressed above clearly reveal that in the existing fiscal structure of the economy agriculture is contributing very little as against the benefits which it receives. The present contribution of agriculture is not merely outmoded, inadequate and irrelevant, but socialiy and economically unjust as well.

Average and Marginal Sectoral Burden of Tax: Another important aspect of "under-taxed" hypothesis is its analysis in relation to inter-sectoral distribution of the average and the marginal tax burden. According to E.T. Mathew's estimates the per capita gross burden of agricultural taxation in the year 1958-59 was Rs. 14.42 which was 6.8 per cent of the per capita income in the agricultural sector. The net burden was estimated Rs. 6.88 or 3.2 per cent of per capita income in the agricultural sector. But, the per capita gross burden of non-agricultural sector taxation for the same year amounted to Rs. 64 or 9.2 per cent of the per capita income and the per capita net burden was 7.2 per cent of its per capita income.[6] This disparity in the distribution of tax-burden in absolute as well as relative terms leads to the conclusion that agriculture is "under-taxed" and additional resources may be generated from this sector.

V.P. Gandhi[7] presents more exhaustive and a clear picture of inter-sectoral disparity in relation to the distribution of tax burden. His estimates show (Table II) that in 1951-52 agricultural sector contributed Rs. 200 crores by way of direct and indirect taxes, whereas the non-agricultural contributed Rs. 450 crores. Thus the ratio between agricultural and non-agricultural sectors was 31:69. In 1968-69 this gap has further widened. Now the agricultural sector contributed over Rs. 907 crores and non-agricultural sector nearly Rs. 2603 crores. The ratio for the two sectors was 25:75.

The per capita taxes on incomes as well as the ratio of taxes to per capita income both are increasing in agricultural and non-agricultural sectors. But agricultural sector has been contributing only 6.1 per cent of its income which is merely one third of the ratio of income contributed by non-agricultural sector. (Table III).

The estimates of marginal rate of taxation show that during a decade — 1950-51 to 1960-61 — the additional income occurred to the agricultural sector was Rs. 1,717 crores, but the additional taxation was Rs. 198 crores. Thus, the marginal rate of taxation was only 11.5 per cent. On the other hand, during the same period, additional income in the non-agricultural sector was Rs. 2420 crores while the additional taxation was Rs. 499 crores. Here the marginal rate of taxation was 20.6 per cent. .

Such disparity has also been estimated on the basis of income group. The estimates shows that the lower group is bearing more burden than the upper income group. In agriculture this burden has been estimated 7 per cent for the upper-income group and 12-13 per cent for the lower income group.

Following conclusions may be drawn from the aforesaid analysis: (i) In general, the agricultural sectors bears for less burden in comparison to non-agricultural sectors; (ii) keeping in view the increasing expenditure on agricultural development programmes and the resulted improvement in income and the standard of living, specially of the rich farmers whose number are increasing, the concessions and subsidies provided by the Government and the increasing trends of agricultural prices, specially of commercial crops, the taxable of rural community has been substantially increased. But the contribution of agriculture in the Government exchequer has been very low; (iii) inter-sectoral average and marginal distribution of tax-burden as well as in terms of income group clearly reveals that agricultural tax system violates the principle of equity and justice; and (iv) there is great scope for increasing agricultural taxation.

SUGGESTIONS FOR INCREASING AGRICULTURAL TAX: AN ANALYSIS

Various proposals for additional agricultural taxation have been made by Raj Committee and the Perspective Planning Division of the Planning Commission. Raj Committee has made five major recommendation. These are: (i) A Progressive Agricultural Holding Tax (AHT) should be imposed on agriculturists who have no assessable income. (ii) Income from agriculture should be included in the total income for the purpose of calculating income tax. (iii) Income from livestock, fisheries, poultry, dairy farming etc. should be subject to tax (iv) An integrated taxation of agricultural property through wealth tax should be introduced. And (v) Capital gain tax on transfer of agricultural lands should be imposed.[9] The Perspective Planning Division proposed a scheme of surcharge on land revenue. Under this scheme small landowners who are paying Rs. 7 as land revenue have been exempted and then on each additional land revenue of Rs. 5, the surcharge increases 40 per cent. The PPD anticipated an annual income of about Rs. 140 crores by this schemes.[10] The Planning Commission has recommended the imposition of highly progressive agricultural income tax.

The aforesaid recommendations have been widely discussed and criticised from various angles. I shall analyse some important points of discussions of two important proposals — AHT proposal of Raj committee and imposition of progressive agricultural income tax (Planning Commission's proposal).

The basic criticism against AHT is that it is either too radical or too cumbersome to implement. The procedure for the computation of rateable value of agricultural holdings which passes through different lengthy procedures prove it well. The steps involved are: (i) A thorough survey of the soil in relation to its nature, quality, suitability to the various crops etc.; (ii) A thorough survey of the climatic condition in different districts/tracts; (iii) Division of the country into soil-climatically homogeneous tracts; (iv) crop-wise production for the past 10-years for each district/tract and crop-wise prices for the last three years; (v) Preparation of Farm Management Studies in each soil-climatic district to compute crop-wise paid out costs of cultivation for each district/tract and (vi) Actual assessment of the operational holdings. All such steps are not only lengthy, complex and cumbersome, but highly costly as well. Besides, a proper thought has also not been given to data at the right time will again be an added problem.

C.H. Hanumantha Rao criticised AHT proposal on the basis of the estimates of yield for the previous 10-years. According to his views such estimates would definitely understate the income of large farmers under conditions of rapid technological progress.[11] But such criticism, however, does not invalidate the imposition of the AHT. If one or the other reasons, a 10-year period for calculating norms of productivity seems to be too long, a shorter period can be adopted. Similarly, if annual assessments are difficult, triennial or any other period convenient for assessment can be made. Rao has also criticised AHT that it is based on operational holdings and hence leaves out the rental income from agricultural taxation. Raj Committee accept this as a valid criticism and mentions different alternatives suggestions, such as ownership holdings as a basis of tax, sharing tax liability of an operational holding between owner and tenants and the amendment of Indian Income Tax so that rental income derived from agriculture is treated in future as non-agricultural income.

Again it is also pointed out that the tendency of division and sub-division of holdings under the impact of population pressure and fixing of land ceilings has been quite powerful throughout the country. Under these circumstances AHT cannot be significant proposal and it may be laps.

There has been, no-doubt, a considerable opposition for AHT proposal. The Government, however, has accepted the Raj Committee recommendation. But the State Government, has finally rejected the proposal on one or the other ground. Planning Commission, however, tried to pursue the State Government and said: "The State Government showed once again consider the imposition of a progressive agricultural holding tax in the form recommended by the Raj Committee. But if this is not considered feasible, surcharges at graduated rates must be added to land revenue in all States....".[12]

The progressive agricultural income tax as recommended by the Planning Commission has been a source of conflict between the central and the States and it has been widely criticised on various grounds as well. The proposal has been turned down by the Chief Minister of States on the ground that agricultural income tax is a State subject. Obviously, the imposition of such a tax by the Central Government is impossible without a constitutional amendment.

The proposal has been criticised on various grounds. Firstly, there is problem in determining farm income. Normally, income is considered the difference between the revenues received and the expenses incurred in raising that revenues. In agriculture, revenue is equal to sale proceeds of various crops and expenses will include the expenses on land, hired and family labour, appliances, implements, fodders, fertiliser etc. It is quite difficult for an ordinary or moderately educated farmers to estimate these expenses. Nor do the farmer keep any records about their incomes and expenses. Besides, wide fluctuations in output and prices of various crops create another problem as it will result in wide fluctuation in farm income as well. Thus, the main criticism of imposing agricultural income tax is that its basis is indefinite. Secondly, it is also pointed out that since land holding and tenancy system in India are different, the problem would naturally arise how to locate the assessees. In many cases, the total agricultural income may come under tax but when it is shared between the landlord and the tenants it may not be subject to tax. Thirdly, the proposal has been opposed from the cost point of view. It has been argued that the cost of collection of agricultural income tax may be vary beary since the farmers are widely scattered. It is, therefore, feared that the cost of collection of revenue will be proportionately higher than the total revenue.

Concluded Remarks: The "under-taxed" hypothesis convincingly proves that there are grave inter-sectoral imbalances in tax-structure which violates the cannon of equity and justice. The agricultural sector, so far as the direct taxes are concerned is actually a "tax-free" sector. This seems to be highly unjustified where the non-agricultural sectors are paying high rate of taxes and the tax-burden-free agricultural sector is enjoying all possible benefits from the increasing expenditures for its development and the concessions land subsidies provided by the Government.

Taking a serious note of this development, Raj Committee and the Planning Commission recommended an introduction of progressive agricultural holding tax which is based on the concept of agricultural productivity and progressive agricultural holding tax which is based on the concept of agricultural income tax. But under the influence of powerful farm lobby the State Governments have shown no inclination to introduce them. For the sake of equity and justice the proposals such as a progressive agricultural income tax, surcharges on income and agricultural holding tax etc. seems to be appropriate. But due to constitutional limitation, their implementation has always been a subject of controversy between the States and the Central Government. The failure is, thus, mainly due to constitutional hitches. The other drawbacks which is usually of economic and administrative nature may be removed by the passage of time and experience. Thus the quick implementation of such proposals is actually based upon how quickly constitutional amendment is being made.

FOOTNOTES AND REFERENCES

1. Intensive Agricultural District Programme (IADP). Integrated Rural Development Programme (IRDP). High Yielding Variety Programme (HYVP) National Rural Employment Programme (NREP). Food For Work Programme (FFW). District Rural Development Agency (DRDA).

Training of the Rural Youth For Self-Employment (TRYSEM). Rural Landless Employment Guarantee Programme (RLEGP).

2. Bansil P.C. "Agricultural Problems of India, Vikas 1977 *p*. 585.
3. Budget speech of the Finance Minister, Feb. 28, 1969.
4. See GOI, Fourth Five Year Plan *p*. 85; Draft Five Year Plan 1978-83, *p*. 60.
5. GOI, Draft Five Year Plan 1978-83, *p*. 60.
6. Mathew E.T., Agricultural Taxation and Economic Development *p*. 25.
7. V.P. Gandhi, Tax Burden on Indian Agriculture.
8. V.P. Gandhi *op. cit.*.
9. See. Report of the Committee on Taxation of Agricultural Wealth and Income (Raj Committee).
10. Economic and Political Weekly, May 20, 1968.
11. Economic and Political Weekly, November 25, 1972.
12. GOI, Draft Five Year Plan 1978-83 *p*. 60.

APPENDIX 'C'

Table 1
Share of Land Revenue and Agriculture Income Tax in the State Tax Revenues (1950-51—1980-81)

(Rs. in crores)

Year	Land Revenue	% of Total State Tax Revenue	Agriculture Income Tax	% of Total State Tax Revenue.
1951-52	48.0	17.1	4.3	1.1
1960-61	97.0	9.6	9.5	1.0
1969-79	108.7	9.2	11.3	1.0
1980-81	166.0	1.7	13.9	0.8

Source: RBI Bulletins.

Table II
Total Tax Incidence on Agriculture and Non-Agricultural Sectors for Selected Years

(Rs. in Crores)

Year	Agricultural Sector	Non-Agricultural Sectors	total	Ratio
1951-52	200	450	650	31: 69
1960-61	399	922	1321	30: 70
1968-69	907	2693	3600	25: 75

Source: V.P. Gandhi, Tax Burden on Indian Agriculture p. 35; The Economic Times, April 2, 1969.

Table III
Average Tax Rates in Agriculture and Non-Agriculture Sectors (1951-52—1968-69)

	Agriculture Sector		Non-Agriculture Sectors	
Year	Per Capita Tax (Rs.)	Ratio of Tax to Per Capita Income (%)	Per Capita Tax (Rs.)	Ratio of Tax to Per Capita Income.(%)
1951-52	8.0	3.8	41.8	9.5
1955-56	9.5	5.4	38.4	8.9
1960-61	13.4	5.6	68.9	13.0
1968-69	26.0	6.5	174.0	19.4

Source: V.P. Gandhi Tax Burden on Indian Agriculture p. 35; The Economic Times, April 2, 1969.

10

THE MICRO AND MACRO DIMENSIONS OF ECONOMIC REFORMS IN INDIA

Indian economy has undergone a major transformation in four years of economic reforms launched by the Government in June 1991. Although the process of reforms is in mid-course, the movement of all economic indicators appears to be positive. Inflation has been brought down from double digit (17%) to single digit (around 7%). Foreign exchange reserves which were barely 1 billion U.S. dollars are now at about 7 billion U.S. dollars. Exports which had shown marginal growth of 3.1 per cent 1992–93, have gone up by about 24 per cent in merely five months of the current financial year. GDP growth which was only 1.2 per cent during 1991–92 has increased to 4 per cent in 1992–93 and may be further high this year. The fiscal deficit which was over 8 per cent of GDP in 1991 has been reduced to nearly 5.6 per cent in 1992–93.

Despite all these favorable trends, our economy is still facing many problems. A major worry is the crunch in balance of payments. Annual trade deficit continues to be in the range of 3 to 5 billion U.S. dollars. Debt-Service-Ratio (DSR) is mounting. To meet the external obligations, our exports in dollar terms need a minimum growth rate of 20 per cent per annum. A major challenge before us is, therefore, to boost export and attract foreign investment in large-scale. India in a short span of two years, stands at the threshold of a leap forward. There is a need to "market" India and its potential abroad.[1]

ECONOMIC REFORMS: MACRO DIMENSION

Economic reforms are not new. Since the beginning of planning era, we have launched various reforms i.e. land-reforms, Community Development Programmes (C.D.P.), Green Revolution, nationalisation of banks. But this time, the effort is multidimensional, more sizeable, more significant and has a world-wide canvas. With these reforms we are transiting from one system to another. If these reforms are sustained and intensified, then the Nehru's vision of a strong, independent India with a sound economy generating growth and reducing poverty will be within our grasp.

The fundamental question about these reforms is: Why the present reforms are necessary? A satisfactory answer to this question will, of course, provide a necessary support for sustaining the steady course of the reforms.

The time when Prime Minister Narsimha Rao's took office, India was engulfed in a severe macro-economic crisis which required immediate attention. The macro-economic crisis which we were facing was actually the outcome of substantial micro-economic (or sometimes called structural) crisis. These micro-economic inefficiencies have actually contributed to the macro-economic crises and actually their reforms had been long-overdue.

The structural reforms were necessary because we failed to generate adequate rate of growth of income and per capita income. Bhagwati J have used data for 21 "high-income" and 88 developing countries since 1960 and stated India's "sorry performance". The failure to grow also undercut our efforts to create more jobs and thus to pull-up more people into gainful employment. This refer to undermining the main objective of alleviating massive poverty. Though our poor and low growth performance cannot be attributed to failure to raise the necessary savings and investment as we did pretty well in that respect, yet it reflects our failure to get adequate returns from these rising investment. In short, our policy framework was inefficient and as a result we had to contend with deep-seated micro-economic flaws.

India's macro-economic crisis was reflected mainly in the growth of public spending which, in turn, increased the budget deficit as a proportion of our GDP. The public debt to GDP ratio increased to almost 60% at the end of 1980s decade. The main reasons were: (i) the failure of the public sector to generate investible resources, and (ii) the explosive growth of the Government current spending that increased the budget deficit as a proportion of GDP from 6.4% to 9% during 1980s.

The failure of public sector enterprises to generate profit is actually an efficiency failure. Further, the restrictive trade and industrial licensing framework also led to serious loss of efficiency by reducing the scale of output, eliminating competition creating bottlenecks and myriad other ways. The result was to reduce the returns from our investments and our growth rate. In a situation of slowly-growing income tax rates may not be raised to increase the revenues. Contrary, the necessity to undertake budgetary expenditure to support the creation of public-sector jobs and for consumption was also increased. All such factors contribute to the budget deficit crisis.

On international front, two OPEC shocks of 1973 and 1979 further deepen the crisis. These external shock administered by the loss of remittances and the expenditure incurred to rescue workers in the aftermath of the invasion of Kuwait in August 1990 certainly accentuated the fiscal crisis at the end.

The rise in foreign borrowing was major component of the fiscal crisis which reflects the excess of domestic expenditure overincome. The external public sector debt, as a proportion of GNP, increased substantially during 1980 and reached upto 21% by 1987–88. Debt service as a proportion of exports increased more than three-fold to 32% in 1986–87 from 1980–81. In fact reserves reduced to less than 10 days of imports by the beginning of 1991. This led to borrow from IMF in January a loan worth of 1.8 billion and again in October 1991 when situation further deteriorated.

The macro-economic imbalances fueled by the budget deficit and financed by external borrowing and decumulation of resources was accompanied by accelerated inflation to double-digit levels. Obviously a stabilization programme and tightening monetary policy, was called for.

Remedial Action: Following areas have been taken into consideration for remedial action.

- Reduction in development expenditure to cut the budget deficit.
- Cut in non-development expenditure and subsidies to public sector enterprises and to agriculture.
- More revenue by expanding the tax base.
- A sound management of monetary policy in the interest of financial stability requires that financial sector reforms be implemented at greater speed.

The reduction in budget deficit, the basic cause of macro-economic crisis, was inevitable. But the basic problem is to choose the best and safest way of reducing that deficit. Two questions are raised: (i) Has the Government raised revenues or relied entirely on cutting expenditure? and (ii) Have the cut in expenditure been too unmindful of the need to take the longer view on developmental expenditure and the need to soften the impact on the poor?

Reduction in budget deficit has been brought about by reduction in development and non-development expenditure. While the over-all development revenue expenditure of the Centre is to remain virtually unchanged in 1992–93 in nominal terms at Rs. 207 billion compared to Rs. 214 billion in 1991–92, non-developmental expenditure is to raise from Rs. 472 billion in 1991–92 to Rs. 538 billion 1992–93. The increase was a Rs. 66 billion in 1992–93 over 1991–92. The major part of it, that is Rs. 48 billion was the interest payment on domestic and external debt.

At the same time, the Centre's development expenditure on capital accounts has also registered only a negligible increase from Rs. 57 billion in 1991–92 to Rs. 63 billion in 1992–93. Thus, the overall Government expenditure during the course of our stabilisation has been significantly at the expanse of developmental expenditure in the revenue and capital accounts. Three consequences are in view:

(i) Since, the developmental expenditures are directly linked with the long-term health of the economy, its reduction is likely to reduce the growth rate and hence built-up pressure to resume excess spending through the budget.

(ii) The reliance on cuts in developmental spending holds danger that must be moderated by reforms in the public sector. These reforms include opening up the areas reserve fully to private sector and for more liberally to foreign investment, a speedier policy on privatisation of a large number of the existing public enterprises, and an energetic demolition of any obstacles in this goal such as price policy restriction, labour laws etc.

(iii) The cut in developmental expenditures may affect adversely the private investment expenditure as the critical infrastructure such as power is in the public sector and private sector on it.

For the sake of improving productivity in the economy cuts in non-development expenditure are also essential. These desirable cuts relate to subsidies of various kinds, chiefly into areas: (i) budgetary support to loss-making public sector enterprises, and (ii) subsidies to agriculture (irrigation, fertilizers and electricity) and to output through the public distribution system.

Indian tax system is also in need of reform. India's fiscal base is narrow and the structure is inefficient. Chelliah Committee report on tax reforms endorse excellent set of proposals.

The internal debt of the Central Government as a proportion of GDP has increased from 35.6% in 1980–81 to 53.3% in 1990–91. Due to control over fiscal deficit, it somewhat decline to 52.1% in 1991–92. Yet the large size of debt refers that interest payments as a proportion of total Central Government expenditure have increased from 5.40% in 1980–81 to 14.8% in 1991–92.

Financial Sector Reform: In 1990–91, nearly half of gross fiscal deficit of the Central Government was financed by the banking system including RBI. Though instruments such as mandatory Cash Reserve Ratio and Statutory Liquidity Ratio, Government has forced the commercial banks to hold a large share of relatively low-yield Government liabilities in their asset portfolio.

It is also argued that the participation of some banks in the recent stock market scandal was actually a reflection of their urgent need to earn a high return from free part of their loanable funds since then profitability was security affected by having to finance relatively unprofitable Government liabilities. Further, our important financial intermediaries such as major commercial banks and Life Insurance Corporation (a monopolist) are in the public sector and that RBI does not have the autonomy like U.K. Federal Reserve and Germany BUNDESBANK. This means that the reforms of the financial sector including RBI must be treated part of the fiscal reform aimed at reducing the likelihood of 1980's discipline and hence to the general reforms of the public sectors in India.

Borrowing: Critics of the reform process says that we are borrowing too much. Reforms that tend to borrow more could be seen as necessary for maintaining our long run credit worthiness so that we could continue to borrow from international capital market for accelerate growth. Hence, the basic question does not relate to much borrowing, but whether overall indebtedness has risen too much altogether, whether we are in the position of Latin American countries with an intolerable external debt burden that would kill their economic growth for nearly a decade or our borrowing prudent as was South Korea's in 1980s.

According to Economic Survey 1992–93, the total external debt—excluding defence but including NRI deposits – is estimated around

72.67 billion dollars. In terms of absolute size of the debt, India is, thus, certainly among the major developing countries to borrowers. However, the debt/GNP ratio is under 30% and the debt-service exports ratio is also around 30%. The corresponding ratio for low income countries other than India and China were 82.6% and 24.9% in 1990. The average interest rate on India external debt was 8%, the average maturity was 25 years and the average grace period of 8 years in 1980. Thus, the average interest rate was not very high while the maturity period was fairly long. These are the cost side of the ledger.

On the benefit side, the returns to the borrowing may be viewed as the marginal returns to the economy. Although there is no direct relation between external loans and investment, as such loans could also finance activities other than investment. Yet, indirectly by releasing resources loans may be considered to add to investment. Again, the marginal returns to investment may be equated to the ratio of investment to GDP brought about by investment.

Consider that india has been investing around 25% of GDP while the rate of growth of GDP sustained by this investment appears, on an average, roughly 5%. This suggests a return in terms of gross value added of 20% to the investment using a net investment rate of 16% of NDP and a NDP growth rate of 5% the return in terms of net value added is about 30%. Thus, assuming a share of capital in value added of about 40%, the realised real rate of return to investment would range between 8 to 12%. If we assume that tne nominal interest rate on marginal loan is of the order 12%, the real interest rate would be about 7% assuming the world-wide inflation rate of 5%.

Thus, the realised rate of interest to investment in the Indian economy is somewhat above the interest costs. If the rate of growth could be increased substantially though better policies, then the realised rate of return would go up substantially. Further, if the real rate on marginal loans were less than 7% then the margin of benefit over cost of external loans would be much comfortable.

Since the real option is not to lower the rate at which the loans are available, but rather to improve our efficiency and income the rate of return over borrowings and investment we can hardly overemphasis the need to get expeditiously with the reform process if we are going to repeat South-Korean experiences rather than get into a Latin American quandary. Successful reforms would certainly improve our credit rating and hence indirectly lower the cost of borrowing.

It is, therefore, of the utmost important to take step such as substantial delicensing of trade and industry and convertibility of rupee.

These steps have led to possible creation of appropriate market incentive in the economy. But much is needed to be done to make them an effective reality. State level restrictions are still existed, powerful bureaucratic machinery is also existed with consequent delays and transaction costs that damage the economy deposits much delicensing. Then, again, with public enterprise still intact, the provision of infrastructural facilities continues to be inefficient. Hence, we urge that the micro-economic reforms should be implemented boldly and as a matter of urgency.

Micro-Economic Dimensions of Reforms

Macro-economic crisis and macro-economic dimensions of reforms, as discussed above, aimed at eliminating the central problem reflected in unproductive policy framework. But macro-economic crisis is actually an accumulation of micro-economic problems, we now turn on micro-economic dimensions of reforms. Micro-economic dimensions of reforms are as under:

- The licensing system which governed industrial and trade decisions has been largely dismantled.
- Privatisation of the large public sector and freeing of the financial sector.
- Opening of the economy wider to trade.

The abolition of industrial and of trade licensing which crippled efficiency in our industry has been attented to with dispatch by the Government so far. The two sets of controls were mutually reinforcing. The removal of one without removing the other would have been infructuous. For instance, if raw material imports were allocated pro rata to capacity, and not allowed to be resold, then the more efficient procedures could not expand production and drive out the less efficient ones even if industrial licensing preventing production expansion were abolished. In the same way, the reform that has led to the rupee trade account convertibility is also critical. If exchange controls continue while import controls are eliminated, the former can create the same restraints as the latter. Thus, removal of industrial and trade licensing must be seen in conjunction with the restoration of rupee's convertibility as having jointly resulted in a freeing of India's economy.

Yet some important conditions must be fulfilled if these reforms are to see truly effective.

(i) The bureaucracy should not become an obstacle to the extended reforms;

(ii) The State-level restrictions on economic decisions, one the Central-level restriction are largely removed, should not be effective constraints.

(iii) The remaining controls, particularly restraints on consumer goods imports, must be removed.

(iv) Institutional changes must support the general feeling of imports that we are moving to.

As we liberalise our trade policy, freeing imports of all types of goods, making international competition an increasing reality, we also need to make institutional changes to accompany and support the new region.

Among the major reforms still awaiting a forceful solution is the reform of India immensely inefficient public sector engaged in productive activity. The problem has arisen in two ways:

(i) Government has acquired several "sick" units to avoid the bankruptcy of failing enterprises.

(ii) for public enterprises the inefficiencies and losses met by subsidies have been the major problems.

In principle, the first one policy can simply be stopped and bankruptcy laws, duly reformed, can be applied to any new enterprises that are failing the market lest so that no new enterprises are taken on as sick unit.

Privatisation and effective competition are the only solution to remove inefficiencies. We require genuine full-scale privatisation. As the privatisation proceeds, the introduction of efficiency-promoting competition can only keep the Government to realise better returns from privatisation. Power, transport, media, industries are the areas whom privatisation and healthy competition may produce better results.

The creation of an efficient mechanism to ensure the flow of resources into the industries and the activities that are more promising by the market lest requires action on several fronts:

(i) Interest rate should be freely determined by the market forces.

(ii) Reduce the role of Government in the allocation of credit.

(iii) Reducing the priority sector lending from 40% to 10% of the total bank loan.

(iv) Reducing the Statutory Liquidity Ratio (SLR) from 38.5% to 25% of the bank deposit and reducing also the "cash-reserve" requirements that similarly taxes the banks in form of the Government.

(v) Proposal for financial opening to the world by permitting private capital inflows, and

(vi) Reduction of existing barriers on private and foreign banks so as to improve efficiency through competition.

Reforms In Agriculture: Agricultural sector has always been very critical to the overall health of the economy. Hence from the efficiency and equity point of view reform efforts must be focused on it as much as on other important areas such as public enterprises, trade, industry etc. Following areas are important for concrete policy reforms:

(i) Foreign trade in agricultural inputs and outputs.

(ii) Public distribution system (PDS) with respect to foodgrains, edible oil and sugar.

(iii) Subsidisation of agricultural inputs such as fertilizers, irrigation and electricity; and

(iv) Agricultural credit.

Foreign trade in most of the agricultural goods is subject to various restrictions such as minimum price requirements, canalisation and GRs etc. and has not been covered by the trade liberalisation measures of 1991 and 1992 to date. As a result, the border prices of the rice and wheat were above twice the domestic price. Edible oil prices were more than twice the world market prices. These price disparities between domestic and world prices reflect export and import restraints.

Inputs into agriculture, on the other side, such as fertilizers, irrigation-water and electricity are heavily subsidised. Further, agricultural income is still not subject to income tax. If the total effect of all subsidies and taxes were calculated, we would/realises that the effect has been to bias the Government provided incentives against agriculture. Hence, a broad-based sweeping set of reforms would favour rather than har, agriculture on the average. There is no reason to continu on QRs and on canalisation of agricultural goods under the new region of liberal trade that the economic reforms plan to implement. It is now time to abolish canalisation and also to convert the QRs into equivalent export and import tariffs. The next step should be toward phased, preannounced set of reductions of these tariffs down to much lower level.

Public distribution system (PDS) has a distributional-equity objectives. This system requires immediate reform because it failed in serving the poor effectively. Instead it has soaked up large-scale governmental revenue while producing limited results.

The PDS supplies specified quantities of rice, wheat, coarse grains, edible oil, kerosene and sugar at prices below the retail market prices to the card-holders through the Fair Price Shops (FPS). The domestic purchases are made at "procurement" prices from the wholesale traders in wheat and from rice millers. A specific proportion (levy) of sugar is bought from sugar mills at the levy price below the open-market price. The FCI and other relevant State Government agencies thus purchase, transport and store the commodities in PDS. In 1988–89, about 16.5% of domestic wheat output and 13.2% of rice output over procured on an average. The pressure for increasing procurement prices year after year has proved politically irresistible. In 1992–93, procurement prices were raised by over 15% in case of rice, wheat and coarse cereals.

As a resuit, the budgetary cost of PDS, that is the difference between the revenue from sales and the cost of purchase, transport, storage and establishment has been growing. In 1990–91, the Central Government above spent Rs. 25 billion or 3.5% of the total revenue expenditure of Rs. 735 billion on food subsidies.

PDS is considered a "safety net" for the poor. Yet according to Economist Subbarao, while 50% of Indian poor live in Bihar, M.P., Rajasthan and U.P., they receive only 10% PDS supplies in 1990. According to Mishas's estimate more than a third of rice and wheat, 40% of edible oil and as much as 75% of sugar sold through the PDS in rural areas were bought by the richest 40%. PDS is thus poorly targeted to the poor, the leakage to the non-poor is very high.

PDS also suffers from leakage of supplies to the open market. Some estimates put such leakages at a third of rice, wheat and sugar off-take from PDS and over half of edible oil. These leakages are effective though sales by Fair Price Shopkeepers to bogus ration card-holders. The shopkeepers earn the difference between the open market price and the sale price to card-holders. These problems of PDS have also clearly recognised by the Government. The Economic Survey 1992–93 paragraph 4.51 explains these problems verywell.

PDS thus, requires reforms. Different alternatives may be considered.

(i) **Better targeting of the poor may be achieved through a means test. A cheap and reliable means test is administratively infeasible in India. Hence we doubt this option has been effectively explored.**

(ii) Better targeting may also be achieved by identifying the poor through local bodies.

(iii) This approach is commodity-based targeting. For example, PDS may confined only on the distribution of coarse cereals which is used only by poor. The case of supplying sugar, vegetable oil through PDS is extremely weak anyway.

Next is the consideration of the design of PDS. Is the choosen method of distribution, assuming even efficient targeting, the least cost way of achieving the objective of supplying the consumption of poor?

Introduction of "food stamps", and allowing the private sector supply the quantity of grains needed for the PDS, at the place and time needed may improve the situation. The abuses of system may be minimized. The food stamp system enables the holders of these stamps to pay for part of the cost of their purchase (from the open market) of commodities covered by this alternative PDS.

Agricultural subsidies on three major inputs: fertilizers. irrigation water and electricity have added to the budget deficit in a big way and also distort the choice of technology in agricultural production. Therefore, they must be removed. Agriculture, on the average, will benefit from these removals instead of being harmed incentive wise.

We finally turn to the question of agricultural credit. The declared objective of agricultural credit policy has been to enable farmers, especially small and marginal farmers, to adopt modern technology and improved agricultural practices. However, despite substantial increase in overall agricultural credit, the problem of mounting overdues has slowed credit expansion, overdues have been around 40–42% during the 3 to 4 years (Economic Survey 1991–92)

Despite substantial increase in the institutional credit in the total rural credit from 20% in 1951 to 80% in 1981, the informal credit (non-institutional credit) continues to be very significant in rural areas. The RBI estimates regarding the expansion of institutional credit, therefore, seem to be an over-estimate. The World Bank estimates shows that in the mid 1980 an average of only 27% Indian farmers used cooperative credit, varying from 9% in West Bengal to 90% in Punjab. Besides, only 4% of the farmers used credit from commercial banks and two third of the term credit goes to the rich farmers.

Thus, it is an open question whether the objectives of the agricultural credit policy are being achieved. The World Bank estimates that farmers cultivating on 5 acres receive an interest rate subsidy on term loans of about Rs. 1 billion per annum.

The situation calls for a corrective policy. It must be understood that the credit subsidies are of little value to the poor farmer since most of them do not get access to credit in the just place; access to credit is really the problem faced by the poor which could be attached along the lines suggested by the Grameen Bank in Bangladesh. The reform in agricultural credit system should be regarded as an important part of the financial sector reforms.

*. Based on Bhagwati J, Srinivasan T.N., "India's Economic Reforms", Survey paper submitted in "Conference on Indian Economy—Challenges and Task Ahead", Federation of Indian Chambers of Commerce & Industry (FICCI) and Indian Economic Association (IEA) held at Delhi 14, 15 October 1993; Dr. Bansi Dhar, Presidential Address, Conference on Indian Economy—Challenges & Task Ahead.

1. Dhar B, Presidential Address, Conference on Indian Economy—Challenges and Task Ahead. op. cit.

APPENDIX 'C'

DUNKEL NEGOTIATIONS : IMPACT ON AGRICULTURAL SECTOR

During past two years the Dunkel proposals have been widely discussed. The Dunkel draft was presented at the Uruguay Round of talk of GATT in December 1991 at the instance of the developed countries, for managing international trade. The uruguay Round of Multinational Trade Negotiations was concluded in December 1993 after seven years of protracted negotiations. Wide ranging apprehensions have been expressed in developing countries. A general observation is that our agriculture which is based on small preasantry class would be ruined. Our farmers would have to buy seeds every year from multinationals. Our Public Distribution System (PDS) would have to be curtailed. Our genetic wealth would be lost. The drug prices would shoot up. Our market would become a heaven for foreign investors, multinationals. A pragmatic evaluation of the implications of such treaty is, therefore, essential. This paper presents an evaluation of the impact of Dunkel Draft on Indian agriculture.

Recommendations for Agriculture

The commendations of the Dunkel Draft (DD) which are most influential for agricultural economy may be broadly divided into two groups: (a) measures in relation to fiscal and trading matters and (b) intellectual property rights (IPRS).

The measures concerning fiscal and trading matters in DD include: (i) Reduction of agricultural subsidy; (ii) Conversion of all barriers on agricultural imports into agricultural tariffs. It is known as tarification of agricultural products; (iii) Guaranteed minimum access for farm imports of between 3 to 5 per cent of consumption; (iv) Reduction of PDS. Subsidised food is granted only to those eligible on the basis of clearly defined criteria related to nutritional objectives; (v) phasing out multi fibre agreement (MFA) which impose discriminatory restrictions on textile imports; (vi) Removal of trade restrictive and distoring investment measures and extension of "equal national treatment" to multinationals; and (vii) Treatment of foreign services enterprise on equal national footing with domestic service enterprise.

Intellectual property rights incorporate the following recommendations: (i) Patents are given for any invention whether products or process; (ii) Patentright is enjoyable without discrimination to the place of invention, the field of technology, and whether products are imported or locally produced; (iii) Life of patents is to be 20 years; (iv) In case of violation burden of proof lies on the accused; (v) Patents are for living organism, (vi) Patents are for plant varieties; (vii) Deletion of provision for compulsory licensing, where a country, and import at par with domestic manufacture for purpose of definition of the working of a patent.

The first and the most widely discussed apprehension is reduction of agricultural subsidy. Fertilizer is the first victim of this clause. We know, fertilizer is the most important input for increasing agricultural productivity and if subsidy on fertilizer is removed or reduced, the cost of production of agricultural output, specially of food item, will increase. Since, food is the most important item of wage-basket in a developing country like India, the increase in the prices of food commodities will increase wages and will reduce profits of all other sectors. This in turn will give boost to inflation. The proposed measure – reduction of agricultural subsidy – has also been opposed by the developed countries like France. The reason is quite justified. Food is the basic need for both the rich and the poor. This is why even developed countries with a small components of agricultural product in their national income try to protect the interests of farmers by providing subsidies in different forms so that adequate marketable surplus may be generated and non-agricultural population may be saved from inflationary pressure. While France opposed the subsidy clause, Japan, South-Korea, Norway, Canada and Switzerland have been against the fertilizer.

This gives an impression that if Dunkel Draft proposals have been accepted, Indian agricultural product will become competitive in the World market and hence agriculture will turn out to be a good foreign exchange earner for industrialization. But, this is, however, not so simple. India, in true sense, is not self-sufficient in food if total nutritional requirement is to be met. More than 30% of the population live below the poverty line and because of this low income, they do not demand even the minimum food. India does not have exportable surplus. she constitutes 17 per cent of the world population and accounts for only about 12 per cent of the total creals and pulses production. The US, on the other hand constitutes only about 5 per cent of the world population and accounts for 13 per cent of foodgrains production. This is a clear indication that exportable surplus of food grains lies generally with developed countries only. And it is quite obvious that these countries are not exporting at the cost of domestic consumption. Hence, the possibility of export earning of developing countries are not bright.

Dunkel Draft and Agricultural Trade: If we look the trade pattern of agriculture products – food, beverage and tobacco – the US, Canada and other Asian countries appear to be net exporters. Tea is major export item of India. Recently, quality rice and horticultural products are also gaining attention in the world market. India has a geographical advantage with neighbouring countries, eastern half of African continent and Middle East countries. Due to low-income, Africa can't import much of high valued cereal crops and other agricultural product from India. Japan's trading advantage is attached with the US and other Asian countries such as Hongkong, Malaysia, Singapore, Europe's geographical advantage lies with Canada, the US with Mexico, Northern Africa and the Middle East. Hence, India has to depend mainly on west-Asia, neighbouring countries and former USSR for her agricultural exports. The reduction of subsidy by the developed countries would therefore not provide much gain to India.

Besides, as has been stated earlier, India does not have exportable surplus of foodgrains because of low soil fertility and input deficiencies. For this either more area has to be brought under cultivation or the yield rate has to be increased. The scope of expanding net area is almost negligible. Only yield rate can be increased by cropping intensity, technological revolution and other scientific techniques. But for this a large amount of investment, specially in irrigation, fertilizer, seeds, mechanization, pesticides, etc. is needed. But they too require proper institutional credit support which does not have much importance in the context of financial sector reforms.

Since food is in most important item of average Indian household budget, rise in food price tends to increase the wage rate, inflation, reduce profitability and the spirit of investment. Since the cost of production will increase, the industrial goods will lose export competitiveness.

IPR and its Impacts

Another important dimension of Dunkel draft is IPR. Indian Patent Act covers (a) process paten for food, medicine, drug and chemicals; (b) product patent for other items; and (c) neither process nor product patent for agriculture. Dunkel Draft requires protection for: (i) product, (ii) plant varieties, and (iii) living organism. The US, has all the above patent facilities. Genetically engineered varieties of seed of food and cash crops owned by multinational bio-technology companies will be sold in India and hence the seeds will have royalty which have so far been absent. Naturally, this increases seed prices. Further, since the seeds are protected by patent, the farmer may not be allowed to save them of their own harvest to sow their next crop. In that case India will not be able to increase the yield rate though high quality seeds to make her product competitive in this world market. The monopolisation of research and gains by multinationals will never allow the benefits to be trickled down.

One more aspect is relevant. Due to the operation of diminishing returns and the pressure from environmentalists, agriculture sector is compelled to move away from the use of chemicals, pesticides to bio-substitutes (bio-fertilizers and bio-pesticides). In India research has been started in this direction. If bio-technology succeeds certain bacteria in the environment can provide the required ammonia to the plant. A group of fungi called myeorrhiza enter the roots of trees, shurbs and crops and solubilise iron phosphate in low fertility soil. Further, they may also mobilise other nutrients like copper and zine. A special kind of bacteria known as Bacillus Megaterium improve the phosphate status in the soil and minimises the need for chemical phosphates. Certain other kind of soil bacteria when injected with methane from the air, release enhanced amounts of phosphorus, potassium, calcium and megnesium. Similarly a whole range of insects and worms have been rediscovered to fight pasts. Further, there are more than 100 kinds known bacteria, virus and fungi which attack insects.

These developments are a clear sign that agricultural technology is entering into a phase of a revolutionary change. In this change a living micro-organisms are going to play an important role. If Dunkel Draft is going to patent all these "micro-organisms" and "micro-biological process", the control over entire range of seed, fertilizer and pesticides will be with the multinationals which not only have a lead in bio-technology, but also have a command on investment. Hence the monopolisation of this technology will make agricultural input costly. In near future agricultural is going to be highly capital-intensive field of technology.

Review

A wide ranging apprehensions of Dunkel Draft in relation to our agriculture are: (a) that our farmers would have to buy their seeds every year from multinationals; (b) that the reduction of subsidy on fertilizers, pesticides and other inputs would increase the inflation, reduce the profit and would make the sector incompetitive. The agro-based industrial sector will also be equally affected adversely; (c) that our public distribution system would have to be curtailed causing immense problem to urgan-poor in relation to fulfillment of basic need; (d) the introduction of bio-technology and bi-engineering as a substitute of chemical fertilizers and chemical pesticides by the multinationals would make agriculture highly capital intensive field of technology. The small and marginal farmers will the have no relevance in the agricultural production; and (e) our agricultural sector would become a heaven for foreigners and multinationals. Since the technology is in their hands, they will command, regulate and control our production, distribution and marketing.

In case of the reduction of subsidy, it is argued that we are under no obligation to reduce any of the subsidies given to our farmers because it is applicable to those whose subsidies exceeds 10 per cent of the total value. And, given the magnitude of our total agricultural production, the possibility of our domestic input subsidies ever reaching 10 per cent of its value is virtually non-existent. But this is the position at present. This means if we want of provide more incentive through subsidies to our marginal and poor farmers, we are bound not to exceed 10 per cent. It is not a control over incentives to poor farmers?

Public Distribution System is in fact not a subsidy for the farmer, but a subsidy for the urban and rural poor to meet their food and other essential requirement. This protection net is mainly for the urban-poor. Farmers generally do not be benefited by PDS. But PDS system is also functioning in rural areas and providing relief to agricultural poors, specially rural labourers which is the true poor segment of the rural society. The curtailment of public distribution system will certainly add in their hardships. A strong argument in favour of Dunkel Draft is that its fiscal measures seem to give Indian agriculture a boost in the international market. But the pre-dominance of poor and the marginal farmers, low fertility soil, application of the law of diminishing returns, low and backward technological level, poor research, institutional and structural constraints and limited foreign markets create strong doubts in the fulfillment of said goal. Our export generation capacity is very low and due to low level of technology we are still not capable of facing world competition. Hence, from the export side as well as from the international competition side we are not in much favourable position.

As a result, the signing of Dunkel Draft open opportunities for the multinationals to enter in our agriculture sector with enormous investment potentials and high-technological level. They will obviously command, control and regulate our agricultural production, distribution and marketing. And by this control, they will also control and regulate the agro-based industrial sector, trade, research and the service sector. In other words, our economy in the name of liberalisation, globalisation and privatisation is actually moving towards, monopolisation. We, in the name of globalisation, have reduced our "commanding heights", but what we are visualising is that we are accepting the commanding heights of multinationals. In the name of making ourselves internally more competitive we have withdrawn the protectionist policies. But the reality is that we have accepted the protection of multinational and of other international agencies. Is it not the beginning of an area of "humble-slavery"?

No doubt we have only one option. Either we leave the Dunkel proposal or accept it. Despite various criticism, Dunkel Agreement has been signed world over. Hence we too can't leave it. The only effort which is sincerely needed at this juncture is to find out a way that could minimise the damages and maximise the benefits.

Reference

Dasgupta, R. Subsidies, patents and markets access in Dunkel Draft. Economic and Political Weekly, May 1, 1993.

SELECTED BIBLIOGRAPHY

1. Heady E.O.: Economics of Agricultural Production and Resource use, (1964) Prentice Hall, India.
2. Robertson, C.A.: An Introduction to Agricultural Production Economics and Farm Management, TMH, Bombay, 1977.
3. Snodgross, M.M. and Wallace, L.T.: Agricultural Economics and Resource Management, Prentice-Hall, N. Delhi, 1977.
4. Martin U.: Agricultural Production Economics and Resource Use, Oxford University Press, London, 1976.
5. Halcrow H.G.: Economics of Agriculture, M.H. International Book Company, 1981.
6. Bishop C.E. and Toussaint W.D. : Introduction To Agricultural Economic Analysis, John Wiley & Sons Inc London, 1958.
7. Adger T.: An Introduction To Agricultural Economics, Thomas Nelson, New York.
8. Black J.D.: Introduction To Economics For Agriculture, Macmillan, 1953.
9. David F.H.: Production Functions, Macmillan, London, 1971.
10. Forster G.W. and Marc L. Leoger: Elements of Agriculture in Economics, Prentice Hall, 1951.
11. Eric Thorbecke [Ed]: The Role of Agriculture in Economic Development, Scientific Book Agency, Calcutta.
12. Tailor C.H.: Outlines of Agricultural Economics, Macmillan.
13. Heady G. L. Johnson & Lowell S.H. [Ed]: Resource Productivity, Returns to Scale, and Farm Size, The IOWA State College Press, 1956.
14. Metcalf: The Economics of Agriculture, Penguin Book, Baltimore, 1969.
15. Kahlon A.S. and Karam Singh: Economics of Farm Management In India, Allied, Delhi, 1980.
16. Mellor J.W.: The Economics of Agricultural Development, Vora & Co., Bombay.

17. Tuck R.H.: An Introduction to The Principles of Agricultural Economics — Longman, 1961.

18. Warren H. Vincent [Ed]: Economics and Management in Agriculture, Prientice Hall, 1962.

19. Saini G.R.: Farm Size, Resource-use, Efficiency and Income Distribution, Allied, New Delhi.

20. Schultz T.W.: Transforming Traditional Agriculture, New Haven and London, Yale University Press, 1965.

21. Singh I.J.: Elements of Farm Management Economics, East-West Press, 1972.

22. Carl Eicher and Lawrence Witt [Ed]: Agriculture in Economic Development, Vora, Bombay, 1970.

23. Cohen R.L.: The Economics of Agriculture, Cambridge University Press, 1956.

24. Southworth H.H. Johnston B.F., [Ed]: Agriculture and Economic Growth, London, Cornell University Press.

25. Khusro A.M. [Ed]: Readings in Agricultural Development, Bombay Allied Publisher.

26. Elements of Land Reforms and Farm-Size in India, Macmillan, N. Delhi, 1973.

27. Eicher C.K. & Staatz J.M. [Ed]: Agricultural Development in The Third World. Johms Hopkins University Press, London, 1984.

28. Ghatak S. and Ingersent K.: Agriculture and Economic Development, Select Book Service Syndicate, N. Delhi, 1964.

29. Sadhu A.N.: Singh A, Fundamentals of Agricultural Economics, Himalaya, 1991.

30. Soni R.N.: Leading Issues in Agricultural Economics, Shoban Lal Nagin Chand & Co., 1992.

31. Wadhva C.D. [Ed]: Some Problems of India's Economic Policies, T.M.H., N. Delhi, 1977.

32. Shah C.H. [Ed]: Agricultural Development of India, Policy and Problems, Orient Longman, Bombay, 1979.

33. Steve Jones and Others [Ed]: Rural Poverty and Agrarian Reforms, Allied, N. Delhi, 1982.

34. Ashok Rudra: India Agricultural Economics: Myth & Realities, Allied, 1982.

35. Fei & Ranis: Development of The Labour Surplus Economiy, Theory & Policy Economic Growth Centre, Yale University, 1967.

36. Hanumantha Rao C.H.: Agricultural Production Functions. Cost & Return to India, Asia, 1965.

37. Mohammad Shafi: Agricultural Productivity & Regional Imbalances. A Study of Uttar Pradesh Concept, 1984.

38. Bimal Jalan [Ed]: The Indian Economy: Problems and Prospects, N. Delhi, 1992.

39. M.L. Dantwala [Ed]: Indian Agricultural Development Since Independence, N. Delhi, 1991.

40. Jagdish Bhagwati and Chakravarthy S.: Contribution to Indian Economic Analysis : A Survey, Bombay, 1974.

41. Uppal J.S.: India's Economic Problems: An Analytical Approach — TMH, N.Delhi, 1987.

42. Mongia J.N.: India's Economic Policies 1947-77, Allied, 1980.

43. Brahmananda P.R., Narayan B.K. and Kalappa A [Ed]: Dimensions of Rural Development in India — Himalaya, 1987.

44. Sau, Ranjit, Indian Economic Growth : Constraints And Prospects, Orient Longman, Calcutta 1973.

45. Kahlon A.K. and Tyagi D.S.: Agricultural Price Policy in India — Allied, 1983.

46. Kahlon A.S. and George M.V.: Agricultural Marketing & Price Policies, Allied, 1985.

47. Allian de Janvry and K. Subbarao: Agricultural Price Policy and Income Distribution In India, Oxford, N. Delhi, 1986.

48. Joshi P.C.: Institutional Aspects of Agricultural Development — Allied, 1987.

49. Ghosh A.K.: Agraian Reforms in Contemporary Developing Countries, St. Martin's Press, New York, 1983.

50. Bergman T.: Agrarian Reforms in India, Agricole Publishing Co., N. Delhi, 1984.

34. Ashok Rudra, India Agricultural Economics: Myth & Realities, Allied 1982.

35. Fei & Ranis: Development of the Labour Surplus Economy: Theory & Policy, Economic Growth Centre, Yale University 1964.

36. Hanumantha Rao C.H.: Agricultural Production Functions Cost & Return in India, Asia, 1965.

37. Mohammad Shafi: Agricultural Productivity & Regional Imbalances: A Study in Uttar Pradesh, Concept, 1984.

38. Bimal Jalan [Ed]: The Indian Economy: Problems and Prospects, N. Delhi, 1992.

39. M.L. Dantwala [Ed]: Indian Agricultural Development Since Independence, N. Delhi, 1991.

40. Jagdish Bhagwati and Chakravarthy S.: Contribution to Indian Economic Analysis: A Survey, Bombay, 1974.

41. Uppal J.S.: India's Economic Problems: An Analytical Approach — TMH, N. Delhi, 1982.

42. Mongia J.N.: India's Economic Policies 1947-77, Allied 1980.

43. Brahmananda P.R., Narayan B.K. and Kalappa A. [Ed]: Dimensions of Rural Development in India — Himalaya 1987.

44. Sau, Ranjit, Indian Economic Growth: Constraints And Prospects, Orient Longman, Calcutta 1973.

45. Kahlon A.K. and Tyagi D.S.: Agricultural Price Policy in India — Allied 1983.

46. Kahlon A.S. and George M.V.: Agricultural Marketing & Price Policies, Allied 1985.

47. Alain de Janvry and K. Subbarao: Agricultural Price Policy and Income Distribution in India, Oxford, N. Delhi, 1986.

48. Joshi P.C.: Institutional Aspects of Agricultural Development — Allied, 1987.

49. Ghosh A. Kumar: Agrarian Reform in Contemporary Developing Countries, St. Martin's Press, New York, 1981.

50. Bergman T.: Agrarian Reforms in India, Agricole Publishing Co., N. Delhi, 1984.